Great God A'mighty! The Dixie Hummingbirds

Great God A'mighty!
The Dixie Hummingbirds

Celebrating the Rise of Soul Gospel Music

JERRY ZOLTEN

OXFORD
UNIVERSITY PRESS
2003

OXFORD
UNIVERSITY PRESS

Oxford   New York
Auckland   Bangkok   Buenos Aires   Cape Town   Chennai
Dar es Salaam   Delhi   Hong Kong   Istanbul   Karachi   Kolkata
Kuala Lumpur   Madrid   Melbourne   Mexico City   Mumbai   Nairobi
São Paulo   Shanghai   Taipei   Tokyo   Toronto

Copyright © 2003 by Oxford University Press, Inc.

Published by Oxford University Press, Inc.
198 Madison Avenue, New York, New York 10016

www.oup.com

Library of Congress Cataloging-in-Publication Data
Zolten, Jerry.
Great god a'mighty! the Dixie Hummingbirds:
celebrating the rise of soul gospel music
/ Jerry Zolten.
p. cm.
Includes bibliographical references and index.
ISBN 0–19–515272–7
1. Dixie Hummingbirds.
2. Gospel musicians—United States—Biography.
I. Title.
ML394 .Z65   2003
782.25'4'0922—dc21   2002005453

1 3 5 7 9 8 6 4 2

Printed in the United States of America
on acid-free paper

To my mother, Betty, my wife, Joyce, and my son, Zach

In memory of my father, Bam

*In memory of my mentors, Gerald M. Phillips, James S. Hill,
Willie "Preacher" Richardson, and Walter Settles*

Contents

Preface

I was one of thousands of white kids who, in my case growing up outside of Pittsburgh in the late 1950s and early 1960s, discovered the exciting and—at the time—exotic world of black music hidden away at the lower end of the radio dial. The station was WAMO out of Homestead, and the music—primarily jazz, rhythm and blues, and doo-wop—was impossible to ignore. In my town, McKeesport, the station and the music came to signify teen rebellion, an intelligent underground alternative to the bland pop that then dominated mainstream airwaves. By the time I graduated from high school, I had amassed thousands of choice 45-rpm records by African American performers the more obscure the better.

It was around then that I chanced on a segment of the WAMO broadcast day that I had never before heard. Sunday mornings, after all, were not prime time teen listening hours. In fact, had I not been out Saturday night from dusk till dawn, I would have missed the Sunday morning broadcast altogether. I no longer remember who hosted the program, but the music was inescapably captivating, emotive beyond anything I had ever heard during regular weekday broadcasts—rocking choirs, screaming preachers, sanctified divas, and sublime vocal groups with a soul feel that at the time was simply not present on the secular side. It was a revelation that fueled my desire to discover the world of black gospel music.

Over the years, I sought out records that pulled me deeper and deeper into the history of the genre. The 12-inch 33–1/3s in the cardboard sleeves and the 45-rpms took me back only so far, but the 78-rpms opened a window on the rich landscape of black religious music stretching back across decades.

In time, I sought out live performances of the music, sometimes at local churches, other times at festivals and concerts where famous acts were scheduled to appear. It was in that context that I first met some of the gospel artists I so admired. My closest association early on was with the Fairfield Four of Nashville, Tennessee, one of the great touring, broadcasting, and recording groups of the prewar era. Starting in the early 1980s, I toured with them, spent nights in their homes, talked for hours, and eventually produced the CD that spearheaded their return to commercial recording. It was on tour with the Fairfield Four in Rochester, New York, that I at last met one of my favorite groups, the Dixie Hummingbirds. We became fast friends, and over the years these men—from the Fairfield Four, James Hill, Isaac Freeman, Willie Richardson, Reverend Sam McCrary, Wilson Waters, Robert Hamlett, and Walter Settles, and from the Dixie Hummingbirds, James Davis, Ira Tucker, James Walker, Paul Owens, Howard Carroll, and Carl Davis— became my teachers.

From them, I learned that black gospel was multifaceted—witnessing to faith, spiritual epiphany, deeply rooted tradition, inspirational entertainment, sophisticated rhetoric, and much more. I saw that the music was culturally bound, its greatest stars barely known outside the African American community, the full measure of its influence on blues, jazz, R&B, doo-wop, and soul appreciated mostly by cultural insiders or those who studied the music.

There was also paradox. This was a realm of music whose players because of religious connotation and spiritual power were perceived as holier-than-thou by the public. As several performers put it to me, "They expected us to be wearing wings." And it was an image that many performers admittedly and necessarily projected—living the life they sang about.

The reality was that gospel, like any other human endeavor, was populated by people of every type and temperament. There was rivalry, jealousy, womanizing, substance abuse, and even violence. But there was also generosity, devotion to family, loyalty, perseverance, sacrifice, mentoring, and a wealth of immeasurable talent. Of all the groups that traveled the gospel highway, none succeeded better than the Dixie Hummingbirds at living up to these latter qualities. It would become the backbone of their reputation and subsequent success.

There was also the Dixie Hummingbirds' unparalleled ability through performance to unite people into a "oneness" that transcended religious belief and even no belief at all. Ultimately, that was the special magic that inspired me to write this book and, in the process, come together with the many people who, by telling their stories, helped me tell the story of the "Gentlemen of Song," the Dixie Hummingbirds.

First and foremost, I want to thank James Davis, founder and patri-arch of the Dixie Hummingbirds, for sharing so much about his personal life and the early history of the Birds, and, along with him, legendary Birds' lead singer Ira Tucker, Sr., who guided me through his early years and key moments in the group's golden years. His wife, Louise Tucker, provided invaluable help, as did his son Ira Tucker, Jr. (vital!), and daughters Sundray Tucker and Linda Lawrence.

Thanks to the many singers and instrumentalists who offered their perspective on the Dixie Hummingbirds. From the Birds, cofounding member Barney Parks, the late James Walker, the late Beachey Thompson, Howard Carroll, Paul Owens, Carl Davis, William Bright, and Joe Williams. Thanks to Minnie Lee Baker and Carrie Thompson, widows respectively of Wilson "High Pockets" Baker and Beachey Thompson.

Thanks to Claude Jeter of the Swan Silvertones, Morgan Babb of the Radio Four, Thermon Ruth of the Selahs, Carey "Squeaky" Bradley of the Kings of Harmony, Isaac "Dickie" Freeman and the late James Hill of the Fairfield Four/Skylarks, Ed Sprouse of the Blue Ridge Quartet, Willa Ward-Royster of the Famous Ward Singers, Margaret Allison of the Angelic Gospel Singers, Horace Clarence Boyer of the Boyer Brothers, Arthur and LeRoy Crume of the Soul Stirrers, Joe Ligon of the Mighty Clouds of Joy, and Marie Knight.

Thanks to Paul Simon, Stevie Wonder, Solomon Burke, Sam Moore, Isaac Hayes, Tommy Hunt of the Flamingos, Otis Williams of the Temp-tations, Prentiss Barnes of the Moonglows, Hank Ballard of the Midnighters, Jerry Butler of the Impressions, "Little" Anthony Gour-dine of the Imperials, and Jimmy Merchant of the Teenagers.

Thanks to Roxie Moore, who wrote great songs for the Humming-birds, and to Evelyn Johnson, who ran the day-to-day business of Peacock Records and the Buffalo Booking Agency. Also to Morris Ballen and Paul Fine of Ballen Records; the late Fred Mendelsohn, producer at Savoy Records; Bruce Bastin, who made available material from Gotham Records, and Andy McKaie, who made available session notes from the Peacock archives.

For background and personal memories of the Hummingbirds, thanks to Dr. Maya Angelou; Reverend Dr. Gadson L. Graham; pro-moter Willie Leiser; Greenville, South Carolina, residents Patria Ross, Mamie Norris, and Blanche McIver; Aurelia and Kazava Smith, widow and son of the late Holden Smith; Curtis Rudolph, lifelong friend to Ira Tucker, Sr.; Darryl Williams, son of Philadelphia disk jockey Kae Williams; and Lula Mae Watts, cousin to Birds bass singer William Bobo.

I am indebted to fellow researchers Doug Seroff and Ray Funk for sharing advice and materials and especially for providing interview transcripts with Beachey Thompson and Robert Hardy. I would also like to thank David Evans, Ray Allen, Alan Balfour, Chris Smith, Howard Kramer, Alan Govenar, Eric LaBlanc, Opal Nations, Anthony Heilbut, David Ritz, Roger Wood, and Alan Young. Special thanks to Phil Klass, aka William Tenn, for inspiring me to write, and Herman Cohen, professor emeritus and valued mentor, for talking out so many of the details with me. Thanks also to Craig and Donna Rothman for the loan of a dock, to Chris Rosenblum for helping me get the balloon aloft, and to old friend Van Dyke Parks for "rah rah-ing" me on. And to my brother Sam for encouragement, hospitality, taking all those pictures for free, and explaining how to get through one end of Philadelphia to the other.

Thanks to Bill Barke who made vital connections; to Barbara Brunhuber and Cindy Mighells, who transcribed many an interview; to Josh Ferko and Kris Kehr, who made rare records available and burned them onto CD; and to my colleagues at Penn State Altoona, especially Dinty Moore, Michael Wolf, Kjell Meling, and Ken Womack.

Special thanks to the Penn State Altoona Dean's Development Fund, the Pennsylvania Humanities Council, the Greenville African American Museum, and, on the home front, to my wife, Joyce, and son, Zach, who spent many an evening wondering when Dad was finally going to emerge from his writing room.

Great God A'mighty!
The Dixie Hummingbirds

In the beginning, after the word, before rock 'n' roll, and before there was rap, hip-hop, disco, punk, funk, metal, soul, Motown, rock-a-billy, before bebop, doo-wop, and the big band swing, there was the Dixie Hummingbirds. The mighty Dixie Hummingbirds.

They sang through the Great Depression, the terms of thirteen presidents, four major wars, five generations of Americans, and seven decades of the twentieth century.

The Dixie Hummingbirds. They personify perseverance, talent, and dedication. Now, the iron men of gospel are celebrating their seventy-fifth anniversary. The Dixie Hummingbirds are indeed an American institution. Ladies and gentlemen, I give you the gentlemen of song—the legendary Dixie Hummingbirds.

—Isaac Hayes

1

"A Wheel in a Wheel, 'Way Up in the Middle of the Air"
(1916–1928)

Ezek'el saw the wheel, 'way up in the middle of the air,
Ezek'el saw the wheel, 'way up in the middle of the air,
The big wheel moved by faith,
The little wheel moved by the grace of God,
A wheel in a wheel, 'way up in the middle of the air.

—Traditional African American Spiritual

"A wheel in a wheel." So go the words of the old African American spiritual. No one knows exactly what the ancient biblical images meant, but they do coincidentally resonate with the life of James B. Davis, founder of the trailblazing Dixie Hummingbirds. His entire existence, so it seems, has been caught up in wheels within wheels.

The first was the circle of racial apartheid. He grew up in a small southern town, part of an African American community forced by the white majority to exist within the confines of institutionalized segregation. The second was gospel music. Though at the center of all African American music, it was always a sphere of entertainment unto itself. Davis and the Hummingbirds would be giants within the genre, but not nearly as well known or as rewarded as they would have been had they opted for the entertainment mainstream. The third and last circle was his life in retirement. No longer active as a performer, he was living once again in a community within a community, the inner city of Philadelphia surrounded by relatively affluent suburbia all around.

The story of the Dixie Hummingbirds rightly begins with the coming of age of James Davis. He is prototypical of the founding fathers of modern black gospel music. His experiences growing up in the 1920s in a black community in the segregated South had everything to do with the Dixie Hummingbirds—the direction they took, the music they performed, and the impact they ultimately had on gospel music as a genre.

As for the music, black gospel is nothing less than communication about culture, far more profound than a mere litany of names, dates, and places. The music is intrinsically linked to life experience and the struggle of African Americans to persevere in a society that, as Bernice Johnson Reagon put it, "debated our worth as human beings."[1]

Without a doubt, seedtime for the Dixie Hummingbirds begins with young James Davis. Looking toward a lifetime of drudge work in his hometown, Greenville, South Carolina, he chose to make music his saving grace. He brought the dignity he found in performance to a personal vision that would ultimately shape the Dixie Hummingbirds.

It was a bitter cold February day in Philadelphia, 1995. Guided by Ira Tucker, Jr., son of the Dixie Hummingbirds' famed lead singer, Ira Tucker, Sr., we were on our way to meet James B. Davis, the group's retired patriarch. Hunkered down in our coats, we walked briskly, trying to minimize the bite of icy cold winds that barreled down the corridors of the inner city streets. Davis had not sung or traveled with the group for years. Nonetheless, he was still—as far as the group was concerned—their guiding light, a man to be treated with deference and respect. In my eyes, he loomed larger than life, a cultural hero of sorts, the rare person whose artistic endeavors had actually become part of the American folk tradition. Quite honestly, I was in awe and nervous about meeting him.

James Davis was a founding member of the Dixie Hummingbirds, and, over the group's seventy plus years as a performing entity, the cohesive force that held them together. As a group, they had come to be so revered within the African American community that calling them "legendary" would not be the least bit gratuitous. Davis was with them in 1928 at the start. He saw them through the Great Depression when they were barely known outside of Greenville County, South Carolina. He stood at the helm through their best years when the Dixie Hummingbirds helped shape the sound of soul gospel music. But the glory days were past and gone, and Davis, now in his 80s, long retired, a bit reclusive, was living in the inner city Philadelphia brownstone he had purchased back when the building and the neighborhood had been top of the line.

When the idea to chronicle the story of the Dixie Hummingbirds originally came up, Ira Tucker, Sr., now the keeper of the flame, was quite clear that James Davis had to be the first person interviewed. As we got closer to the Davis home, Ira, Jr.—"Gramp," as his closest friends called him—continued prepping to make sure everything started off smoothly. "Mr. Davis is eccentric," he said. "Odd. He has strong ideas." Davis had always been remarkably, sometimes mystifyingly, firm in his beliefs, stubbornly insistent about the "right" way to do things. For the moment, that meant no four-letter words of even the mildest kind or anything that might upset his sensibilities.

Even though he was not a member of the Hummingbirds, Ira Tucker, Jr., was also raised within the orbit of James Davis's influence. He was the kid who stood in the wings at Harlem's Apollo Theater back in the 1950s, watching and absorbing as his father, Davis, and the others worked their soul-wrenching magic on the crowd, people screaming and shouting, some doing holy dances right there in the theater aisles. The Hummingbirds were at the top of their game and James Davis was calling the shots. Even then, Ira, Jr., knew that James Davis was a force to reckon with. Now, back on the cold streets of Philadelphia, as we at last approached the house, Gramp's respect was evident in how, even outside the man's presence, he still talked about him as *Mister* Davis.

"There seemed nothing 'odd' about the man who greeted us."

The house stood in a block-long row of connected narrow brownstones in a neighborhood that had been upscale when Davis had originally bought there but was now rundown and shabby. The Davis house, though, was an exception, well maintained in the midst of abandoned boarded-up buildings, the gang-turf graffiti spray-painted on every available surface.

Davis was a man who had never permitted racism to block his progress, so it seemed fitting that he lived in the shadow of a 100-year old stone wall that had come to represent a victory over racism in the City of Brotherly Love. The wall surrounded the Girard School, isolating the institution, hiding its grounds from public view. Philadelphia financier Steven Girard founded the school in the 1830s and stipulated in its charter that room, board, and a free education be provided to orphan boys—*white* only. African Americans were to be excluded. The policy remained intact for decades and, for the African

American citizens of Philadelphia, came to symbolize institutionalized segregation. By the 1960s, with the neighborhood around Girard School almost entirely black, the stone wall stood as a constant and bitter reminder of those prejudices.[2] But through the efforts of an African American attorney, Cecil B. Moore, the Girard School policies, like the walls of Jericho, came tumbling down. Today, Cecil B. Moore Boulevard runs through the neighborhood, and the wall, no longer symbolic of a barrier to overcome, now signifies a battle fought and won. An apt setting for the residence of Mr. James B. Davis. We at last arrived at his door and knocked.

There seemed nothing "odd" about the man who greeted us. James Davis was tall, handsome, elegant, and most gracious. He was soft-spoken, a bit raspy as if all those years of singing had taken a toll on his voice. His clothes were heavy against the chill he evidently felt even inside the house. He invited us into a long dimly lit narrow living room. A lifetime of career mementos stood on shelves and hung on walls all around the room—fading sepia-toned photographs, trophies, gold records, and the Grammy award won in 1973 for the Humming-birds' version of Paul Simon's pop hit, "Loves Me like a Rock." We sat back, Davis across from us on the sofa as he began reflecting on the beginnings of the Dixie Hummingbirds and the days of his youth in Greenville, South Carolina, in the 1920s.

"No connection with the whites at all!"

Greenville is a city on the Piedmont plateau near the foothills of the Blue Ridge Mountains. In the 1920s, when James Davis was growing up there, almost 29,000 people lived in Greenville, more than a third African American.[3] Mamie Norris, born there in 1906, knew James Davis by reputation and has vivid memories of Greenville from their childhood days. Her family had a house near the train station. "Right at the Southern depot," she says. "We had a lot of trains then. The Southern Railway—that was the biggest mode of transportation at the time. From New York to New Orleans, right through Atlanta, Birmingham. It was called the main line. Greenville also had 18 cotton mills, one of the largest cotton mills in the world under one roof."[4]

But while the jobs were plentiful for African Americans in Greenville, as in every other southern city, segregation was the law of the land there, and civil rights were routinely denied to African Americans.

James Davis, founder of the Dixie Hummingbirds, 2000. Photo by Sam Zolten.

A story in the *Greenville News* circa 1928 exemplified the circumstances. One Bishop Hall, "a Negro," had been caught "making whiskey." The judge ordered Hall to sign "an agreement to permit police officers to search his home at any time day or night, with or without a warrant and search for whiskey."[5] This was the Greenville that James Davis knew. The city's African American community lived as well as they could within those parameters, closing ranks against the outside hostility. People worked around it, rose above it, and pressed on at their own pace and terms. "Wholly segregated," said Mamie Norris, resignation in her voice. "No connection with the whites at all."

Barney Parks has similar recollections. He and Davis teamed up as singing partners when they were kids, forming the core of what would become the Dixie Hummingbirds. Parks sang with the Birds until he was drafted in World War II, but continued after the war to work with them and other gospel artists as a booking agent. Nowadays, Parks was long retired and grappling with serious illness. He talked matter-of-factly about the past, laughing occasionally, but even after all these years he was still bitter about his experiences as a person of color in segregated Greenville. "Greenville was a prejudiced town, very much so."

> See, we didn't have any problems because we knew the situation. We knew how things were, and it didn't bother us. We knew how to stay in our place. When you know something and just go ahead, you're looking for trouble. But you can avoid that. We just didn't have any dealings with whites. [laughs] That was off limits! [laughs harder] Yeah, I'm telling you! We knew how to act around people.

In the 1920s, Greenville's African American community pulled together, formed a circle unto itself as protection from the indignities and pitfalls that existed on the outside. Blanche McIver, who grew up with Parks and Davis, has never forgotten how the lines were drawn, but she underscores that family and community helped everyone get through.

> They had black movie houses—I went to those. When they opened up the theaters, the blacks sat in the balcony. I didn't think nothing about it. They had stores uptown on Main Street that wouldn't let you try on clothing. The hell with them, 'cause when they put the money in the drawer, it is all green, isn't it? I didn't know Greenville was segregated. Didn't make any difference to me. That's the way it was.

We got everything we wanted within the black community. I give all the credit to my mother. She used to say, "Be yourself and you don't have to bow down to anybody!"[6]

This was the world in which James Davis and his family and friends lived. The irony was that institutionalized segregation, at least in Greenville, clearly had an unintended result. True, blacks may have been deflected from the mainstream, but the result was the flowering of a distinctly African American homegrown culture. The black people of Greenville had their own social activities, entertainments, shops, markets, businesses, schools, and churches. From all accounts, the African American community of Greenville in the 1920s and early 1930s functioned as an extended family, the "village" that raised the child. The children of Greenville, as much as one can generalize, were taught a healthy respect for their elders.

This certainly seems to hold true for James Davis. To this day, he credits the teaching of his elders—parents, teachers, clergy, and friends—with providing the foundation he brought in later years to the Dixie Hummingbirds. Even with their faults, he speaks respectfully of what he learned from his parents, John and Jannie Davis.

"My daddy was smart. My mother said he was a 'pimp.'"

James Davis was born in Greenville on June 6, 1916. The Davis home was on Meadow Street, a neighborhood of shotgun houses across the Reedy River from downtown Greenville. Even though it was west of the city, that part of town was called the Southern side because the Southern Railway tracks ran close by. The neighborhood itself was called "Meadow Bottoms" because it flooded every time the Reedy River overflowed. The houses were built up on high foundations so that floodwaters could pass harmlessly underneath. "My mother, Jannie, was a dark woman. John, my dad, was light-skinned, about my color. There were three of us kids, but only my sister lived. My brother died." John Davis had a profound impact on young James. "My daddy caught himself preparing me for everything. He sat me down and told me how things were."

John Davis offered lessons in both physical and spiritual survival. Times were financially tight for African American people all across the rural South. "Think about this time," says James Davis. "It was very poor. I think my mother made about seven dollars a week. She was a cook." But John Davis always seemed to have what he needed. "My daddy was smart," says James Davis. "My mother said he was a 'pimp, a good looking old pimp of a daddy.'"

Of course, Mrs. Davis meant what she said more figuratively than literally. John Davis was in fact strictly honorable and religious. She labeled him a "pimp" because he masterfully maintained the illusion that he worked for a living. With no visible ties to any job, he always seemed to have a dollar in his pocket. James Davis, like most members of the community, had a great deal of respect for his father, recalling, "Everyone thought he was a preacher. He was always glad, and I never heard him use a bad word. He didn't drink, didn't smoke, didn't curse, but he liked to go when he wanted to, come back when he pleased, work when he wanted. My mother, she just about had my daddy right in some kinda way."

Although he was not a preacher, John Davis was a spiritual man with firm ideas about right and wrong rooted in the Bible. He and Jannie were avid churchgoers. "My mother spent her whole life in church," says James Davis.

> My mother believed in growing wings, so to speak. But my dad was a guy that couldn't be pinpointed too well. Most people thought he was a preacher. But he wasn't a preacher. He was a guy with *his* kind of integrity. I'm a lot like him—a little odd. Most people think I'm odd. Never been interested in blues and stuff like that. Never been to a dance.

James Davis seemed to take a certain pride in being labeled "odd." For him, it meant he measured up to the ideals his father had planted in him all those years ago. To James Davis, being "odd" was synonymous with having "integrity," meaning he had a clear set of righteous rules and the discipline to stay true to them. Determined to be a man of unusual principle, James Davis would bring these values to his work and his music. "I'll tell you, my daddy made sure that I had my feet on the ground solidly."

The summers found James Davis away from home working on his mother's family farm in nearby Lawrence County. All he gained from the experience was the certainty that physical labor was not for him.

> They'd be working on the half, what they called "sharecropping," one of these set-ups where you work all year, and at the end of the year,

the men that owned the land would come in and say, "Well, we barely broke even, but we'll make it up to you next year." In other words, we barely got fed or paid off.

I don't remember having received a quarter in three years, but I ate better there than I did at home. One day the boss man said, "I wish I had your appetite." And I said, "You mean you want that, too!"

"If you don't know where music came from . . . you don't know anything about it."

Music was an important part of community life in Greenville, and especially so within the Davis family. As far back as James Davis can remember, his father was caught up in religious music and singing. "My daddy was a master of music—period!"

> He was one of those guys who would come up and say, "If you don't know where music came from, where it's going, and how fast it's traveling, you don't know anything about it!" Now that's the kind of fellow he was.
>
> He liked church music. He was a singer. He would sit down, sing the notes first and then the words of the song. And he loved to be able to sing it four or five different ways. When he was finished with that one, the next day, another song. I guess he knew so much about how a song was made. He didn't ever become attached to no song. But he loved all of them. Maybe he'd get another book, wherever it opened, that was his song.

Unlike his son, John Davis never thought to earn a living in music. For him, the reward was in the sheer mastery and in the intensity of the commitment. Although James was too young to understand his father's philosophy of music, he did learn some musical skills, such as the technique of "shape note" singing. "The reason it's called 'shape note' is because, like the words say, there are shapes for each note."

> Like "doh" was a triangle, go to "re," a half moon, and what not. The shapes were a standard thing from church to church. And that was a short way to learn music. You associate the shape with the note.
>
> He called me in the house one day, he says, "Bodee, [a nickname his closest friends still call him today] this is a 'doh.'" He was making shape music. "This is the foundation of music, right here, this note." It was shaped like an Indian teepee. So, he said, "This is a 'doh.' It's the

first letter in music. It's the last one in music. This is the foundation. You always come back to this."

I wasn't certain what he was talkin' about. I had a pocket full of marbles. I just looked at him and went back outside and began to shoot my marbles. He called me back in about 15 minutes and asked me what that was. And I said, "I don't know." He snatched me up off the floor and looked at me. When he got angry his eyes danced, you know. He'd say, "I'm your daddy. Hear me when I talk to you."

"If you could sing, even though you might be black, people like you anyway."

While James Davis may not have immediately picked up his father's passion for music, he was intrigued by the many styles he encountered around town. First and foremost, there was church. He loved the harmonies and the big sound of the choir, a group that, in a few years, he would be old enough to join. He was also taken with the solo singers, the unself-conscious souls who, without benefit of training, threw themselves totally into hymns they sang in church on Sunday, the entire congregation rocking and swaying as they kept time with hands and feet and the occasional tambourine.

Then, there were the needle-worn Victrola records his parents played at home, a cappella quartets just beginning to explore the emotive possibilities of the old spirituals. James Davis also remembers encounters on the streets of Greenville with itinerant sanctified singers, some accompanying themselves with guitar, some starkly solo voice, but in either case trying to entice any spare change they could from compassionate passers-by. But the performance that he remembers really first caught his attention was by a nameless preacher who had been invited to sing at his school.

> When I first fell in love with singing, a guy came to our grade school—a preacher—and he was singing a cappella—by himself. He had so much feeling that the people there went crazy over what he was doing. Now, he wasn't even singing in time. He sold his music through expression and feeling. You talk about soul. Man, that old man had some soul! I can almost hear him now.

James Davis was drawn to the idea that music could touch its listeners' emotions. Music was a way to connect to people and possibly even earn a decent and respectable living. Davis was aware of a handful of black gospel quartets who had become famous, at least within the confines of the African American community, because of their phonograph records. He took notice of the local performers busking on the streets of Greenville and the entertainers who passed through town in medicine shows, minstrel troupes, and jazz and blues tent show revues. Davis particularly remembers the Gulf Coast Singers, a street ensemble sponsored by a soft drink company. "Boy, could they sing!"

Even way back then, they were good enough to sing for Pepsi Cola or one of those. They had a sponsor. One thing about the South. If you could sing, even though you might be black, people liked you anyway. That group made an impression on me, though, and I saw *that* was a way. When I first started singing, I wasn't thinking in terms of making no living. That wasn't it. I was just singing 'cause I liked it.

Davis also took notice of the "big name" talent that occasionally passed through Greenville. "One thing I recall vividly, Cab Calloway coming there. And he was so big at that time, they had to have officers keep the people off of him. Everybody wanted to get to 'em, you know." Textile Hall was the place where performers of Calloway's stature appeared. Davis liked that the shows at Textile Hall were open to anyone. At smaller venues, race mixing was outlawed. There might be a "prime time" show for whites and a late show for blacks. Or, as Mamie Norris remembers, there would be a "main floor where the dancing was, and whites would be the spectators in the balconies. But when whites were on the dance floor, blacks would be watching from the balcony."

Given Greenville's strict segregation, James Davis is still incredulous thinking back on the open door policy at Textile Hall. He wondered if the lax rules had somehow carried over from the Catholic Church that stood next door. "Way back then, whoever—black man, white man, beggar man, thief—could go to that church. They'd been a standout all that time. And Cab was playing right next door and anybody could come! I just wonder if the people who ran Textile Hall were motivated by that Catholic Church? Anybody in town could come." The philosophy evidently made a lasting impression on James Davis. Over the years, his Dixie Hummingbirds always strived to reach the broadest spectrum of people. Black or white. American or European. Believers or nonbelievers. The Birds would be a group for everyman.

"It was singing about Jesus that kept us in everything."

As for his own performing preferences, James Davis never seriously considered secular music. From childhood, he was taught there was purity and morality in spiritual music and singing for the Lord. "We came out of the church, and that's all we had. It was singing about Jesus that kept us in everything." Davis learned in church how to sing and perform in front of audiences. He started as a soloist and then joined the junior choir where he would meet other singers and befriend a group of older boys who had already organized their own quartet. He impressed them with his high voice. "I used to sound like a woman when I sang. I was around 10 or 11, so naturally, I did have a real high voice." In fact, that high voice would be Davis's mark of distinction throughout his career. The "older boys" who wanted him to sing with them were his cousin, Andrew Lloyd, and friends Cleve Willis and Furman Haggard. "Andrew got me to sing tenor for them. That helped me get interested in quartets."

The first time Davis sang on a program with the young quartet, though, turned out to be his last. They were invited to perform at a church in Asheville, North Carolina.

> I went off with those guys after having rehearsed with them for about six months. That was my first program. And two of them decided they must have some whiskey. And it got back to my mother. By the time I got back to Greenville, she dropped that on me. She said, "Yeah. They tell me some of the boys were drinking." I said, "Well, you're right." I didn't mess with those guys again. I got out that night. But by that time I had come to like the idea of the quartet, the harmony, you know. I liked that part, so I formed my own group. Oh yeah! And that would be our first rule. No drinking. That was a "no no."

From that day forward, as far as Davis was concerned, "no drinking" would be number one in the Dixie Hummingbirds' rulebook.

"We called it the 'Junior Choir,' and then we started to be the 'Junior Boys.'"

Davis drew the members of his new group from within the junior choir. Among the first to join was Barney Parks who had moved to Greenville from Willington, South Carolina, where he was born to James Tate and Maggie Parks on July 15, 1915. "James Davis and I grew up together.

We were raised in a sanctified church, the Bethel Church of God Holiness in Greenville. The membership wasn't too large and the choir wasn't too large. We called it the 'Junior Choir,' and then we started to be the 'Junior Boys.' There were just four of us."

The old wooden church stood on the corner of Meadow and Bailey, just down the street from the Davis house. The services there could really rock, upbeat and roiling with emotion. "Very spiritual," remembers Barney Parks.

> Oh, there was a lot of shouting, a lot of "hallelujahs" and "amens" and testifying. Just having a good time spiritually. At that time, people looked down on Holiness churches. They called us "holy rollers." They didn't understand. They always carried the Holy Bible, but they didn't understand the meaning of holiness. And we connected with holiness through those spiritual services.

In 1928, twelve-year-old James Davis organized baritone Barney Parks, bass Fred Owens, and lead Bonnie Gipson, Jr., into a group called the Junior Boys, the first incarnation of the Dixie Hummingbirds. "We were real tight," says James Davis. The Junior Boys were well practiced and drew a crowd when they sang. "We used to pack the church out every Sunday night," said Barney Parks. "We had a pretty good little group." Mamie Norris remembers that other churches started inviting the Junior Boys to sing on their programs.

> I would hear 'em in the church down below us, but then too, they would be citywide. People would want them on different occasions. They were just four little old black boys. That's all! Nobodies. Didn't even have uniforms. And they didn't do the rocking like these fellows all do now. They didn't have that rhythm and stuff like that. They just sang spirituals mostly. They sang from their hearts. People would get to hand clapping, jumping, and shouting. [laughs] They sang everywheres and just rose to fame.

"It was the only black high school in Green County at that time."

Sterling High School launched the Junior Boys on their career. "Sterling was the only black high school in Green County at that time," says Mamie Norris, "and Sterling was special." Founded in 1896 by former slave, the Reverend Daniel Minus, and named for antislavery activist

Mrs. Emeline Sterling of Poughkeepsie, New York, Sterling was known for its committed teachers and supportive community.[7]

Sterling High nurtured and encouraged the boys' ambitions. Soon after their arrival, the Junior Boys changed their name to the Sterling High School Quartet. The boys attracted a lot of attention from the start. "The kids had it in for us right away," says Davis, "just because we came in as a group."

> They felt we had a chip on our shoulders because people [were] talking about the singers and all. And we thought we looked cute and we must of made a show of it, see. [laughs] Man, the initiations! They beat me up something terrible.
>
> We all stayed together, that's what got to them. And all the females! I remember I had to hide under one of the little chairs in school, and some girl found me. Boy, she was hot! [shouts] "Here he is! Here he is!" Boy, they wore us out.
>
> And then the coaches. We were just coming in, you know. And at the end of the line were the coaches. They really wanted us to get on the football team. And I had played football when I was in grade school. Some guy threw me and a bunch of guys came and got on top of him and I was on the bottom. When I got up, I was finished with that game!

At Sterling, Davis, Parks, and the group received formal training as singers from one of their teachers, Professor Hickson. Hickson had already arranged for other Sterling students to study music on scholarship at Morris Brown University in Atlanta and was thinking along the same lines for the Sterling Quartet. Davis and company, however, had other ideas. Impressed by the quartets they had been hearing on phonograph records and in live local performances, the Sterlings were thinking about becoming professional gospel entertainers like them. "The first professional group that I heard," says Barney Parks, "was the Heavenly Gospel Singers with their bass singer, Jimmy Bryant, who was already famous back then. The Heavenly Gospel Singers took things by storm. Back then, you know, it was 10 and 15 cents at the door. When they came, it was 25 cents. We would stand outside and listen through the window, me and Davis and the others, 'cause we didn't have money."

The members of the Sterling High School Quartet admired those singers' lifestyle as much as their music. James Davis in particular understood that the profession of quartet singing was one of the few occupations open to persons of color that offered a measure of dignity and promise.

"All the way from Greenville to Atlanta. But we were traveling!"

The annual Church of God convention in Atlanta, Georgia, where thousands converged for a weekend of meeting, testifying, preaching, and singing, was the quartet's first big public performance. The Sterling High School Quartet made the trip with every intention of breaking out in a big way. "We gonna travel some!" says Barney Parks. "All the way from Greenville to Atlanta! [laughs] But we were traveling! And that year, we were gonna get famous."

Their performance was an enormous success. Riding on a cloud of inflated assurance, that night after the program the quartet drove out of Atlanta and kept on going. "We just took off," says Barney Parks.

> We were in a borrowed car. No money. We headed for West Virginia. Not able to buy the gas we should have, we cut the ignition and coasted down the hills. Nothing! Just nerve. Sleeping in the car. Standing on the corner not knowing anybody. Hungry. Stayed in Chattanooga and had to pawn one of Bonnie Gipson's suits to get away from there.
>
> But we got along all right because we was just a clean religious group. We ended up in West Virginia with a Mr. Briggs. And Mr. Briggs would tell us, say, "Look, you all got a good little group, but you got too much harmony." He wanted us to holler. We couldn't holler, see. In school, we were in the glee club and all that. We were kinda refined. We didn't know all that hollering gospel. We got into it later because we had to for variety and in order for the group to be successful on the road. But back then, no.

Determined to stay the course, the Sterling High School Quartet returned humbly to Greenville and struggled to make a name for themselves from home. As James Davis put it, "We thought we could make a living at it, but we had to learn how."

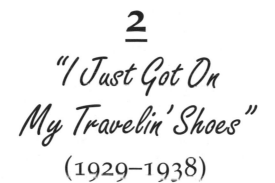

2

"I Just Got On My Travelin' Shoes"

(1929–1938)

I just got on my travelin' shoes,
I'm doing my duty,
Oh, Lordy, yes, yes, yes.
Because I just got on my travelin' shoes.

—"Traveling Shoes"
Mitchell's Christian Singers, 1934

The 1930s—with the Depression, migrants from the Oklahoma dust bowl, and the mass exodus of black Americans from the Deep South to the urban North and West—were difficult for many Americans, but the decade ultimately brought success to James Davis, Barney Parks, and a revolving lineup of the Sterling High School Quartet. They benefited from the old formula—when times are hard, the entertainment business thrives—as well as from the increasing popularity of African American performance style among Anglo-Americans. The mass migration of African Americans from the South created a nationwide market for black entertainers of all kinds. In a short time, the whole face of American pop culture would come under the sway of what Langston Hughes called "black magic," the alluring mass appeal of African American performance style.

Perhaps the most important factor favoring the fledgling Sterling Quartet was the development of radio and phonograph records. Performers who formerly could only build a fan base through direct personal appearance could now reach greater numbers than ever before. Even the poorest families—including most African Americans—found a way to own a radio, a wind-up Victrola, and a pile of well-played phonograph records. It was a luxury that would significantly improve the quality of almost everyone's life.

During the early 1930s, Americans warmed to President Roosevelt's homey "fireside chats" and forgot their troubles in the music, drama, and comedy offered up over the course of the broadcast day. Despite the demeaning images of African Americans perpetuated by radio programs such as *Amos 'n' Andy*, the medium also provided African American musical performers extraordinary opportunities to reach the broad audience. Over the airwaves, one could hear the works of African American bands fronted by leaders like Cab Calloway, Jimmy Lunceford, Erskine Hawkins, Fletcher Henderson, and many others.

Out of radio's intermingling of musical styles, numerous ironies arose. Tunes like "Brother Can You Spare a Dime" stood in sharp contrast to pop fare like Bing Crosby's relatively insipid signature song, "Where the Blue of the Night (Meets the Gold of the Day)." With compositions derived from African American tradition, George Gershwin rose to the top of the entertainment world while black composer Duke Ellington continued to struggle for every ounce of mainstream recognition. "Empress of the Blues" Bessie Smith fell out of fashion as subtler jazz stylists like Billie Holiday moved into the spotlight. American popular music was in flux with the blending of black and white musical styles as up-and-coming artists created new amalgams from the old genres.

In 1932, after both his wife and son died in childbirth, down-and-dirty blues singer Thomas Dorsey wrote the first and most enduring of his hymns, "Take My Hand, Precious Lord."[1]

> Precious Lord, take my hand,
> Lead me on, let me stand,
> I am tired, I am weak, I am worn;
> Through the storm, through the night,
> Lead me on to the light,
> Take my hand, precious Lord, lead me on.

In this new style, labeled "gospel," Dorsey fused the elegant emotionality of spirituals with the lowdown beat of barrelhouse blues.

By the 1930s, major record companies, labels like Victor and Columbia that for decades had specialized in the music of Anglo America, released selected styles of African American religious music. These labels recorded black preachers like the Reverend J. M. Gates and the Reverend J. C.

Burnett. Their sensationally titled records—"These Hard Times Are Tight Like That," "Don't Hide from Your Furniture Man," "Scat to the Cat and Sooey to the Hog," "Is There Harm in Singing the Blues," "Straining at a Gnat and Swallowing a Camel"—sold tens of thousands of copies, encouraging the recording of other types of religious performers.

Recordings by a cappella gospel quartets helped the style spread in popularity throughout the Deep South and along the eastern seaboard. Groups like the Famous Blue Jay Singers of Alabama and the Norfolk Jubilee Quartet of Virginia broke beyond regional bounds through the reach of phonograph records. These quartets performed in the spiritual tradition but with unorthodox harmonies and vocals that overflowed with emotion. Like Thomas Dorsey, they sang with a beat, moved around on stage, clapped their hands and tapped their feet—flirting with the devil as far as conservative members of the African American religious community were concerned.

Taking advantage of this rapidly changing music scene, the Sterling High School Quartet launched an ambitious campaign to succeed as professional gospel entertainers.

"I figured that was the only bird could fly both backwards and forwards."

The members of the Sterling Quartet could still hear the applause from Atlanta, were still intoxicated by the adventure of the spontaneous road trip that followed. James Davis and the others understood, however, that a Sterling High diploma meant a great deal to both family and the community that nurtured them. Greenville's African American community considered each student who graduated a small victory in the fight against racism. But the bitter truth was that a diploma ultimately could not help a person of color to secure honorable work with decent pay anywhere in or around Greenville. The young singers, though, irreversibly hooked on the excitement of their quest, felt that the possibility of a musical career was preferable to the mundane low-paid drudge work that seemed the inevitable alternative.

James Davis had learned from his father that singing for the Lord was in and of itself honorable and respectable, although ironically the elder Davis would not have approved of singing as a way to earn a living. There was, however, simply not enough money coming in to feed and clothe the entire Davis family. "My mother was the only one at the house working," he remembers. "We were having such a problem. It was too tough."

Davis's ultimate decision was also helped along by a chance encounter with one of his former teachers at Sterling High, a man whose counsel he respected. "It was the last time I saw him. He was riding a bicycle delivering drugs for a drug store."

> It broke my heart to see him, but you know what he told me? He said, "There is not enough room for all of us to be teachers or professors." And that's all you could do down there unless you wanted to be an undertaker. Or leave home. Or be a football or baseball player, and then you couldn't go far, couldn't get in the major leagues. There was no use even to think about making a living with baseball, football, or boxing. Joe Louis had everything in boxing tied up anyway. My teacher made me see that I'd have to get out of there if I ever hoped to make my own way.

Davis was also encouraged by his mother who told him, "If you think you can make it, go on out and try." With his father off on one of his perennial mystery excursions, Davis sought approval instead from his church pastor. "The pastor said, 'I don't see anything wrong with it.' Of course, we did have a little controversy. Some of the other ministers in the church . . . wanted people to secure our services through *them*. They were serious about that!" The quartet, however, had other ideas. They wanted to be independent.

James Davis, a year or two younger than the others, would have graduated from Sterling High School in 1934. Instead, he dropped out to pursue the dream of becoming a professional spiritual entertainer. Now that they had cut their ties with school, the group decided a name change was in order. They came up with the "Dixie Hummingbirds."

Davis takes credit for the name. "I came up with the Hummingbirds because I saw how the hummingbirds were down there in South Carolina."

> I figured that was the only bird could fly both backwards and forwards. Since that was how our career seemed to be going [laughs], I figured that was a good name, and the guys went along with it.

The group wanted people to know where they were from, so their first impulse was to call themselves the South Carolina Hummingbirds, but the name seemed too long. They shortened it by substituting "Dixie," and the rest was history. "They always said the Dixie Hummingbirds was the first of the 'bird' groups," says James Davis.

By "bird" groups, Davis meant street corner vocal ensembles like the Ravens and Orioles who, in the postwar 1940s, turned professional and charted the stylistic course later followed by so-called doo-wop harmony groups. By the middle 1950s, bird names were the fashion in rhythm and blues. The Wrens, Crows, Cardinals, Swallows, Quails, Parrots, Robins, Penguins, Flamingos, and even the plain old Five Birds were some of the best known, and all would be part of the first great wave of the music that came to be called "rock 'n' roll."

In fact, these "bird" groups appropriated more than a naming convention from the Dixie Hummingbirds. They also drew on melody lines, rhythms, complex harmony weaves, and the stirring lead vocal styles perfected by the Birds and fellow gospel quartets. Davis was proud that the Hummingbirds had an impact outside gospel and that they had a reputation as innovators, right down to choosing a group name. An uncommonly savvy choice in those days before media consultants and market analysis, the name "Dixie Hummingbirds" was at once charming, expressive, and memorable.

The "Dixie," with its association to the minstrel song of the same name, imparted to the group an inescapable southern connotation. The technique had been used numerous times before by record companies that arbitrarily tacked "Dixie" to a group's name hoping that the implied southern authenticity would spur record sales. The device was also pressed into service when recordings were re-released on budget subsidiary labels. So, for example, in the 1930s, the Pace Jubilee Singers on Gennett became the Dixie Jubilee Singers on Champion, and Bryant's Jubilee Quartet on Gennett became the Dixie Jubilee Choir on Supertone.[2]

Most gospel groups chose flat functional names that reflected number, origin, or affiliation: the Southernaires, the Norfolk Jubilee Quartet, the Birmingham Jubilee Singers. The trend derived no doubt from the Fisk Jubilee Singers, the group that had first sparked worldwide interest in the almost forgotten slave spirituals.

In an effort to raise money for Fisk University in Nashville, the Fisk Jubilees had traveled the world performing spiritual classics like "Swing Low, Sweet Chariot," "Nobody Knows the Trouble I See," and "Steal Away." The African American press regularly chronicled their international movements. "The Fisk Jubilee Singers are in Calcutta, India, where they are winning golden opinions as usual," reported the *Detroit Plaindealer* in 1890, and in the *Indianapolis Freeman*, "having completed their tour through Australian colonies, India, Burma, Singapore, and China, will after visiting Japan, return to America after an absence of more than six years on a journey around the world."[3] With their early success on tour and on records, the Fisk Jubilee Singers had been the role model for African American vocal group names, at least in the realm of religious singing.

Secular African American groups, on the other hand, competed to out-name one another. The Mills Brothers chose a straightforward designation, but most of the best-known groups—the Ink Spots, the Delta Rhythm Boys, the Charioteers—alluded obliquely to race, with lesser-known groups picking delightfully inventive names such as the Four Pods of Pepper, the Four Blackbirds, the Jones Boys Sing Band, the Five Jinks, the Bronzeville Five, Tim Brynn's Black Devil Four, Rollin Smith's Rascals, the Mississippi Mud Mashers, the Pullman Porters Quartette, or the Grand Central Redcap Quartet.

The Dixie Hummingbirds achieved both a degree of novelty and a measure of dignity, avoiding heavy-handed puns or allusion to their race. In two intuitively well-chosen words, they managed to convey a sense of place and the sweet singing style that would define them early on. Equipped with a catchy name, the Dixie Hummingbirds set out to sell their reputation and build a following. James Davis, very much in his father's style, assumed control, making certain the group held to a professional course and was strategic in its ambition.

Throughout the 1930s, the Hummingbirds toured vigorously. Among the first groups in black gospel to fuse spiritual sensibilities with commercial appeal, they hoped to reach African American audiences on a broad regional scale by delivering consistently powerful and memorable performances.

"We started off singing spirituals."

By the 1930s, recreational a cappella vocalizing was already an "old and venerated African American art form."[4] Basic freedoms won in the Civil War—the right to choose an occupation and move freely about the countryside—had made it possible for African Americans who had been enslaved to pursue careers as itinerant performers. White America had responded by evolving a degree of tolerance for African Americans who were skilled as entertainers and even a genuine affection for black performance styles. A turn-of-the-century story in the African American newspaper, the *Indianapolis Freeman*, quoted a white theater manager: "Negro music is the sweetest music in the world. If you don't believe it, go and see some of the success made by the singing pickaninnies in the various theatres in New York at the present time, to say nothing of the Negro quartets in the 'Uncle Tom's Cabin' shows."[5]

By the twentieth century, African Americans had become an integral part of the American popular entertainment scene, appearing as minstrels and medicine show shills, blues and sanctified singers, operatic divas, collegiate chorale groups, dancers, and jazz and brass and fiddle and jug bands. Minstrel shows, a genre that cultural historian Hans Nathan called the "national art of the Nineteenth century,"[6] featured grotesque and demeaning caricatures of African Americans. Traveling minstrel shows, however, ironically provided African American vocal groups the first opportunities to display and perfect their skills as performers. Black minstrel troupes, redundant in blackface, toured countrywide, portraying the stereotypical characters to black, white, or mixed audiences. In this context, African American a cappella harmony groups first found opportunity to perform and be paid. Vocal groups with their complex harmony and rhythm were the stars of black minstrel shows.

Poet and songwriter James Weldon Johnson wrote in 1929 about the early African American quartet tradition. He began with a scene conjured up from slavery days. "When the folks at the 'big house' sat on the veranda and heard the singing floating up through the summer night from the 'quarters,' they were enchanted." Johnson remembered how as a "small boy" in the 1870s, he enjoyed hearing crack quartets made up of waiters in the Jacksonville hotels. "Each of the big Florida resort hotels," he wrote, "boasted at least two quartets."

He recalled days when "every barber shop had its quartet, and the men spent their leisure time playing on the guitar ... and 'harmonizing,'" putting forth his view that the "barbershop chord" and Anglo harmony group tradition had their origins in these African American vocal traditions.[7] In closing, Johnson described how competitions and cash prizes motivated quartet singers to experiment, in the process obliterating conventions of vocal group arrangements, harmonies, and rhythms. "I have witnessed some of these explorations in the field of harmony and the scenes of hilarity and back-slapping when a new and peculiarly rich chord was discovered. There would be demands for repetitions, and cries of 'Hold it! Hold it!' until it was firmly mastered. And well it was, for some of these chords were so new and strange that ... they would never have been found again except for the celerity with which they were recaptured."[8]

Among those drawn to the quartet enterprise were James Weldon

Johnson himself, who sang competitively in the 1890s, and Scott Joplin, the "King of Ragtime," who got his musical start as one of the Texas Medley Quartet.[9]

When the Dixie Hummingbirds began touring earnestly in the 1930s, they were entering a long-standing performing arts tradition, one that unlike other entertainments afforded African Americans the opportunity to present themselves with dignity. In fact, quartet competitions played a vital role in spurring initial cross-cultural interest in black performance style. Noted the *Freeman* as early as 1894, "the National Contest between the Tennessee Warblers, the Chicago Quartette, and the Hoosier Quartet will be an eventful occasion. . . .The Y.M.C.A. Hall will be crowded. . . . A great many white people will attend the contest, . . . the masses of the young people are elated over the coming contest."[10]

In contrast to the performers in minstrel shows, African American quartet singers projected a positive image. Brilliance and originality were permissible—in fact, encouraged. The Dixie Hummingbirds would carry on that rich tradition as they progressed toward professionalism. As group leader, James Davis would always concern himself with image, intuitively extending the legacy of nineteenth-century African American vocal groups such as the Excelsior Quartet, the Black Diamond Quartet, the Buckeye Quartet, the Darktown Quartet, and the Beethoven Quartet, whose names had long been forgotten.[11]

"We rehearsed in motels and even on the highway in the car."

In the 1930s, African American vocal groups called themselves "quartets" no matter how many individual singers they had. The idea was that the four standard voices—tenor, alto, baritone, and bass—were represented in the harmonic mix.[12] When there were five or more in a group, parts were doubled, or leads were handed off like a baton in a relay race; the objective was to avoid straining the lead voices and to bring variety to the overall group sound. In their earliest days, however, the Dixie Hummingbirds remained a true quartet, with James Davis in his distinctly high tenor handling most of the leads.

Strict adherents to the quartet tradition, the group performed in their Sunday best, dark suits and ties. They stood in a straight line and simply sang without moving, instead allowing the emotion to come through in the expression of their voices and the words of the song. Their harmonies were homespun, made up in their heads, but drawn from every harmony group they had ever heard in or out of church. They were serious and mindful of tradition, singing, really, the only way they knew.

They performed a cappella, no instrumental accompaniment at all. On the road, if there was a piano, the odds were it would be out of tune. With voices only, the Hummingbirds could practice anytime, anyplace. "We rehearsed in motels," recalls James Davis, "and even on the highway in the car." And if a singer did not work out—which in those days happened often enough—he could be easily replaced with minimal disruption.

By 1937, only Davis and Barney Parks remained of the original four. Bad habits, personality clashes, and unreliability all factored in to the turnovers. "We had a lot of guys, a lot of talent back in the very beginning," said Davis, "but we couldn't do anything with 'em."

> Fred Owens was our original bass singer. You couldn't handle Fred Owens. Number one rule in the group, you had to carry yourself like gentlemen. He had a bunch of habits that we couldn't tolerate. Made the group look bad.
>
> J. B. Matterson sang bass with us for a short while.
>
> Bonnie Gipson, Jr., and I were very tight. We were tight as boys. But Bonnie didn't have a sense of pitch. Oh, he had a wonderful voice, wonderful personality, as nice a fellow as you'll ever meet, but he didn't have a sense of pitch. And boy, it broke my heart, really broke my heart to have to let him go.
>
> Barney Parks was the one who stayed with the group. Now, I was a funny guy. I didn't fall out with a person because we were incompatible, though we were. If a guy did his job, I'd try to make it with him, and that's how it was with Barney.

The Hummingbirds remained in a state of flux as they struggled to reach a consistent level of professionalism. "Lots of great singers came and went," says Davis.

> There was O. D. Hill. He was good, but he was one of those guys who wanted to stay around home. He didn't stay with us but a little while.
>
> Luther Chriswell, the same thing. He was some kinda bass singer. One of the best I ever heard anywhere! Our problem would have been singing low enough for this guy. He was too much! He had fallen in love with some woman. And he says, "Ah, you know, I'd like to go with you all, and stay with you all, but you see that little woman there? I ain't leaving her no way." His woman told him to get off that, but he stayed with her anyway.
>
> We had another singer, Wilson Baker. Called him "Highpockets"

because he was so short. He's the only guy I know who would hit out a note and miss it a mile! But he had a way with the people. He'd sell it man, have the people giving him a big hand! Boy, he was too much. I guess he sang with us a couple of years.

Sam Briggs, he was one we fell out with because we couldn't do nothing about him and his whiskey. That's one of the reasons why it was hard to keep singers. One time we had us a bass singer that was out of this world. And the first program we went off on, a deacon of all people, came to us and wanted to know, did we want a little refreshments. We asked what did he mean. He says [taking on the voice of the character], "Something to wet your whistle, give you a little nerve." I said, "We don't drink." But this bass singer, he just kept on watching the guy. After then, I said to myself, we sure going to have to get rid of him. But he sure could sing.

"He was a real handsome dude, and he knew he was handsome."

Of all the singers to move in and out of the Dixie Hummingbirds during those formative years, none impacted them more than bass singer Jimmy Bryant. "He was a member of the group twice," remembers James Davis. When Bryant first joined the Hummingbirds in the late 1930s, he had been with the Heavenly Gospel Singers, a group that had recorded over sixty sides for the Victor budget subsidiary label, Bluebird.

The Heavenly Gospel Singers, originally from Detroit, were headquartered in Greenville's sister city, Spartanburg, South Carolina. They came to Spartanburg through a series of unfortunate events. Organized by lead tenor Fred Whitmore, the group had been touring the South when they were involved in an automobile accident that resulted in the death of a white judge. The entire group was jailed and after their release, fell apart. Whitmore returned to Detroit where he put together a new lineup that included Roosevelt Fennoy, Henderson Massey, and Jimmy Bryant. This was the configuration that became famous for their recordings on Bluebird Records.[13]

Once again on tour, the Heavenly Gospel Singers were in the South when leader Fred Whitmore unexpectedly died. Henderson Massey, a Spartanburg native, steered the group to his hometown, and that became their new base of operations.

The Heavenly Gospel Singers had a substantial following in the Carolinas, even though they had a different sound from the local groups. Carolina quartets had a distinctive approach that Tony Heilbut described as "harmony over expression."[14] With tight harmony as the focal point, Carolina quartets tended to sing as a team, no single voice standing out, a style that certainly described the early Dixie Hummingbirds. The Heavenly Gospel Singers, on the other hand, rooted in a northern urban tradition, favored a more expressive technique. But mostly the difference could be attributed to Jimmy Bryant. His approach to bass singing was unique. He was neither a profound bass nor a particularly great singer, but he brought personality to the role. "I never thought Jimmy Bryant could sing a stroke," says James Davis, "but the people did. He'd go to a schoolhouse, he'd turn the place upside down! He would clown and do a lot of things to get that audience. He could sell it. You know, singers back then didn't move around too much. But Bryant did. He was one of those guys who could almost go over backwards to the floor. Tall and limber. The people ate it up!"

Bryant's antics and percussive style drove the Heavenly Gospel Singers and set them apart from the local quartets. As a result, the group, noted gospel historian Ray Funk, "took the area by storm . . . and caused everybody to imitate them."[15]

"People wild about 'em back then," says James Davis.

Before Bryant's move, the two groups had a long-standing rivalry in the Carolinas. In fact, they would often set themselves up on the same bill, figuring the competition would be a good draw. At first, the Heavenlys were the top attraction. With the Birds improving over time, though, they eventually got to a point, as James Davis tells it, when they consistently outperformed the Heavenlys.

The two quartets egged each other on with new songs, more striking harmonies, hotter arrangements, and stage movements. "It was a matter of each group trying to be the best at what they were doing," says James Davis.

The Heavenly Gospel Singers had made a lot of records, and people *crazy* about their records! And we were on a lot of dates with them. And most of those dates *we* took. We could get by the Heavenly Gospel Singers by outclassing them. We could sing their style, but they couldn't sing ours.

If a group in front of you goes over well enough, the last thing you want to do is the same type of stuff they're singing. A group get up and raise a lot of sand, you get up and be as sweet as you can get! Get sweet as a honeycomb before you get up there hollering. Show the people you have some voices. And we could sure enough do that because that was how we started.

As far as James Davis was concerned, Jimmy Bryant had simply made a move to the better group. But the instability that befell the Heavenly Gospel Singers following the unexpected death of their leader, Fred Whitmore, may have played a role. In addition, Bryant may have been more trouble to the group than he was worth. Barney Parks remembers him as "kind of wild and just not stable." James Davis concurs. "He could be hard to get along with at times."

I know he was dissatisfied with something that had gone on with the Heavenly Gospel Singers and he wanted to get with us. Bryant was one of those guys who liked to be in the spotlight. When he gets all up in the air, he some *kind* of salty! But when he got to the program, all that is under the table. That was his best night. He worked harder that night! But, oh man, when he got back in the car, he start up right again! He was a lot like that fellow who plays basketball in Chicago— Dennis Rodman. He was a lot like Rodman! A bad boy.

As for the Heavenly Gospel Singers, they did not mind losing Bryant because they had discovered a local bass singer, William Bobo, who they thought might be even better for the group. Bobo did not growl out the notes like Bryant, but instead sang with the deep luster of a fine bass fiddle. Davis still recalls the first time he heard William Bobo, because it was the rare occasion when the Heavenlys got over on the Dixie Hummingbirds. "We were in Gaffney, South Carolina. Bobo decided to take over that night—and boy, he did! He was blowing *every*body out of the place—and the people went crazy!"

In 1938, replaced by the smooth-singing William Bobo, Jimmy Bryant left the Heavenlys and joined the Dixie Hummingbirds. The Birds benefited from his rugged driving style and popularity. "Jimmy Bryant, he was a real handsome dude," says James Davis, "and he knew he was handsome. Kids just went wild over him. They knew him. Some people didn't even want him to come around. He was very popular. Jimmy Bryant. Oh, man!" Bryant immediately boosted the Hummingbirds' popularity locally and used his connections in the record business to land them their first professional recording opportunity

"The dissonances are . . . not to be ironed out by the trained musician."

The addition of James Bryant to their lineup set off a decade of stylistic evolution for the Hummingbirds. "We didn't start off singing gospel," says James Davis. "We started off singing spirituals." The Dixie

Hummingbirds stayed within the parameters of the tradition in which they were raised. They were not out to develop a new repertoire but to bring as much originality as they could to the singing of the staid old spirituals.

So-called hard soul gospel—the intense bring-down-the house style the Birds would become famous for decades later—was not yet fully formed. The ingredients, though, were already present in the shouted sermons of emotive preachers, the cross-rhythmic hand-clapping of church congregations, the flatfoot dancing of Carolina and Georgia sea island Gullah ring shouts, the "catch-on-fire" style of Alabama quartets, and the jubilant prayer services in the Birds' own Holiness Church.

In the years between 1935 and 1939, though, the Dixie Hummingbirds stayed with the tried and true to win over the widest possible spectrum of listeners as they traveled from town to town, church to church. Mostly, they performed for African Americans, but often enough audiences were mixed and on some occasions entirely white.

When they performed for whites, they began with at least one song that conformed to white expectations of what blacks ought to be singing before moving on to the rest of their show. The song they used as a "placater" was Stephen Foster's "Old Black Joe," a melancholy pseudo-hymn about an aged slave yearning for old times and friends long gone. "Jimmy Bryant brought the song into the group," recalls James Davis. "He'd take the house with 'Old Black Joe.'"

> Gone are the days when my heart was young and gay,
> Gone are my friends from the cotton fields away,
> Gone from the earth to a better land, I know,
> I hear their gentle voices calling, "Old Black Joe."
> I'm coming, I'm coming, for my head is bending low.
> I hear those gentle voices calling, "Old Black Joe."
> Where are the hearts once so happy and so free,
> The children so dear that I held upon my knee,
> Gone to the shore where my soul has longed to go,
> I hear the gentle voices calling, "Old Black Joe."

The 1860 song's romanticized vision of slavery was especially popular with white audiences in the South. The Dixie Hummingbirds were aware that they were validating white stereotypes, but they viewed it as part of the price paid for the privilege of accessing wider audiences. "Even whites got to be crazy about us back then," says James Davis.

We used to sing "Old Black Joe" on the radio, and, oh man, you talk about letters. We got all kinds of letters. A lot of our people wondered why we didn't sound the same when we were broadcasting. But we knew the audience was mixed, so we were trying to make enough harmony and do it in a way that everybody would buy it, you know.

We sang different to white audiences. We just didn't figure they would like us as well. We were blessed because we could sing sweet and get very sweet. We would dress it up. They just went for that. Same songs, and they bought it. We weren't trying to get them worked up or anything because we figured they didn't know where we were coming from. "Old Black Joe" might not have been a song we did a whole lot, but we did it then. It was just a song white folks went for.

When they performed for African Americans, though, the Hummingbirds moved the songs differently. "Folks wanted old spiritual favorites like 'Swing Low, Sweet Chariot' and 'Ezekiel Saw the Wheel,' that kind of thing," says James Davis. "If you couldn't sing those, well then, you couldn't get over. They were crazy about 'em."

African American folklorist Zora Neale Hurston wrote about "real" spirituals, describing them as "variations on a theme," songs "bent on expression of feelings. The jagged harmony," she wrote, "is what makes it, and it ceases to be what it was when this is absent."

The composers were unknown, the words and melodies evolved out of the experience of slavery, biblical verse, and African spins on the eighteenth-century hymns of English cleric Isaac Watts. From those hymns twisted to a perversely utilitarian interpretation of Christianity[16]— "Servants, obey in all things your masters," Colossians 3:22[17]—arose the buoyant hopeful spirituals. The songs, never schooled or written down by the singers, were an ever-changing oral inheritance passed on from one generation to the next. Their "truth," wrote Hurston, "dies under training like flowers under hot water. The harmony of the true spiritual is not regular. The dissonances are important and not to be ironed out by the trained musician. The various parts break in at any old time. Falsetto often takes the place of regular voices for short periods. The congregation is bound by no rules. No two times singing is alike, so that we must consider the rendition of a song not as a final thing, but as a mood. It won't be the same thing next Sunday."[18] As a body of song, the spirituals represented a great awakening of African American identity. The Hummingbirds celebrated this tradition when they performed for black audiences.

"I would say that Davis was the brains as far as singing."

While the early Dixie Hummingbirds worked in the spiritual tradition, they made changes, sampled, borrowed, and built on melody lines and ideas, adding nuances to make the songs their own. When they started as young boys, Davis and the others learned the traditional arrangements and melodies. As professionals, though, they were open to influences from outside the region and fed on competition from other groups. They had to find ways to put their own spin on the old formulas.

The Birds were inspired in part by what they were hearing on radio and phonograph records. Groups that a decade before had no hope of being heard outside their hometown communities were now, thanks to a thriving media industry, being heard over wide areas. The expanded exposure was helping popularize innovative ways of using the voice, constructing harmonies, and arranging songs. Records and radio were putting a lot of fresh ideas into the air, and the Dixie Hummingbirds found they had to respond if they wanted to attract and keep audience interest.[19] They began to shape their own sound by reworking the spirituals, breaking them down and reassembling them in unique and appealing ways.

The Hummingbirds were able to draw on a variety of traditional a cappella performance techniques—African American vocal conventions like stretching and playing on notes, switching leads, carrying the rhythm along in the bass voice, adding soaring falsetto ornamentation, shifting tempos, and introducing counterpoint harmony weaves. As always, the first and foremost goal of any Dixie Hummingbirds performance was to sing for the Lord and guide listeners to spiritual epiphany. But now as professionals, they also had to think about putting on a show. There was room for spontaneity and improvisation, but they had to be highly practiced.

James Davis continued to provide the group's leadership, demonstrating a clear vision about how things ought to be done. "I give Davis credit," says Barney Parks. "Davis knew more about music in a sense than anybody. I would say that Davis was the brains as far as singing. I give him that credit."

"We were all very young back then," reflects James Davis.

> The main thing we'd do, we'd get an old song and rearrange it. We always did it ourselves. I'd sit and write a song down, get the words

together and everything. When I first started, I'd do it in shape notes. But later I didn't have to. I would just write the words down, and once I go over it one time, I could throw it away. That's the way it was at first.

And we would never let anybody else be in our rehearsals. Never did. That way, you're protecting the guys' feelings. I wanted them to feel comfortable. We were not in that big a hurry because we weren't making any money. See what I mean? A whole lotta rehearsing, and it'll come to you. Especially when you had already been singing in the choir.

While Davis may have written out the words or taught the basic melody, the working out of harmonies and arrangements remained a group effort. To succeed in the Dixie Hummingbirds required more than just a good voice or a pleasant stage personality. Each person had to have the ability to work out his own part in the mix. That was the key to a man's worth to the group, what it was all about. "If you didn't have an ear," says Barney Parks, "I don't care who teach you."

If you're in a group, though, and you hear something, if you've got an ear for it, you can pick it up. In other words, if someone would hit something, and we're in the car, we could chime right in because we knew our parts. I was a baritone singer, but we each knew all the different parts.

If we heard a song that we liked, we'd rearrange it some. We got ideas like that. When you've got an ear, you can do it. Right now, I can follow just about anybody I want to. Start up a song in church, if I want to sing a part, I just follow. Once it's in you. But if you don't have that ear, you just as soon get on somebody else's tune or anything else.

"Oh, motherless children shall see it's hard when mother is gone."

One of the songs performed by the Dixie Hummingbirds in the late 1930s and typical of their a cappella style was, as the published title read, "Motherless Children Has a Hard Time." The song had already been recorded as both a blues tune and a spiritual. Texas-born guitar evangelist Blind Willie Johnson recorded a sanctified version for Columbia in 1927. Josh White, also from Greenville and a childhood friend to both Davis and Parks, recorded it as a blues for the American

Record Company around 1933. Both featured solo voice and guitar self-accompaniment. The Birds' version, however, was built around their configuration of four unaccompanied voices.

The group laid it out slow and somber, James Davis taking the lead. In the starkest terms, the lyric bemoaned loss, loneliness, and isolation. The element that distinguished the Birds' version from previous bluesy renditions was the spiritual subtext, the repeated phrase "Have mercy, Lord," interwoven as a harmony backdrop throughout the performance. Though the message was simple, the means of communicating it was musically intricate and beguiling. Davis began in his high voice, taking his time, singing the opening lines in his own indeterminate tempo.

> Oh, motherless children, [hesitates]
> Shall see it's hard, [holds the note, then hesitates]
> Hard when mother is gone.

The others then begin chanting in three-part harmony, "Have mercy, Lord." Lead voice and backup become intertwined as the story unfolds. The rhythm of the syllables imparts to the song a steady beat. Davis lets his emotions come through and the harmony voices respond in kind, building intensity as he does, backing off when he cools down.

> When mom is gone,
>> Have mercy, Lord.
> Now, motherless children,
>> Have mercy, Lord
> Shall see that it's hard,
>> Have mercy, Lord
> When mom is gone.
>> Have mercy, Lord
> When mom is gone.
>> Have mercy, Lord
> They don't have,
>> Have mercy, Lord
> No where to go,
>> Have mercy, Lord
> They've got to run,
>> Have mercy, Lord
> From door to door.
>> Have mercy, Lord

Now, motherless children,
>   Have mercy, Lord
Shall see it's hard,
>   Have mercy, Lord
Hard when mother is gone,
>   Have mercy, Lord
When mom is gone.
>   Have mercy, Lord

Davis keeps the song at an even emotional level until this point. He then turns up the intensity. "Father does the best he can when mama is gone," he sings, then mournfully cries out the next line, "WHEN MOM IS GONE!" taking it up into a moaning falsetto. In response, Jimmy Bryant pumps up the background as he growls the words "Have mercy, Lord—Have mercy, Lord." Bryant then eases back, setting the mood for one final crescendo.

Father does,
>   Have mercy, Lord
The best he can,
>   Have mercy, Lord
Oh, but he does not,
>   Have mercy, Lord
Understand.
>   Have mercy, Lord
Now, motherless children,
>   Have mercy, Lord
You will see that it's hard,
>   Have mercy, Lord
When mother is gone,
>   Have mercy, Lord
When mother is gone.

Davis moves into the last verse.

Now, friends don't treat you,
>   Have mercy, Lord
Like your mama did,
>   Have mercy, Lord
When mother is gone,
>   Have mercy, Lord

He turns it up a notch.

> Now, friends don't treat you,
>> Have mercy, Lord

Then shouts the next line, the background right with him.

> Like your mama did!
>> Have mercy, Lord,

And then settles the song down as he winds it to a close.

> Now motherless children,
>> Have mercy, Lord
> Sure see it's hard,
>> Have mercy, Lord,

And finally Davis breaks tempo, taking his time as he draws out the notes of the last line.

> When mom is . . . ,

His voice reaches up to a final high note.

> go-o-o-ne.

He holds the note, and then shifts it down lower. The background catches up with him and they join together on a last augmented chord. The performance is complete.

"We invented something we called 'wildcattin'."

In addition to "Motherless Children," highlights of the Birds' late 1930s repertoire included titles like "Wouldn't Mind Dying," "I Looked Down the Line," "What a Time," "I'm Leaning on the Lord," "The Stone That Was Hewed Out the Mountain," "Where Was Moses," and "Moving Up That Shining Way."

The songs were all steeped in tradition, but uniquely arranged by James Davis and the group. They were performed in a generally easy-going style, but laced through with moments of emotional intensity accomplished through changing dynamics and qualities in the lead singer's voice. Their style evolved in response to their perception of what listeners wanted and needed from them as spiritual entertainers, very much a product of particular place and time. Their performance skills were pointless, however, if nobody came out to the programs. Inspired by their initial forays into the Carolinas and beyond, the Dixie Hummingbirds worked without pause throughout the 1930s to build their reputation and expand their audience.

The Birds began working small Carolina towns and country churches, eventually taking chances on long road trips to Florida, West Virginia, Pennsylvania, and Michigan where they were entirely unknown. The roads were poor, the car unreliable, and around every bend lurked the threat of a racially charged encounter. The Humming- birds were savvy, though, and understood they would not go far as professionals if they stayed too close to home.

"During that time," says James Davis, "we were practicing *all* the time, working on something, and we just loved what we were doing enough to sacrifice." Perhaps the biggest sacrifices came in their personal lives. The extensive travel and time commitment required for musical success obliterated any possibility of a normal family life. The situation that confronted James Davis was typical for all. He knew from the start the price he would have to pay. "I was so wrapped up in singing at that time."

What little education I had gotten wasn't enough to carry me, and as far as I could see, there was no way to make it around Greenville. I thought I could do it singing, but that meant I'd be gone a lot.

That's what I told my wife when I met her. She wanted to get married. She said [Davis puts on a high female voice], "You do love me?" I say [back to normal], "Oh, yeah. I love you all right. But, honey, I really don't know how I'm going to make a living. I got to learn how first."

I told her in advance that I had to figure out a way to make a living.

Back when I was coming up, it was hard for people to understand that you could make a living as a singer because everybody had a job, and singing wasn't considered a job. So I said, "OK, suppose I marry you? We're fixing to leave here. In fact, I'm leaving here tomorrow. I mean the day after our wedding!" She say [back to the high voice], "Well, I'll be here when you get back. And I know you will be back. I'm with you. I'm with you." [In normal voice] And, hey, I'd go back and hadn't done too well. I'd go back and tell her, "We didn't do so hot." She'd say, "Oh, don't worry about it, baby. You'll do it, you'll do it alright."

I was gone for three months after we got married. I give her credit. She had more sense. She knew me better than I did. When we started doing pretty good, got into *Ebony* magazine, *Sepia*, and all those magazines, she was more proud than I was. Hortense. That was her name. She was fifteen and I was twenty-one. We got married in 1937. And that's the greatest thing that happened to me besides this group!

Each of the Hummingbirds did his best to juggle career with family, friends, and romantic relationships. As for traveling, they had not so much a precise plan as a general strategy, a take-it-as-it-comes campaign of touring and self-promotion. James Davis laughs when he thinks back on it. "We invented something we called 'wildcattin'!"

We would go into a neighborhood, into a pretty good-sized town, and work out from that town. We'd go out in the country and solicit and ask people if they'd be interested in sponsoring the program. Most of the time, there would be someone in the church who would help us with promotion, and we'd go along with that. Sometimes we had little promoters who would set things up for us. We did it all kinds of ways, you name it, we saw it. It's like I told some guy, if it's anything about gospel, we tried it one way or another. We've been it and we've been through it! That's how we came to be successful.

By the late 1930s, James Davis had firmly established himself as group leader and musical director. Barney Parks oversaw the bookings and business affairs. The group stayed on the road for weeks and even months, performing any place that would have them, but mostly in small African American country churches. They took whatever money came in the collection plate or when the hat was passed. Getting from place to place was difficult. "We'd borrow cars," says Davis. "Anybody's! Mostly old Fords. 'A' models. We had one man's car two months! He knew we'd take care of it, though."

"You could go down and try to get on a radio station."

The wisest move the Birds made was to get involved in the growing trend of live local radio. Throughout the 1930s, far-reaching 50,000-watt stations and nationally syndicated radio networks had made celebrities of many entertainers. A number of African American vocal groups had already made significant progress in that direction. The pop-oriented Charioteers and Delta Rhythm Boys, and the more purely gospel Golden Gate Quartet out of Norfolk, Virginia, were breaking through to mainstream America by regular network radio broadcasts and subsequent record sales. While these groups had their constituencies within the African American community, they were presented to white America more as representatives of respected "Negro" tradition. They chose selections and sang in a technically brilliant but minimally expressive style designed to appeal to the broadest audience. These groups, however, did not garner their widest popularity until the 1940s. Even the Golden Gate Quartet, by far the best with their tight harmonies and swing arrangements, never did achieve the level of fame and success of their secular counterparts like the Ink Spots or the Mills Brothers.[20]

The Dixie Hummingbirds, rather than transforming themselves into a secular group, chose to remain true to music that celebrated the Lord and promoted spiritual well-being. But their ambition was still to reach the widest expanse of listeners by performing live on radio.

Radio during the Great Depression came to hold a special place in rural southern households. Local stations were unencumbered by metropolitan marketing concerns and could originate programming tailored to community tastes and needs.[21] At the same time, "network" radio offered people isolated in "towns, farms, and mill villages" a welcome voice from "distant cities" that provided "release from the demands and rituals of labor."[22] Depression-era radio became a "principal escape for millions . . . on the edge of poverty. Losing oneself for a half-hour or an hour or an evening in jokes, laughter, and song was a welcome alternative to total despair."[23] Through programming that originated locally, low-powered regional stations were able to develop distinctive broadcast identities. Program hosts, sponsors, and especially performers were homegrown and familiar to listeners, and this helped make small town radio a smashing success. The trend of showcasing local talent started in 1922 when station WSB out of Atlanta began broadcasting in-studio performances by country fiddler John Carson and blind gospel singer and minister Reverend Andrew Jenkins. Rural radio was quick to follow suit.[24] So it was that through hometown radio, the Dixie Hummingbirds first became aware of quartets like Nashville's Fairfield Four and the Golden Gates.

Even when folks could not afford to own a radio, the locals could "grapevine," a method of transmission that was especially popular around Greenville. A wire connected to a radio in a local storeroom would be extended cross-country over fences, phone poles, bushes, and trees. Anyone along the route was welcome to tap into the signal, providing they paid a fee to the system owner at the point of origin. Of course, subscribers had no control over the programming or even the tone or volume. But they had radio in their homes.[25]

The Dixie Hummingbirds used the smaller stations scattered throughout the region as pivotal points for their own networking. "What we started to do," says James Davis, "was to go to any place that had a station in the area. Just walked in cold. And we would work in that area and popularize ourselves.

> After we stayed there and everyone in that whole vicinity knew us one way or another, then we'd go to another one a long ways from there. Oh, yeah! Groups would try and get on the radio. It was new and the people were crazy about it. We did millions of that even before we left Greenville. Started out on WFBC, did broadcasts every Sunday morning. We were not even thinking about making or selling records. We were making our way on the radio.
>
> We were being heard all down in South Carolina, Georgia, and, after sustaining over that station, we'd go to another. That's how we built us a route all the way to Florida and up to Boston. It was really something we had cultivated. They had four or five groups down in Raleigh, but we were on the radio—WPTF—and we had the people!

There was another distinct advantage to radio as far as the Dixie Hummingbirds were concerned. Skin color was simply not a factor. Station owners cared only that listeners stayed tuned, heard the advertisements, and bought the products. Radio also regularly put black performance style in close proximity to white Americans. When they took to the radio, the Dixie Hummingbirds were connecting to a diverse audience and winning fans across racial lines. "Back then," says James Davis, "it wasn't like it is today. If you could make harmony—and we got that real good while we were in school—you could go down and get on a radio station."

> We never tried a station that we couldn't get on. Go up to the station manager and say, "We got a little quartet here, and we would like to sustain awhile if you have a spot."
>
> One station we went in, and the man say, "Well, let me get a level

on you." And we got up to the microphone, got in position, and we hit the song and hollered loud. And right back in there, oh man, we could hear them saying, "Boy, they know what they're doing!"

Through radio, the Hummingbirds became part of a cultural revolution that would change the shape of American popular music. Live local radio contributed powerfully to the cross influence between black and white musical styles.[26]

"People used to come to our programs just to see what we would wear."

While radio was enormously helpful to the Dixie Hummingbirds, they recognized that they had to succeed in live performance as well—in looks and behavior. This was especially obvious to James Davis who became a stickler for appearances. He believed unwaveringly that how they looked and behaved was as important to their success as singing. It was a lesson that had come to him from a myriad of directions: his parents, the teachers at Sterling High, every church service he had ever attended, every spiritual program he had ever witnessed. James Davis was committed to the idea that the group had to sustain a positive public image.

Spiritual entertainers were particularly held up to public scrutiny. To those within the African American community, the Dixie Humming-birds and groups like them were seen as walking talking advertisements for the rewards of the good life. The Birds understood and delivered, taking great pains to look their best. No matter how short they were on funds, some amount was always put aside for clothes. "A whole lot of our money went into clothes," says Davis.

> Suits. Ties. And they had to be just alike, down to the socks! Every-thing! We just felt like appearance played a part. People used to come to our programs just to see what we would wear. Schools, audito-riums, churches. We did them all. Years later, we'd have a *couple* new outfits. *Every* year. And every year people come out to see what we'd be wearing. We were dressing when we didn't know where the money was coming from.

How group members behaved in public was also essential to James Davis. "Just like appearance," he says, "your character played a part. One is as important as the other." He unequivocally reminded the others that they were role models, expected to at least *act* like they lived the life they sang about. They may have been gospel singers but, like anyone, each had his own strengths and weaknesses. Life in the sanctified spotlight demanded more. Davis made it clear that anyone who strayed would be out of the group.

"It's the way you carry yourself," says Davis, "especially with a gospel group, if you want to go far. Now, if you just want to get out there and raise a little sin until the people find you out, that's another thing. But our people want you to be growing wings if they're going to hear your program. In other words, you got to have sense enough to know how to carry yourself."

Davis imposed strict rules and penalties, soon developing a reputation for running the group with a strong hand. "The news got out how tough I was on the gang," says Davis. "I mean all *kinds* of news went out about me." Davis was toughest on drinking. He had never forgotten when drinking behind the pulpit derailed his first group. Even in this early stage of the group's career, Davis had already lost a number of talented singers to the bottle.

> No drinking was number one! And, of course, had things been like they are now, no dope would have been number one. But the main thing was, we had to keep a cool head. That's what that rule was about whiskey. No drunkard's gonna pay to hear you sing and you drunk as he is. No way. Not our people.

Reliability was another essential in the Davis rulebook. He knew that starting late, canceling, and, worse yet, not showing up at all, could destroy a group's reputation. News of this sort spread quickly. "'Integrity' was a key word," says Davis. "If you say you're going to do something, do that! If you say you're going to be there, then be on time and do your show. Integrity comes first."

Davis also imposed on the group strict rules concerning women. "I didn't let *no* woman ride in the car," he says with righteous indignation, an incident from the early days of touring still fresh in his mind. In truth, the situation was probably inflamed more by racism than appearances of impropriety, but Davis blames it on the latter. "Jimmy Bryant had married this girl." She was black but looked as white as any white woman you ever saw.

> We had come into this little town in Florida and arranged with people to sing at their church. We were just gonna make a little bit and go on over to Gainesville.

Now, Bryant and this girl, they were acting like they were in New York City. And, boy, the two of them, they had gone and driven the car downtown. Raised up quite a stir.

Well, some lady found out where we were stopping and she came down there running, almost out of breath, and she said, [in a high panic-stricken voice] "They're figuring on getting you all tonight!"

[Back to his normal voice] Downtown with that white woman, you know! And, boy, by day's end I was getting myself together and getting outta there. We got *away* from that place, man. We dismissed that place. Told the man at that church, sorry, we'll try 'em later when things cool down.

As far as Davis was concerned, from then on, no women other than wives in the car. Davis was the enforcer, the caretaker of the group's reputation, stability, and sometimes even physical survival. His strictness became the rudder that steered the Hummingbirds toward the consummate professionalism that would be their hallmark in years to come.

"[We've come] into some kind of precarious situations."

Traveling from radio station to radio station and performance hall to performance hall, the car came to serve as both a living space and rehearsal hall for the Hummingbirds. "Drove around sometime for months!" bemoans Davis. "Driving 'til you feel you like to rest, another guy take over. Sitting on pins and needles 'til we got back home."

In the car winding along the highways, the Dixie Hummingbirds worked on their style and began the evolution away from sweet singing into something a little more emotional. "One time we went to West Virginia, we sounded like a college group, the sweet music, you know, all the sweet stuff."

Some of the people say, "You know, you all got some beautiful voices. You make so much beautiful harmony. But, I don't know, you need a little something."

That's how we learned to holler. On the road out in the cars. Scream. Holler. They just figured we needed a little something extra.

But I'll tell you one thing. One of the things that made the group versatile was the fact that if a guy had a range just so far, we would switch parts with him. Somebody else would do his part at a given place. And switch all through the song. And we did that for years. Everybody in the group can sing four parts.

The Dixie Hummingbirds worked the coal towns of West Virginia and from there occasionally headed up to Detroit, but the group traveled most often into the South, through the Carolinas, down into Georgia, and especially the area around Jacksonville and North Florida. "Florida was our best state when I was with the Birds," says Barney Parks. "We used to headquarter down in Jacksonville quite a bit. Tampa. Sometimes Orlando. People liked us and they still follow us in Florida."

It was on the road in Charlotte, North Carolina, in 1937 that the Hummingbirds first crossed paths with the Golden Gate Quartet. The Birds had heard the Gates on the radio and admired their percussive a cappella jubilee style. The Gates were in town to cut in a makeshift hotel room studio the records that would soon propel them to nationwide popularity.[27] "The Golden Gates gave us a lot," says Barney. "We looked them up. They were big, but they were very nice. Bill Johnson, the leader, was very nice. They gave us some pointers. We got some good tips, information from them."

Though there were rewarding moments on the road, the experience generally brought mixed blessings. They were making money and winning fans, but as James Davis puts it, travel also "landed us into some kind of precarious situations."

We were in Florida one time, and that's supposed to have been a nice neck of the woods. Just had our program and we were on our way back to the motel, and I saw a joint, a place where I thought I could get a sandwich. Started in there, they wanted to know where was I going. Asked me if I think this looked like a [hesitates] damn nigger joint. You know.

So I say, "No. No, we just hungry and would like to get anything to eat."

He said, "Well, you go across [puts on exaggerated accent] hyeah, and over theah, and ovah behind that railroad, and that's where they are." So, we did that. Got whatever we wanted, and then kept going.

Another time, we were working out of Albany, Georgia, and we came through Tifton. Back at that time, everybody in the group had a rifle, a .22 you know. That's because when we get to a program early—we sang in a lot of country places—we could get out in the woods and target practice. We were on our way through there and some guys came up right along beside us and started calling us names. I just told the guys to cool it and act like they're not there. They followed us about two miles and went on back.

And there would be many times where we would be charged for speeding when we hadn't been speeding. One night they charged us $50.00 a car. That night we were traveling in two cars. And wasn't even speedin'!

"I'll always remember when we left to go to the recording studio."

By 1938, the Dixie Hummingbirds came to realize that all their performances, radio broadcasts, and constant touring would still only get them so far. One promoter even suggested they get out of gospel altogether. "Well, we were sure enough singing for a living now!" says James Davis.

> But I remember this one guy used to book us said, "The people around here are crazy about y'all! They love the way you carry yourselves." He said, "But let me tell you something. I've been in this business a long time. What you need to do is start singing the stuff that the Ink Spots sing. Go on to New York and make that money! That's where it's at!" He said, "Gospel, they want that for nothing!" He said, "Now, you can stay with it if you want to, if you just love it that well, but you're not going to make but so much money."

The advice may have been well intentioned, but the Birds were simply not willing to abandon their commitment to spiritual entertainment. It was the music they knew best and the direction with which they felt most comfortable. The commitment ran deep.

The Birds, while they chose not to stray from their religious roots, did however take note of the advice about New York City. They felt they had come as far as they could on the regional touring circuit. The major recording companies were in New York. The Hummingbirds needed to make records and get their music out through a company with nationwide distribution. In those days, records did not create immediate significant income for performers. There were no "signing bonuses," royalties, or in some cases, even expense cash up front. "Race" records—the industry-coined term for recordings by black artists marketed to black record buyers—had been on the scene since 1920 when blues singer Mamie Smith hit with "Crazy Blues" on the Okeh label. Most "race" performers were paid a modest flat fee for the session, while the record company made the profit on sales volume.

For the Dixie Hummingbirds, income from sales was not the immediate incentive to make a record. "We did those recordings," says James Davis, "because they legitimized us and it helped us make money on our programs." A record brought prestige to a group and meant not always having to perform live to be heard over the radio. For the Dixie Hummingbirds, records functioned more as advertisements that helped spread reputation and draw crowds. Requests for appearances might now come in from points outside the usual territory. Even at home, a group with a record could anticipate more bookings, an increased draw, and higher admission prices. Instead of the usual nickel, people might be willing to pay a dime, fifteen cents, even a quarter, to see a professional recording group.

The Birds were ready, and they had an inside track not available to other groups. Bass singer Jimmy Bryant was a studio veteran, having recorded numerous sides for the Bluebird label as a member of the Heavenly Gospel Singers. "Jimmy was the one," says James Davis, "who had the contacts for that."

Neither Davis nor Parks remembers much about the sessions themselves. Davis recalls that a single microphone was used. "They would place us around it. The lead and the bass would get closer, one on each side of the mike and the others back further."

While the sessions themselves may have faded into a blur, the trip from South Carolina to New York City has remained indelibly etched in their minds. "I don't know today how we made it to New York," says Barney Parks, "because those tires, you could almost see through 'em." James Davis remembers it the same way.

> We left from Florence, South Carolina. And when we left there, one of our tires on the car had gotten down to those things that the rubber's on! All the rubber was gone! I could see that little spot when we left Florence.
>
> That was our first time to New York to do those records. Naturally, it was the biggest place we'd ever seen. It was a strange place. You know, I've even forgotten where we stayed. But we went to New York and got back to Florence. When we got home, I said, "Gentlemen, the Lord has been with us a long ways. Let's get us some tires."

"I remember doing it and at the time being so scared," says Barney Parks. "We didn't know nothing! Jimmy got us in there. We just cut. I don't remember any pay. If there was anything, I guess Jimmy got it. It wasn't about money anyway. Just wanting to record."

James Davis recalls that the group did get a little money for expenses, but no more. No fee, no royalties, just the self-satisfying knowledge that at last they had made a record.

Thermon Ruth was with the Selah Jubilee Singers, a group of Brooklyn-based spiritual singers who also recorded for Decca during the same period. The Decca sessions, he recalls, were coordinated by legendary "race" producer, J. Mayo Williams. "The Decca recording studios were at 50 West 57th Street near Fifth Avenue," says Ruth. "All the big bands and everybody recorded there. Andy Kirk and Louis Jordan. Everybody!"

As for the money, Thermon Ruth is blunt. "Mayo Williams took our money. They gave me $12.50 a side. Never did see any of it. Never did get royalties."[28] Most likely, a similar fate befell the Dixie Hummingbirds.

According to the discographical account, the Dixie Hummingbirds recorded sixteen songs that day in New York City, a Tuesday, September 19, 1939.[29] James Davis disputes the date. He says the Dixie Hummingbirds actually went into the studio in 1938 and that the records were released in 1939.

Though Davis may question the exact date, the more important fact is that the initial recordings by the Dixie Hummingbirds were issued on the prestigious Decca label, a powerful company with national distribution. Decca got its start in 1934, an American offshoot of British Decca. Almost immediately, the label began releasing records by African American artists in what they called their "Sepia Series" with label numbers in the 7000s.

The two most popular secular groups of the day, the Mills Brothers and the Ink Spots, recorded for Decca. The label was also open to religious singers. Decca would be the first to issue the recordings of Sister Rosetta Tharpe, one of the major figures in gospel's coming decades. In 1938, Decca would set up a field studio in Charlotte, North Carolina, and record a number of vocal groups, including the Norfolk Jubilee Quartet, the Spartanburg Famous Four, and the Shelby Gospel Four. Decca would launch a "Sepia Series" that played a significant role in getting the music of black America out to the nation at large.

"The recording came out pretty nice," says Barney Parks. "Jimmy

1939 Decca label; one of the Hummingbirds' first recordings.

Bryant heard it before I did. We were in Florida and he asked me had I heard it. You know, we were just country boys out there, didn't have any business sense. And they wasn't pushing gospel like they're doing now. We didn't go after it in a business way. But we had a record out there and they were playing it!"

"I can always remember our first hit number," says James Davis. "'Joshua Journeyed to Jericho.' Man, this was records! The first record we ever made. Everybody had 'em!" He sings out a line from the song. "'I was shouting around the walls of Jericho.' You couldn't outrun that record. I don't know where the song came from. I just know we did it."

The lineup at those first sessions included tenor leads James Davis and Wilson Baker, baritone Barney Parks, and bass Jimmy Bryant. The records would change their lives, but not immediately. The Hummingbirds drove home from New York City in triumph, but back in Greenville, they still had to scuffle for work, singing when and where they could. In time, though, the records found their way south and gave the Birds the stability and edge they needed. Now they were a group with credentials, truly professionals at last. James Davis remembers how he felt when his father finally came out to a program to hear them.

That was the onliest time he came up and said, "I believe you gonna make it." He'd been saying, "Man, you not doing nothing." But this night he came and couldn't get in! I didn't think nothing about what he thought by then because I knew we were getting over.

Did I see the big picture? No, I didn't see that far. But I thought it could probably help me run into something. And after we were out here a little while, I figured we could make it.

3

"Ain't Gonna Study War No More"

(1939–1942)

I'm gonna lay down my burden,
Down by the riverside,
Ain't gonna study war no more.
—"Down by the Riverside"
Traditional Spiritual

It was a hot summer day at the shore in Avalon, New Jersey, August 1998. Ira Tucker, Sr., was decked out in full fisherman's regalia as we stood on a dock overlooking the bay. That year marked his sixtieth with the Dixie Hummingbirds. Tucker joined the group in 1938 shortly after they returned from making records in New York City. "The head of the house, . . . the virtuoso" who "looks to seduce his audience vocally," writes Anthony Heilbut about him.[1] Ira Tucker would be as important to the success of the Birds after the 1930s as James Davis had been before. Davis had seen the group through its first decade with his vision and stern leadership. Ira Tucker would help the group break through on the national scene with his warm personality and singular lead vocal style. But on this hot summer day, he was out on the water trying to catch fish.

Tucker loves fishing because, as he says, "It puts me into another dimension." He first learned how to fish as a young boy when the man he worked for took him out regularly on the local river. Later, when the Birds traveled the East Coast and headquartered in places like Jacksonville, Florida, Tucker would spend his off time fishing the ocean waters.

He looked comfortable in well-used fishing clothes. The air was warm, the wind was up, and the squawking seabirds were a constant and welcome distraction. Tucker was equipped with an arsenal of fishing poles, a battered bait box, and all the trappings of a serious fisherman. He lit up talking about fish—"flounder," "croakers," "spot, the ones with the spot on each side of their head—and whatever." So far, that was all he had caught—whatever. But it was the act of fishing that he loved best, simply being on the water, looking out to sea, thinking, figuring which fish were biting, mulling over life, and in the process, coming up with ideas for songs.

Tucker had always had his best song ideas while out fishing. But for him, songs could be as fleeting as the fish. To be sure none got away, he always carried a mini–tape recorder all loaded and ready to go. He had been doing that for years. "When I'm out fishing," he says, "songs come to me. If I don't put them down on my tape recorder right away, one or two hours after that—gone with the wind."

Curtis Rudolph, Tucker's longtime friend, stood within earshot on the other side of the dock. He laughed and then sang out a line about disciple Simon Peter the fisherman from "He Cares for Me," one of the songs he liked most to hear Tucker sing. "I'm going to do like Simon Peter, when he was fishing on the sea. I'm going to cast all my cares on him. He cares for me."

Rudolph has known Ira Tucker for more than fifty years. They first met at a Dixie Hummingbirds concert in Columbus, Georgia, in the mid-1940s. Rudolph was a fan, the Dixie Hummingbirds the headliners on the show. "When I first met him, they were all in nice black suits," says Rudolph. "There were a lot of people trying to get to Ira. I had to work my way up. I told him how much I admired his singing and that he was my favorite singer in the group. He said anytime I see him at a program and want to talk, just come on." Rudolph took him at his word. They have been friends ever since. It was that kind of warmth along with his inimitable singing style that helped put the Dixie Hummingbirds over the top in the 1940s.

"As long as I've known the Dixie Hummingbirds, even back then," says Rudolph, "they always had a top reputation and Ira Tucker was the main man that everybody would talk about. He had that scream." Rudolph attempts to imitate Tucker's hallmark corrugated growl and laughs at himself as he falls far short. "That was it! That was Ira Tucker."[2]

"I could lay in my bed and speak to people out on the street!"

In 1938, after the Decca sessions in New York City, the Dixie Hummingbirds were back in Greenville, touring and increasing their draw. Crowds were turning out, people were buzzing about their records, and ticket prices had accordingly gone up to ten, fifteen cents, and on occasion a quarter. As a group, the Birds sounded better than ever, but the cohesion was short-lived.

Jimmy Bryant, due to the usual internal squabbles and control problems, abruptly exited the Hummingbirds.

The group found themselves in an unanticipated period of instability. But with bookings continuing to come in, the Birds needed a new spark in their lineup. They heard about a young singer, thirteen-year-old Ira Tucker, from nearby Spartanburg, a town known for nurturing its singers. Like Davis, Tucker grew up struggling against poverty in a home where his mother was the rock and foundation. James Davis at least had a strong bond with his father. Ira Tucker barely knew his.

Ira Tucker was born on May 17, 1925. "My mother's name was Maggie and my father was Douglas," says Tucker. "But I did not know my father's side. I got strayed away from my daddy. It was a thing where I didn't even know him until I got a certain age." While he may not have had a relationship with his father, Tucker did have the benefit of an extended family that included his mother, grandparents, and brothers.

The Tuckers lived in a shotgun house on Golden Street. "A white lady named Miss Cease would rent you the house," says Tucker, "but you had to fix it up yourself."

We had an oak tree in the yard and when you first come in the front door, you're going to step on big acorns. Then, through the hallway, to the right was a bedroom and to the left was a bedroom, then into the kitchen where we had an icebox. I cut a hole in the floor and put a galvanized pipe where the water would leak out, and then took it on down from under the house. We had kerosene lamps, wooden floors, and an outhouse. The lady my mother worked for kept us up in pretty good furniture.

The house was up on props on account of flooding. There was no pavement or nothing. It was all dirt roads.

None of the houses were too good. One evening, we heard this great lumbering growl. There was this old man named Mr. Jacob Gray, and the house he lived in—the whole thing—had fell down, and Mr. Jake crawled out the window with a bucket of quarters he had saved.

I've even seen times where I could lay in my bed and speak to people out on the street! [laughs] I remember my grandfather used to rub his back on the door. You could look out through a crack he wore from scratching his back off!

Maggie Tucker had come to Spartanburg from Newberry, a small town about sixty miles to the southeast, where her family had labored as sharecroppers. "My mother began seeing ads for jobs in the Spartanburg paper, " says Tucker, "jobs for cooks and maids and all that. So, she wrote and got a job as a maid. This was before I was born. She was making something like ten dollars a week. Big money back then, ten dollars a week."

In time, there would be three children, Ira in the middle, a younger half-brother, Eddie Eugene Gallman, and an older brother, Johnny. "Eddie was one of the best singers I ever heard," says Tucker. "I couldn't hold a light to him! He was around sixty when he died in Philadelphia. Now, my older brother Johnny, he couldn't carry a note to the mailbox! But he was a natural born artist. He could draw. He died young, too."

Tucker's father, Douglas, was rarely present. "My daddy, he would come in, go out, stay sometimes two or three weeks. So, my mother got so she quit worrying about him. Forget it. He wasn't too good anyway." Maggie's father, Ed Moore, became the patriarch of the family. "My grandfather worked for the W.P.A.," says Tucker. "He did top-soiling and other kinds of hard physical work. He did all of that and then some."

Tucker's memories of his grandfather are tempered with a mixture of reverence and affection. "My grandfather was an angel," says Tucker, "but if he would tell you to do something and you didn't, o-o-o-h, he was really mean." The stories come welling up.

> He called me "Ketta." Bought me a pair of boots and a shotgun, and he says, "Ketta, when I come home from work, I want a rabbit for dinner." Gave me a box of shells. Now, I had never killed a rabbit in my life, but when he spoke, he spoke with authority. So, I went out with that shotgun and I saw a rabbit and shot him, and didn't have nothing but his back legs—and that was after the gun had knocked me down. Got up and practiced how to shoot, and then I shot another rabbit running. I came home that night with a rabbit and a half!

Then, there was the story about the peas at the dinner table, a favorite that Tucker delighted in telling about his youth. "I was a little kid about the age of five or six."

He was playing in the yard when he overheard his cousins out on the road talking. One of them had just come from shelling "crowder" peas and told the other, "I'll be so glad when I get these damn peas home." "And me, being a little kid," says Tucker, "I thought that's what you called them."

> I guess a couple of weeks after that, my mother cooked some of those peas and I said, "Poppa, pass me the damn peas, please."
>
> He looked up and said, "What'd you say, boy?"
>
> I said, "Pass me the damn peas."
>
> "Get up from the table young man!" He took me out in the yard and he put as many knots on me as an artichoke! Oh, I'll tell you, back then you say anything bad, you got it, man!
>
> But my grandfather died trying to provide for us. He worked himself to death.

"I've never been with an attitude about what I didn't have."

As a boy, Tucker also had to carry his share of the family load. Maggie Tucker was ill and poverty necessitated that everyone had to work, and with no equivalent to Greenville's Sterling High in Spartanburg, he never received any significant education. "Didn't have the best of speech because I was denied of schooling when I was coming up," Tucker says matter-of-factly, no trace of bitterness in his voice.

> All blacks went to the same school, Dean Street School. It went up to the seventh grade. After that, you had to go to Cummings Street School, a big old high school. When I got to where I *could* go to school, I had to quit because my mother got sick. I had to teach myself. From the age of fourteen, I have been on my own.
>
> But, you know, I've never been with an attitude about what I didn't have. Always prayed for what I had and I wasn't jealous of nothing. When I sit down and write songs like "The Mood That You Be In," it signifies where I come from. Just like when you hear all these blues, these guys from the Delta and the lower part of the South. They worked. They were out in the fields. They sung what they felt.
>
> Same is true with gospel. Gospel came from loneliness, bewilderedness and shortchanged in life, cursed out and knocked down and everything. And then after all that, you go to church and thank God for another day.

Tucker's patient and upbeat temperament helped him face the thousands of indignities that confronted him as a young black man in 1930s

Spartanburg. "To me," says Tucker, "South Carolina is one of the most beautiful states in the world because I was born there, but it could be trouble, too."

> They had names for the neighborhoods in Spartanburg like John's Alley, Jim's Alley, Highland, Baptist Side, Niggertown. And *everybody* said these names, whites and blacks. "Yeah, let's go down to Nigger-town, man." You know, it was just a word. I didn't even think about it. "I have to go to Niggertown, man." Different times.

The work available to Ira Tucker was also fraught with indignities. A local storeowner, Mr. Turner, taught Tucker how to butcher. "I did a lot of butchering by the time I was ten."

> I cut up meat and made all kinds of sausages. He told me, "Boy, one day you're going to like me for this. I'm paying you a dollar a week but I'm learning you a job you can have for the rest of your life!"
>
> Turner would send Tucker by bus to butcher on weekends at a farm he owned in nearby Campobello. "Mr. Turner would pay me off in chitlins, and he would make me get on the bus with them."
>
> I said, "Mr. Turner, I can't get on the bus with these here chitlins."
>
> He says [Tucker puts on a gruff voice], "Get on the bus! If anybody say anything, tell 'em that *I* told you to get on the bus!"
>
> So, I get on and these white guys start hollering, "Get that nigger off the bus with them stinkin' chitlins!" And one of the other guys on the bus said, "Let 'em alone. Turner told him to get on here."
>
> Well, that shut 'em up because Mr. Turner owned almost everything around and employed so many people. They had to get used to me. I think about it now and I just laugh. Soon after, I quit that one-dollar-a-week job and got one for two dollars a week in a grocery store.

Spartanburg could also be a dangerous place. "Anywhere you would go could be risky," says Tucker. "Those guys in Spartanburg, they didn't take any tea for the fever. They would fight to the end!"

> A policeman might come around and demand to know where you work and everything. And if a black guy had a job, the first thing he would say is, "Hey, look, I'm a working man." And then the policeman would say, "Nigger, you need to say 'mister' to me!" Trying to get something going.

But those black guys in Spartanburg, when they were in the right, they were kind of tough to deal with. The white cops, when they would get ready to arrest a black man, it would take three or four of them. If they came into a neighborhood to arrest somebody for nothing, black people would fight back. Now, if a black man had done something wrong, people would help the police to put the man in jail—if he was wrong. If he was right, though, he'd fight back.

Now, things were different in Greenville. They had a cop over there named Hugh Chisel and he had a bad way. If it was a black guy or woman, he would knock the hell out of you and then ask you your name. So, they sent him over to Spartanburg figuring that because he'd calmed down all the blacks in Greenville, maybe he could quiet down all the guys over there. Biggest mistake they ever made.

Tucker realized that if he remained in Spartanburg, this would be the life he too would face. He credits his aspirations and clear sense of direction to a strong religious faith and resiliency learned from his mother, Maggie.

I've heard some people say, "I get up sometimes in the morning and can't even stand myself." I've never been like that. I never wake up with a frown or a groan. Always, always, ever since I was a kid. I wake up halfway singing. Just my life. The way I am.

My mother was like that, too. She was one of the most friendly women on earth. Never met people that she didn't like. Anybody could get along with my mother. I'm the same way. Always have been.

"That man could play that thing!"

Spartanburg also offered Tucker good times, local characters, and a world of music, starting right in his own home. "My grandfather used to play a little old accordion," says Tucker.

I still have it somewhere up in the attic. It was a German accordion. And, man, that man could play that thing! My mother used to sit on his knee when she was a kid and even then that accordion was thirty-six years older than she. Then, when I was a kid, I would sit on his knee.

Everyone called him Uncle Ed. My front porch would be full of people. "Uncle Ed, when are you going to play?" And he would pick up that accordion and sing! I remember him singing songs like "Let's Go 'Round the Walls of Zion" and making up verses to "Dig My Grave with a Silver Spade."

My grandfather was also a great bass singer, yes he was. He used to sing in the choir. My mother was in the choir, too. The Metropolitan Methodist Church over on Dean Street, and then later, Golden Street Baptist on Crawford Avenue. My mother had a beautiful voice, a soprano, but she only sang in church because she had to work to keep us going. Both of them learned with shape notes. Me, I never could understand shape notes. [laughs] Never could understand it and I never even sang in the choir.

Tucker did sing, though. He learned from his family, but he acquired most of his musical education in private homes and on the streets of Spartanburg. In the 1930s, the town was full of musical characters and situations. Tucker remembers "Trotting Sally." "They called him 'Trotting Sally' because people said he was marked by a horse."

His mother when she was pregnant carrying him was either afraid of or scared by a horse. However it happened, he would neigh and then start running. When the spirit hit Trotting Sally, he would jump up like a horse. I mean a racehorse! He wasn't just going to be running. He would be burning the wind, man. But he would play that violin. He was an excellent violinist. Nothing but strings and his fingers. He had that violin almost sounding like it was talking. If you said "Good Morning," he would make that violin say, "G-o-o-o-d M-o-o-o-rning." He could make that thing sound like people talking. I never will forget that.

The blues were also part of the musical life of Spartanburg. "I used to love the blues. Back then, it was one of the dominant styles. People played the blues and bought a lot of the records."

He remembers being impressed by an old man who sang and played the guitar. People called him "Blind Simmie." This was most likely Blind Simmie Dooley who played picnics, fish fries, parties, and storefronts around town in the 1920s and 1930s. "He played and sang so well, it's a shame he never got a break," bemoans Tucker.

In fact, Simmie Dooley had already had his moment in the blues spotlight. In the 1920s, he and another Spartanburg-based blues singer, Pink Anderson, had teamed up to perform with Dr. W. R. Kerr's Indian Remedy Medicine Show. In 1928, the duo traveled to Atlanta, Georgia, and cut four sides for Columbia records:[3] "Every Day in the Week Blues," "C.C. & O. Blues," "Papa's 'Bout to Get Mad," "Gonna Tip Out Tonight." Their "C.C. & O. Blues" captured a small piece of local history, describing hopping rides on the Carolina, Clinchfield, and Ohio, a coal hauling line that ran trains between Spartanburg and Elkhorn City, Kentucky.

On the streets of Spartanburg, "Blind Simmie stayed around a little street called Short Wolford. There were a couple of juke joints on it, and Blind Simmie would be outside in front of the juke joints. He would play his guitar and sing and then stop for maybe a half-hour and eat some peanuts. He had peanut hulls everywhere!"

Ira Tucker, though he enjoyed the blues, never performed the secular genre. "I was brought up in the church. I didn't sing anything else around my mother, nothing but gospel. If I did, she would have whipped my butt. She didn't like the other type of stuff."

"I just wanted to sing, that's all."

Tucker remained true to the spiritual tradition. Gospel was uplifting and wholesome and he felt better about himself when he sang that music. He also saw how the community revered spiritual singers. Gospel entertainment was certainly valued within Tucker's family and circle of friends, a staple of everyday life. "Down through the years as far back as I can remember," reflects Tucker, "there were always gospel singings."

> During my time, there was no kind of activities for our young people to get in. You went to church. You went to work. We *had* to make our own entertainment.
>
> So, we had for enjoyment what we called a "silver tea." For ten cents admission, you get tea, crackers, wafers, sandwiches, cinnamon rolls. You paid your dime and that's why they called it a silver tea.
>
> And they would have two or three groups inside of a house. Always on Sunday. Always spiritual. My cousin—"Brown" Rogers— had a quartet, and they would sing. We would all be sitting around singing. The Heavenly Gospel Singers were real popular and we would sing a lot of their songs. "The Sun Didn't Shine at Calvary."

"When My God Was Hanging on the Cross." "Working on a Building." Songs like that.

Tucker loved the singing and begged his cousin to teach him. "I must have been 6 or 7 years old. And he kept shooing me off, but I said I'm going to show him. [laughs] I just wanted to sing, that's all. So, my mother taught me. Those silver teas were my first experiences singing."

In the late 1930s, Spartanburg overflowed with gospel talent, including the Heavenly Gospel Singers and another recording group, the Spartanburg Famous Four. Like the Hummingbirds, the Famous Four also cut twelve sides for Decca, all traditional spirituals such as "Go Where I Send Thee," "I Know My Time Ain't Long," and "John Wrote the Revelations."

"The people loved them," says Tucker. "They would sing songs like 'Let the Church Roll On' and 'Take the Deacon Off the Board and Put the Board on the Deacon.'" Tucker heard the Famous Four every Sunday on local radio and was impressed by their lead tenor, Buster "Bus" Porter. Tucker loved how Porter extracted every drop of emotion out of a lyric. He stretched notes, jumped in and out of falsetto, moaned, cried, and improvised scat vocals all around the melody line. Tucker paid close attention and would in time absorb Porter's bag of tricks into his own singing style.

"If you could sing, you would go there to rehearse."

Most of all, though, Tucker loved the impromptu sessions that took place sometimes on the street corner, and other times at the home of Mr. Belton Woodruff. "One place where all the groups got together was in my neighborhood—they called it Jolly Street—under the light at the intersection of Crawford and Golden."

> That's where a lot of great singers lived. Like Arthur Prysock and his brother Red. Anyway, the light was the place where all the guys would meet to sing. And somebody would be there seven nights a week. I mean *seven* nights. They would get off work, go home and eat and come back and, "See you at the light!"
>
> Nobody never bothered us about congregating under that light. Even the cops. We would sit sometimes 'til twelve or one o'clock in the morning.

I went back not long ago to look over the place. I had to shed a few tears. There's nobody there now. The whole place is grown up.

The other important singing spot was the Woodruff home. "'Mr. Belt,' we called him," says Tucker. "That was the place, if you could sing, you would go there to rehearse."

The gatherings at Mr. Belt's took place on Sunday afternoons. Singers crowded the front room and porch, learning new tunes, experimenting with harmony and chord changes, determining their vocal range. Along with Tucker, there was the younger Julius Cheeks, who would someday make a name for himself as lead singer of the Sensational Nightingales. Also present would be Mr. Belt's grandson, William Bobo, the same Bobo who would replace Jimmy Bryant in the Heavenly Gospel Singers.

Two other regulars at the Woodruff house, semiprofessional singers Plato "P. D." Petty and Robert Hardy, would have a significant impact on the singing of Ira Tucker. Their quartet was called Hardy Blue Steel. "My brother [Willie] was the bass singer," explained Robert Hardy, "and he came up with that. I guess . . . he figured . . . blue steel was something that was pretty tough." Hardy was a lead tenor, P. D. Petty a baritone lead. At the Woodruff gatherings, the two threw out pointers and coached one-on-one. Tucker learned by example from Petty, whose baritone was close to Tucker's own vocal range, but Robert Hardy personally taught him the art of lead singing. "I trained him," said Hardy. "He came up younger than I was, but he liked singing and he always would be around us, and he'd come over my house and I'd sit down and teach him."[4]

And like so many other young singers around Greenville/Spartanburg, Ira Tucker was also taken with Jimmy Bryant's showmanship. "He really knew how to put on a show. He worked the audience. All the women were crazy about him. I saw that singing was a way to be popular. It would do me good to be around Jimmy Bryant—and everyone else who could sing!"

"You could hear a group live, but nobody played gospel records on the radio."

Tucker was influenced not only by the singers who worked his own home turf but also by out-of-town groups he heard through radio broadcasts and phonograph records. Tucker became a fan of the Mills Brothers and developed a fondness for white country gospel performers like the Chuck Wagon Gang and Tennessee Ernie Ford. Even though

they were a local group, Tucker paid more attention to the Dixie
Hummingbirds after he heard them on the radio and on the record
player. "They were playing records by the Dixie Hummingbirds everywhere," says Tucker.

> I even had some of those records. But back then, there was no such
> thing as a black disk jockey who played gospel. You could hear a
> group live, but nobody played gospel records on the radio. They were
> playing those records in record shops and in people's homes.
>
> You could buy phonograph records in a lot of places. Ten-cent
> stores. Furniture stores. They didn't have special record shops like
> they do now, at least not in Spartanburg. But you could buy records
> anywhere.

Motivated by hearing their records, Tucker still recalls the effort he
made to see the Dixie Hummingbirds in person for the first time. "I told
my boss man—I was working at the grocery store—said, 'I'm going to
hear one of my favorite groups singing tonight. The Dixie Hummingbirds.' I thought they had a beautiful style of singing."

> The place was packed with people. The admission to get in was fifty
> cents. It had moved up from a quarter. Of course, I didn't have the
> money. My seat was a tree! [laughs] I could climb up that tree and see
> right over into the church, the whole action just like you was in
> church!
>
> I remember they had on nice uniforms. Suits. Ties. They had this
> one really short fellow, so they called him "Highpockets." Wilson
> Baker was his name. Well, he just walked the aisle and smiled. He had
> a little technique with the crowd.

As impressed as he was with the Dixie Hummingbirds on the home
front, of all the groups Tucker was hearing on radio and records, none
bowled him over more than the Norfolk Jubilee Quartet featuring lead
tenor Norman "Crip" Harris.

From the Tidewater region of Virginia, the Norfolk Jubilees were one
of the first African American quartets to make records. Between 1921
and 1940, they cut well over a hundred sides for labels such as Okeh,
Paramount, and Decca. In Tucker's estimation, Norman Harris pointed
the way to the future of black gospel lead singing. "This guy impressed
me because he had the group singing like twenty, thirty years ahead of

their time. They were doing barbershop chords in gospel. It was so much different from what other gospel singers were doing 'til they stood out like a sore thumb." As far as Tucker was concerned, the Norfolks made other quartets sound "gut-bucket" raw. "Harris was the only one," says Tucker, "who could take eight different groups and give them completely different arrangements of the same songs. You know the Four Freshman and the Hi Los? You'd hear that very same sound. It might be a little bit different, but you could hear it like you hear my doorbell ringing!" Tucker still grooves on the time years later he would meet his idol in New York City. "I was living in an apartment," he recalls, "and I heard somebody singing in a high voice. Now, I said to myself, ain't but one man can sing like that. Crip! So I went up to his door and said, 'Crip, you don't know me, but I got everything you did on records.' Me and Crip got to be friends just like that. Living in the same apartment building in New York City!"

"When he was singing he almost bent himself all the way backwards."

In 1938, Ira Tucker had a local reputation as the precocious young man who knocked door-to-door offering to sing for spare change. He had already penned his first original tune, a novelty called "Jazzbo Jackson" about a high-stepping character that not coincidentally resembled Jimmy Bryant.

Tucker also had his own quartet, the Royal Lights, with a friend, Rayford Simms, handling the leads; Tucker and Mark Scott, a half-brother to William Bobo, covering the middle; and an out-of-towner, Jimmy Brown, from Detroit, singing bass.

Brown's real name was John Carwell, but he used "Jimmy Brown" on stage. He had landed in Spartanburg through his friendship with William Bobo, whom he had met on the road when Bobo was touring with the Heavenlys. Brown and his quartet, the Gospel Carriers, were traveling with the Heavenlys as the two groups worked their way across West Virginia. The Carriers, however, broke up in mid-tour, and Bobo invited Brown to visit him back in Spartanburg. There, Bobo arranged for Brown to board with the Tucker family. The timing was perfect. Ira Tucker was looking for a bass singer and Jimmy Brown promptly joined the Royal Lights. With Brown in the lineup, the Royal Lights made the rounds singing at local church programs and occasionally out of town. "There were always guys around trying to set up things," says Tucker.

Meanwhile, as the Royal Lights were making progress, the Dixie Hummingbirds were about to hit a snag. Late in 1938, Jimmy Bryant left the Birds permanently. His departure was not a complete surprise. Once, James Davis had fired Bryant on the road, and they had to meet their program obligations with a last-minute substitute, Claude Jeter, who years later would gain fame in his own right as a lead singer. Bryant's departure this time, though, was of his own volition. Heading first to Florida and then back to his hometown, Detroit, Bryant finished out his career with the Evangelist Singers, also known as the Detroiters.[5]

The Hummingbirds scuffled to find a new bass singer. William Bobo told Davis about Jimmy Brown of the Royal Lights. Barney Parks caught up with Brown at a Royal Lights performance and took him to meet Davis. They talked and Davis offered Brown the job. It was an opportunity he could not pass up. The Royal Lights were simply not in the same league with the Dixie Hummingbirds. With the Birds, Brown could travel, earn decent pay, and establish himself as a singer on the professional circuit.

Although Tucker was at first distraught, he ultimately gained, too. "Here I had my own group," Tucker still laments, "and the Dixie Hummingbirds came over to Spartanburg and picked up my bass singer! But do you know what happened?"

> Jimmy Brown told me, "Look, I'll go now, but we'll be back, and I'll get you in the group." A few months later they came back to sing with the Heavenly Gospel Singers. It was fifty cents to see the two groups. I borrowed the money out of my pay and went in to see them. Jimmy had done what he said. He'd told the fellows about me. So, at the end of the show, Davis came up to me and said, "Hey, can you sing tenor?" I told him I'd never sung tenor and never sung no lead. He told me it was a tenor he needed. So I said I would try it out and if I couldn't do it, I would be on my way back home. To be honest, I didn't figure I could do it. But I went by and asked my mother. She said I could go and I left with them that same night.[6]

Barney Parks recalls Tucker's audition. It took place at night in the parking lot of the House of Prayer Church in Spartanburg. The program was over and the crowd had gone home. The Birds were standing around the car listening as Tucker sang. "Tucker was a little nappy headed boy right there in Spartanburg, still riding a bike," says Parks.

"But he had it! I remember when we tried him out. He wanted to make it so bad, when he was singing he almost bent himself all the way backwards. He had that drive and he still does."

"I just had that kind of nerve," says Tucker. "I just loved the idea of standing up before people. I just wanted to get out there." Maggie Tucker was willing to let him go. Failing health made it difficult for her to sustain the family, and she knew that with the Dixie Hummingbirds, her son would be in good hands and headed in a promising direction.

"We just turned the car back over and came on home."

The Hummingbirds headed back to Greenville. With James Davis, Barney Parks, Jimmy Brown, and now Ira Tucker, they were a true quartet. In Greenville, Tucker and Brown shared a room in a house owned by Barney Parks and his wife.

Tucker picked up his vocal parts quickly and during those first few months worked strictly in the background. As soon as Tucker was ready, the Birds resumed touring. "We worked all around South Carolina after I first joined," says Tucker. "Places like Darlington and Laurens." As they fanned further out, the need for a car of their own became apparent. They bought a serviceable DeSoto for a few hundred dollars and took to the highway. Mobility brought mixed blessings. They could travel, but they were now placing themselves more at risk.

Tucker and Davis still bicker about who caused more near-fatal accidents. Tucker brings up the late night rollover coming back from a program in Laurens. "Davis was driving. I don't know whether he went to sleep or what, but I know we turned bottom upwards! Somehow, nobody got hurt." Davis brushes it off. "I *did* turn the car over. I had driven all night long and hit a slick spot, and the car wanted to go in the Enoree River. So, I decided I'm just going to let it turn over. Just turned the car over and came on home."

Davis then counters with the time Tucker ran the car off the road. "We were coming from Detroit," says Davis, "and I had driven all day long and had gotten sleepy, so Tuck said, 'Oh, I'll drive. I'm wide awake.'"

About forty-five minutes later I'm asleep and the next thing I hear is Tuck hollering, "It ain't my fault, Jim!" We had gone off the side of the road and into a creek. Water was coming in. Boy! You talk about a man coming out of a car. But we didn't hit anybody and we all got out, wet, but okay.

Tucker shoulders full responsibility for that one. The main thing, they both agree, is that by the grace of God, the Hummingbirds survived and lived to sing another day.

"Can't be worrying about what 'Sister Flute' like!"

During Tucker's first few months, the Dixie Hummingbirds continued to stay relatively close to home, working the broad region of the Carolinas. James Davis remained the principal lead singer. With Jimmy Brown in place of the gruff Jimmy Bryant, the Birds retained their sweetness, sounding even smoother than ever. As they moved from town to town, though, Tucker was noticing the stylistic differences between the Birds and other groups. He was taking stock of which groups and lead singers were going over best with the crowd. He was thinking about what he would do if he ever got a shot at singing lead.

Of all the groups the Birds crossed paths with back then, Tucker was most taken with the General Four. "We used to travel around and have contests with them," says Tucker. Their lead singer Holden Smith opened Tucker's eyes to the changing tastes of the time and the stylistic possibilities. "They were the ones that started turning the tide from us singing just sweet to more hard gospel."

> The General Four were from Shelby, North Carolina. They had sewed up that part of the country. But they came to sing over in Greenville, and we had a contest with them with judges. And the judges gave it to us. But the crowd didn't go for that. I've never seen that many dollars thrown on the stage—for *them* in protest! Right there in the hometown of the Hummingbirds. They were singing all that hard cornfield stuff and the people done got into it. And I told Davis we were going to have to do some of that stuff. Can't be worrying about what "Sister Flute" like!

Tucker explains about "Sister Flute." "Bill Johnson [of the Golden Gate Quartet] came up with Sister Flute. Sister Flute was the staunch church lady that didn't believe in no party stuff, none of that hard gospel."

"Sister Flute" came to be Hummingbirds' code for the staid old-time style of gospel, the kind that they and the younger generation were gradually leaving behind. There would always be a place for Sister Flute, but more as a jumping off point, that laid back moment on the emotional roller coaster ride of gospel performance that made the high-flying moments seem that much more dramatic. As the 1930s rolled over into the 1940s, African American tastes were changing and gospel performers were gradually making the adjustments. Tucker sums it up succinctly. "Can't no longer be thinking about what Sister Flute wants."

For him, Holden Smith and the General Four signaled the turn-around. Says Tucker, "Holden got to be a very popular black country singer who sang black country gospel."

> He didn't do all this screaming like some traditional gospel groups. He had a way of singing which was different from anybody else's. He was a showman. He had a strange voice and when he held a note, you know, he would start walking with the note. Then he had his sister, his family in the group. It was traditional but it was a unique style. They were unbelievable. They were terrific! They wrote their own material. They had odd sweet harmonies. They were great!

What it came down to for Tucker was that Holden Smith had his own style. When you heard him, you knew it was Holden Smith and nobody else. Also, he was not about just one thing. Smith injected variety into his performances. He finessed the crowd, played them, used his vocals to evoke a range of emotional responses. Even in the late 1940s after the Hummingbirds had achieved a modicum of fame, they still looked forward to their trips back to the Carolinas to perform with Holden Smith and the General Four.

Smith's cousin Patria Ross, now in her eighties, remembers the glory days when the Dixie Hummingbirds and the General Four sang head-to-head in contests. "Holden and the General Four were very popular in Shelby."

> They sang on radio a lot. Once a week on Sundays on WHOS. Besides Holden, there was his brother who sung bass, and Thomasine Marr, he sung tenor. For a while James Husky sung alto with them. Then they kind of reorganized and Holden's sister, Christianellen, started singing with them. Their manager was Mr. C. Zed Accor.

The Dixie Hummingbirds and the General Four would often sing together at the Armory Auditorium in Shelby. They would sing in Spartanburg. They would sing in Gaffney, South Carolina. They'd sing in Charlotte, they'd sing in Gastonia. Both groups just sang all around.

The times I would go to see them were at the Armory. It would usually be on a Sunday afternoon. I remember one show when the Dixie Hummingbirds and the General Four sang with Rosetta Tharpe. Tickets were around $3.00. That was a lot back in the 1940s.

When the groups sang together, the General Four would come out first. One song they would be sure to sing was "Little Boy, How Old Are You." That was the song that Holden was best known for.

The place would be crowded. At least a couple hundred, maybe even five hundred. Whites came to the show too. Everybody would be all dressed up and crowded in together. The Birds had uniforms. I remember they had maroon suits. The General Four usually wore dark clothing, black or dark blue suits. Because of Holden, we always got to meet the Dixie Hummingbirds. We would shake their hands and congratulate them. They were nice. They were always really nice.[7]

Tucker held on to what he learned from watching Holden Smith. In time, he approached James Davis and asked if he could have a try at singing lead. "When I first got with the Birds, I *wanted* to sing baritone," says Tucker.

I didn't feel like I could stand out as a leader. I told 'em, I said, "I don't know how to sing lead or tenor." I said, "But if I can't do it, I know my way back home." So, they gave me a try, and Davis said, "Oh, that's good! You can do it." But I had never sung anything but baritone in my life.

Says James Davis, "We actually reached our peak after we got Tucker."

I was doing the lead at the time, but down the road Tuck wanted to get out front. He told me, he said, "Man"—he could sing just about as high as I did—"you sing too high for me. You killin' me."

Years later, Davis would explain the situation this way: "I had a very high voice and Tucker's excuse was that it was killing him because he had to sing too high to sing tenor behind me."[8]

"Let me have the lead," Tucker said. I say, "You can have it! It doesn't make any difference in here. If you can do it, you got it!"

So he picked it up and kept going, kept going, kept going. When he sang, he'd get way down like he was riding a horse! He was very progressive. He wanted to be right out front.

Davis really had no problem sharing the leads with Tucker. Even though Davis had a high-pitched voice, he never really thought of himself as a lead singer. Since tenors traditionally carried the lead, he more or less fell into the job by default. The truth was, he preferred supportive or second tenor and the job of keeping time.

"Tucker was just more apt," says Barney Parks. "He really changed things around. By me and Davis having sung in school together, we had harmony. But Tuck brought rhythm in it, different style. Tucker came in, it was a different ball game."

With Tucker alternating on leads with Davis, the Birds were able to broaden their point of attack. They could lay it down mellow, lay it down hard, or lay it down anywhere in between. Tucker had come to realize that, as he called it, the "backwoods hard-working rawer" performance style was "what everyone wanted." "And they still do," he is quick to say. "The 'sweet' stuff is the 'brain' stuff," he says, "but the 'hard' is 'heart' and 'emotion.'" Back then, Tucker wanted to be in the business of "stirring up emotions," connecting people to their "spiritual side." That was important to him then and throughout his career, the intangible that made gospel singing a worthwhile endeavor.

"We did a lot of rehearsing back then."

In the late 1930s and into the 1940s, the Birds continued fine-tuning their style. "We did a lot of rehearsing back then," says Tucker. Short, efficient sessions. "We didn't rehearse like other folks," says Davis. "Only about an hour's worth. Whatever we wanted to do, we'd do then." No single person took charge at rehearsal sessions. "Everybody would put his little bit in," says Davis. "Tuck, we found out, had the gift of arranging songs. He was real good at that." The Dixie Hummingbirds were gearing up to return with Tucker to places like Florida and West Virginia where they had been well received in the past.

The 1930s had been difficult for the music industry throughout the United States. At mid-decade, record sales totaled less than five million.[9] "Race" labels like Paramount and Black Swan had gone under completely. By 1939, the industry had grown more stable, with record sales increasing threefold to almost fifteen million per year. Radio broadcasting had contributed to the increase, but Decca Records—the Hummingbird's own label—was a major player with their affordable price of only thirty-five cents a disk. Within a short time, other labels followed suit with budget lines aimed at ethnic and regional markets.

The recording industry maintained its interest in African American music, releasing "hot" dance sides of the bands of Duke Ellington, Count Basie, Cab Calloway, Louis Armstrong, and Jimmy Lunceford. Meanwhile, the most popular bandleader in America, Benny Goodman, was schooled in swing through arrangements he commissioned from African American instrumentalists like brothers Fletcher and Horace Henderson, Benny Carter, Mary Lou Williams, and Edgar Sampson.[10]

In 1938 and again in 1939, John Hammond, Benny Goodman's brother-in-law, produced history-making "Spirituals to Swing" concerts at Carnegie Hall in New York City. Hammond had a mission. His goal, he wrote, was to "present a concert that would feature talented Negro artists from all over the country who had been denied entry to the white world of popular music."[11] Those New Yorkers who paid the price of admission were treated to an array of black talent from across the nation. Count Basie, Sidney Bechet, James P. Johnson, Charlie Christian, and Lester Young were among those who represented swing and jazz traditions. Big Joe Turner, Ida Cox, and Sonny Terry each performed in their own unique blues styles.

Hammond took an active interest in all forms of African American music and did not neglect to include spiritual entertainers. Two groups and one soloist got the call, Mitchell's Christian Singers and Sister Rosetta Tharpe in 1938, and the Golden Gate Quartet in 1939.

Mitchell's Christian Singers of Kinston, North Carolina, were a home-spun quartet with coarse harmonies and arrangements unfettered by conventional patterns and time signatures. They were brilliant in their naiveté. In spite of thirty releases on American Recording Company labels,[12] they had no designs on a professional touring career and seldom performed away from home. When not singing or cutting records in New York City, they returned to their jobs as a mason, a tobacco factory worker, a coal dealer, and a truck driver.

On the 1938 program, they performed three traditional spirituals in their own inimitable a cappella style: "Are You Living Humble," "What More Can Jesus Do?" and "My Mother Died A'Shoutin'." Their untrained voices chugged along, falling into call and response patterns, their lead singer mellow, a strident second tenor piercing through over top, a middle harmony voice, and a bass who in actuality sang in the baritone range. Their performance was a folk art masterpiece.

Of the gospel artists represented on the bill, none better represented the growing schism between religious and secular music and the crossover to white audiences than Sister Rosetta Tharpe, born Rosetta Nubin in Cottonplane, Arkansas, in 1915. Sister Rosetta sang out the gospel in a high, clear, pitch-perfect voice. She infused her performances with a rocking beat and her own self-assured guitar style laced with single note runs that sounded more like the blues than church. Just a few months before in October, Sister Rosetta had recorded four sides for the Decca label. The songs were gospel, but the instrumental backup was by Lucky Millinder's jazz orchestra. As musicologist Horace Boyer described it, "The members of the sanctified church were shocked, but the record-buying public went into a frenzy for this new singer with the new sound. Her popularity was so great in New York City that she was included in John Hammond's first extravaganza of African American music, 'From Spirituals to Swing.'"

Sister Rosetta was backed by boogie-woogie pianist Albert Ammons on her two selections, "Rock Me," a reworking of Thomas Dorsey's "Hide Me in Thy Bosom," and "That's All," with its refrain, "And you better have religion, I'll tell you that's all!" Sister Rosetta's appearance at Carnegie Hall was well reviewed and led to a successful tour throughout the Northeast. Appealing to record buyers both black and white, Sister Rosetta Tharpe would not only fuel the taste for rocking hard gospel within the black community but would propel a growing interest in black religious music among whites, especially in the urban East.[13]

The 1939 "From Spirituals to Swing" concert featured the group long admired by the Dixie Hummingbirds, the Golden Gate Quartet. They had first crossed paths back in 1937 when the Gates were broadcasting from and recording in Charlotte, North Carolina. The Gates were, in a way, a model for the Birds, not so much for their sound as for their commercial success. By 1939, the Gates had sold multi-thousands of records and been heard nationwide on NBC's radio variety show, "Magic Key." Now, with the appearance at Carnegie Hall, the Golden Gates were, for a black gospel group, experiencing success in the mainstream on an unprecedented level.

The Gates, with Bill Johnson, Henry Owens, William Langford, and Orlandus Wilson, performed three numbers on the show: "Gospel Train," "I'm on My Way," and "Noah." They opened with their signature tune, "Gospel Train," a fast-paced pumping railroad ride to salvation with voices simulating the sound of rolling wheels, whistles, steam, and bells. As the song wound to a close, the tempo slowed and

GOLDEN GATE QUARTET ENTERTAINS AT VETS HOSPITAL

From Huntingdon post 24, American Legion, where they are appearing in shows this week-end, the Golden Gate quartet came yesterday afternoon to give a half-hour show for the patients at the local vets hospital. The men, Orville Brooks, Orlandus Wilson, Clyde Riddick and Alton Bradley, with Glen Burgess at the piano, are well known in radio, TV and the screen, according to George Prendergast, manager of the Huntingdon Legion home, who has been supplying hospital shows from the talent appearing there.

The Golden Gate Quartet, with a new line-up, perform in Huntingdon, Pennsylvania, November 11, 1950.

the lead voice called out "All Aboard." Then a sudden and stunning shut down on sharp bright harmony chords. A long "w-a-a-a-a-a-ah" and then a rapid-fire "wa wa," and finally a drawn out "o-o-o-oh" as the song train came to a halt.

They quickly followed with "I'm On My Way," the story of Job tempted by the devil. The performance was more typical of the Gates rapping jubilee swing style. Though the song had all the lyrical earmarks of an old spiritual, it was in fact the work of Bill Johnson. He was the innovative master of creating song stories based on tales from the Bible. Johnson begins with a call and response opening. "I'm on my way," he sings, and the group repeats each of his lines in smooth tight-fitted harmony.

> To the kingdom land,
> And if you don't go,
> I'll journey on,
> I'm on my way, Lord, Lord, I'm on my way.

At this point, the arrangement transforms. The background vocals jump into double time, imparting a bouncing rhythm via punctuated and clearly enunciated syllables. As they transit from verse to verse, the bass voice pokes through with short connecting phrases. Bill Johnson rides along on their rolling harmony as he talks out the story. His words come fast.

> You know Job was the richest man,
> That lived in the land of Nod,
> He was the only man for miles around,
> That kept the commandments of God,
> Well the devil he got jealous of Job,
> And came to God one day,
> Said, "Remove your hands from around the man,
> He's gonna curse you to your face one day,"
> God said, "There's nothing you can do to turn him around,
> Because he done signed up, made up his mind,
> He's on his way, he's on his way.

And so the story unfolds in rap, rhythm, rhyme, and harmony.

Both the Golden Gate Quartet and Mitchell's Christian Singers were representative of the state of the art of black religious music in the late 1930s. Mitchell's Singers, though, were a stylistic throwback to the past, while the Golden Gates were the wave of the future. The Gates were moving forward on momentum set into motion by the "roots" music of Gullah prayer house "shout" dancers and Alabama quartets and contemporaries like Thomas Dorsey who was bringing rhythm, emotion, and original composition to the forefront of black religious music. Within a few years, the term "spiritual" would be displaced by "gospel" to describe the new style of African American sanctified music.

The Dixie Hummingbirds, inspired by these innovations and encouraged by audience reactions, adapted their style as well. They had to, realizing that exclusively sweet would no longer cut it. They experimented by featuring different leads on different songs and switching leads in mid-song. They began thinking in terms of the whole program, starting out easy, building, catching fire, and leaving the audience hollering for more.

In spite of Tucker's increasing ability to handle the lead, James Davis retained a couple of numbers as exclusively his own. "I had an arrangement on 'I Want Jesus to Walk Around My Bedside,'" says Davis. "I was also singing a tune called 'Tell It Wherever I Go.' Either one of those numbers I could turn the place out with."

Tucker, meanwhile, was developing his own repertoire. "The first song I ever led with the Birds," he says, "was 'Feed Me Jesus.' I got that song from Sister Rosetta Tharpe." He breaks into the first couple of lines. "Jesus, give me bread. Feed me Jesus." "I also used to sing 'Cooled Down by Chilly Jordan.' That was another."

Davis was especially impressed in those first years with Tucker's ability to "pitch a song." He remembered how his old friend Bonnie Gipson, Jr., the Bird's original lead singer, had no sense of pitch. "Bonnie had a wonderful voice, and if you pitch it for him, he could sing up a blue streak."

> But his problem was he just could not pitch a song, and we had to let him go. As long as we were out there, though, I don't remember Tucker ever having pitched a song too high for himself. And we were out there many a year. You had to know to not pitch a song so high that you couldn't sing it. Or too low. And nine times out of ten, Tuck hit that song right on the head. But that's something that some people just do not have.

By 1940, the Birds had evolved a sound that would take the show no matter how far afield they might travel.

"During the day, we'd go fishing and at night we'd sing."

Just as the Birds were preparing for their first long road trip with Tucker, they invited Wilson Baker back into the group. Baker's ability to charm audiences had so impressed Tucker when he first watched the Birds perform from his tree-top perch back in Spartanburg. Baker had tired of the road, as he perennially did, and gone to Hickory, North Carolina, where he worked as a clothes presser. Now, he was ready to sing and travel again. The Hummingbirds headed immediately to their favorite destination, Florida.

There, they had a faithful following from years back, and the Birds enjoyed the warm weather and the fishing. Also, the Birds had a broken down old car and, unlike South Carolina, Florida had no automobile inspection laws. "There was one guy," says Tucker, who called them "the singing-est most unprepared-to-travel guys he had ever seen."

Our car was so low, we couldn't hardly cross a manhole cover! And when we got out, we had to dust ourselves off. And we had leaking gas. We had a pan that we would whip under the tank when we got out and a "no smoking" sign we would put in the window.

The Birds headed first to Gainesville and, with the poor roads and rickety car, it took them four days to make the trip. When they arrived, they sought out their usual accommodations. "We'd stay at people's houses or guest houses," says Tucker. "Rooms for rent, and all that."

Immediately, they began lining up performances. "The news that the Hummingbirds were in town would get around fast," says Tucker. "From the barber shop to the beauty parlors to the churches." Gainesville, though, was too small to sustain them for long. Fortuitously, they were approached by a preacher, Elder Williams, who suggested they try Jacksonville. "Elder Williams was about the biggest preacher in Gainesville," says Tucker, "and he had this big Cadillac."

He said, "Hey guys, there's a big program over in Jacksonville and do you all want to go?" Said, "It won't cost you nothing."

Well, we all said, "Yea-a-ah!"

So he said, "You got uniforms?"

We had but one uniform, so we put that on. We knew we wouldn't have no place to change. Just wore that uniform all day.

We got over there that evening and man, that church was jammed! I'll never forget. It was the Day Spring Baptist Church on Jefferson Street. They had about 15 groups there, all local. We wrote our name down on a piece of paper and gave it to the person in charge. The paper made its way to the front and someone said, "We got a card here for the . . . ah . . . Dixie Hummingbirds. J'all ever hear of them?" People yelled out, "Let 'em sing!"

Man, we worked that place down! Afterwards, everyone came up to us and said, "Why don't you all move over here!" We went back to Gainesville that night and the next morning moved on over to Jacksonville. We'd have six shows in a day in Jacksonville—and we'd have crowds at every one of them. After about two months, we bought us a Lincoln Zephyr. Used, but it was sleek!

From then on, Jacksonville became home base for the Dixie Hummingbirds when they were in Florida. They worked the town and all the crossroads communities within striking distance west and south, all the way down to Fort Pierce. "We were singing almost every night," says Tucker. "That was a good life. During the day, we'd go fishing and at night we'd sing."

Minnie Lee Baker was a young girl in 1941 when she first heard the Dixie Hummingbirds in Florida and met her husband-to-be, Wilson Baker. "He and the Birds were singing in a little town called Tangerine, Florida, just north of Orlando."

> They played in a little wooden Baptist church out in the country, and they were already famous. All they had to do was put up a little flyer that said the Dixie Hummingbirds were coming and the people would come out.
>
> It was a weekday night, and when the Hummingbirds pulled up in their car, the church was already crowded. Maybe about a hundred people.
>
> The Birds looked fine. They wore suits and ties. Tucker was the one who moved around most. Wilson picked a little guitar and sometimes played it with them. One song I remember that featured Wilson singing was "Standing by the Beside of a Neighborhood."
>
> After the show, Tucker invited people to come up and meet them. That's how I met "Highpockets." We got married in 1942.[14]

Back then when the Birds appeared, they had no written contracts. "We used to get by on a nickel and a promise," says Davis. Tucker kept one of the tickets from those Jacksonville days. The admission price was fifteen cents. "We got to where we were bringing home forty, fifty, maybe even sixty dollars on a really good night," says Tucker. At those prices, that meant more than three hundred people had paid to see the Dixie Hummingbirds. "The split," says Tucker, "was always even. No one got any more than anyone else."

There were no bank accounts, and once each got paid, the money was theirs to do with as they pleased. Most they kept for expenses, and the rest was sent home to family. In the process, James Davis developed a reputation for extreme frugality. Claude Jeter, referring to his brief time as a fill-in with the Birds, loved to joke with Davis about it. He'd say, "You know why I left? Because when I was in there, Davis was the only one who could save any money. We were making a dollar and a half a day and he was living off his fifty cents! Can't nobody live off fifty cents a day. That Davis can sure hold some money!"

Tucker, though, sees it another way, because Davis always used his money to make sure the group had what they needed. "If it wasn't for Davis," says Tucker, "we would never have made it because nobody else had any money!" Says Davis, "That's why I was trying to save. They knew I was always going to have enough to meet expenses and make it to the next show."

Low funds were not the only hazard the Hummingbirds faced on the road. Even in a church setting, there were the attractions and temptations difficult to resist. "You had to try to get away from it," says Davis. "You had to be strong. People expected us to be above that. You had to know when to run, when to stand." Tucker affirms. "You had to walk the line," he says. "If you didn't, the church people would take you down."

There were also con artists and rip-offs. Sometimes the man with the money disappeared before the show was over. Sometimes the promoter skimmed the receipts. James Davis still rankles over the time his suit was stolen. "Brand new suit," says Tucker, "and it was beautiful. Fitted him like a glove." Davis sensed trouble halfway through the program. "Something just hit me and I ran back to check. That suit was gone!"

Tucker puts on sanctified airs as he imitates the less-than-charitable response of the church preacher. "This is the House of Prayer for *all* people. *Every*one comes in here. I can *not* be responsible for your clothes!" At this, Tucker and Davis both laugh out. "After that," says Davis, "wherever I went, my clothes were someplace where I could see 'em."

Then, of course, there was always the hostility endemic to racism. Says Tucker, "I remember in Tavares, Florida, a guy pulled a .44 on me. I walked into a store and started to get me a Baby Ruth candy bar. He pulled a gun on me and said, 'Back out, nigger.'"

"Whenever we traveled," says Davis, "we had to know how to deal with prejudice. We had it down to a science. There were times, say, when we'd walk into a restaurant and they'd stop us at the door and ask where in the so-and-so did we think we were going. We knew we had to stay cool and just get on out of there."

But hostile encounters were far outweighed by good people they met who helped them on their way. Tucker remembers the Giles family, who he roomed with in Jacksonville for more than nine months. Then, there was his landlady, Fanny Boatright. "Man, that woman would fix the biggest dinners. She was just so-o-o nice. When my oldest brother, Johnny, passed away, I told her, . . . and she bought me a roundtrip bus ticket and gave me fifty dollars."

Back home, wives and families waited patiently. "If you got the right woman," says Davis, "even if you're not home, you could be feelin' good about each other. Maybe that could have been the reason my wife and I were as close as we were. I'd go off and stay a couple of months, come back, and like we were on a honeymoon."

In Jacksonville, the Hummingbirds would also meet Otis Jackson, who sang with them briefly and maintained an association with the group as a songwriter and producer for years to come. "Otis Jackson came out of Cochran, Georgia," says Tucker, "which is not too far out of Jacksonville."

He was at that big program in Jacksonville, but we didn't know it. Jackson was singing with a group called the Great Pilgrims. They were all there that night when we worked that place. We messed it up. Otis came up afterwards. He said he wanted to book us guys. We said ok, and later on, about a month after that, he said, "Man, I need to be in there with you." So we took him in the group.

Otis sung with us for about six months. He was the biggest pro-moter down there. He also wrote songs. He wrote a song that went "Tell me why you like Roosevelt, he wasn't no kin, great God a'mighty, he was the poor man's friend." He also had a song about Madam Mary McCleod Bethune. She organized the college in Daytona Beach.[15]

Jackson's tenure as a singer with the Hummingbirds was short. They were ready to move on from Florida and Jackson was not yet ready for life on the road.

"If you black, they figure you have to know how to do something!"

Florida was the Hummingbird's choice of destination when northern climes were cold. But when the seasons changed, the group headed back to the Carolinas and points north. "We liked Florida because we were dodging the weather," says James Davis. "Florida in the winter. Up north in the summer." Pivotal on their northern tour circuit was West Virginia with its coal mining towns and substantial number of African Americans who had migrated there for the work.

The towns of southern West Virginia—Welch, Gary, Beckley, and small company towns like Coalwood, Hawk's Nest, and Ansted—all had sizable African American communities. Workers were involved in every aspect of the industry from mining, transporting, and crushing to the brutal labor of burning down coal to make the more efficient industrial fuel, coke. "The heat, smoke, and dirt from the ovens" would settle into the West Virginia hollows, making them unpleasant places to live. Nonetheless, determined black laborers migrated in from all parts of the country because they needed the work. Movie theaters, restaurants, lunch counters, and schools were segregated. For the most part, though, "blacks and whites lived and worked together in relative peace, while maintaining a distance from each other."[16]

Claude Jeter was one of those African Americans who came to West Virginia to work, which is how he first encountered the Dixie Hummingbirds and wound up singing with them briefly. "I was born in Montgomery, Alabama, in 1914, but I went to West Virginia when I was old enough to work in the coal mines."

> I was in my twenties then. There were a lot of blacks working around Coalwood, Carratha. People came there from everywhere. They called West Virginia the "billion-dollar coalfield." Blacks and whites worked together in the mine, but outside the coalmine, whites lived in one place, and blacks lived in another.
>
> I was singing with a group in West Virginia called the Harmony Kings, a group I organized. But I knew the Dixie Hummingbirds. They were singing around, coming through all the local coalmining towns. All the towns had their little churches. The Birds were a wonderful group, one of the best. They were more "soul" singers, sang old songs that contents people, you know. Davis contacted me when they needed a replacement for their bass singer.
>
> Eventually, I quit coal mining and went to Knoxville, Tennessee. Two of the guys from the Harmony Kings went with me. We started singing for the Swan Baking Company and we sent for another one of the guys from the Harmony Kings. He came up and we sang for them as Swan's Silvertone Singers for five and a half years.[17]

In West Virginia, like anywhere, music was part of community life, a means to entertain, pass the time, lift the spirits, and let off steam. Black gospel quartet singing flourished. The local coal community churches had their groups, and of course, well-known itinerant professionals like the Heavenly Gospel Singers and the Dixie Hummingbirds regularly passed through.

Religious entertainment was presented in a variety of settings: company-owned auditoriums, schools, outdoor parks, and churches.

"We always did well in West Virginia," says James Davis. "Sometimes we would go out to a high school and just talk to the principal." More often, though, the Hummingbirds relied on a local promoter, R. S. Briggs, a white man who arranged programs for them around the region.

"Briggs did a lot of booking up there," says Tucker. "He was from Beckley. Give him a certain amount of dates and he would set things up." And in West Virginia, like nowhere else, the Birds found themselves performing for both black and white audiences. "Briggs would set us up in places that had the money," says Davis. "And one more thing. The white folk didn't have to know you. If you black, they figure you have to know how to do something! And singing is one of those things they think. They liked our material because it was sweet and it was real. We could sing as sweet as a honeycomb."

Touring in both the Northeast and the South, the Birds became seasoned and polished professionals who could succeed with any audience. They learned to read a crowd, adjusted their style for each audience, and developed a solid reputation for reliability and punctuality. It was a philosophy that was essential, as far as James Davis was concerned. "There was something about me . . . about us, the Hummingbirds," says Davis. "Nine times out of ten, if we were supposed to appear anywhere, we were there before any other group. We still have a rule that we are supposed to be at a given place to sing one hour before time, and if one of the members is late, he has to pay a fine." Typically, the Dixie Hummingbirds arrived hours ahead of time, giving themselves an opportunity to mingle and meet the people. It was a policy that won them fans in West Virginia, Florida, the Carolinas, and anywhere they played. Their professionalism endeared them both to show organizers and to fans.

The Dixie Hummingbirds—James Davis, Barney Parks, Ira Tucker, Jimmy Brown, and Wilson Baker—continued wildcatting throughout the remainder of the 1930s and into 1941. Basically, they got along. There were some tensions between Parks and Davis stemming from boyhood days, a rift over an old girlfriend, differences about who should be in charge. But they persevered and continued to successfully win over loyal fans in the Southeast. In 1942, however, the group would make a momentous decision that would ultimately put them on the path to national success.

4
"Twelve Gates to the City"
(1943–1944)

Oh, it's a beautiful city!
Yes, what a beautiful city!
Oh, what a beautiful city!
Twelve gates to the city, ha-lay-loo.
—Traditional Spiritual as sung
by Sister Rosetta Tharpe

As the Dixie Hummingbirds continued to make their mark regionally, other performers were experiencing success on a national level, their efforts gradually fomenting change in the outward stylistic character of black religious music. Any constraints of Anglo performance style lingering from the earlier spiritual tradition were being cast aside. The performances, always laden with somber emotion, were now being sung with all stops pulled, invested with stylistic devices designed to electrify, to transport to a state of spiritual bliss, and in the best moments, even to raise to a frenzy. Throughout the 1940s, the staid spiritual style was giving way to the more free-spirited African American "gospel." The term "gospel" had been used for years to describe religious music, but now it was coming more to mean the new upbeat style with its increasing reliance on instrumental backup in place of pure a cappella. The growing confidence of African Americans as a people seemed to give rise to the unfettered celebration in the new gospel.

The migration of African Americans from the South begun in the 1920s and 1930s continued into the 1940s. "People came from the South," remembers Maya Angelou. "Some people seemed to have tied their mules to the trees and came out to work in the war plants—shipbuilding plants. They brought their music, their records with them, and they also brought the culture." With mobility and opportunity came the confidence that liberated African Americans' religious performance style. Whereas spirituals had been calming, gospel was pure jubilation. "Freedom might account for it," reflects Angelou. "The freedom of a different location, change of venue and some money in the pocket might account for the release, the liberation into being freer and shouting, and some of that shout is jubilation."[1]

The changes were in what notes were sung and how, the structure of harmonies, song arrangements, and the use of musical instruments. Emotive and rhythmic components were not Anglo but more African in origin. These characteristics marked a trend that evolving professional groups like the Dixie Hummingbirds could not ignore.

Gospel did not emerge whole cloth in any one place or time. The scattered strands were pieced together over decades from homespun rituals played out in tiny country churches throughout the South. By the 1940s, rocking soulful gospel had spread west and north, becoming the prevailing fashion in both rural and urban congregations. In his novel, *Go Tell It on the Mountain,* James Baldwin captured the essence of a 1940s sanctified service in a scene set in an African American fundamentalist church in Harlem, New York City:

> The sisters in white, heads raised, the brothers in blue, heads back; the white caps of the women seeming to glow in the charged air like crowns, . . . the gleaming heads of the men seeming to be lifted up— and the rustling and the whispering ceased and the children were quiet; . . . then Elisha hit the keys, beginning at once to sing, and everybody joined him, clapping their hands, and rising, and beating the tambourines.
>
> > The song might be "Down at the cross where my Savior died!"
> > Or: "Jesus, I'll never forget how you set me free!"
> > Or: "Lord, hold my hand while I run this race!"
>
> They sang with all the strength that was in them, and clapped their hands for joy. . . . Their singing caused [belief] in the presence of the Lord; indeed, it was no longer a question of belief, because they made that presence real. . . . For them it was the very bread of life. . . . Something happened to their faces and their voices, the rhythm of their bodies, and to the air they breathed; it was as though wherever they might be became the upper room, and the Holy Ghost [was] riding on the air. . . .

On Sunday mornings the women all seemed patient, all the men seemed mighty. . . . The Power struck someone, a man or woman; they cried out, a long, wordless crying, and, arms outstretched like wings, they began the Shout. Someone moved a chair a little to give them room, the rhythm paused, the singing stopped, only the pounding feet and the clapping hands were heard; then another cry, another dancer; then the tambourines began again, and the voices rose again, and the music swept on again, like fire, or flood, or judgment. Then the church seemed to swell with the Power it held, and, like a planet rocking in space, the temple rocked with the Power of God.[2]

Tableaus like Baldwin's were actually taking place in African American churches in northern cities like New York, Boston, Philadelphia, Washington, D.C., Baltimore, and west to Pittsburgh, Cleveland, Detroit, Chicago, across to Los Angeles and in between. Cutting-edge performers like Sister Rosetta Tharpe and the team of Thomas Dorsey and Sally Martin were propelling the trend with original songs that combined inspiring lyrics with the good-time feel of jubilees and the beat of barrelhouse blues.

Thomas Dorsey, having helped start the commercial gospel trend, was in the 1940s doing more than anyone to fuel the growing popularity of the style. He would champion gospel through a Chicago-based company operating on multiple fronts that encompassed composing, publishing, marketing, and the organization of gospel choirs.

A partner, Sallie Martin, helped Dorsey in his efforts. Martin arrived in Chicago from Pittfield, Georgia, in 1927. Her spontaneous and emotional singing style quickly built her a following in local Chicago churches. On the strength of her local popularity and diligence in making herself known to Dorsey, Sallie Martin became a song demonstrator on the Dorsey team. In a short time, her flair for business emerged and put the Dorsey operation over the top. "She organized his music store, hired assistants to work at the counter, and kept records of the inventory. After a few short months . . . she was able to show a profit for his business—a feat that had eluded Dorsey." In 1940, she organized the Sallie Martin Singers, and adopting the "sanctified style of shout singing," she became famous for "her Holy Ghost jerks and steps. When taken over by the spirit, her dark alto would soar above a shouting crowd . . ."

Throughout the 1940s, the team of Dorsey and Martin contributed significantly to the propagation of the sanctified gospel sound. As

Horace Clarence Boyer noted, "By 1945, it was difficult to avoid gospel music in the African American community."[3]

During this period, while jazz and blues proliferated and found a fan base outside the African American community, gospel remained for the most part culturally confined. Perhaps the religious nature of the music limited its commercial appeal, or perhaps white America was simply not ready for the performance histrionics of the genre. Nonetheless, African American musicians on the secular side freely borrowed from gospel performance style.

A case in point was vibraphonist Lionel Hampton, swing era legend and pioneer of postwar rhythm and blues. Hampton drew deeply from the well of sanctified church music. "I was brought up in the Holiness church . . . where I'd always try to sit by the sister who played the big bass drum. Our church had a whole band, with guitar, trombone, and different drums. That sister on the bass drum would get happy and get up and start dancing up and down the aisles, and I'd get on her drum: boom! boom! I always had that beat in me. That heavy backbeat is pure sanctified, Church of God in Christ."[4]

Then again, in the 1940s, already a star, Hampton was impacted by an encounter with Whirlin' Willie at a faith-healing service in Little Rock. On tour with his swing band, Hampton had the night off and out of curiosity, wandered into a revival service. "Whirling Willie's band started to play. What a band! First I wanted his trumpet player to join my band; then I wanted to just hire 'em all. They got to swinging, started feeling the Holy Spirit, and man, did they hit a groove. Of course, they wouldn't go out with me. They just wanted to play the Lord's music. And I can't blame 'em, they had the spirit and the power. . . . After they got really going, a door opened in the back, and Whirlin' Willie came in whirling, just whirling around and around, and he didn't stop once! The band started groovin' even harder, and the people just started rising up. . . . When I couldn't hire any of his musicians, well, I started working on my musicians, getting them to play with that kind of inspiration. And I think I was the first to bring all that music from the Holiness church—the beat, the hand clapping, the shouting—out into the band business."[5]

While gospel music swept the land, not every congregation welcomed it. "I know there were those, the Purists . . . who didn't want Gospel music," remembers Maya Angelou, "that only wanted Spiritual music."[6] But what could not be accepted publicly, radio and phonograph records permitted to be embraced privately in homes. And though not open to the whole sweep of the music, Anglo America, too, was beginning to be receptive to a handful of gospel artists. Sister Rosetta Tharpe, for one, high profile from her radio and Carnegie Hall "Spirituals to Swing" concert appearances, became popular with general audiences. Her driving style and flirtation with jazz and blues instrumentation, while scandalous to many religiously conservative African Americans, won her more fans—both black and white—than she ever stood to lose.

These were times of transition. World War II had been in a rolling boil since 1939. The United States would enter the fray in 1941. Americans of every ancestry would put their lives on the line. At the war's end, returning African Americans, having served valiantly, were no longer willing to tolerate institutionalized segregation. The fight for freedom would take a different turn as African Americans and those who stood with them fought on the home front for social equality. Gospel music would become a soundtrack in the battle for civil rights.

The Dixie Hummingbirds would be swept up in the shifting tides, doing what they must to stay afloat. As tastes in religious entertainment changed, so too did the Hummingbirds. Audiences were looking for more of an emotional impact, and the Birds had to learn to deliver. Ira Tucker would emerge as the powerhouse who moved the group further in that direction. South Carolina continued to be their base of operations, but by the early 1940s, even that had to be reconsidered.

"You got twenty-five on the ground!"

For more than a decade, the Dixie Hummingbirds had spent the bulk of their time on the road, a lifestyle fraught with inconveniences. Income was always uncertain. They lived away from family and friends for months at a time, functioning ultimately as a family unto themselves. Confined together in the car for hours on end, they often drove to the point of exhaustion, sometimes sleeping in the car overnight, bodies slumped uncomfortably against one another.

Prejudice and segregation forced them to take precautions, like carrying sandwich-makings or leftovers from last night's church supper in case no restaurant could be found to serve them, or filling the car up with gas when the tank was only half empty, in case they could not find a station that would sell them gas when they needed it.

As the Birds motored along, they defused the normal tensions that arose from constant proximity by philosophizing, working out songs, telling stories, and joking—but, of course, the jokes had to be "clean" because that was the Davis rule. Ever the enforcer, James Davis made it his responsibility to see that the group "didn't get out of line," reprimanding each according to his own temperament.

The unremitting companionship compromised individual members' privacy but also helped maintain solidarity. They shared in-jokes, experiences, and even a special way of talking, a patois that marked them as partners, a lingo that was also known to fellow travelers on the gospel highway. Jive talk lightened things up, sugarcoated the down side. So, someone might say, "I'm gonna check me out some chorus girls," meaning they were about to eat some canned sardines lined up all in a row, the poor man's lunch, back then a staple of the touring life. Davis laughs thinking back on it now. "The 'gig,'" he says, "that meant the 'job.'"

> You hear that all the time now, but we were sayin' it before other folks knew what we were talkin' about. "Gators," that meant shoes. A "brim" was a hat. A "short," that was a metaphor for a car.
>
> And you think *we* were something, you should have heard the Harmonizing Four! One of them would walk up and say, "You got about twenty-five on the ground!" He was talking about your shoes. In those days, twenty-five was a lot to pay for a pair of shoes! I still remember the last time I saw the Harmonizing Four, I walked in and someone said, "Hmm. Look like you dropped about twenty!" That meant I looked older than the last time he'd seen me.

Periodically, the Birds would return to South Carolina for weeks at a time. They would have stayed longer, but maintaining a steady income demanded live performances, and there were only so many places to play and only so many times people would pay to see them. They had to stay on the road to generate a living wage.

Starting in the 1940s, war rationing restricted the consumption of gasoline and automobile tires, and in September of 1942, the American Federation of Musicians imposed on its members a "300-mile jump limit," the distance traveled between performance sites. In addition, as *Billboard* magazine remarked in 1942, "In the gas-rationed East, ... patrons find it increasingly difficult to reach the spot of entertainment,"[7] a circumstance that reduced the size of audiences.

Moreover, the "wildcatting " that had been such an adventure in their earlier days was wearing the Hummingbirds down. "We loved what we were doing, but we constantly had to figure out how to make it pay," says James Davis. They were coming to terms with the idea that radical changes would have to be made. The solution lay to the north. The Dixie Hummingbirds would first move to Washington, D. C., and then to Philadelphia, Pennsylvania.

"I got you guys a job in Philadelphia if you can come up here to stay."

The move north was trying for the Birds. The only affordable approach was to once again leave family behind and hope that success would eventually allow their families to join them. In 1941, they headed to Washington, D.C., where Davis had an aunt with whom they could room.

There had been another close call in the automobile on the way up. "All I know," says Tucker, "it was morning and we were in a cornfield!" Davis, who had been driving, never admitted to Tucker whether he had fallen asleep at the wheel or intentionally pulled over for the night. That day, they drove into the city.

Washington was an eye-opener for the Dixie Hummingbirds, especially for Tucker. It was the first time he had ever traveled out of the South. "I thought Washington was the biggest place in the world. It was certainly the biggest place I had ever been." The Birds worked in and around Washington for those few months. Then, after a brief reprieve in Greenville, the Hummingbirds set out for Philadelphia, where Barney Parks's father lived.

"Back then," Tucker said, "Philadelphia was a home base to a lot of gospel singers—The Angelics. The Ward Singers. The Sensational Nightingales[8] organized right here in Philadelphia. In the 1940s and 1950s, quartet singing was top shelf."[9] In addition, the city was strategically located along the Boston–New York–Baltimore–Washington corridor. The highways were decent and they provided easy access to the big northeastern cities. Also important to the Birds, given their propensity for fishing, Philadelphia was close to rivers, lakes, and both the Chesapeake Bay and New Jersey ocean waters.

Philadelphia also offered a fairer brand of justice than the Birds were accustomed to in the South. Northern courts at least seemed willing to consider the civil rights of African Americans.[10] And as they were often on the road, the Dixie Hummingbirds ran less risk of being incarcerated or lynched in Philadelphia than they did further south.

In fact, by the early 1940s, Philadelphia had become a favored destination for many African Americans migrating from the Carolinas,

enough that an eatery called the South Carolina Boys restaurant maintained a viable business for years, first at 4140 Lancaster Avenue and
later at 1802 South Street. Philadelphia was in many ways ideal as a
"home away from home" and eventually, for the Dixie Hummingbirds,
a permanent home for themselves and their growing families.

The single most important factor that drew the Hummingbirds to
Philadelphia, though, was the offer of steady work from Charlie
Newsome, a booking agent they had met in Jacksonville, Florida, where
he had been managing a group called the Royal Harmony Singers.
"They were also from South Carolina," says Tucker, "and had this guy
named Julius Ginyard—he went on to be with the Golden Gates for a
little while."[11]

The Royal Harmony Singers performed as singing waiters at a downtown hotel, a common attraction in Jacksonville and many southern
hotels at the time. The group wore "white duck pants . . . with a red
streak down the side," says Ginyard, "and a little red vest like the
Phillip Morris boy used to wear." Tucker remembers, "They'd stand
right in between [the tables] and do a song. I'd never seen anything like
it before."[12] The hotel owner, according to Ginyard, gave them a used
Chrysler Royal automobile, a thousand dollars up front, and twenty-
five to thirty dollars a week at the hotel.[13]

"The Royal Harmony Singers were working down in Jacksonville,
Florida," says Tucker, "and we came in on their territory and got the
best of them."

> So they left Florida and came up to Philly. Charlie Newsome was
> booking them and after they got to Philly, he got them a radio show
> on WCAU. But they had a big argument and fell out with each other.
> Charlie wrote and told me I got you guys a job in Philadelphia if you
> can come up here to stay. So, I told the guys and we got together and
> we came on up.

At the time of the Hummingbirds' arrival in 1942, WCAU, a 50,000-
watt clear channel station, was the ratings leader in Philadelphia. A CBS
network affiliate, it aired most of the popular radio shows of the day—
Amos 'n' Andy nightly at 7:00, serials like *Easy Aces* and *Mr. Keen, Tracer
of Lost Persons*, Fred Allen's *Texaco Theater*, *The Romance of Helen Trent*,
and *Vic and Sade*, among others. WCAU offered live broadcasts of
sporting events, nightly war reports, and a variety of musical programming that included classical, big band, and the *Lucky Strike Hit Parade*, a
countdown of the top tunes of the week.

Mindful of the growing population of African Americans newly arrived from the South, WCAU and its competitors regularly aired Sunday morning programs of black gospel music. Most of these shows were nationwide network broadcasts carried by local affiliates. In design, they were intended to remind listeners recently arrived in the city of life back home in the rural south. The Southernaires, for example, had a program called *The Little Weather-Beaten Whitewashed Church* that aired at noon over NBC affiliate WFIL.[14] The Deep River Boys could be heard on both WEAF and KYW. WCAU broadcast the popular Wings over Jordan at 10:30 A.M. Wings over Jordan was a thirty- to forty-voice choir organized in Cleveland, Ohio, that in 1942 had already been a mainstay on the CBS network for almost five years.[15] According to a *Billboard* report on competition between Philadelphia radio stations, "religious programs on Sunday mornings" had the highest ratings in that time slot, with WCAU's broadcasts of Wings over Jordan one of the "outstanders."[16]

These programs were certainly popular within the African American community, but over time, listeners of any and all backgrounds increasingly tuned in. A 1941 article in New York City's African American newspaper, the *Amsterdam News,* attested to, for example, the cross-cultural appeal of the Southernaires on radio.

> Originally their audiences were almost exclusively colored because of the nature of their work, but the good word spread and the caliber of their performances made them ambassadors of the spiritual to all Races. . . . Their work is nationally loved because it is so essentially American.[17]

In Philadelphia, the appeal of African American music across color lines—and that included gospel—was evident in the range of performers appearing in the early 1940s on film or in person at city theaters, cabarets, and clubs that catered either primarily or sometimes exclusively to whites.

The film *Cabin in the Sky,* Vincente Minnelli's 1942 directorial debut, with its spotlight on performers like Ethel Waters, Louis Armstrong, and Duke Ellington, drew filmgoers black and white into city movie houses. That same year, pianist Fats Waller appeared in person at Fay's on 40th and Market with the gospel quartet, the Deep River Boys, as his opening act.

A year later, Waller would himself be featured on film along with blues singer Ada Brown in *Stormy Weather,* Twentieth Century Fox's answer to *Cabin in the Sky*. *Stormy Weather* also starred Cab Calloway, Bill "Bojangles" Robinson, Lena Horne, Dooley Wilson, Eddie "Rochester" Anderson, and the Katharine Dunham dance troupe. The film's concept was to transport audiences back a decade or so into the world of black music. Waller's scene took place in a Memphis juke joint set on legendary Beale Street. As the leader of a hot jazz combo, Waller and company reenacted the look, feel, and sound of the late 1920s.

That Hollywood believed *Stormy Weather* would have mainstream appeal was further testament to the broadening allure of black entertainment—or at least the white community's perception of it. In spite of the film's good intentions, some African American critics were still put off by the stereotyped characters. Wrote a reviewer for *The Philadelphia Afro-American*, "Cab Calloway and Bill Robinson were made into clown princes, . . . Oscar Smith and Charles Moore get boot-licking and tramp-act note, . . . Jess Lee Brooks, Rita Christina, . . . and Willy Best as happy-go-lucky eye-rollers."[18]

Meanwhile, the year the Dixie Hummingbirds came to town, two other black gospel groups with national reputations were performing in Philadelphia. At the Swan Club at 5725 Broad Street, the Charioteers were playing. The newspapers touted their appearance in *Hellzapoppin'*, a recent film hit starring slapstick comics Olsen and Johnson. The Delta Rhythm Boys were also in town at Kaliner's Rathskeller on Spruce Street. Their frequent guest appearances on vocalist Kate Smith's syndicated radio program had earned them widespread popularity. Unfortunately, African Americans could not attend the shows, as both the Swan Club and Kaliner's were "white only" venues.

There were places in Philadelphia open to "mixed" audiences, like the Earle Theater and Fay's that offered auditorium seating and a combination of live stage shows and movies. In 1942, the Earle presented a "sepia stage bill" that featured in person Ella Fitzgerald and Bill "Bojangles" Robinson opposite a John Wayne film, *In Old California*. "As dapper, limber, and delightful as ever," wrote an *Inquirer* reviewer about Bill Robinson. "Making light of his 64 years, 'Bojangles' was in fine form capering, clowning, telling stories—and going through a number of the soft shoe routines he has made famous with the agility of a youngster. . . . Miss Fitzgerald, looking quite charming in a full-skirted white summer dinner dress, brought her popular, thoroughly individual vocal style to 'Knock Me a Kiss,' 'All I Need Is You,' 'Mr. Paganini,' and, of course, 'A Tisket, a Tasket.'"[19] Fay's also took out ads in Philadelphia's black press offering "all colored" stage shows and appearances by top names like Fats Waller, the Earl Hines Orchestra with Billy Eckstine, and Louis Jordan.[20]

With the move to Philadelphia in 1942, the Dixie Hummingbirds had entered a city brimming with opportunity for African American performers in all musical styles.

"I couldn't see the difference between 'Swanee' and 'Dixie.'"

In the months before the Birds made the trip to Philadelphia, there was one major shift in their lineup. Bass singer Jimmy Brown would leave the group. The circumstances were not the best. "Brown left us in Florida," says Tucker.

> He got married and took the group's whole treasury with him! Took what little money we had and we didn't feel too good about it at all. When we got back to South Carolina, there was a guy named William Henry who was singing with a group called the Brown Brothers, no relation to Jimmy. I got him over to the side and said, "Hey, you wanna sing with the Hummingbirds?" "Yeah, yeah, man! When we leaving?" I said, "Can you come up to Spartanburg?" He said, "Tell me when." Packed his bag, and in a couple of days, he was there. He had the voice, we learned him how to sing bass.

Wilson "Highpockets" Baker had also been moving in and out of the group in recent years as he wavered about earning his living on the road as a singer. He decided, at least for the time being, to once again cast his fate with the Dixie Hummingbirds and make the move with them to Philadelphia.

So, in 1942, the Dixie Hummingbirds—James Davis, Barney Parks, Ira Tucker, Wilson Baker, and William Henry—made the journey from South Carolina to Philadelphia. In style and repertoire, they sang as they always had—traditional a cappella spirituals, James Davis leading on the sweet songs, Ira Tucker handling the up-beat shouters, Wilson Baker fronting one or two, but with Barney Parks mostly covering the middle and William Henry holding down the bass.

The Birds were not entirely unknown in Philadelphia. Thanks to phonograph records and appearances in town, they already had a bit of a following. At first, they looked to those fans for performance venues. "We were singing mostly in churches and schools," says Tucker. Once the Birds began their regular radio broadcasts, however, those circumstances would change. "When we got on that radio, then people were calling up from everywhere because it was a 50,000 watt station. We had all the work we could do. In some ways more, because it was wartime and a lot of people were in the army."[21]

The success of nationally syndicated black gospel radio shows had created a market in Philadelphia and other cities for programming that originated locally. The radio program listings published that year in the *Inquirer* reveal a number of stations airing generically billed "Negro male quartets," sometimes as fill-ins between shows and other times in their own spots at the start of the broadcast day or as guests on other local shows. The Dixie Hummingbirds were quickly incorporated into WCAU's broadcast schedule. According to Tucker, "a month after we got to Philly, we were on WCAU."[22]

In the beginning, the group was given featured spots, a song or two here and there at various times on the schedule. Within about two months, though, they were invited to perform on a popular local show, *Ninety Minutes from Broadway*. The title alluded, of course, to Philadelphia's proximity to New York City. "The show was a half hour long," says Tucker. "Right there at WCAU. 'Bon Bon'[23] was the singer and Miss Haven was an organist and the musical director at WCAU. Miss Haven told somebody about us, and they put us on." Says Tucker, "We were the first black group to have ever been on *Ninety Minutes from Broadway*."

The opportunity was just the break the Dixie Hummingbirds needed. The only drawback was that station management wanted to call the group something other than the Dixie Hummingbirds. "WCAU did not like the idea of us calling ourselves 'Dixie,'" says James Davis. "So one of us said do you want us to make it the Swanee Quintet, and they said yeah." No one ever explained to them exactly why the change in name. "I couldn't see the difference between 'Swanee' and 'Dixie'," says Davis. "Both of them meant 'south.' At least that's what we thought."

Ultimately, they concluded that station management thought the name "Dixie Hummingbirds" was too black to appeal to WCAU's white listener base. "Swanee Quintet" was more neutral and in keeping with white expectations. As far as the Dixie Hummingbirds were concerned, they could live with the name change and marketing ploys as long as management permitted the group to stay true to themselves and their fans. The arrangement suited both parties. WCAU got what they wanted in an expanded audience and increased advertising revenues, and the Dixie Hummingbirds cum Swanees found a new home base, steady income with less travel, and the opportunity to reach more listeners than ever before. In fact, a recording of one of their WCAU performance spots would lead to the career breakthrough they had been hoping for—a chance to perform at a major venue in New York City. The club, Café Society, was the brainchild of political activist Barney Josephson and his musical consultant and booker, John Hammond.

"An integrated night club with mixed entertainment and mixed audiences."

Charley Newsome had done well by the Dixie Hummingbirds when he got them on WCAU. Now, he took them an important step forward by bringing the group to the attention of John Hammond, producer of the 1938 and 1939 "From Spirituals to Swing" concerts at Carnegie Hall. Hammond was uniquely positioned in both New York City and the national music scenes.

Born in 1910, John Hammond's father was a lawyer, his mother a Vanderbilt. As Hammond himself wrote, his path was "smoothed by inherited wealth (Mother's share of the hundreds of millions accumulated by *her* mother's Vanderbilt forebears and of her father's mercantile fortune), and by a tradition of accomplishment whose momentum had been well begun four generations before him."[24]

In 1922 when Hammond was twelve, he had already begun collecting 78-rpm phonograph records. "All music fascinated me, but the simple honesty and convincing lyrics of the early blues singers, the rhythm and creative ingenuity of the jazz players, excited me most. It was not long before I discovered that most of them—certainly all those I liked the best—were black."[25]

Hammond made the transition from collector to producer in 1931. That year he produced a jazz recording by Garland Wilson, an African American pianist he had heard at Covan's Morocco Club. "He wasn't nearly as good as I thought he was, but he was flashy."[26] The tracks were "St. James Infirmary" and "When Your Lover Has Gone." Hammond's ties with Columbia began with Frank Walker, the label's recording manager. Walker made the last recordings of blues singer Bessie Smith with Hammond paying the $125 production costs out of his own pocket. Hammond's association as both producer and talent scout with Columbia records lasted his entire lifetime. Over the years he had a hand in the recording careers of performers as disparate as Benny Goodman, Count Basie, Billie Holiday, Aretha Franklin, Bob Dylan, and Bruce Springsteen.[27]

Although his efforts for Columbia earned a great deal of money, Hammond had no need to rely on it as income. He lived well on a yearly stipend provided by his family. In spite of his life in the comfort zone, however, Hammond was drawn to the disenfranchised. He became what he called a "New York social dissident."

> My dissent from the social order started with my objection to the discrimination I saw everywhere around me.... Despite the influence of early teachers, the books I read, and what I had seen for myself in the South, the strongest motivation for my dissent was jazz. I heard no color line in the music. While my early favorites were white players, the recorded and live performances of Negroes excited me more. The fact that the best jazz players barely made a living and were barred from all well-paying jobs in radio and in most night clubs, enraged me....To bring recognition to the Negro's supremacy in jazz was the most effective and constructive form of social protest I could think of....
>
> Recording offered a unique opportunity for creative casting; the stage provided the spontaneity of live performance; the music and liberal press gave me a platform for constructive criticism. The times themselves [in the 1930s] imposed insurmountable odds, particularly for Negroes, against achieving any sort of recognition without help. The opportunities for me were clear.[28]

"The money had very little to do with it, actually," Hammond would tell interviewer John Koenig, "and I was determined to integrate the music business."[29] To that end, Hammond would use his position and musical knowledge to stage the "From Spirituals to Swing" concerts. As the concerts were designed to spotlight the best in African American talent, Hammond gathered together on the stage of Carnegie Hall performers from across the nation representing genres ranging from blues to jazz to gospel. "My own idea for 'From Spirituals to Swing,'" wrote Hammond, "was to present artists not widely known to jazz fans, artists whose music had never been heard by most of the New York public."[30]

Hammond intended the concerts to be more than mere entertainment. For him, they were a sociopolitical statement, a slap in the face to the racist attitudes that had infected American entertainment from its very beginnings. The concerts were about righting wrongs, giving credit where credit was due, and redirecting mainstream focus to performers

Hammond rightly believed had been overlooked and exploited and were deserving of recognition. With "From Spirituals to Swing," Hammond hoped to throw a long overdue spotlight on a broad spectrum of African American performance style. Even the stature of Carnegie Hall was factored into the message he hoped to send.

The concerts were a smashing success and even before the curtain came down on the first of them, Hammond and like-minded others knew they wanted to keep the idea alive, if not in form, at least in spirit. To that end, in 1938, a unique nightspot opened in the city. Called Café Society, Hammond described it as "one of the most successful and controversial night clubs in New York City."[31] Like numerous other nightspots around town, Café Society offered an array of African American talent. What made the club different, however, was its nondiscriminatory policy. Anyone, black, white, or otherwise, was welcome through the doors for dinner, dancing, and, of course, the stage show. As one of the first integrated clubs in New York City, Café Society was perceived at the time as nothing less than radical.

The tone of racism had been set more than a decade before by perhaps the most famous of New York City's venues showcasing African American talent—the Cotton Club. It typified segregationist policy, not only in New York City, but also in similar urban clubs all across the nation. The Cotton Club thrived almost from the beginning when it opened at a site on Harlem's Lenox Avenue in 1923. Outstanding African American artists like Duke Ellington and Cab Calloway as well as numerous singers, dancers, and comedians used the Cotton Club stage over the years as a springboard to commercial success and nationwide fame. The performers may have been black, but by design, the audiences were almost exclusively white. As jazz singer Billie Holiday put it, the Cotton Club was "a place Negroes never saw inside unless they played music or did the shakes and shimmies."[32]

The show room at the Cotton Club was done up to look like a jungle replete with fake palm trees and tropical backdrops. Customers had the illusion of viewing a primitive spectacle from a safe vantage point. "Among those who were considered undesirables," wrote Jim Haskins in his history of the Cotton Club, "were blacks, even in, or perhaps particularly in, mixed parties."

Carl Van Vechten reported: "There were brutes at the door to enforce the Cotton Club's policy which was opposed to mixed parties." Only the lightest-complexioned Negroes gained entrance, and even they were carefully screened. The club's management was aware that most white downtowners wanted to *observe* Harlem blacks, not mix with them; or, as Jimmy Durante put it, "it isn't necessary to mix with colored people if you don't feel like it. You have your own party and keep it to yourself. But it's worth seeing. How they step!"[33]

Like night to day, Café Society was completely opposite in concept. Barney Josephson, Café Society's owner, took great delight in flaunting his nonracist policies and, for that matter, in mocking elitist attitudes across the board. The very choice of name was born in sarcasm. The term had been in use by noted editor and playwright Clare Booth Luce to describe the upper crust of the New York City nightclub scene. Café Society, the club, was a place that drew no lines, where the riffraff and the elite were free to mix without prejudice. Barney Josephson copyrighted the phrase and touted his club in ads as "The Wrong Place for the Right People."[34] And Josephson practiced what he preached. One night, John Hammond and his wife came to the club with Paul Robeson. "Robeson and Mrs. Hammond danced," Josephson would tell *New Yorker* columnist Whitney Balliett.

> The headwaiter told me that the people at Table 41 would like to see me. There were two couples at the table, and one of the men said, "Do you allow niggers to dance with white women in this place?" "Sir," I replied, "we do not use that word in here. Furthermore, there is a law in this state against discrimination, and we abide by it. But it's still a democracy and you have a right not to like what you see." "Well, we don't like it at all," he said. They walked out, but I made sure they paid their bill in full, even though they had just begun eating their shrimp cocktails.[35]

That was the spirit of Café Society, what cultural historian Michael Denning called "a remarkable synthesis of the radical political cabarets of Berlin and Paris with the African American jazz clubs and revues of Harlem."[36]

With six thousand borrowed dollars, Barney Josephson took a "shuttered-up basement in Sheridan Square" and redecorated it to fit his political purview. He hired three W.P.A. artists "to do some murals." The murals would become one of the best-remembered features of Café Society. There was a "debutante surrounded by . . . little bald guys with pot bellies," a "stylish lady, her head a gramophone machine, with her nose on a record playing the music—it represented a yak-yak, talk society girl," and behind the bar a portrayal of "cabaret types as 'all animals, all kinds in a menagerie, dressed like humans . . . and the mural was as if it were a mirror.'" Finally, "topping off the décor [was] a plaster cast monkey in 'Hitler mustache and hair' hung from one of the pipes 'with a noose.'"[37] For most of the first year, patrons were greeted at the entrance by a doorman in a tattered coat and white gloves with the fingertips out.[38]

Since Barney Josephson knew next to nothing about music, he needed an advisor, and John Hammond stepped into that role. "Barney and I hit it off immediately. He wanted what I always wanted: an integrated nightclub with mixed entertainment and mixed audiences. . . . It would be a place . . . where blacks and whites could hear the best music in the city." Prices were deliberately scaled down to make the room inviting to clientele of even the most modest means. "Dinner cost $1.50 and there was no minimum at the bar adjacent to the bandstand, so people could sip a 75-cent beer and listen to the best jazz talent in New York." Café Society became an extension of Hammond's "From Spirituals to Swing" concerts, "a place where known and unknown performers could appear, where Negro patrons were as welcome as whites."[39]

Café Society in the heart of Greenwich Village started off slowly. "Village people came," said Josephson, "and so did uptown types and the college kids."

> It was a grand success, but I was losing money. I simply didn't know enough about this sort of merchandising. . . . I began to think that I had opened the club in the wrong part of town, that I should move uptown. I found a place on 58th street which had changed hands a lot. My press agent, Ivan Black, sent out a release saying that Café Society was so successful I was opening an uptown branch. Actually, I planned to dump the original club, but when people heard about the uptown club the crowd doubled downtown and I suddenly began making money. Café Society Uptown opened on October 8, 1940. . . . Uptown had cost me almost thirty-thousand dollars to put in shape, all of it borrowed, but it started making money immediately, and by the end of that year I had paid off every cent.
>
> I moved the Downtown show to the Uptown when it opened, and brought new people in Downtown. . . . In time I had a steady, floating company of musicians and comedians and dancers and singers that moved back and forth between the clubs and that worked on a nearly

permanent basis. It was a new concept in nightclubs, and it gave the performers a sense of security most of them never had before. It also gave them time to try out new routines and ideas.[40]

The original location at Sheridan Square became Café Society Downtown, the new location on 58th between Lexington and Park Avenues, Café Society Uptown. "Downtown was a basement holding 210. Uptown was a fancier two-story affair with 350 capacity."[41] "Café Society became a club for intelligent people with a social consciousness who were concerned about political, social, and racial justice."[42]

Even with the best intentions, however, there were those, as evidenced by a cynical critic for *The Jazz Record*, who simply did not buy into the formula.

> Café Society Uptown isn't one of those places that you can arrange to meet your friends in. No, this pretentious club . . . is so big that you are liable to get lost in it yourself. It looks strictly like a joint out of a Hollywood production with all the fancy trimmings straight from a wild exhibit at the Modern Museum of Art. . . .
>
> Let it be said for the record that the entertainment is among the best in town, if not the best. Café Society Uptown is about the only fancy club these days where you can get terrific entertainment without having to step over swooning women who have just listened to Sinatra or [Dick] Haymes and so on ad nauseum.[43]

"Gimme some corn bread, baby! . . . Gimme some of that hard stuff!"

Both Café Society Uptown and Downtown delivered some of the finest music in town. This was the world the Dixie Hummingbirds were about to enter thanks to Charlie Newsome and his efforts with John Hammond. Within a little more than a year, the Birds had made a rapid transition from a provincial southern quartet to Philadelphia radio stars. Now, it looked like they would become featured performers in one of New York City's hottest, most liberated and controversial showrooms.

The Dixie Hummingbirds would be in distinguished company at Café Society. Among those who regularly performed there were vocalists Lena Horne, Sarah Vaughan, and Mildred Bailey; blues singers Joe Turner, Big Bill Broonzy, and Josh White; and some of the hottest piano players in the land, Art Tatum, James P. Johnson, Mary Lou Williams, Hazel Scott, and the boogie-woogie trio Albert Ammons, Meade Lux

Lewis, and Pete Johnson. Two of Café Society's most memorable performers were Billie Holiday and the Golden Gate Quartet. Both would play vital roles in politicizing the music heard at the club.

Billie Holiday's engagement at Café Society would take her to new heights. "I opened Café Society as an unknown," she wrote in *Lady Sings the Blues*. "I left two years later as a star."[44] Holiday would be most remembered at Café Society for her performances of "Strange Fruit," a song that she called her "personal protest." The lyric, about lynching in the South, was written for her by a fan, Abel Meeropol. "He suggested that Sonny White, who had been my accompanist, and I turn it into music. So the three of us got together and did the job in about three weeks." Holiday feared that the crowd would hate the song. "The first time I sang it I thought it was a mistake.... There wasn't even a patter of applause when I finished. Then a lone person began to clap nervously. Then suddenly everyone was clapping."[45]

> Southern trees bear a strange fruit,
> Blood on the leaves and blood at the root,
> Black bodies swinging in the Southern breeze,
> Strange fruit hanging from the poplar tree.

At successive performances, Josephson insisted that Billie Holiday close the show with "Strange Fruit." "Lights out, just one small spin-light, and all service stopped," recounts Josephson. "There were no encores after it. My instruction was walk off, period. People had to remember 'Strange Fruit,' get their insides burned with it."[46]

The great Golden Gate Quartet, the Tidewater Virginia group so respected and admired by the Hummingbirds since their earliest days in the gospel business, had in the early 1940s also become a mainstay at Café Society. The Gates had been a sensation at the 1939 Carnegie Hall "From Spirituals to Swing" concert, and now John Hammond had arranged a long run for them at Café Society. The idea of spiritual enter-tainers in a secular room was at the time cutting edge—some in the black religious community would consider it scandalous—but Hammond had succeeded at Carnegie and would do the same at Café Society. In essence, Hammond was opening doors for religious performers, providing a rare opportunity for them to be appreciated for the music's sake and draw a generous paycheck to boot. The Gates, with their slick personable manner and alluring musicality, were perfectly suited to Café Society. "John brought in the Golden Gate Quartet," recalled Barney Josephson, "and they made the blood rush up my arms, which brought the goose pimples out, when they sang—and here I was a disbeliever—'As they were driving the nails in His feet you could hear the hammer ringing in Jerusalem's streets.'"[47]

The Gates had built their reputation within the African American community via the usual reworking of classic spirituals. By the late 1930s, they had broken through as one of the top groups in the country in part on the strength of captivating original songs written by founding member and baritone lead, Bill Johnson. Johnson's songs spun out stories about biblical characters like Noah, Jonah, Job, Shadrack, Nicodemus, Daniel, and Jezebel. At Café Society, the Golden Gates began performing songs with political overtones, like "Comin' in on a Wing and a Prayer," a Harold Adamson/Jimmy McHugh collaboration, and "Stalin Wasn't Stallin'," a lyrical tour de force written by Bill Johnson. The song, loosely based on the old religious novelty "The Preacher and the Bear," was about the Russian premier's efforts, seen at the time as heroic, to thwart the Nazi invasion of his country. John Hammond produced a recording of the song for Columbia Records in 1942. The Gates rapped it out in pulsing rhythm and rhyme:

BILL JOHNSON:
> Now, Adolph got the notion that he was the master race,
> And he swore he'd bring new order and put mankind in its place,
> So he put his scheme in motion and was winning everywhere,
> Until he up and got the notion for to kick that Russian bear.

GROUP:
> Now, Stalin wasn't stallin' when he told the beast of Berlin,
> That they never would rest contented,
> 'Til they'd driven him from the land.
> So he called the Yanks and English,
> And proceeded to extinguish,
> The Fuehrer and his vermin, this is how it all began.

"Loose-boned gospel songs and spirituals," was how one critic described the Golden Gate Quartet.[48] They were so well received at Café Society that Josephson and Hammond immediately began looking for other gospel quartets, especially when Josephson opened his second club. The Dixie Hummingbirds were perfectly positioned and ready to roll. Their regular broadcasts over WCAU in Philadelphia had helped them fine-tune their style. The Birds had also begun training with a vocal coach named Charles Williams. "He was a classically trained music teacher who worked within the school system," says Ira Tucker.

> He was into music and he taught us vocals. He was the first and only instructor we had. We needed him because we wanted to learn how to phrase, do crescendos, vocal techniques, you know. Charles Williams was a great man. He knew singing backwards. He was real strict on us saying your words. He believed in perfect lyrics. Charles Williams came in handy for us. Years ago, he booked us into programs he used to put together in Atlantic City at the convention hall.

In October of 1942, the Birds went head-to-head in a highly publicized concert engagement with the Royal Harmony Singers, their old rivals from Jacksonville and now also relocated to Philadelphia and broadcasting on radio. A photograph of the Hummingbirds dominated

The Dixie Hummingbirds over WCAU. Photograph from the *Philadelphia Afro-American*, 10 October 1942. Wilson Baker in front; from left: Ira Tucker, James Davis, Barney Parks, William Henry.

the top of a page in the *Philadelphia Afro-American*. "To compete with Harmony Singers," read the caption. "Members of the Swanee Singers of radio station WCAU, also known as the Dixie Hummingbirds of Greenville, S.C., will meet the Royal Harmony Singers of station KYW in a singing contest on October 14, at Mother Bethel AME Church for the city radio championship." "Quartet War Declared!" Adult admission to the "song battle" was sixty-five cents, thirty-five cents for children. A month later, the Dixie Hummingbirds would make their debut at Café Society in New York City.[49]

Charlie Newsome had arranged the audition that would win the Hummingbirds the gig. The timing was perfect. Hammond and Josephson had been looking for a gospel quartet to cover for the Golden Gates when they were on the road or working the opposite Café Society location. Bill Johnson of the Gates had also spoken up on the Birds' behalf. "Charlie Newsome could talk the horns off a billy goat," says James Davis. "He just went in there and talked with Hammond and told him about us."

Newsome brought Hammond a recording of the Birds performing on WCAU. The way Tucker tells it, Hammond said, "Hey man, what the hell are you waiting on. This is the group I want. I want them up here yesterday!" The Birds traveled to New York City and auditioned for Hammond and Josephson. "We went in there and sang all that polished up stuff," says Tucker.

"Mt. Zion." "I'm On My Journey Now." We had about ten beautiful songs. Davis came up with them and I had arranged them. But Barney Josephson, you know, was something like an atheist. He said as long as we're singing, he felt good. But as soon as we got through singing, it was over for him. [Tucker laughs at that]

But John Hammond, he was the man who had the feeling for hard gospel. He didn't like too much of this real sweet stuff. John said, "Now hold up! Is this all you all got?" And we say, "Oh no, we can come through the woods with it!" He said, "You all from the South I know. Gimme some corn bread, baby! [Ira shakes his fist in imitation of Hammond] Gimme some of that hard stuff! I want gutbucket, man. I want to hear what you all about. You can't get too wooley for me!"

And, man, we got to singing that cornfield stuff. We came down on him with songs like "Don't Drive Your Children Away," and "New Jerusalem." Hitting them hard, gutbucket! [Tucker laughs]. "Now that's what I want," said Hammond. "N-o-o-o-ws you're doing it!"

I was shocked, man. I went home and couldn't sleep that night, him picking them kinda songs over the ones we had really put our hearts in, you know. I was really knocked out to know that he would choose those songs over the other ones.

The Birds, with all their experience, were certain they understood the taste of white audiences. Hammond's reaction had thrown them for a loop, and it would mean a bit of a stylistic turnaround for the Hummingbirds. They had worked hard smoothing out their style with vocal coach Charles Williams and they had been "rehearsing every day from seven to seven," but, as Tucker noted, "Williams was too polished. The people—black or white—wasn't going for it." At WCAU, the Birds had succeeded by conforming to white expectations of black performance style. In New York City, though, they realized that some whites—Hammond, at least—wanted "authenticity," "emotion," and the "real thing." "Back when we started," says Tucker, "we beat 'em to death with that sweet stuff, man. We'd whoop 'em. That's how we got over on the Heavenly Gospels. They was nervous when they came around us." And now all that was changing.

John Hammond would prove to be a tough critic. All or nothing. He either loved it or hated it. "I would be so nervous when John Hammond came into the club," says Tucker.

When John Hammond would . . . [Tucker demonstrates by sitting up and clapping his hands vigorously] . . . you knew he liked it, and everybody would do the same. But when he . . . [Tucker sits back and claps slowly and unenthusiastically] . . . that meant you wasn't going to be there long! If he didn't like an act, you didn't stay at Café Society. Everybody would be waiting for his fast clap!

There was one other hitch before the Dixie Hummingbirds could begin their engagement at Café Society. Barney Josephson did not like "Swanee Quartet," the name they had been using on WCAU. "Oh, I can't stand that Swanee!" Tucker remembers him saying. He guessed that Josephson was repelled by the Old South "whitebread" connotation imparted by the famous Stephen Foster song. For similar reasons, neither Hammond nor Josephson cared for "Dixie Hummingbirds" either. The word "Dixie" reminded them too much of the pro-slavery South sentiments in the song of the same name. Not that anyone flat out said so, but that was the impression Davis and Tucker had, knowing Hammond and

Josephson as they did. So," says Tucker, "we took on another name—the Jericho Quintet." Tucker can no longer recall who came up with the "Jericho," but apparently it was deemed neutral and authentic enough to pass muster. "For a short time, we were going by three names. The Dixie Hummingbirds when we were singing at churches, the Swanee Quintet in Philadelphia, and the Jericho Quintet at Café Society."

Tucker and the others were taken with Josephson's comments on the occasion of their hiring. "He would explain it to you when you first got in there," says Tucker.

> "This is my place and whoever come in here, whether it's black or white, as long as you are amenable, come right in. I can put anyone in or out of here." And he did have him some boss bouncers. Oh, they'd throw you out of there!
>
> He told us, "Gentlemen, this place here, you are free. If a woman wants you, if she's white it doesn't matter. You are free. But don't mess up with somebody that don't want you. Don't make no scene in my business."

On November 11, 1942, the newly anointed Jericho Quintet performed for the first time at downtown Café Society. For the time being, they would resettle in the Sugar Hill neighborhood of New York City.

"We did that slide and then we did a switch."

Café Society afforded the Hummingbirds a steady income and a stable lifestyle. They were reaching wider and more sophisticated audiences. At Café Society, they were playing to secular audiences and realizing that their gospel style had real currency beyond a religious setting. As long as Hammond and Josephson did not ask them to betray their gospel roots, the Birds were comfortable with the situation.

"I remember one night the Coleman Brothers[50] came in," said Tucker.

> They came in and said they heard we were singing "pop." After they heard us, though, then they say, "No, whoever said that told a lie. They ain't singing pop. They're sticking with gospel."
>
> A lot of other entertainers would come in especially to see what we were really singing. It was an issue because you were supposed to be a big time gospel group and they catch you there singing pops. But

you know the Gates started out in the South singing pop and gospel together. The Gates sung that until they died. "Sweet Sue." Stuff like that. "Sweet Georgia Brown." They mixed their program up. They did that all through Europe and everywhere else. Of course, when they went to church they didn't sing no pop.

At Café Society, the Birds were being seen by and meeting people in the highest echelons of New York show business and public life. Davis remembers Adam Clayton Powell, Paul Robeson, and Lena Horne coming in often. "Lena called us her boys!" Davis says, radiating delight at the memory.

Blues singer Josh White also frequented the Café Society shows. He had been performing there himself since 1940 and had introduced his famous novelty hit, "One Meat Ball," at Café Society. He often stopped by to catch the Jericho Quintet.[51]

The Café Society appearances were making show business professionals of the Dixie Hummingbirds. With daytime practice and nightly performances, they were perfecting their entertainment skills like never before. They were learning how to make the most of their brief time in the spotlight. Tucker glows at the recollection of those glory days. "The stage at Café Society Downtown was not that big," he says.

Man, that place stayed loaded every night! You could get about 60–65 people in there. The club was beautiful. Floodlights on the floor. Then they had lights when they had soft music, when they were serving champagne. And the rich people would be in there dancing to Lester Young's band. Lester would be out there the whole time blowing himself away! It was great. It was a plus.

And the pay was good. We was doing $600 a piece a week! That was good money. People had to pay something like 5, 6, 7 dollars to get in. You had to pay a cover charge. When you sit down, that's five dollars gone. And then a bottle of beer would cost you 3 or 4 dollars. They had all kinds of good food.

The rigorous three-shows-a-night schedule and the need to develop new material had the Birds rehearsing almost daily. "We were tight," says Tucker. "We would rehearse from 11:00 to 7:00."

The nature of the shows at Café Society also introduced a new element of instrumentation into the Dixie Hummingbirds' sound.

Before, they had sung a cappella, or with piano or to Wilson Baker's guitar accompaniment at most; but now they would be working with a full band—Lester Young's sextet.[52] "Lester Young was a guy that, if he liked you, he would spend a lot of time talking and laughing with you," says Tucker.

> He stayed mostly to himself and practiced on his horn, and you know he was great with that horn. Lester Young's band would be playing. His brother Lee Young was on drums and Lester was on saxophone.
>
> We didn't do every song a cappella. We had the band backing us up. They'd be playing soft behind us. Red Callendar would be on the upright bass. And when we did a cappella, he'd just give us the key.
>
> What we would do, we would go in early and get with Lester's band in the club and work it out. We'd work it out at our hotel first and get the stuff together, and we'd get to the club early enough to work it out with Lester's band. Man, those guys, they liked that. They looked forward to playing behind us.[53]

As the Jericho Quintet, Hammond and Josephson had the Birds kicking off the show each night. Following them were Pete Johnson and Albert Ammons, the boogie-woogie piano kings. "Each one," remembers Davis, "would have a piano that he was playing with his back to the other."

Pete Johnson was a veteran of the Kansas City, Missouri, club scene. At the "From Spirituals to Swing" concerts, he sat in with Benny Goodman's sextet and later backed up blues shouter Big Joe Turner. Albert Ammons worked the Chicago clubs before moving to New York City where he teamed up with Johnson. Ammons, Johnson, and Meade Lux Lewis were a triple boogie-woogie piano sensation at the "From Spirituals to Swing" concerts. Now, Ammons and Johnson were riding their success into Café Society.

Typically a comedian or some type of novelty act followed Ammons and Johnson on the bill, and then the finale would be Lester and Lee Young. "Prez was the cream of the crop," says Tucker, "and he would always close the show."

Billboard magazine published a review of the Downtown Café Society show in September 1942. Lester Young had just opened his run and the Jerichos were not yet on the bill. Filling in the gospel spot was a soloist in the style of Paul Robeson.

Latest show-change at this haven of hot licks finds two new items on hand; the fine jazz band of Lee and Lester Young, and the impressive basso of Sam Gary. The Revuers are held over, as are the perennial boogie-woogie piano pulverizers, Ammons and Johnson.

The show is a good one, because the Revuers are in rare form. Opening night throng couldn't get enough of the attractive Quartet's lampooning, and made them run through quite an assortment. They satirized pop songs and the frailties thereof, did a devastating take-off on "The Banshee Sisters," fem trio, [The Andrews Sisters?] and also stuck pins in the cavalcade-type radio program, old-time girlie shows, impersonators of Lionel Barrymore, etc. Very clever and well received.

Sam Gary, nice looking young Negro with a rich carefully trained voice scored nicely with "Joshua Fit the Battle of Jericho," "Asleep in the Deep," "John Henry," and "Waterboy." Delivery lacks feeling, but the voice itself is so resonant and the singer so serious as to win listeners over.

Lee and Lester Young's band blew the roof off with a few jump numbers to deafening cheers from the assembled hipsters and Ammons and Johnson also clicked with their familiar poundings.[54]

The talent lineup on the Café Society shows often turned over quickly, and within two months, Sam Gary and the Revuers were off and the Jericho Quintet on. A review in the November 11, 1942, issue of *Variety* read, "New show at this spot adheres to the pattern perfected in five years of operation. Negro talent built around a small orch. [*sic*], a hot pianist and a vocal group, all seasoned with social significance, are still the stand-bys here."

Holdovers in the new show were Lee and Lester Young ("The Orch. provides a neat, if not exceptional brand of dansapation . . .") and Ammons and Johnson ("The pianists beat it hot and hard and pleasurable . . ."). Joining the bill were pianist Connie Berry ("She'll need a different hair-do . . . to enhance her personality . . . Her pianoing is a definite asset and ranges from 'The Man I Love' to 'Twelfth Street Rag' . . .") and vocalist Helen Humes ("a so-so blues singer. . . . Voice and delivery are light").

About the Hummingbirds, the reviewer had this to say: "The Jericho Quintet (New Act) fresh out of the Carolina church-sing circuit, do spirituals, straight and swing, and old character songs."[55]

At Café Society, the Jerichos were expected to heat up the audience and put on a show. They moved rapid fire through a short set—seven or eight songs—that ran from traditional spirituals to topical message songs. If the songs did not get them, the Jerichos won them over with their snug harmonies, roller coaster arrangements, and lead vocals that alternated between sugar and fire.

As openers, their job was to take the audience on a ride from the minute they stepped out on stage. To that end, the group put some thought into the visual dimension of their show. They began wearing expensive matching suits in the latest cutting-edge style. "Zoot suits," says Davis. "We had on the zoot suits, man—with the long watch chains hanging down." No longer did they simply walk out on stage. Now, they came running from side stage, sliding in synchronized formation to their places, one in front of each microphone. "Lester's band," says Tucker, "would already be out there playing."

> Lee Young was the announcer and he would say, "GOOD EVENING LADIES AND GENTLEMEN AND WELCOME TO DOWNTOWN CAFÉ SOCIETY!! NOW PRESENTING THE JERICHO QUINTET!
>
> The band would hit "Da Da Da—Dow Dow Dow Dow" and we would run out and slide. Man, we busted our butts learning to do that, but we got it down pat. We did that slide and then we did a switch.

The "switch" was the Birds' take on a choreographic move they had seen the Golden Gate Quartet do. The idea was to take their positions, act like they were about to sing, and then at the downbeat, abruptly spin out, cleanly swap places, and then kick into the song. The shift was pure visual enjoyment and it got audiences going before even a note had been hit.

The Birds had never before consciously thought out the physical aspects of their stage show. They did what came naturally. Now, on the New York night scene and expected to deliver on a caliber with the best, the Birds had to plan more methodically. There was little room for spontaneity and they had to succeed not only with audiences but also under the watchful and critical eye of John Hammond. The choreographed moves they first developed at Café Society would become forevermore integral to their act. The "switch" was the start of it all. "We'd do that switch right after we would slide out on stage," says James Davis.

> We'd slide into our places and then move around into different spots. I found out from doing it that anything you could do on stage could

get the audience going. Later, we'd work that kind of stuff into our show. We'd give any set of groups a hard way to go.

I remember one time I got a standing ovation for flipping up on the stage. Now, that was something! Someone had gotten the microphone out of synch some kind of way and they had us on the very tail end, in the worst place on the show, after the people had sat there so long. When they finally called us, I thought, "Boy, I got to do something about that mike." So, I ran down and adjusted the microphone. Then I looked up and saw that the stage was almost as high as I was tall. I don't know what made me do it. Something just told me I could. I was inspired to do it so I just did. I made a flip up on that stage and the people went crazy. I couldn't wait to get back to my wife. She was back by the door. I told her, I say, "Hey baby, somebody here seemingly think I'm getting old! And they gave me a standing ovation for flipping up on the stage." It got a big hand.

There were other physical moves that first surfaced at Café Society that would become hallmarks of the Birds' act in later years. "One thing we did," Davis says, "was we would wave our hands in the air." He had seen some groups actually keep time that way, but Davis thought that looked "unpolished." When the Birds used hand motions, they did so only at predetermined moments and strictly for dramatic effect. The job of marking time also became a visual aspect of the show. "I was the one who carried the beat and I did it by stomping my feet. A lot of times I had corns, and they were hurting, but I did it anyway." The idea was to provide visual zing.

The Hummingbirds were convinced they were doing things right. "We were applauded back nine times one night," says Davis. "We couldn't get off the stage. Every time we would finish singing we would run off and then have to come sliding back out on stage."

"Now be careful. You might get shot out there with Paul Robeson!"

Café Society was, of course, a leading nightclub, an entertainment venue foremost; but there was also the political agenda, part of the Josephson/Hammond plan from the beginning. None of the performers who worked there could or necessarily wanted to escape that. Some took part out of personal commitment, others were less committed; but one way or another, political point of view found its way into the content of every show, if not every act. The strategy was to pull in the crowd with great entertainment and sway them with the political message. The formula turned out to have great appeal. Of all the Dixie Hummingbirds, Ira Tucker would be the one most attuned to the political overtones of Café Society. The music he heard, the people he met would open him to the possibilities for the Dixie Hummingbirds and their music to be forces for change and hopefully for good. Of course, Tucker had always known that, since that was intrinsically the nature of gospel, but Café Society would broaden his horizons and prepare him for his own future as a songwriter.

Café Society must have seemed an oasis of radicalism in those racially charged times. Social inequality in the context of segregation or the plight of the working-class poor in America or the victims of fascism overseas had become a cohesive concern. This evolving climate of solidarity would be necessary for Café Society to succeed at its inception and on into the 1940s.

Barney Josephson brought to the Café his dream of replicating the antifascist blend of politicized cabaret musical performance he had so enjoyed in his pre–World War II travels through Europe; Hammond brought his outrage over racial inequity and his belief that music could effect change. Had they stood alone, the Café Society experiment would have collapsed soundlessly, but thousands of New Yorkers, particularly among the white intelligentsia, stood with them. The numbers were enough to keep a steady flow coming into Café Society. "On Friday nights the place looked like Princeton, Yale, and Harvard rolled into one," Josephson told interviewer Whitney Balliett.[56]

In his book, *The Cultural Front*, Michael Denning uses the term "Popular Front cabaret blues" to describe the musical/political mix that characterized Café Society. Rooted in the outrage that arose from the 1931 "Scottsboro Boys" trial, a miscarriage of justice in which an all-white jury wrongly convicted a group of nine young African American men for raping two white women, the movement coalesced with Billie Holiday's performance of "Strange Fruit" in the spring of 1939. Denning characterizes the "Popular Front" as an "insurgent social movement forged out of the common interests of a number of American factions." Among them, he includes the labor movement, Roosevelt Depression-era "New Dealers," the working classes for whom the "New Deal" was designed, African Americans fighting for equality, antifascists, and those Americans—primarily Jews, Catholics, and immigrants—affected by the fascist-driven persecution then beginning to overtake Europe.[57]

In New York City, black performers, working-class whites, and intellectuals, both black and white, had come together in mutual sociopolitical interest. Denning roots the "complex alliance" in the campaign to free the Scottsboro Nine and the "working-class musical culture of hot jazz and swing." The Scottsboro case nudged many Americans, especially blacks, into the arena of activism. "The rallies and campaigns to free the [Scottsboro] defendants mobilized black communities across the country, as well as black artists, including jazz musicians."[58] Café Society was able to capitalize on this newfound solidarity between disparate groups. By 1942, the United States and communist Russia were war allies and at Café Society, the Golden Gate Quartet's "Stalin Wasn't Stallin'" was well received as a patriotic rallying hymn.

Paul Robeson, perhaps the most important African American performer on the New York scene at the time, reflected on his politico-musical philosophies in the liner notes to his album, *Songs of Free Men*.

> As one brought up on the songs of my own people, who expressed in them their sorrows, protests, and hopes, I early felt closer to that music which comes directly from folk roots.
>
> The particular songs in this album have that folk quality and show in no uncertain way the common humanity of man. Beyond this, they issue from the present common struggle for a decent world, a struggle in which the artist must also play his part.
>
> These songs are a very important part of my concert programs, expressing much of what I deeply feel and believe.[59]

Ira Tucker shared Robeson's respect for "roots" music and his struggle to create a more decent world. "One time we sang together on a program at Carnegie Hall," says Tucker, "and he hung out with me that whole day."

> And people would say, "Now be careful. You might get shot out there with Paul Robeson!" But he was a gentleman, a great man. People didn't understand. Paul had gone to school in Russia. They were asking him questions, so he told the truth. He said, "Look, I was treated better in Russia then I was at home." Some people over here, they took it out of context. He was just telling the truth, but they said, "Well, get your so and so back to Russia!" Everybody got flamed up, and people will kill you and don't even know what it's about.
>
> Now, Paul Robeson was a nice looking guy, well kept. He was right there in New York City with us. We never did talk about politics, but

he would tell me how he loved our harmonies. He was a guy who kept his mind on his work, and he could sing!

Josh White, best known to Café Society audiences for the novelty message-song, "One Meat Ball"—about the "little old man" who had money enough for only one meat ball—along with Robeson and Billie Holiday, enhanced the Café Society's reputation as a venue for politically charged music. White was at his most political with self-penned tunes like "Jim Crow."

> This is a land we call our own,
> Why must the Negro ride alone?
> It's Jim Crow!
>
> This is a land of democracy,
> Why isn't everybody free?
> It's Jim Crow![60]

The Dixie Hummingbirds also incorporated political material into their act or occasionally lent their services as performers to political causes that took place off the Café Society stage.

"We were just singers. We didn't know too much about that political stuff."

At Café Society, the Hummingbirds found themselves working opposite the Golden Gates—the Birds uptown, the Gates downtown—or in their place when the Gates were out of town. Hammond also had the two groups covering the same material. Both performed spiritual standards like "Swing Low Sweet Chariot" and "Shadrack." The Birds/Jerichos, of course, put their own spin on their renditions. "The Gates would do it strictly jubilee, but we would put a little more gospel to it, a little more shouting and rocking. And the other entertainers would say, 'Don't go out there now. It's still the Jericho's time!' We were really doing it!"

There were also occasional novelties to "break the monotony. 'Hambone is sweet, possum meat is good,'" says Davis. "You never heard that one, I bet." And then there were what Davis called the "war songs." "Patriotic numbers that we had arranged," remembers Barney Parks.

"During the war time," says Tucker, "we'd do a song like 'Praise the Lord and Pass the Ammunition.' And we had a thing called 'Hold On Soviet Union . . . Joseph Stalin . . . The Second Front Is Open . . . Hold

On.' Tucker credits the song to Bill Johnson of the Golden Gates. "Bill Johnson was a guy who could be very political."

> Yes, he was. He used to do a whole lot of writing. Bill Johnson didn't let the white man or nobody else outtalk him about the money. Bill Johnson kept his group going. He said that's it or forget it. Bill was something else, man.
>
> They tried to say that the Gates onetime was into some kind of stuff with Barney Josephson. The communist thing. They branded Josephson as a communist because he did not segregate in his business. Somehow integration added up as communism in some people's minds.

Although the Dixie Hummingbirds were familiar and more comfortable with their spiritual and gospel repertoire, at the urging of Hammond and Josephson, they incorporated political material as supplied by writers like Bill Johnson of the Golden Gate Quartet into their programs.

The Dixie Hummingbirds were willing to do what they had to do to put on a good show, as long as it did not compromise their principles. The songs they sang in support of war allies or of the war effort in general were, in their view, compatible with the spiritual/gospel mission to uplift, to provide hope and support through song. As a composer, Bill Johnson was writing a kind of secular gospel rich in biblical reference, praising of God, and condemning of the Devil and his minions of evil. The Dixie Hummingbirds were perfectly comfortable with the material.

Indeed, Michael Denning points out, "The Piedmont musicians ... were inheritors of an ... open tradition of black labor activism and political radicalism in the Carolinas and Virginia. . . . Textile mills and tobacco factories were not only a center of southern industry but also of southern labor radicalism. . . . The industrial towns of the Southeast were also the home of working class black gospel quartets, sponsored by unions, companies, schools, and churches."[61]

In making his case, Denning cites performers like Josh White from the Carolinas, the Golden Gates from coastal Virginia, and Sonny Terry and Brownie McGhee, a blues duo from the Carolina Piedmonts. They would go on to become popular in New York City and on the national scene during the folk music revival of the 1940s and 1950s. Sonny Terry performed at the 1938 "From Spirituals to Swing" concert. As a duo, Terry and McGhee performed in the early 1940s on bills with Paul

Robeson; Texas blues singer, Leadbelly; and at "rallies, parties, concerts, benefits, strike meetings, and on street corners. They sang out against fascism, the excesses of capitalism, the oppression of minorities, and the ills of organized society."[62] As to how consciously folk artists brought a political agenda to the table, at his hearing in 1947 before the House Un-American Activities Committee, Josh White judiciously suggested that "artists are not often smart about politics," and are "easy prey for anyone who appeals to our sense of justice and decency."[63]

The Dixie Hummingbirds, while aware of the political agenda surrounding them, and in spite of their "Jim Crow" experiences, were utterly dedicated to being spiritual entertainers. As always, their desire was to spread the good word, whether the message was about God and faith or the suffering of allied troops and the need to stand in solidarity behind them.

Beyond their "political" tunes, the Birds, as the Jericho Quintet, were also asked to take part in Café Society–sponsored fund-raisers for causes ranging from the Scottsboro Boys to antiwar and election campaigns to raising money to buy wristwatches for Russian allies.[64] The group saw nothing wrong with what they were asked to support, and they wanted to be seen and heard as much as possible. If Hammond and Josephson were using them, as far as the Birds were concerned, the benefits were mutual. "We knew what was going on," says Tucker.

> One time we were on a show with Maxine Sullivan and the Delta Rhythm Boys. All of us on the show were raising money for Russia. And a pint of liquor would cost like five thousand dollars. Somebody would say, "Do I hear five? Do I hear six?" And that liquor would get up to five thousand a fifth! It was all millionaires raising that money for Russia. John Hammond was involved in that sort of thing.

More than the others, Ira Tucker was intrigued by the fusion of politics and music. The rest of the group was simply not that interested. "We were just gospel singers," says Barney Parks. "We wasn't involved into anything and frankly, we didn't follow anything political. It was just a matter of entertainment." Parks himself felt rather distant from the Café Society crowd. "We weren't generally too friendly with anyone anyway. We were different from those people. You know, they drank and what not and we didn't. We kept our standards."

"We couldn't have been political," says James Davis. "We were just singers. We didn't know too much about that political stuff."

"I had an ace in the hole—William Bobo."

During their run at Café Society, the Birds would return on off-nights to perform in Philadelphia. Toward Christmas, on a Monday, December 14, 1942, the Birds drove home to mark their fourteenth anniversary with an evening concert at McDowell Presbyterian Church, 21st and Columbus Avenue. Interestingly, the ads never mentioned that the Birds were performing in New York City, nor, for that matter, that they now called Philadelphia home. "The Dixie Hummingbirds of Greenville, S.C.," read the ads. "This group is known as the Suwanee [*sic*] Singers and will broadcast over station WCAU the same day at 3:20 P.M. Tune in." Admission was 55 cents for adults, 35 cents for children.[65]

In 1942, still none of the Birds had been affected by the draft. Ira Tucker at seventeen was underage and twenty-six-year-old James Davis was sole support of a now large family. "Every time they would call me," says Davis, "when you had too many children, that's part of what kept me out."

> But also every time they sent for me, I would be out on the road. I would send them a letter and tell them where I was. And they would say check in when you get home. So, every time I would get home, I would check in and they would say we don't need you right now. But then, the group was making appearances at fund-raisers for the war effort. We did quite a bit of that.

The first to be drafted was bass singer William Henry. "When William Henry left," says Tucker, "we had to go back and hit the drawing board."

> We knew that John Hammond was a strict man and wouldn't want us to go on without a bass singer. We had to get somebody else. But, I had an ace in the hole—William Bobo. That's when I called Bobo.
> Bobo had broken up with the Heavenly Gospels, and at the time, he wasn't doing anything. He came up and met us in New York. We had such a tight harmony and background and we had to train Bobo. He had a different way of singing than we did, different arrangements, songs, that kind of stuff. It was going to take some time.

"We liked William Bobo," says Barney Parks, "because he had an unusually heavy voice. We thought that would be outstanding for the

Birds. No musical instruments. Just the four of us and Bobo with that deep bass."

Within a week, the Birds had worked Bobo into the act. Unfortunately, though, they discovered that John Hammond had a special liking for William Henry and was not pleased with his replacement. "He was crazy about William Henry," says James Davis.

> Mr. Hammond was sitting down there in front of us and looking, you know, and enjoying the singing, and his eyes fell on Bobo. After the show he say, "Hey, where's Henry?"
>
> "He's in the army."
>
> "What! I don't like that one you got up there."
>
> I don't know. Something about him he didn't like. Bobo could sing very well, but Mr. Hammond didn't like his looks. He told us, "Well, we'll just call it a day."

That quickly, the Dixie Hummingbirds were finished at Café Society. "Because of that," says Ira Tucker, "John and we all agreed that we needed to get on out and let him put another big act in there." The Birds closed at Café Society on January 20, 1943.[66] By then, Lester and Lee Young had already departed and been replaced by the lesser-known Georgie James Band. The Hummingbirds were disappointed. They would have to return to Philadelphia and begin rebuilding their lineup and their career.

Meanwhile, the draft was about to strike again. Barney Parks would see the Dixie Hummingbirds through their transition back to Philadelphia and a few months beyond, but then he would also be called to serve. Parks had been a Dixie Hummingbird from the start. "The only reason I left the group," says Parks, "was because I was drafted into the service."

In the military, Parks was assigned to Special Services, the entertainment branch of the armed forces. In that capacity, he was able to continue singing and put his own ideas about quartet performance into play. "I was singing and I also started a little group there. We were doing patriotic numbers about bombs, the Japanese, and like that."

Parks would never again perform with the Dixie Hummingbirds, though he would be linked to their fortunes in later years. After the war, he would become a manager and promoter working with some of the biggest names in gospel. Parks would set the Birds up with concert appearances that helped make them one of the most popular attractions on the gospel circuit.

Wilson Baker would also leave the Dixie Hummingbirds during the war, spending a brief period with Thermon Ruth's Selah Jubilee Singers before he too was drafted.

James Davis, Ira Tucker, and William Bobo returned to Philadelphia in 1943 and would begin looking for new singers and a fresh direction. Café Society had presented a rare opportunity to stay in one place and work to broad audiences. Back in Philadelphia, the Birds would return to local radio, hometown concerts, and the grueling tour circuit of churches, schools, auditoriums, whatever it took to sustain. It had also been four years since they had last cut a record, and that too would be a pressing goal.

5
"Move On Up a Little Higher"
(1915–1949)

Move on up a little bit higher,
Going to meet the Lily of the Valley,
I'm going to feast,
With the Rose of Sharon,
It'll be always howdy, howdy and never goodbye.
—"Move On Up a Little Higher"
As performed by Mahalia Jackson, 1948

The years after World War II were glory days for African American gospel as inventive performers built on tradition. An overall healthy economy spawned thriving record and radio industries as more slots on the radio dial were allotted to the entire spectrum of black music from jazz to blues to gospel.

By the late 1940s, urban radio stations were beginning to introduce programs hosted by and directed to African Americans—although anyone could and did tune in. Chicago radio featured pioneering record spinners Al Benson and Jack Cooper. New York City had "Smiling" Henry Copeland and Henry Newbie. Nat D. Williams could be heard over WDIA in Memphis, Tennessee, and the station also pioneered gospel radio with hosts like Ford Nelson and Theo "Bless My Bones" Wade, who also served as master of ceremonies for the famed gospel group, the Spirit of Memphis.

Ebony magazine reported that in 1947, there were only sixteen African American disk jockeys out of at least 3,000 "wax spinners" on the air nationwide. By the early 1950s, the number had increased to more than a hundred, including Vernon "Poppa Stoppa" Winslow in

New Orleans; Phil "Doctor Jive" Gordon and Jack Walker, "the Pear-Shaped Talker," in New York City; James "Alley Cat" Patrick in Atlanta; "Daddy Rabbit with the Do Rag Habit" in Jacksonville, Florida; Maurice "Hot Rod" Hulbert in Baltimore; and Lavada "Doctor Hep Cat" Durst in Austin, Texas.[1]

Philadelphia too had its share of African American air personalities. In 1947, former pro football player Ramon Bruce hosted "Ravin' with Ramon" on station WHAT. His program offered blues, rhythm and blues, and jazz during the week and gospel on Sundays. WDIA had Douglas "Jocko" Henderson, and on other stations, Georgie Woods, the "Guy with Goods,"[2] and John "Lord Fauntleroy" Bandy, "the Lord of Rhyme bringin' the sound from out of the ground to your part of town!"[3] Kae Williams was another important figure in Philadelphia radio. In addition to hosting a program, he produced concerts and records and scouted local talent. Among his discoveries were the Silhouettes and their quintessential rock 'n' roll hit, "Get a Job."[4]

Recordings were more important than ever to performers' careers as airplay enticed listeners to buy their disks and sparked demand for in-person appearances nationwide. The new media created a cross-regional genre of black music, and the industry began using terms like "race," "sepia," and "Harlem Hit Parade" to differentiate the market. Later, those terms would be displaced by "rhythm and blues," a racially neutral term coined by Jerry Wexler of the New York City-based independent label, Atlantic Records. By the late 1940s, independent labels had become indispensable vehicles for the music of America's regional and ethnic communities.

Jazz had once again become the province of African Americans as young blacks discarded "swing" in favor of "bebop," a new style characterized by improvisation, angular melodies, rollicking tempos, eccentric rhythms, and unconventional chords. "Bebop was triumphant," observed Bob Koester, owner of Chicago's Jazz Record Mart, "and the party line was that everything before bebop was junk."[5] The genre relied on forward-looking independent labels. In 1945, trumpeter Dizzy Gillespie released his seminal "Be Bop" on Newark-based independent label Manor Records, while saxophonist Charlie Parker released his classic "Koko" on Manor's cross-town rival, Savoy.

Meanwhile, rhythm and blues was crossing color lines as young whites were drawn to records like Fats Domino's 1948 debut, "The Fat Man." Distancing themselves from their parents' music, teens in general were choosing upstart vocal groups like the Ravens and Orioles over old

The Soul Stirrers in the white tuxedoes that inspired the Dixie Humming-birds. From left to right: Heywood Medlock, R. B. Robinson, R. H. Harris, Senior Roy Crain, Jesse James Farley, and Thomas Bruster.

favorites like the Mills Brothers and the Ink Spots. Both B. B. King and Ray Charles released their first commercial recordings in 1949. Within a few years, Ray Charles would revolutionize pop music by fusing gospel and blues to create a new kind of rhythm and blues—"soul."

In his autobiography, *Brother Ray*, Charles wrote, "I . . . knew many of the gospel men and women. . . . Among them were the best singers I had ever heard in my life. And the very cream of the crop—for me at least—were cats like Ira Tucker of the Dixie Hummingbirds, Archie Brownlee of the Five Blind Boys of Mississippi, and Claude Jeter of the Swan Silvertones. These guys have voices which could shake down your house and smash all the furniture in it. Jesus, could they wail! They sung for real, and I loved their music as much as any music in the world!"[6]

In the late 1940s, women were the top draw in gospel. Among the best known were Sister Rosetta Tharpe; Sally Martin; Clara Hudman Gholston, the Georgia Peach; Ernestine Washington; Dorothy Love Coates; Mahalia Jackson; and from Philadelphia, the Angelic Gospel Singers, the Davis Sisters, and Clara Ward and the Ward Singers.

Male quartets were on the rise with Rebert "R. H." Harris and the Soul Stirrers leading the way. Their performances, consistently infused with the intensity of a sanctified church service, helped sway tastes away from the reserved traditional style. The Stirrers popularized gospel showmanship and used the trade-off between dual tenor leads to spur audiences on to emotional heights.

The Dixie Hummingbirds, with Café Society behind them, adapted to these new postwar tastes and styles through personnel changes and the maturation of Ira Tucker as a lead singer, songwriter, and arranger.

"We would tell people to bring old records."

After their stint as the Jericho Quintet at Café Society, the Birds—now a quartet of James Davis, Ira Tucker, Barney Parks, and William Bobo—returned to Philadelphia to resume their career as the Dixie Hummingbirds. Abandoning their political material and other Café Society trappings, the Birds returned to performing pure gospel for African American audiences, working venues in northeastern cities along with their usual tried and true southern circuit. They also looked more than ever before to radio and recording to advance their career.

Billboard, the entertainment industry magazine, offered an optimistic report on African Americans in these endeavors in the early 1940s. Columnist Paul Denis decried radio's stereotypical portrayals and the absence of "great Negro artists" like Paul Robeson and Marian Anderson. But he also noted that "Negroes have made progress on the radio," pointing out that the Golden Gate Quartet had been appearing regularly over a two-year period on the CBS network.

There was even more promise, reported Denis, in the record industry. "Negroes are discriminated against the least, if at all, on records, and records are important because other build-up mediums such as publicity, network wires, hotel locations, and films are often closed to them."[7]

The Dixie Hummingbirds were clear about their direction. In April, three months after their Café Society closing, entertainment reporter Leroy Haden wrote about the Birds in "This Is Radio," his daily column for Philadelphia's mainstream newspaper, the *Inquirer*. "Listeners who heard the Jericho Quartet on the Monday and Wednesday stanzas of WCAU's 'Open House' may not have recognized the rich voices of those a cappella singers. But they have sung on the station before—as the Swanee Singers. They were heard regularly from last July until they went to New York, where they scored a smash hit at ... Café Society."

Haden offered readers a nutshell history of the Hummingbirds and plugged "their additional stints on 'Open House,'" as well as a fifteen-minute program that WCAU would air on Sundays at 1:30 P.M. The columnist also mentioned that the Hummingbirds had recently "made a number of recordings for the Office of War Information which will be short-waved to our troops overseas."[8]

Overseas wartime broadcasts provided opportunities for African American performers that otherwise would not have been available. In May 1943, for example, the Special Services Division of the War Department produced *Jubilee*, a program of spirituals and gospels performed by the extraordinary contralto Marian Anderson and the Charioteers Quartet.[9]

In Philadelphia, the Dixie Hummingbirds took part in similar broadcasts, although on one memorable occasion, their efforts were derailed by the racist policies of the local musicians' union. The Birds, along with popular local vocalist, Bon Bon, and piano stylist Betty King, had been invited to perform live on a WCAU-produced program, *Dixiana Revue*, that would be broadcast simultaneously overseas. Originating from the South Broad Street USO, the show came to a grinding halt when the all-white orchestra, members of Philadelphia's segregated local, refused to broadcast with "Negro musicians." Eventually, the broadcast was scuttled and the show went on, but only for the audience at the USO. The Dixie Hummingbirds, disappointed but not defeated, moved on to other ways of lending their talents to the war effort.[10]

The Birds frequently appeared, for instance, as the main attraction at "shellac drives." Shellac, a prime ingredient of both phonograph records and explosive weapons, had between 1942 and 1944 ostensibly been restricted for military use.[11] Shellac drives became a common sight on the streets of Philadelphia. "We had, on Germantown Avenue, twice a week, in the back of a big truck," says Ira Tucker, "microphones, speakers, and everything. We would sing up there about an hour and a half. And we would tell people to bring old records—that's what they would bring—and put 'em in the truck. They were recycling old records in those days to get the shellac for the war."

That first year back in Philadelphia proved to be eventful for both the Birds and the city's gospel community. In August, Paul Robeson performed a concert at the Robin Hood Dell to an audience of approximately nine thousand. The program was rich with spirituals such as "Sometimes I Feel Like a Motherless Child," "Every Time I Feel the Spirit," and "Ezekiel Saw the Wheel."[12]

On November 29, 1943, a Monday, the Dixie Hummingbirds celebrated their anniversary with an 8:30 P.M. concert at the Olympia Theater, 711 South Broad Street. They had been experimenting with the lineup, and second tenor George Graves sang with them that night.

Opening the program was the Willing Four of Baltimore, Maryland—lead tenor Beachey Thompson, baritones Joseph Johnson and George Thomas, and bass Vincent Simpson. Local singers and the "best quartets of the city" were also invited to participate. Tickets were available in advance at numerous locations for 75 cents and at the door for $1.10. Service men and children were admitted at half price.[13]

The Birds were acting as their own promoters. Over the past few years, a number of gospel entrepreneurs had emerged in Philadelphia, setting themselves up as middlemen between the performers and the public. The promoters were the ones who made the big money. The Birds, however, had the experience and the name that allowed them to eliminate the middleman. They took control of their career, working as both promoter *and* performer. And when they appeared in Philadelphia, the Birds always—and rightly so—played as the star attraction.

Although the Dixie Hummingbirds were enjoying local success, it had been four years since their last commercial recording. The Birds had to cut a new record if they wanted to compete in the new national market. They were also thinking about a second tenor lead to complement Ira Tucker. George Graves had not worked out, but they were keeping their eyes open.

"You want to pull off those overalls and ... go with us?"

Just as the Hummingbirds were gaining momentum, they weathered a few blows to the lineup. The Golden Gate Quartet, having gotten to know Tucker from Café Society, offered him a spot in their group. "Tuck told me they were interested in him," says Davis. Not wanting to hold him back, Davis urged Tucker to give it a try.

"Go over," I told him. "Stay a few days. See if you like 'em. If you do stay, I'll have to replace you. Simple as that."

So, he went over there, stayed about a day and a half and came on back. He said, "No good, cuz." It was something he didn't like. They had a different life style than the Hummingbirds, so he came on back."

"I did three shows with the Golden Gates," says Tucker, "but I just couldn't leave the guys. It didn't feel right, what with Davis giving me a break and all. The Gates ... took me in, trained me to see if I could make it. I told them if I couldn't, I know my way back home."

"Tucker could have left us," says Parks, "but he wouldn't leave the Birds. It was just something there, a closeness, I guess. But if he had left the Birds, Birds would have been dead then."

With Tucker firmly back in the fold, Barney Parks would be the next to go. Drafted in late 1943, Parks helped the others locate a replacement before he left. Beachey Thompson of the Willing Four, the Baltimore quartet that had recently opened for the Birds on their anniversary program, proved the best candidate. Parks recalls, "At the time, we did a lot of singing in Baltimore. We'd go into Baltimore probably stay four or five days, sing at different churches. And I got to know Beachey through that. I heard him at the programs and I just liked his singing."

Thompson was a versatile tenor with a clean clear high tone, a bit of a trill at the end of his vocal phrases, fuller in voice than Davis, and with the ability to switch from backdrop to lead and even lower parts if necessary. "A utility man," he called himself, able to shift easily between voices.

He was born "Beachey" on October 12, 1915, in Newberry, South Carolina. "Even though I grew up on a farm, I always did want to be a singer. I started a group and we learned songs from records—on an old windup Victrola—when we weren't in the fields. Gospel was all I knew. Popular singers didn't come our way."[14]

In the 1930s, Thompson was living in Charlotte, North Carolina, and singing lead tenor with a group from nearby Shelby called the Five Gospel Singers—Lee Thomas, bass; Ezell Wells, lead; Paul Saunders, second tenor; James Thompson [no relation], baritone; and Pete Samuels, manager.[15]

"I was with this group for quite a good while. I must have been about nineteen, give or take. Around 1933–34. We used to broadcast from Gastonia, North Carolina, between Shelby and Charlotte. WGNC. Every Sunday from 2:30 to 3:00. A funeral home out of Shelby ... sponsored us."

Like so many other groups, the Five Gospel Singers took to the road, traveling in a rundown jalopy Thompson called their "struggle bus."

The coal country was a favorite destination. "Stone Gap, Kentucky. Lynch, Kentucky. Virginia . . . up and down those hollows." The roads were so narrow, "you had to pull over to let a guy by."

The coal mining towns were company owned, and when Thompson performed there, the group got paid not in dollars but in "scrip." "It was what they used in the coalmines at the store they call the commissary, the company store. . . . I could take that scrip—it had six slots in it . . . like a trolley token—I could . . . trade it in the next morning and get fifty cents. . . . I had never seen anything like it before."[16]

"The Five Gospel Singers used to do battles, contests against the Heavenly Gospel Singers and the Dixie Hummingbirds," recalls Thompson. The Birds would stop by Thompson's work place and tease him about joining the group. "They'd say, 'You want to pull off those overalls and . . . go with us?' They'd arrive in a new car. 'We must be doing something right. Look at us. We got new clothes. We have money in the bank.' I was a mail clerk for railway express for Southern Railroad. I wanted to keep my job until I was sure of that."

Thompson stayed with the Five Gospel Singers about four years before moving on, first, briefly, to Norfolk, Virginia, where he sang with a group called the Southern Stars, and then on to Baltimore where he joined the Willing Four.[17] He recalls, "Baltimore, that was where the Dixie Hummingbirds got me. They got me to sing baritone in place of Barney Parks. I can sing baritone, lead, and tenor. "

Reluctant to burn all his bridges behind him, Beachey Thompson kept his room, his money, and even his day job back in Baltimore. "I wasn't sure I was going to make it with them." Six months later, though, he moved all his belongings to Philadelphia.[18]

In 1944, the Dixie Hummingbirds consisted of Davis, Tucker, Bobo, and now Beachey Thompson, with Davis maintaining his leadership role.

William Bobo, meantime, was attracting notice as one of the most profound bass singers on the gospel circuit. He loved to tell fans and reporters how, as a child, he had been a tenor, but that upon being revived from an accident in which he nearly froze to death, his voice had mysteriously plummeted to bass. Bobo had an extraordinarily heavy voice and was perfecting his skills at what gospel professionals called a "moving" bass style. Bobo could "ooh" and "aah" with the best, but he could also pop out single notes that, like a big bass fiddle, provided a beat as he moved up and down the scales on the bottom.

Beachey Thompson, like Ira Tucker, was also vocally flexible, having come into the Birds as a tenor but now leading songs more in the baritone range, shifting high or low, foreground or background, as needed. With their combined versatility, Thompson and Tucker began evolving the approach to harmony that would give the Dixie Hummingbirds their unique and identifiable style. "We had a sound all our own," says Thompson.

> I found it is hard to duplicate our songs. One of the reasons is, we can start into a note, I'm singing tenor . . . and before I finish my note, I'll switch from that to a lead, a "background" lead, and from that to what they call a "background bass." From tenor, I'll slide right into a background lead and that is what is confusing.[19]

The Dixie Hummingbirds were building versatility into their style around the art of switching parts. Thompson might start a song in his tenor lead, Tucker holding back in the baritone range. A dozen measures in, the tempo would double-time, Thompson retreating into the background as Tucker took over, drawing on his vocal bag of tricks to "up" the emotional level. The song spun and turned, transformed and captivated as each singer worked his particular brand of magic. When Tucker and Thompson were not taking it over the top, Davis would step in and lead the group in a mellow sweet song. The Birds were distinguishing themselves from the pack and, by 1944, had earned the right to once again enter the recording studio.

"He just said that he could put us out because we didn't have nothing out."

In the middle and late 1940s, the recording industry saw a proliferation of independent labels. Although independents such as Paramount, Black Swan, and Black Patti, focusing on the music of African Americans, existed as early as the 1920s, the new, inexpensive electric recording process and healthy postwar consumerism allowed plenty of new independents to flourish. These labels became specialists in regional music for regional sale—combo jazz, rhythm and blues, and gospel in the larger cities, hillbilly and country and Western in rural areas and in the South.

The "indie" labels, as they were called, operated on modest budgets and offered performers an alternative to the major labels. They became indispensable as stepping-stones to broader fame. From the late 1940s into the mid-1950s, over a thousand new labels came into existence.[20]

New York City became a hotspot for many newly emerging labels like Atlantic, Apollo, Jubilee, and Blue Note, and in Newark, New Jersey, Savoy and Regis, the latter started in 1943 and later renamed Manor.

The Dixie Hummingbirds agreed to a one-record deal with Regis and recorded four songs in July 1944. For Ira Tucker and Beachey Thompson, the Regis sessions would be their first commercial recordings.

Regis was owned by Irving Berman, a Newark businessman and nightclub impresario. Like most other independent label operators in the Northeast, Berman directed the bulk of his musical product to the African American market. His greatest success was with rhythm and blues balladeer Savannah Churchill. Berman managed Churchill's career and co-wrote songs with her, including "Daddy Daddy," her 1945 break-through hit.[21] In addition to Savannah Churchill, the Regis/Manor roster would eventually include former Ink Spot Deek Watson and his group, the Brown Dots; the jump blues of bandleaders Tab Smith, Gene Phipps, and Tiny Bradshaw; swing vocalists the Cats and the Fiddle; balladeers the Four Tunes; contemporary jazz combo Sid Catlett and the Regis All Stars, featuring jazz pianist Oscar Pettiford; and comedian Pigmeat Markham.

The Regis imprint, with offices at 162 Prince Street in Newark, was first mentioned in *Billboard* in February 1943. "Another Disk Manufac-turer; Spirituals Only," read the banner over a short article.

> G & R Record Shop . . . has started to produce waxings of spiritual numbers . . . under the Regis label.
>
> Irving Berman, president of the corporation, claims four records a month are being produced. To date, 2000 copies of each have been made, and Berman feels no reorders will be necessary until the end of this month.
>
> Local talent is used to make disks . . . retailing for 53 cents. . . . Regis is stimulating sales by sponsoring programs over stations WHOM, Jersey City, and WPAT, Paterson.[22]

The Dixie Hummingbirds were among those spiritual artists signed early on to the label along with the Coleman Brothers, the Silver Echo Quartet, the Reverend Utah Smith, the Skylight Singers, the Willing Four—minus Beachey Thompson, of course—and old friends Thurman Ruth and his Selah Jubilee Singers.

By late 1944, the label was advertising itself as "The Elite in Sepian

Blues–Spirituals–Jazz,"[23] and in 1945, the operation moved to 313 West 57th Street in New York City, changing its name to Manor Records.

At Ira Tucker's suggestion, Sister Ernestine Washington, the "Songbird of the East" and a Regis/Manor recording artist in her own right, recorded two sides with the Birds at their July sessions. "Ernestine Washington," says Tucker, "was the wife of Reverend Frederick D. Washington in Brooklyn. He was a big man at Washington Temple. That's where all the big programs would be—at Washington Temple in Brooklyn. The idea to record with her was partly mine. I told her that I wished she'd make a record with us. She said she'd love to."

Tucker, though he did not think about it in those terms at the time, was taking his first steps as a producer.

Sister Ernestine was the epitome of the earnest Sunday morning church soloist, proper and somber, standing in the crook of the piano and pouring her soul into heartfelt spiritual renditions. She drew on the extremes of her soprano range, carrying the melody in the full-toned low end of her voice, jumping to a high thin nasal with rapid trills on the phrase-ends when she wanted to drive home the point of the lyric. She lent her good name to the Dixie Hummingbirds by recording with them that July.

The Hummingbirds' records—10-inch 78-rpm discs—were originally released on the Regis imprint and then, with the company's move to New York, on Manor. The price was 79 cents.

Later, label owner Irving Berman further capitalized on the Hummingbirds' sides by leasing them for second and third releases on the Arco and Kay-Ron labels. The Hummingbirds were paid little or nothing for their work. In lieu of payment, Berman offered them free copies to sell at their concert programs. "With Berman," says Tucker, "he just said that . . . if it sold, he would give us a certain amount of money. And if not, he would give us some records." The Birds kept all the money they made from selling their records. It was an arrangement they could live with until something better came along. "We felt that it was a start, better than not having nothing out."

The sides they shared with Sister Ernestine were "Savior Don't Pass Me By" and "If I Could Just Make It In," released as Regis 1007, Manor 104, and Arco 1244. Both were arrangements of traditional spirituals with piano and acoustic guitar accompaniment, Sister Ernestine's regular backup musicians, according to Ira Tucker.

"Savior Don't Pass Me By" begins with a few downstrokes of acoustic guitar in the style of the Mills Brothers. A tinkling piano takes up the melody and then Sister Ernestine comes in singing "Sav—ior . . . Sav—ior . . . Sav—ior," carefully leaving space between and stretching out the words. Then, the phrase, "Don't you pass me by." The Birds fill in between the spaces with the repeated line "Savior don't you pass me by," imparting the song with the rhythm that Sister Ernestine works against with her staccato phrasing. As she moves from chorus to verse, the Birds revert to harmony "oohs" and "aahs," staying very much in the background, but providing depth and an easygoing medium tempo. The overall effect is precisely what one might expect to hear in a Sunday morning church service. "Savior Don't Pass Me By" would later be recorded by the Flying Clouds of Detroit and become a signature tune for them.

The other side recorded with Sister Ernestine, "If I Could Just Make It In," is less complex in vocal interplay and puts more of a spotlight on the Birds. Again, there is a brief acoustic guitar introduction, but then we hear the unaccompanied pleading voice of James Davis.

> If I could just, Lord, make it in,
>
> If I could just—just make it in,
> If I could just—just make it in,
> Into the heaven—heavenly gates.

Sister Ernestine picks up the lyric from there and the performance becomes pure a cappella with the Birds literally humming the backdrop. The tempo is slow.

> I won't mind,
> This load I'm carrying.
> I won't mind,
> The clothes I'm wearing.
> I won't mind,
> The way I'm staring,
> If I could just, just-a make it in.

She sings several more verses and then the Birds reenter to bring the song to a conclusion. They sing in parallel harmony, Bobo's bass punctuating lightly on the bottom, with subtle volume swells and varying brightness that give the effect of an old-time pump organ.

> If I could just, Lord, make it in,
> If I could just, Lord, make it in,
> I won't mind the load I'm carrying,
> If I could just make it in.

The performance is subdued, not rocking gospel, but still old-fashioned in style.

The two other songs recorded at that July session featured the Dixie Hummingbirds alone. [Regis 1008, Manor 1074, and Kay-Ron 1004] Although their harmonies remain conservative, the arrangements are a departure from pure traditional. Ira Tucker is credited on the label with arranging both tunes, "I Just Couldn't Keep It to Myself" and "Book of the Seven Seas." "We called it 'The Book of the Seven Seals,'" says Tucker, "but they put 'Seven Seas' on the label."

James Davis carried "I Just Couldn't Keep It to Myself" in his high sweet tenor as the group provided a chugging repetitive "doo wah" backdrop. The material was unremarkable, the performance competent in a slow ballad tempo. The message was a straightforward testament to the joys of finding Jesus.

> I love to tell about the day,
> My sins and burdens were rolled away.
> Since then, I just couldn't keep it to myself alone.
> Since He came into my heart,
> Made my sorrow to depart,
> Lord knows, I just can't keep it to myself alone,
> Myself alone.

"Book of the Seven Seas," on the other hand, was fresh, upbeat, a swinging jubilee reminiscent of the Golden Gate Quartet. The song, sometimes titled "John the Revelator," had been a standard in the gospel repertoire for decades.

The lyric drew from the biblical story in the Book of Revelation about John and the visions revealed to him in a heavenly scroll secured with seven seals. As John breaks each seal, a new revelation about the power of God on earth springs forth in rich mystical images.

In the version recorded by the Hummingbirds for Regis records that day, Ira Tucker raps out the lead, tells the tale in a rapid fire delivery, and, just like John, becomes a vehicle for revealing fundamental truths about Jesus and the good life. The song rides along on the alphabet, each letter unfolding wisdom in primer-like sequence, taking on the same clipped rhythms as the original biblical passage.

The performance is Tucker's to carry, his first on record leading the Birds. Each word is clear, his phrasing masterful. The signature opening is traditional call and response, but then the group retreats into the background coming in with punctuated "a-a-ah o-o-o-m-m-ms" as Tucker spins out the lines.

> Tell me who is that writing?
> John the Revelator,
> Tell me who is that writing?
> Oh, John the Revelator,
> Now, what was John writing?
> Oh, he wrote the Book of Revelation,
> He wrote it in the Book of the Seven Seals.

Then Tucker takes over.

> Hey, John, now you read your Bible, you will understand,
> Just what it takes to carry you through this land,
> You read St. Luke, you read the Book of Psalms,
> Read the alphabets one by one,
>
> "A" is for Almighty, that is true,
> "B" was the baby like me or you, well the
> "C" is Christ, the Son of God,
> "D" is the doctor, the man of war,
> "E" is for an evil with the watchful eye,
> "F" is for fire that he dodged at his trial,
> "G" is for God, and everyman know,
> "H" is the healer to the dying soul,
> "I" is intelligent, and He's very wise,
> "J" is Jehovah and he can not lie, church,
> "K" is for Kings, I'm prepared to say.
> "L" is for lawyer, He will plead your case,
> "M" is for master of this world,
> "N," He's noble and He can be heard,
> "O" for Omega, the first and the last,

"P," He's the prophet, just hold him fast and,
"Q," He's quick, he is slow,
"R," He can rise where no man know,
"S" is for savior, the Son of Man,
"T," He can talk and you can understand, and,
"U," He's useful, He takes his time,
"V," He's strong as a running vine,
"W" for water, he knows all streams,
"X," He will save you from your extremes,
"Y" is for you, and you is for me,
"Z" is the son of Zebedee.

With that, the tale is told and the group joins in again, twice repeating the opening verse before bringing the song to a close. The performance is winning with its rolling meter, stellar lead vocals, and mantra-like litany of biblical references.

Ira Tucker remembers first hearing the song from Otis Jackson, his old friend from Florida. "Otis had been singing the 'Book of the Seven Seals,'" says Tucker, "and I told him I was going to record it. So, he said okay." Tucker pointed out that in those days, singers helped each other and expected nothing in turn but a favor in kind when the situation arose. "That's how it was with recording that song. No big deal."

"Book of the Seven Seals" can be traced to sources other than Jackson who were also close to the Dixie Hummingbirds. As early as 1938, the Spartanburg Famous Four featuring Tucker's early mentor, Bus Porter, recorded a version for Decca records [Decca 7543] called "John Wrote the Revelations." Porter's take on the song did not use the alphabet, but the opening verses were identical to the ones used by the Birds.

The alphabetical verses do, however, appear on a 1941 Decca recording [Decca 8628] by Julius Ginyard and the Royal Harmony Singers, the Hummingbirds' old rivals from Jacksonville. The Royal Harmonies called their version "The Alphabet of the Bible," and Tucker's words were almost identical to Ginyard's. The difference was in the feel. The Royal Harmonies performed it in stodgy rhythm, but the Birds, thanks to Tucker's brilliant phrasing against a precise rhythmic backdrop, made it rise up and swing.

The world of professional gospel had become crowded and competitive, but the Hummingbirds' recording of "Book of the Seven Seas" put them firmly back in play. "The record wasn't a hit," says Tucker, "but it was a good seller."

During that time, there wasn't any real hard gospel hits. They were good sellers, but people didn't have that much money. Later, after the 78s, then it took off. But not when we first started.

"Ring Bobo's Bell ... Ring Tucker's Bell ..."

Fueled by release of their Regis sides in the summer of 1944, the Birds found ready audiences in and out of the city. The group traveled to New York, Baltimore, Washington, and points along the East Coast where their reputation had preceded them. Churches were still a mainstay, but with the popularity of their records, they were now able to work small auditoriums and similar public forums.

Radio had also re-emerged as a force in expanding their audience. The Birds had been broadcasting sporadically in guest spots on WCAU, but by the summer of 1944, they returned to regular broadcasting with an 8:00 A.M. Sunday morning program on station WIP.

That fall, they appeared in a self-produced "personal battle of song" at McDowell Community Presbyterian Church at 21st and Columbus. Tickets, a dollar and under, could be purchased at the door or at Fennell's Beauty Shop on Diamond Street or from the Birds themselves. The ad read, "1608 Masters Street, Ring Bobo's Bell, 1526 North 18th Street, Ring Tucker's Bell," a small thing but an indication that the Birds had not forgotten that friendliness and accessibility had always played a part in their efforts to win over audiences.

Throughout that year and into 1945, the Birds continued to perform up and down the northeast corridor. On Monday, January 22, 1945, the "Dixie Humming Birds" [*sic*] presented their first local concert of the year at Mt. Sinai Baptist Church at Highland and Steward Avenue in Lansdowne, just west of Philadelphia. Ticket prices were now 75 cents in advance, a dollar at the door. A photo in the *Tribune* showed Tucker, Davis, Thompson, and Bobo sitting in symmetrical formation, each with a hand on his knee, identical fine suits, perfectly folded handkerchiefs jutting out of breast pockets at precisely the same angle and level, a picture of dignity, warmth, and goodwill.

Two months later in March, the Dixie Hummingbirds performed on two successive nights at Philadelphia's Mercantile Hall at 1410 North Broad Street, a special Easter program on Holy Thursday and Good Friday. Sharing the stage with them, a showing of Cecil B. DeMille's 1927 silent film classic, *The King of Kings*.

By mid-August 1945, World War II had at last come to an end. All the newspapers carried banner headlines and for months following were packed with stories about battles won and fighting men returning home. V-E and V-J festivities abounded. In September, the *Tribune* advertised a moonlight boat ride, a "celebration cruise" featuring the dance music of local black bandleader Jimmy Shorter and his orchestra.

On the same page was a story criticizing the presence and portrayal of Negroes in Hollywood films. "The white person is made more at ease in the knowledge that he is on top," read the article. "The Negro is made to feel that whatever he does counts for naught, because he is still in the crap-shooting and watermelon-eating bracket of life. . . . Of course, we know and realize that this is not so. There are Negroes in competition with the white man in every phase of life, and many excel in invention, ingenuity, wisdom, and social graces. But Hollywood does not accept this. . . . Instead, they emphasize the lower aspects of the Negro while accentuating the theory that white is right."[24]

In the column next to the story was the photo of the Dixie Hummingbirds that had appeared the previous January picturing them in elegant suits, ties, and jutting handkerchiefs, as if they were a living example of the issues raised in the article. The caption touted their new radio show. "The Dixie Hummingbirds, who have been heard over Mutual Network, CBS, and NBC, will be heard every Saturday over station WFIL 1:45 P.M."

These were times of great irony for the black community as a whole and the Dixie Hummingbirds in particular. The Hummingbirds, for one, were among those African Americans excelling in inventiveness and ingenuity, defying the odds as they moved up the ranks in their chosen realm of entertainment, affected by but working around the negatives that surrounded them. As for the African American community, though the war was over, racism was still an issue on the home front. Thousands of African American soldiers who had fought bravely for freedom were unwilling to tolerate restriction back home. These concerns would help fuel the postwar civil rights movement.

As professional singers, the Dixie Hummingbirds dealt with racism by establishing themselves as a unique voice to the black community. The Hummingbirds were symbolically flaunting the racial myths of the oppressors, countering the stereotypes with musical brilliance and physical elegance. In public appearances and on record, they made it their business to be uplifting, inspiring, always models of dignity, intelligence, and civility. As a group, they were poised to capitalize on the increasing opportunities for black performers in the prosperous postwar decade.

At war's end, new nightspots, often black owned and catering to African American tastes and clientele, were opening in cities across the country. Dozens of clubs, bars, restaurants, and cabarets blossomed in Philadelphia. Fay's Theater, in business before the war, continued to present the best in live black entertainment back to back with the latest films. New clubs and concert venues, including Catharine's New Postal Card Bar and Grille on South Street, the Macombo on Diamond, the Coronet on Broad, the Uptown Dreamboat, the Zanzibar, Butler's Paradise, Maxie Spector's King Kole Club, the Showboat, and Pep's featured the coolest in blues and modern jazz.

The city also had its share of larger concert venues that in the years before the war primarily showcased mainstream popular and classical entertainment. Now these facilities were opening their doors to the whole pantheon of African American talent. In 1945 and 1946, Duke Ellington and His Orchestra would appear at Convention Hall, Louis Armstrong at Mercantile Hall, Count Basie at Town Hall, Billie Holiday at the Academy of Music, and Louis Jordan and his Tympany Five at the Armory.

Gospel, too, would find a place in Philadelphia's "better" concert halls. The Dixie Hummingbirds had already performed at Mercantile Hall. On Sunday, November 11, 1945, they would stage an ambitious self-produced anniversary concert event at the Metropolitan Opera House, one of the city's most prestigious venues. Called "the Met" by locals, the multistory brick building with high windows all around stood at the corner of Broad and Poplar. Intended as an opera house when it was built in 1908, it had shifted in focus and by the mid-1940s, after some years as a vaudeville theater, it was now open to other possibilities.

"Gospel wasn't a big thing, then," Ira Tucker recalls. "When we first rented the Met, that man like to have a fit! He said, 'What you going to put in there? Ain't no gospel singer going to pack this Met!'" Tucker chuckles about it now. "Yes. The Metropolitan Opera House. I'm the first black to ever get the Met. It was two hundred and seventy five dollars to rent. And it seated 5,500. And I had it so packed they had to put some people out because of the fire marshal."

The bill that night featured the Birds and a host of out-of-town performers—the Shelley Quartet of Danville, Virginia; the Seventh Trumpet Quartet of Charlotte, North Carolina; the Pearly Gate Female Quartette of New York City; the Pearly Gate Quartette from Wilmington, Delaware; plus a piano soloist and both steel and Hawaiian

Ira Tucker and James Walker at the Met in Philadelphia.

guitar soloists. The show started at 7:00 and tickets were a dollar in advance and $1.25 at the door. Always mindful of promotion, the Birds also put in newspaper ads that they could now be heard every Saturday night at 11:15 over station WFIL.[25]

The Dixie Hummingbirds' Easter concert at the Met would become an annual tradition, one still vividly and warmly remembered by the elders of Philadelphia's African American community.

Senior Wheels East is a care center for the aging housed in a church off Broad Street not far from where the Met still stands, its windows boarded up, its glory days long past. The neighborhood is in the heart of Philadelphia's African American community.

On a hot day in July 2000, Iula Austin, Cleora McKeever, Emma Lockett, Ruth Sherman, Eula Otey, and Robert Jackson, in their seventies and eighties, sit around a large circular table talking animatedly, reminiscing about the Dixie Hummingbirds and those magnificent concerts at the Met.

"I used to go to the Met in the late '40s, maybe even into the 1950s," said Ruth Sherman. "Me and my husband would go to see the Hummingbirds. . . . The line would be stretching around the block. We'd get there around 5:30 and when the doors opened the people would go in there like a herd of horses! It was a big place. There were a couple of balconies and the room could hold thousands. Everybody would be waiting to hear the Birds. It was a pretty fancy kind of thing and being on Easter Monday, everybody would dress up in their Easter outfits. People would be seated like at a big church."

Robert Jackson remembers the radio broadcasts originating from the Enon Church on 8th and Brown. "The Birds . . . was on for about half an hour. The church used to pay about fifteen dollars for airtime. I remember many a time they used to say, 'We need a couple more dollars!'"

"And the pastor," says Eula Otey, "would let me be the announcer. And I would say, [shouts it out] 'Here are the Dixie Hummingbirds!' They were outstanding. The Birds weren't like the groups today that's making a whole lot of motions. They sung from their hearts and you could hear what they were singing! They sang old fashioned gospel."

And after the program, folks would head to restaurants like the South Carolina Boys or Ida's on 19th and Columbia. "That's where all of the famous gospel singers used to meet after the show," says Robert Jackson. Philadelphia's Carolinians constituted a close-knit gospel community.[26]

"Known throughout the country for their wonderful renditions of spirituals."

Although they enjoyed deep admiration in Philadelphia, where their Regis/Manor recordings circulated among friends and neighbors, national popularity still eluded the Birds. Other quartets were faring better. The Golden Gates, for example, were recording for Columbia Records, a famous label with a nationwide reach. Another quartet, the

Deep River Boys, received nationwide press over their purchase of an airplane. "The Deep River Boys, popular singing stars of radio and records, take off on their three month nationwide concert tour in late November, and will inaugurate a new era in modern transportation of theatrical attractions, when they travel exclusively by air to fulfill their engagements in 83 midwest, southwest, and southern cities."[27]

But these "big money" groups cultivated a sound that had more mass appeal. The Golden Gates, for example, employed harmonies and arrangements that were pleasing, slightly exotic perhaps to those unfamiliar with the tradition, but in no way challenging. Their song lyrics often deemphasized religious faith and spoke to the broader concerns of mankind, bordering sometimes on the secular. The Hummingbirds, conversely, stayed true to a performance tradition, loyal to religious ideals and the spiritual needs of their core black constituency.

Even without appealing to white audiences, the Hummingbirds got a boost from the increasing buying power of African Americans. More and more, ads and articles about black artists appeared in national trade magazines like *Billboard* and *Variety*. Postwar issues of *Billboard* now included within the "Music Popularity Chart" a subsection called "Most Played Juke Box Race Records" that listed sides by artists like Lionel Hampton, the King Cole Trio, the Ink Spots, Louis Jordan, Big Joe Turner, and Bull Moose Jackson.

The number of ads in African American newspapers for record stores and records-by-mail also increased markedly after the war. By 1946, businesses dealing in recorded music had sprouted up all across Philadelphia—Sherman's, Dee's, Premier, and Bergin's, to name a few. Savoy Music called itself "North Philadelphia's Largest Race Record Shop," and Sherman's touted "Philadelphia's most complete selection of sepia records." When the Golden Gate Quartet came to Philadelphia in January for a concert at Town Hall, they stopped at Sherman's to autograph their latest Columbia release, "I Will Be Home Again."[28]

Other operations, like CR Department Stores, listed as many as fifty titles in their newspaper ads and offered them for sale by mail. "Watch for our weekly top numbers in this and other papers.... We ship records anywhere. Send only $1.00 with your order. Pay balance to postman on delivery." Local promoters, meanwhile, made a point of placing ads for up-and-coming concert events in close proximity to the record store ads. So it was that when the "famous Six Soul Stirrers" played Turner Hall in May, their picture appeared in the *Tribune* directly alongside the ad for the CR Store's record department.[29]

The city, meanwhile, was alive with major gospel concerts that first year following the war. Wings Over Jordan played the Met in April, and in May, the Clouds of Joy came to town, with The Live Wire Quartet of Cleveland for an opener. On Mother's Day, Newark-based promoter Roney Williams staged "The Devil's Funeral" featuring a showcase of regional talent that included the NBC Shelly Quartet, the Silver Echoes, the Willing Four, and the Bay State Gospel Singers, a popular mainstay on the Philadelphia scene. "Lucky ticket holders" stood a chance to win a brand new Ford and "$50.00 Cash to the Oldest Mother Present."[30]

The Dixie Hummingbirds maintained their high hometown profile. They began the year with a concert at Mercantile Hall, a "Grand Prize Concert" with "$1,250 in Prizes from Leading Department Stores." Opening for them were the Euphon Chorus, a touring community choir, and local favorites, the Bay State Gospel Singers.[31]

In the spring, the Hummingbirds booked Mercantile Hall at Broad and Master and set themselves up in a singing battle with the Live Wires, the latter group remaining in the area as they continued their tour of the East.[32] Competitions of this sort were a common practice. Not only were hometown crowds treated to a charged concert atmosphere, but also, in reality, the two groups were helping each other. The Birds would introduce the Live Wires to the Philadelphia audience and, at a later date, the Live Wires would return the favor, sponsoring the Dixie Hummingbirds in Cleveland.

Their battle was given prominent play in Philadelphia's African American newspapers. Both groups were pictured in stylish attire. "The Dixie Humming Birds [sic]—Known throughout the country for their wonderful renditions of Spirituals—ARE CONTESTING THE FAMOUS Live Wire Gospel Singers . . . rated as Ohio's best quartette." In spite of the buildup, however, locals understood that the Dixie Hummingbirds would come out on top.

In securing live performance dates, the Birds excelled, but as recording artists, they needed a breakthrough.

"Bess Berman gave us a better deal."

Two years after recording with Regis/Manor, the Birds sought to cut a new record with a label that could offer better promotion and sales. In February 1946 the Birds signed with Apollo Records, one of the more successful independents, a growing company based in New York City. The operation was an offshoot of a white-owned Harlem record store, the Rainbow Music Shop at 102 W. 125th Street.[33] The company was only in its second year of operation, but label owners Bess and Ike Berman, Sam Schneider, and Hy Siegel knew of the Hummingbirds from the buzz on the street and sales of their records at the Music Shop.

Apollo, with Bess Berman primarily calling the shots, was recording black, white, and Latino acts, jazz, blues, hillbilly, swing, Caribbean, and gospel—a remarkable representation of the city's cultural mix. They had popular dance bandleaders Charlie Barnet, Georgie Auld, and Ray Eberle. They offered hillbilly by Tennessee "Slim" King and Curly Perrin and his Boys; calypso by Sir Lancelot, the Duke of Iron, and King Houdini and his Calypso Parliament; the "samba-polka" style of the Jose Morand Orchestra; and the Latino rhythms of Pancho and his Orchestra and the combo of the Laszlos and Pepi. Apollo released Yiddish comedy by Fyvush Finkel, the Barton Brothers, and Sam Levenson; Polish polkas by the Eddie Gronet and Joe Meresco Orchestras; and jazz by Luis Russell, Coleman Hawkins, Erroll Garner, Earl Hines, Dinah Washington, Blue Lu and Danny Barker, Cee Pee Johnson, and Arnett Cobb. Apollo had down home blues by Josh White and the duo of Jelly Belly and Slim, and urban jump blues by Duke Henderson, Rabon Tarrant, and blues shouter supreme, Wynonie Harris. In gospel, they had the Golden Tones, the Reliable Jubilee Singers, the Ivory Gospel Singers, Prophet Powell and Congregation, Roberta Martin, and Clara Hudman Gholston, also known as the Georgia Peach, formerly a vocalist with the ubiquitous recording artist, sermonizer Reverend J. M. Gates.

Apollo also had Mahalia Jackson—perhaps the most important and certainly one of the most renowned gospel artists of the twentieth century. When she signed with Apollo in 1946, Mahalia Jackson was just beginning her prolific and illustrious career. An admirer of blues singer Bessie Smith, Jackson melded the expressiveness of secular styles with traditional gospel repertoire and became Apollo's major breakthrough success, soon to earn billing as the "world's greatest gospel singer."

The Dixie Hummingbirds decided to affiliate with Apollo because they thought this company was precisely what they had been seeking. "Bess Berman gave us a better deal," says Tucker. "The Manor label was a statewide thing. It didn't go anywhere, but Apollo went just about all over."

They would record their first sides in February, all featuring Tucker's vocal leads. He remembers Hy Siegel driving them back and forth from Philly to New York. The four songs, cut at a single session, were "My

Record Will Be There," "In the Storm Too Long," "Every Knee Surely Must Bow," and "Amazing Grace." There was no outside producer. Siegel simply delivered the group to the studio. The Birds—Davis, Tucker, Thompson, and Bobo—gathered in a close semicircle around the microphone, and at the engineer's signal, performed what they had already meticulously rehearsed. Few takes were required. By summer, the records had been released—the label a warm light green, the name emblazoned over a regal profile of Apollo, god of light, healing, poetry, and music. In an August *Billboard* ad announcing "new Apollo releases," the Dixie Hummingbirds were pictured alongside pop mainstreamers Ray Eberle and Bill McCune.[34]

"My Record Will Be There" was a compelling track, a fast-paced piece in parallel harmony with William Bobo's resonant bass breaking out of the pack as a fill and in the verses as a response to Tucker's understated leads. "Amazing Grace," however, was the musical standout, a masterwork of a cappella performance that in a scant three minutes took listeners on an emotional ride from the somber to the glorious.

The song begins in free meter, Tucker's pleading vocal glissandos guiding the group through a harmonic series, each phrase ending in a bright and unconventional sustained chord. The open cadence continues for a few bars, and then the Birds fall into a defined upbeat rhythmic pattern, Tucker in the lead, Davis, Thompson, and Bobo in response.

> TUCKER: A-may   zin' grace
> GROUP: A-may   zin' grace
> TUCKER: Lord, how sweet   the sound
> GROUP: How sweet   the sound.

The Birds play the groove out a few measures more, and then shift to a different pattern. Tucker moves into the upper range of his voice and by doing so boosts the intensity. The background rises to the moment by singing more syllables per measure, in effect, double-timing the beat.

> TUCKER: Oh, Lord,   a-may,   may-zin'   grace,   oh lord,
> GROUP: A-may-zin' grace, oh lord, how sweet, how sweet the sound,
> TUCKER: That saved   a wretch   a wretch   like me,
> GROUP: That saved, that saved a wretch, saved a wretch like me.

Now two minutes into the song, the Birds move into the resolution, once again changing the rhythmic texture, Tucker and the vocal background gliding and pirouetting in their complex harmonic dance. In the last moments, Tucker kicks into his growl and steers the song into the home stretch. "Amazing Grace" finishes with Tucker sliding up to a sustained high note as the backing vocals slip in underneath. The Birds succeeded in transforming the familiar Anglo hymn into something uniquely their own.

Interestingly, while Apollo pushed "My Record Will Be There" and "Amazing Grace," the side that caught on most with the public was Apollo 104, "Every Knee Surely Must Bow." In Philadelphia, Bergin's and the Record Shop listed only that title in their weekly ads, as did the Record Haven, a mail-order operation based in Brooklyn that regularly advertised in Philadelphia's African American newspapers.

"Every Knee Surely Must Bow" was Tucker's arrangement of an old spiritual, and its appeal resided in its lilting bounce. A true team effort, no one voice stood out, only a roiling harmony so dense that at times the words were difficult to distinguish.

> This evening our heavenly father,
> Once more and again,
> A few of your hand made servants,
> Have bowed down before thee.
>
> You said you'd be a mother for the motherless,
> A father for the fatherless, too,
> You said if I would serve you,
> You'd be my father, too.
>
> Now, throw your lovin' arms around me,
> Prop every leanin' side,
> Every knee surely must bow.

"Sometimes when we'd do a song," says James Davis, "the words could be hard to make out. We'd throw in phrases and repeat words just to give it a rhythm. Many a time a good beat would win out over great words."

By the end of 1946, the Birds were getting radio play and record sales nationwide, each 10-inch shellac disk an advertisement that further spread the name and sound of the group. The Dixie Hummingbirds were now prime players in the world of traditional gospel and requests for personal appearances began pouring in.

"When you come behind the Birds, you had your work cut out for you."

The Dixie Hummingbirds toured extensively throughout 1947. They continued to work their usual circuit as headliners, but also picked up dates as openers for Sister Rosetta Tharpe, at the time, one of the hottest acts in the business. Back from the war, Barney Parks no longer performed but rather established himself as a manager and booking agent. "When I got out of the service," Parks recalls, "I was kind of a playboy, in a sense, and I was going with Rosetta."

> I kinda got into money with Rosetta and what not. We'd be taking in money so fast it'd be all out on the floor! And I started doing some booking with the Birds. And Rosetta really brought them out. I took over the business and that's when the Birds got on their feet. I booked them by themselves and booked them on shows with Rosetta. Because of Rosetta, I got them in armories in the Carolinas that blacks hadn't been in . . . places like the Bell Auditorium in Raleigh. I was booking ahead of them, keeping them busy.

Tharpe, meanwhile, had succeeded in broadening her appeal by performing not only in churches, but also on records and in nightclubs, cabarets, and concert stages backed by the jazz combos of bandleaders like Lucky Millinder and Sam Price. She was walking a fine line and in late 1946, the *New York Amsterdam News* reported that her indecision was costing Tharpe some credibility with her religious constituency.

> Sister Tharpe . . . wavered between being a true gospel singer and a nightclub chirper. For a time, it was hard to tell which side had the strongest appeal. Early this year after she announced she was through with nightclubs and would sing only in churches, Foch Allen, of Allen Artists Bureau, signed up as booking agent for Sister Tharpe and set out to line up some church dates.

Allen booked more than thirty-two engagements, but then, according to the story, Sister Rosetta put them on the back burner while she was "out west doing a few nightclub dates on the q-t."[35]

By the summer of 1947, though, Sister Rosetta had by all appearances returned to the fold. She was back working churches under the auspices of New York City promoter Johnny Myers. He staged most of his gospel programs at the famed Golden Gate Ballroom at 142nd

Street and Lenox Avenue, dubbed by locals the "Madison Square Garden of Harlem,"[36] and presented Sister Rosetta in New York on two successive Sundays, June 22 and 29. The concerts were heavily promoted. Newspaper ads proclaimed, "SISTER THARPE IS BACK IN THE CHURCH—TO STAY."

On the bill with her, the National Clouds of Joy, the Victory Boys, Mme. Marie "The California Nightingale" Knight, the Two Gospel Keys, and, according to the buildup, "SPECIAL INVITED GUESTS, YOUR SINGING FAVORITES, The Champion of Champions—World Famous DIXIE HUMMINGBIRDS."

The schedule was grueling. On June 22 at the Golden Gate Ballroom, there were two shows: one at 3:30, the other at 8:30. A week later there were four shows, two in the afternoon at the Jamaica Arena on Long Island and two in the evening at the Holy Trinity Baptist Church in Brooklyn. The appearances with Sister Rosetta gave the Dixie Hummingbirds a tremendous career boost, and when they were not on the bill with her, they played the usual venues in the urban North and on the southern tour circuit they had built up over the years.

In New York City, the Birds appeared at least once a year as head-liners at the Golden Gate Ballroom. Isaac "Dickie" Freeman of Johns, Alabama, one of the most distinguished bass singers in quartet gospel, had made his name in the 1940s with the Fairfield Four. He had just joined the Kings of Harmony when the Alabama-based group performed at the Golden Gate Ballroom with the Dixie Hummingbirds. Freeman recollects, "When people came out to the Golden Gate auditorium on a Sunday, it was like going to church. It was a big place, very alive spiritually."

The Birds performed about four or five tunes before calling up the Kings of Harmony. "They always started off with something light," says Freeman, "and built from there. And if a group really shook the house up so bad, they'd have to wait for the people to settle down before the next group was ready to come up." The Kings, though, as Freeman recalls, did not "worry about that too much." They had their own secret weapon. "We had a guy in the Kings at the time, Charlie Carver, Little Charlie. Hey, you better sing all you're going to sing, because when he come up, we're going on! He was the 'house man,' we call him, the 'housewrecker.' Everybody just sit back and wait for Little Charlie." In Freeman's telling, "this particular Sunday, people just fall off the benches, fall out of their seats. One lady fainted and never did come back. They rushed her to the hospital!"

Freeman remembers that when the Birds sang, Tucker was the man who could "take the house." The guy could sing anything, man. He could do it all. He would get down low like a boxer, ball up his fists, hold his head up and really work the song." Then, there was Freeman's counterpart, bass singer William Bobo. "Bobo actually owned that part of the country," says Freeman. "Anywhere . . . headed that way, all you could hear about is Bobo. . . . I wasn't as deep as Bobo back then, but I was one of his followers. I wrote my name behind his."

When the Hummingbirds were not working close to home in the northeast, they traveled south, their popularity propelled by radio disk jockeys who gave their records plenty of air time. Curtis Rudolph, a longtime friend of Tucker's, came to know the Birds precisely through that route. Stationed at Ft. Benning, Georgia, in 1947, Rudolph was a regular listener to the Dr. Jive radio show. "At the time," recalls Rudolph, "Dr. Jive was broadcasting over WDAS out of Columbus, Georgia. He came on about 4 o'clock in the evening, 'cause I remember his theme. 'The clock on the wall say half past four, here come Dr. Jive, let's jive some more!' He would play blues, rhythm and blues, and gospel. Dr. Jive mixed it all up together, and he always had the Birds on."

Dr. Jive also produced local concerts, and when he brought the Dixie Hummingbirds to town, Rudolph was excited about seeing them in person. "The Hummingbirds concert was advertised in the paper and on the radio and posters on telephone poles. Tickets were only about 25 cents, but people would be lookin' around for that quarter, man, like they was hunting for five dollars. A quarter was a big ticket in those days!"

The concert took place at the Columbus minor league ballpark. "All kinds of people would come," says Rudolph. "But they would segregate the audience, blacks on one side, whites on the other. The stage was out on the field, made from two flat-bed semitrailers backed up side by side against each other."

Rudolph made sure to get there ahead of time because the Birds had a reputation for showing up early, and Rudolph wanted to meet them. "Some of the other groups would come in late. Off and on, you'd have a group that wouldn't show. But with the Dixie Hummingbirds, you knew they would be early. They'd be standing around and that's how I got a chance to meet Ira."

The program that night was typical of the Birds' southern tour work. Three or four local groups came on first. "They'd each play for about twenty minutes to a half an hour," remembers Rudolph. "All a cappella." It was evening by the time the Birds took the stage. The announcer would bring them on "and the Hummingbirds would just walk out and Davis would introduce the group right away. 'Ladies and Gentlemen, we are the Dixie Hummingbirds and we are glad to be here to bring you gospel through songs.'"

The show was divided into two parts. "They would do one section, say maybe half an hour, and they would go off. The break was about 15 minutes. Then they would come back on."

And the Birds always put on a show. Davis had this move, was a windmill circle with his hand. [Rudolph does a circular motion, slapping his leg each time his hand comes round.] Ira was more of a stomper. He'd get his foot going. Bobo would mostly keep his hands to his sides and just pop it out. Beachey never moved much, but he was one of the greatest tenors I ever heard. The Dixie Hummingbirds would always wreck the house. Everybody would take to screamin' and hollerin.' The Birds got the house. And it was hard for anybody to come behind the Birds. When you come behind the Birds, you had your work cut out for you![37]

"Everything you do goes back to your heritage, always a referral back."

Between 1946 and 1949, the Dixie Hummingbirds propelled their career with the release of eighteen sides on Apollo. The Birds flourished on the label and the label flourished with the Birds. In fact, the early success of Apollo was without doubt built up on the solid rock of the label's gospel catalog. Of course, the Dixie Hummingbirds were only one of the gospel performers who contributed substantially to Apollo's rise as a leading independent. Mahalia Jackson was certainly the clear standout, but there were others like the Roberta Martin Singers who in 1949 sold a million copies of "Only a Look."[38]

By the late 1940s, Bess Berman and her partners began urging many of their spiritual acts to cross over to the secular side. Some, unable to resist the temptation of a major payday, were willing to translate their gospel expertise into a new pop style.

Certainly groups like the Ink Spots and the Mills Brothers remained popular, but now, to some younger African Americans, they seemed old-fashioned, even sellouts to white mainstream tastes. There was a new vocal group sound in the air, one that reflected the grit and rhythm of the postwar urban experience, and young blacks, looking for music to call their own, were attracted to it. Attitudes were changing, and in 1950, veteran lyricist Andy Razaf, famous for songs like "Ain't Misbehavin'" and "Black and Blue," captured the turnaround in a poem that challenged the music industry's concept of a category called "race records."

> I chanced to stop at a music shop,
> Where I looked up to see:
> Above a rack, "Race Records,"
> The wording puzzled me.
>
> I thought they meant recordings,
> Of horses at the track,
> So quickly I selected one,
> And played it front and back.
>
> But it was just a pressing,
> Of a singer and a band;
> Why were they called "Race Records?"
> I could not understand.
>
> I finally got the answer,
> From the owner of the place:
> Said he, "It means the artists,
> Are of the colored race."
>
> So, even in the field of art,
> Mean Jim Crow shows his face,
> Where genius is set apart,
> And sold in terms of race![39]

Music and civil rights were increasingly intertwined. The younger generation, raised on jump blues, jazz, the holy shout, and gospel quartets, wanted a contemporary sound. They found it in "bird" groups like the Ravens and the Orioles—names inspired by the Hummingbirds—now on the ascendance. In 1947, Symphony Sid, popular jive-talking disk jockey on New York City station WHOM, presented the Ravens an award, the "foursome" having been "polled the best new singing group of the year."[40] At Apollo, Bess Berman took note and steered a number of the label's gospel groups in that unsanctified direction.

The Royal Sons—Windsor King and two sets of brothers, Eugene and John Tanner, and Clarence and Lowman Pauling—of Winston-Salem, North Carolina, had been successful on Apollo with recordings like "Bedside of a Neighbor" and "Journey's End." At the urging of Bess Berman and Apollo artist and repertoire man Carl LeBow, they soon transformed themselves into a rhythm and blues group, the Five Royales. By 1952, they would have a nationwide hit with "Baby Don't Do It," written by group member Lowman Pauling.[41]

At Bess Berman's urging, Thermon Ruth and the Selahs, old friends of the Birds and also signed to Apollo, would take a similar route. "According to Bess and other record company executives," says Ruth, "this style of music would generate higher profits." So, as the Larks, Ruth, Gene Mumford, Pee Wee Barnes, Allen Bunn, Hadie Rowe, and David McNeil recorded tracks like "Coffee, Cigarettes, and Tears," "Eyesight to the Blind," and the suggestive "Little Side Car" for Apollo.[42]

Rhythm and blues recordings simply had a better chance of becoming breakthrough hits. The music received more exposure and the market was larger, especially with young whites beginning to listen.

The Dixie Hummingbirds had been quite successful for Apollo, and Bess Berman accordingly tried to persuade them to cross over. As before, the Birds would not give up their traditional roots. James Davis always calls up the same story when asked why they stuck with gospel. "There's something about the Dixie Hummingbirds we found out when we were very young," he says.

> First trip Tucker and I took together, somebody who'd been traveling a lot came up to us and said, "I've traveled all over the world.... I like you fellas, but if you want to make a real good living, really get rich, go up there to New York City and join Bill Kenny and the Ink Spots, the Mills Brothers." He said, "You all can do it. All you got to do is practice a little bit on that stuff. You got the voices for it. You'd kill 'em!" But didn't nobody want to go.

Tucker explains, "When you do a song, it signifies where you came from. We all have roles and Jesus said that before the end of time, the bottom will be on top and the top will be on bottom. There is a right and a wrong way." Gospel was simply the right way for the Humming-birds. Tucker saw it as their calling, and to stray would have been a

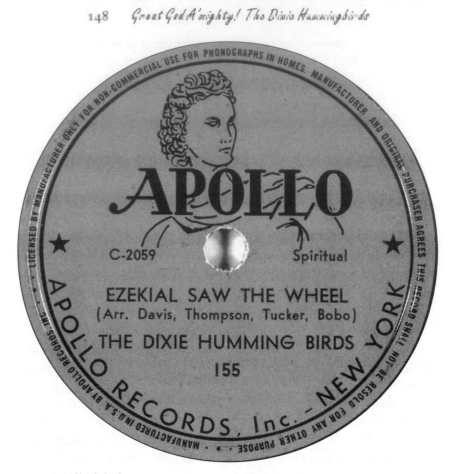

1947 Apollo label.

betrayal of God and heritage. "Everything you do goes back to your heritage, always a referral back." The Birds stood for religious values, tradition, and commitment. Their fans expected them to remain true to those ideals.

During the Dixie Hummingbirds' tenure at Apollo, they recorded a number of signature pieces, all tried and true public domain a cappella gospel. Fourteen additional sides between 1947 and 1949. "I still wasn't writing at that time," says Tucker. But he was arranging, and that was the gift he brought to the Apollo recordings. While the songs were familiar to the buying public, the arrangements were striking and fresh, infusing old standbys with new flavor.

The label issued their third release in 1947. Apollo 132 paired "One Day," a melancholy ballad-tempo performance featuring James Davis in falsetto, with "Don't You Want to Join That Number," a buoyant spiritual with bright chords and Tucker's defining leads. Then came Apollo 155, "Just a Closer Walk with Thee" b/w "Ezekiel Saw the Wheel," and Apollo 183, "Wrestlin' Jacob" b/w "Nobody Knows the Trouble I've Seen."

James Davis performed the classic hymn "Closer Walk" in his sweet tenor style, but turned it over to Bobo who concluded in his contrasting low rumble. "Ezekiel" bounced along as Tucker traded off leads with Bobo. "Wrestlin' Jacob" was similarly arranged.

Of the six sides released that year, "Nobody Knows" would become a Hummingbirds classic. They would record it again years later, but the Apollo track was their seminal version. The performance was a Tucker tour de force destined to become a standard in their on-stage repertoire. The group comes in chording like a pump organ, somber, deliberate in pace, Tucker over top with a long high note, gentle, then carefully enunciating the lyric and intoning the words with the "cry" in his voice that would become one of his hallmarks. No shouting, no breaking tempo. The song moves solemnly forward and ends on a deep rich chord with Tucker closing it out gracefully in a series of high vocal flourishes.

> Nobody knows the trouble I've seen,
> Nobody knows the trouble I've seen,
> Nobody knows the trouble I've seen,
> Glory ha-lay-loo,
>
> Sometimes I'm up, sometimes I'm down,
> Glory ha-lay-loo,
> But still my soul is heavenly bound,
> Glory ha-lay-loo.
>
> Now, old Jordan River is so chilly and cold,
> Well, it chilled my body but it didn't chill my soul,
> And when I get to heaven, I'm going to put on my shoes,
> I'm going to walk around in glory and spread the news
>
> Oh children, nobody knows the trouble I've seen,
> Nobody knows the trouble I've seen,
> Nobody knows the trouble I've seen,
> Glory ha-lay-loo.

There would be eight more Apollo releases before the Hummingbirds left the label. Of them, three were particularly outstanding. "If We Ever Needed the Lord Before" backed with "Journey to the Sky" was issued as Apollo 191. "If We Ever" was simply a beautiful song, a mellow performance, warm chords with Tucker spinning and wheeling over the top, skywriting a filigree over the rock solid harmony backdrop, the message bound to set the listener nodding in agreement.

> If we ever needed the Lord before,
> We sure do need him now,
> We sure do need him now,
> We sure do need him now.
>
> Well, if we ever needed the Lord before,
> We sure do need him now,
> We need him every day and every hour.

"Journey to the Sky," on the other hand, was reassuring in its message, an ethereal treatment of a classic spiritual. The pace was calm and performed by Tucker in mellow voice. The surprise comes in the last verse when James Davis takes over and ends the song on a high note that jumps up three levels to an impossibly high falsetto.

> There's only one thing,
> That I long for,
> When I reach my home on high,
> To see Jesus in his glory,
> And to reign with him on high,
>
> I'll be so glad to see my mother,
> Who has gone on to the land,
> But I long to see my savior,
> And by his side to stand.

Finally, Apollo 220, "The Holy Baby," was an original take that combined two standards, "Go Where I Send Thee" and the popular Christmas hymn, "Last Month of the Year," also known as "When Was Jesus Born." The arrangement was set up as call and response, a new element added with each verse, the lead, in this case bass William Bobo, then repeated the entire sequence in reverse as the song built to the end.

TUCKER: I'm gonna send you glad news.
BOBO: What is your glad news?
TUCKER: I'm gonna send you two two.
BOBO: What is your two two?

GROUP: Two was
BOBO: Paul and Silas
GROUP: One was
BOBO: Little bitty baby
GROUP: Wrapped up
BOBO: In the swaddling
GROUP: Lying
BOBO: In the manger
GROUP: Born in Bethlehem

The lyric progressed by the numbers. Three is the Hebrew children, four, the four that stood at the door; five, the gospel preachers; six, the six that couldn't get fixed; seven, the seven that couldn't get to heaven. At seven, the song breaks from the arrangement as the Hummingbirds jump to twelve and shift into a rapid-fire harmony weave so dense that the lyrics become unintelligible. As the group counts back from twelve, Tucker comes bouncing in overtop on long high notes before the group comes together as one and ends on the phrase, "Born in Bethlehem."

With the Apollo recordings, the Dixie Hummingbirds established themselves as one of the best traditional quartets in the business. They used the quality of their voices, their harmonic blend, the allure of rhythm, the message, the melody, and the inventiveness of their arrangements to invest the material with an originality that put them a cut above the rest.

They might spotlight a voice—Ira Tucker's, for instance—with his ability to sing high or low, hot or cool. They might trade leads, contrasting the highest highs of James Davis with the lowest lows of William Bobo. The rhythm might be easygoing, it might bounce and rock. They might sing call and response, or chug along in background, the lead voice overtop. By the late 1940s, the Birds had become masters of the art of engagement, and in their hands, the old spirituals were revitalized. Though none of their Apollo singles ever sold a million, the titles sold well, even among younger listeners.

Tommy Hunt was one of them. Best known for his work with doo-wop legends, the Flamingos, he was profoundly influenced by postwar gospel and the Dixie Hummingbirds in particular. Hunt grew up in Perrysville, a small town north of Pittsburgh, where he learned to sing "in a little Baptist church out in the country, Peace and Heaven Baptist Church. I was so young that I had to beg the minister to let me be in the choir. That's where I learned to sing harmony parts."

In his teens, Hunt lived in Pittsburgh's Hill District. "Pittsburgh was a great town for gospel, a very religious town. People liked the Soul Stirrers, the Delta Rhythm Boys. The Swan Silvertones were based out of Pittsburgh. But the Dixie Hummingbirds were very big, one of the top groups when they came to town." Hunt heard them at the Roosevelt Theater. "We didn't have the money for me to go see the shows." But he would listen through the back door and wait in the alleyway to greet them as they came out.

Ira Tucker and the Dixie Hummingbirds were Hunt's special favorites. He knew their music mostly from hearing their records on the radio. "Radio played a very important part in our lives, especially to kids in those days. We didn't have as many activities as kids have today, so we found our fun in listening to the radio and waiting to hear what new songs were coming out. It had a big effect on us."

Mary Dee was their favorite disk jockey. "Mary Dee played everything on her show." The station was in a "little storefront shop" that Hunt passed every day on his way home from school. The kids hung out in front of the picture window and listened to the music. "And whenever I had the money, I used to go out and buy gospel records by the Dixie Hummingbirds and other groups. I would listen and learn all the words. It was always the rhythms and the lead singers I liked, the way they were phrasing the words." Hunt would bring the vocal skills he learned from gospel records to the Flamingos, their sound—rich harmony backups and pleading mellow leads—lifted straight from the a cappella gospel stylebook.

In the 1956 film, *Rock, Rock, Rock,* Tommy Hunt and the Flamingos performed their hit song "Jump Children" to an all-white teen audience. The Flamingos took the stage with fire in their eyes. They screamed and shouted, performed acrobatic dances, and did double splits before going out full throttle on the phrase, "Ro-o-o-ck, rock 'n' roll, Ro-o-o-ck, rock 'n' roll." The camera cut to the crowd and clearly the Flamingos had brought them to the light. "Gospel funk" is the phrase Tommy Hunt uses to describe doo-wop performances like these. "It was a gospel thing in the days when those rock 'n' roll boys were coming up and that's what they brought into their music."[43]

"You sing what I want you to sing!"

Certainly it had not been the intention of the Dixie Hummingbirds or their fellow gospel travelers to inspire a secular style that would revolutionize pop music and be embraced across color lines by a younger generation. But gospel artists with their personalized performances and adherence to a powerful tradition had great appeal to the architects of rhythm and blues and its outgrowth, rock 'n' roll.

The Hummingbirds and their fans enjoyed the purity of their performances and would not sacrifice that quality for crossover success. So in January of 1949, with the release of Apollo 196, "Guide My Mind" b/w "God Is Now Speaking," the Dixie Hummingbirds cut their ties with the label.

The break with Bess Berman came following a triumphant performance by the Birds with Mahalia Jackson at Carnegie Hall. At that point, Berman "had become very controlling," Tucker says, "trying to pick our material, trying to make us contemporary in flavor, suggesting we record other than gospel. 'You sing what I want you to sing!' and 'I happen to know what's best for you!' She was saying these kinds of things." The Dixie Hummingbirds were so committed to their course that they willingly walked away from the label that had most helped them move on up a little higher. By early 1949, the Dixie Hummingbirds were once again free agents.

In November, the Philadelphia papers carried ads and a story about a "Gala Anniversary Program and Battle of Music" to be staged at the Met on December 9 at 8:00 P.M. "Philadelphia's Beloved Dixie Hummingbirds" would headline an extravaganza that included a host of "famous guests that you love to see and hear." The accompanying story attested to the stature of the event.

> Philadelphia will hear the Dixie Humming Birds [sic] present their 1949 anniversary program on Friday evening. . . .
>
> Among the featured guests are the "Selah Jubilee Singers" of Raleigh, N.C. This group will do their new recording of "I Cried Holy."
>
> Guest unit will be the "Two Gospel Keys" of Augusta, Ga. [Emma Daniels and Mother Sally Jones]. The Gospel Keys have not appeared in Philadelphia for quite some time and the two ladies, age 63 and 74, created a sensation at their last appearance here with their unusual style of singing.

The "Davis Sisters," who are now recording and "The Sacred Four" of Columbia, S.C., a popular male quartet now residing in Philadelphia, will also appear.[44]

In the ad copy, there was a star beside each group name along with a record company affiliation. The Davis Sisters were on Apex and the Selahs and Sacred Four on Gotham, all imprints of the Philadelphia-based Ballen Record Company. As 1949 wound to a close, the Dixie Hummingbirds, as the ad indicated, had also signed with Gotham. In label owner, Ivin Ballen, Ira Tucker would find a kindred spirit willing to teach him the art of recording and the skills of music business entrepreneurship. The Dixie Hummingbirds were poised to meet the new decade.

6

"My Record Will Be There"

(1950–1951)

I'm singing,
Oh, my record . . . will be there,
Singing,
Oh, my record . . . will be there,
I'm singing,
Oh, my record . . . will be there,
Oh, pages, pages, dark or fair.

—"My Record Will Be There"
The Dixie Hummingbirds

Five years after the end of World War II, a new conflagration flared up, this time in Korea. In June 1950, northern communist forces invaded the south, and President Truman committed U.S. troops to turning back the tide. Over the next three years, the bloody confrontation brought heavy casualties to both sides, and the war became a source of dark subject matter for many a blues and gospel lyric. For decades to come, communism would be America's official enemy designate.

On the domestic front, the civil rights movement continued to gain momentum. African Americans were, at this late date, still treated under the law as second-class citizens. Segregation permeated education, occupation, and even recreation. Stories of violence against African Americans—murder, lynching, burning—surfaced regularly in print and broadcast media. The African American press—regional and nationally syndicated newspapers and magazines—offered a telling ethnic perspective on issues of the day. Most often, the NAACP (National Association for the Advancement of Colored People) acted as the collective voice of protest for America's black community. In urban areas, especially in the north, some African Americans were turning to the more proactive Nation of Islam and the teachings of its leader, Elijah Muhammed.

American popular music continued to mix and meld and percolate. By 1950, big band swing was far less the thing, as small combos and solo singers like Frank Sinatra, Nat King Cole, Tony Bennett, and Ella Fitzgerald took over the spotlight.

Black jazz remained cutting edge and culturally defining. The music was never conceived for the broad market; musicians played for themselves, their community, and the challenge of stretching musical boundaries. Nevertheless, black jazz had its devotees across race and region. By 1955, though, saxophonist Charlie Parker, bebop's genius and first great star, was dead. Within four years, both Lester Young and Billie Holiday would also be gone. The music moved forward into the era of "cool" jazz through the efforts of survivors like Dizzy Gillespie, Thelonious Monk, Miles Davis, and John Coltrane.[1]

Of those jazz giants, John Coltrane had special ties to both Philadelphia and gospel. Like the Hummingbirds, he, too, migrated in the 1940s from the Carolinas to that city. As he matured as a saxophone player, Coltrane took inspiration from among other influences Philadelphia's rich gospel scene. He was especially taken with the sermons of the radio preachers. In time, he would construct one of his most poignant compositions, "Alabama," around the phrasing and feel of the sermon delivered by Martin Luther King, Jr., in remembrance of the four young girls killed in the 1963 bombing of the Sixteenth Street Baptist Church in Birmingham, Alabama.[2]

On another front, rock 'n' roll was beginning to coalesce. In 1952, Bill Haley and His Comets, a white group from Chester, just outside Philadelphia, released "Rock the Joint" in a style that melded the Western swing of Bob Wills to the Kansas City blues shouting of Big Joe Turner. The record was a foretaste of music to come.

That same year, Cleveland-based disk jockey Alan Freed started an after-school radio show aimed at white teenagers. Called "Moondog's Rock 'n' Roll Party," the music Freed righteously played in disregard for color lines—black rhythm and blues and vocal doo-wop groups— would constitute the first great wave of rock 'n' roll. The vocal groups so favored by Freed and his listeners drew heavily from black quartet gospel, usurping rhythms, harmonies, performance style, and, with minor word changes, even lyrics. Black gospel would not only influence early rock 'n' roll, but also provide a training ground for some of the emerging genre's brightest stars.

Prentiss Barnes, for example, sang with the Moonglows, one of rock's great pioneering vocal groups. Harvey Fuqua, nephew of Charlie Fuqua of the Ink Spots, was the Moonglows' leader. Prentiss Barnes sang bass. Like most young African American vocalists who made their mark in doo-wop, his path to stardom had its origins in late 1940s and early 1950s gospel.

Prentiss Barnes was born in Magnolia, Mississippi, in 1925. "We were kids when we started out in church. We listened mostly to spiritual groups like the Fairfield Four and the Seven Stars out of McComb, Mississippi. The Seven Stars never recorded or anything. They just . . . used to come out and sing in the school, churches, around the neighborhood."

Barnes eventually moved to Louisiana and then to Detroit, where gospel quartet singing continued to be the primary music in his life. "It was in Detroit that I joined a group. We sang a lot of spiritual songs."

Then, on to Cleveland where Prentiss Barnes hooked up with the Moonglows. "I just heard them singing in the apartment house we all lived in. Danny Carter and Harvey Fuqua. Harvey had a little guitar playing with it, so I went over and knocked on their door. And we just all got together, we three, and started singing." Their sound was rooted in gospel. "When I joined with Danny and Harvey, what they were singing was spirituals, but I wanted to move into R&B [rhythm and blues], and that's what we did. I didn't think there was too much difference between gospel and R&B."

"Back when the Moonglows first recorded," says Barnes, "we relied on vocal backdrops, and we picked up quite a few from spiritual groups like the Dixie Hummingbirds and the Harmonizing Four. It wasn't that hard to pick up the sound from these spiritual guys and Harvey had a good ear. Even our idea of wearing matched suits came out of gospel, but in R&B, they were louder colors—reds, greens, blues." By the late 1950s, the Moonglows, taking inspiration from gospel, had established themselves as prime role models in early rock 'n' roll.[3]

Perhaps the most compelling story of the link between gospel and R&B belongs to Sam Cooke of the Soul Stirrers. R. H. Harris had been the guiding force behind the Soul Stirrers, but by 1950, he had quit the group, some say because he was put off by too much soul stirring of the sinful kind. "All the hysterical 'carrying on,' gimmickry and showboating from the performers," wrote gospel scholar Dave Law, "which caused equally hysterical reactions from the female audience in particular, became too much for Harris to handle.... Harris took his high morals and gentlemanly ways and left the sinful temptations of the road and the Soul Stirrers."[4]

However, Bobby Womack, one-time guitarist for Sam Cooke, tells it differently. "Traveling around, Harris got to a point where he couldn't perform in different cities because he was always under arrest for child support. He had children everywhere.... They'd say, 'He does one-nighters on stage and one-nighters with the women.' It got so bad that he couldn't go on the road anymore."[5]

Whatever the case, R. H. Harris left the Soul Stirrers, and in 1951, Sam Cooke took his place. With youth and good looks, Cooke soon developed an incongruous stage persona—gospel performer as sex symbol. The combination was not new in gospel, but Sam Cooke made it more prominently. Old-line gospel fans mostly disapproved, but younger congregants flocked to see the rejuvenated Soul Stirrers and bought their records in unprecedented quantities.

By 1957, however, Sam Cooke's run with the Soul Stirrers was over as he left the group for the more lucrative world of rock 'n' roll. Cooke took control of his career, writing songs, arranging, producing, publishing, and even establishing his own label. For young African Americans, he came to represent independence and black entrepreneurship. Sam Cooke blazed on until 1964 when he was gunned down in a Los Angeles motel lobby. Authorities attributed the shooting to a jealous boyfriend, but in gospel circles, the talk was that Cooke had paid the price for crossing over to the devil's music. In other circles, speculation linked the shooting to mob or racist factions that had no toleration for a black man controlling his own destiny.

In the first years of the decade, though, the climate for African American music was rife with opportunity. The allure of fame and fortune attracted performers into both the secular and sacred sides of the genre. In gospel, there was money to be made, but only a handful of the top performers would find it extravagantly profitable.

"Our platters had been left to simmer on the back burner."

In 1949, gospel was thriving in Philadelphia. Perhaps inspired in part by the Dixie Hummingbirds' success, other local groups were vying for attention. A number of Philly gospel entertainers earnestly pursued the elusive record deal and a hit song that would put them on top. Good fortune must have been in the air, because that year a striking number *did* manage to take important first steps in that direction. They were helped by proximity to the many independent labels in nearby New York and New Jersey and to one in their own backyard. Ballen Records, established in Philadelphia just after the war, was growing in regional stature and market clout. Some Philadelphia gospel groups found a home with Ballen; others went with labels like Savoy or, in the case of the Sensational Nightingales, Coleman.

The Sensational Nightingales was one of the most important local groups to debut on records in 1949. Philadelphia-born guitarist and vocalist Howard Carroll organized the Nightingales in 1946. Originally called the Lamplighters, the personnel also included Jerome Guy, Theodore Price, Sam Whitley, and Junior Overton. As the Lamplighters, they worked in a variety of genres—gospel, blues, and jazz—before deciding to go strictly gospel. Ultimately, according to Howard Carroll, they simply felt more comfortable in the spiritual realm—good news for good people.

By 1949, the Lamplighters had changed their name in "bird group" fashion to the Sensational Nightingales, made some personnel changes, and hired a professional manager. Howard Carroll would be the only remaining Lamplighter in a group that now included Ben Joyner, former Dixie Hummingbird William Henry, and Paul Owens, an experienced and versatile tenor.

Owens had been with several Philadelphia gospel quartets, including the Israelite Gospel Singers and the Bay State Gospel Singers,[6] the latter frequently an opening act for the Dixie Hummingbirds. Paul Owens brought needed strength to the Nightingales' vocal mix when he joined them in 1949, and they would be his entrée into the recording studio.

The Nightingales hired former Hummingbird Barney Parks to build their reputation as he had for several up-and-coming groups, largely, as with the Dixie Hummingbirds, by placing them on programs with megastar Sister Rosetta Tharpe. Spartanburg's Julius "June" Cheeks, childhood friend to both Tucker and Bobo, would prove to be the turning point in the Nightingales' success.[7]

"I had the Nightingales on a radio station in Wilson, North Carolina," says Parks. "They wanted to make it. Badly. And they listened to me." Parks ran the group like they were in the military. "I had them just like they were in the army."

When I set up practice, we'd have the mike there, and we'd work on showmanship! We'd excite the people. When I got June Cheeks in there, they was unstoppable. Any group, I don't care how famous, they knew just to get up and sing, 'cause June Cheeks and those guys going to turn out on you. Spirit-killers! If they didn't get you one way, they'd get you another. They were just that hard.

Barney Parks arranged for the Sensational Nightingales—Carroll, Joyner, Owens, and Henry—to record for the Newark-based Coleman label, owned by old friends from the gospel circuit, the Coleman Brothers, a rare African American gospel group that had eliminated the middleman and were in the record business for themselves.[8]

Of course, the 'Gales were far from the only act in town. While they made their debut that year on the Coleman label, other Philadelphia groups launched recording careers with the hometown operation, Ballen Records. It was, in fact, Ballen's success with local groups that drew the Dixie Hummingbirds' attention to the label in the first place, though, ironically, those Ballen successes were not with male quartets but rather with the remarkable array of female talent that abounded in Philadelphia at the time. No other city could boast as high a concentration of female gospel talent as Philadelphia, and leading the way were the Ward Singers—mother Gertrude, sisters Clara and Willa, Henrietta Waddy, and Marion Williams, later distinguished in her own right as a soloist.

The Wards started out in 1934 as a family trio, the Consecrated Gospel Singers. By the early 1940s, Gertrude Ward had moved from performance to management as daughter Clara stepped in as the lead. Soon, they were touring countrywide as Clara Ward and the Famous Ward Singers.

By 1948, though seasoned touring artists, the Wards had yet to make a record. "People had been telling us about Savoy Records," recalls Willa Ward-Royster. "So we went in person to the Savoy offices in Newark and auditioned for Mr. Herman Lubinsky and Mr. Fred Mendelsohn."[9] Savoy Records signed the Wards and in January 1949 released their first sides, "Jesus" b/w "Stretch Out." Over the course of the year, Savoy released a dozen more sides, which reached a modest audience. The Wards, meanwhile, were on tour at the time and tearing it up with their take on W. Herbert Brewster's "Our God Is Able." Clara Ward had modified the words and was singing it as "Surely God Is Able."

"The first series of our songs pressed by the company were very good," says Willa Ward-Royster, "but had not been enthusiastically pushed. In fact, religious recordings in general lagged behind secular ones, and our platters had been left to simmer on the back burner. Now,

The Sensational Nightingales, 1947. Back row: Ben Joyner, former
Birds bass singer William Henry, Howard Carroll; front row: Paul
Owens, Julius "June" Cheeks. Photo by Powell Photo Service.
Courtesy of Howard Carroll.

when we let the Savoy people hear our rendition of 'Surely God Is Able,'
they raved over it—yet they dragged on with excuse after excuse for
their delay in recording it."

Frustrated and disappointed, the Wards took the song to Ivin Ballen.
His operation was not yet as far-reaching as Savoy, but the label had
picked up some steam thanks to a hit by another of Philadelphia's
female gospel groups, the Angelic Gospel Singers. Ballen moved quickly
to record the Wards. "Surely God Is Able" b/w "I Need Thee Every
Hour" was released in 1950. The Wards' studio performance captured
the rollicking energy of a sanctified church service in the dual
organ/piano backup, the chugging rhythm, and Clara and the group
shouting back and forth to each other.

From the first, the record sold well. The Wards had only been paid a
flat fee of $125.00, but the real payoff came in the form of increased
demand for bookings countrywide, all stoked by sales of the record.

Clara Ward and the Ward Singers.

Savoy, meanwhile, caught off guard, finally noticed that one of their contracted groups had a hit on a rival label. They sued and eventually won the right to release "Surely God Is Able" on Savoy—but not in time to reap the full rewards of the record's popularity.

In the end, the Ward Singers were legally bound to return to Savoy and over the course of a decade released most of their finest material on that label. Ballen, however, maintained his ties with the Wards, later releasing a number of sides by the Clara Ward Specials. Clara Ward did not sing with the Specials, but she did handpick the lineup, train them in her style, and sanction them with her name. The arrangement was of mutual benefit. Ballen continued to capitalize on records featuring the Ward sound, and the Wards expanded their profits and reputation by in effect franchising their good name.[10]

Even before the Wards signed with Ballen Records, however, the label had already scored significantly with two other prominent Philadelphia female groups: the Angelic Gospel Singers and the Davis Sisters. The Davis Sisters—Thelma, Ruth, Audrey, and Alfreda—were of an offshoot Pentecostal Holiness sect whose very name—the "fire baptized"—suggested the ardor of their performance style. With Curtis Dublin on piano, his approach "midway between the sanctified church and the nightclub," the Davis Sisters rocked the house when they performed.[11] They too launched their recording career in 1949, releasing "I'm Going to Tell God" b/w "Thy Holy Will Be Done" on Ballen's Apex label. The Davis Sisters would eventually release an additional twenty-five sides with Ballen, finally hitting big in 1952 with an Alex Bradford composition, "Too Close to Heaven." By 1955, the Davis Sisters, like the Wards, had also gone over to Savoy and would record with them well into the 1970s.

Finally, the Angelic Gospel Singers, though never quite achieving the prominence of the Davis Sisters or the Wards, gave Ballen the breakthrough hit that attracted other groups like the Ward Singers and, in time, the Dixie Hummingbirds. Like the Davis Sisters, the Angelics were also Pentecostals, but of a more mainstream sect. The Angelics were to "Pentecostal congregations," notes Horace Boyer, "what the Ward Singers were to the National Baptist Convention."[12] Pentecostals tended to be unrestrained in performance style; their singing was more spirited and laced with shouting and the instrumental backing of piano, organ, guitar, or tambourine.[13] Baptist performance style, on the other hand, was a more reserved approach "that sought to capture the ecstasy" of Pentecostal singing "but without the excesses." The difference was evident in their church services. "Excesses," says Boyer, meant "singing in the extremes of the register," "interpolating additional words into the text, hand-clapping, and occasional spurts of shouting."[14]

Margaret Allison organized the Angelic Gospel Singers in the early 1940s. Born in McCormick, South Carolina, Allison, like so many other Carolina African Americans, migrated to Philadelphia. She was ambitious and a visionary, the concept of her group, right down to the name, coming to her full-blown in a dream. Allison played piano, composed, and arranged. She organized the Angelics around her sister, Josephine McDowell, and two other former South Carolinians, Lucille Shird and Ella Mae Morris, the latter from Greenville, James Davis's hometown.

The Angelics were well known in Philadelphia and had an established touring circuit of Pentecostal churches. In 1949, with several years of performing experience behind them, they finally auditioned for Ivin Ballen, who signed them and released their first recording, "Touch Me, Lord Jesus" b/w "When My Savior Calls Me Home" as part of a new "600" gospel series on a label he had just acquired, Gotham. The record was a hit and brought immediate countrywide recognition to both the Angelics and the Gotham imprint.

"He bought the label for the act."

In the wake of the Angelics' success in late 1949, the Dixie Hummingbirds signed with Ballen. The decision was bold. They had fared well with Apollo, but with Bess Berman trying to steer them in a secular direction and control how and what they recorded, they decided to end their association with the label. Ballen Records, with a track record of commitment to Philadelphia gospel, caught their attention. Owner, operator, and engineer Ivin Ballen had a reputation as being forthright; he was willing to risk the upfront production costs and would not question his performers' artistic choices.

The Dixie Hummingbirds appreciated both the creative freedom and the studio's proximity to home. For Ira Tucker, the association proved to be especially fortuitous. Ivin Ballen, respectful of his talent without regard to skin color, was willing to work closely with Tucker and teach him the business. "What I was trying to do at that time," says Tucker, "was get into the field. When we were with Ivin Ballen, he showed me how to do things."

By keeping his eyes open and working directly with Ballen, Tucker learned how to be a deal maker and a producer. He learned technicalities like designing an acoustically effective recording studio, placing microphones, and operating the control board. "Ballen showed me all kinds of things. He'd have foam rubber on the walls and glass hanging around, cut glass on the studio walls to get that reverb sound."

Ballen also took Tucker seriously on creative issues like whom, how, and what to record. With Ballen, Tucker would hone his skills as an arranger and producer of recording sessions. In the long run, Tucker's development would serve the Dixie Hummingbirds well. James Davis had always handled business and steered the group in keeping with the righteous vision planted in him by his parents all those years ago. Davis would continue in this guiding role. Tucker had been a creative force within the Hummingbirds since he joined, but now he would get the chance to mature as a professional, and in the process, solidify his role as the creative half (with Davis) of the team at the helm of the Hummingbirds. In late 1949, the Dixie Hummingbirds, ready to draw on the full measure of their abilities, joined the diverse roster of talent on Ballen's Gotham label.

Ivin Ballen followed a common route into recording African American music. He was born in Philadelphia in 1909 to Jewish immigrants from Ukraine. In these years, many Jews were immersed in the world of African American music. As journalist Mark Lisheron has noted, "Jews either owned or were a major part of almost every important independent label of the time."[15]

Over the years, the Dixie Hummingbirds had worked with a number of Jewish producers including Barney Josephson at Café Society, Irving Berman at Regis Records, Bess Berman [no relation] at Apollo Records, and now Ivin Ballen at Ballen Records. Indeed, Jews owned a significant number of the independent labels then recording the music of emerging African American artists and participated in every aspect of the enterprise from talent acquisition to song selection to session production. Herman Lubinsky and Fred Mendelsohn at Savoy, Herb Abramson and Jerry Wexler at Atlantic, Syd Nathan at King/Federal, Phil and Leonard Chess at Chess/Checker, Art Rupe at Specialty, and the Mesner family at Aladdin were among the most influential Jewish businessmen in the music industry.[16]

Jews identified with African American culture in a variety of ways. There was the shared legacy of slavery and the social discrimination prevalent in the 1950s. For some Jews, the bond grew out of the circumstances of poverty.

Art Rupe recorded outstanding African American artists like the Alabama Blind Boys, Sam Cooke with the Soul Stirrers, Guitar Slim, Clifton Chenier, Joe and Jimmy Liggins, and Little Richard. Born into a family of poor immigrants, Rupe grew up in the shadow of steel mill smokestacks in the town of McKeesport, just southeast of Pittsburgh. He described it as "what you might call a ghetto area.... We were all poor and whether white or black our culture was the same. The music I heard was black.... What bonded us was a culture shaped by our similar economic status, not our ethnicity."[17]

But perhaps the music itself was the most powerful draw. Most Jewish label owners came to black music first as fans, then later as businessmen and women. The music resonated with Jewish temperament.

"There's an affinity between blues and Hebrew music," said Ralph Bass, trailblazing producer of R&B greats like James Brown, Ike Turner, the Dominoes, and Etta James. "I hear the blues in a minor key, and, hey, baby, I'm back in synagogue."[18]

Then there were the lyrics to the traditional spirituals with their allusions to ancient Jewish culture—"Go Down, Moses," the "Hebrew Children," the "Battle of Jericho," and the "Balm in Gilead." Abraham, Joshua, Job, Jacob, David, and Noah. "Canaan Land" and the "River of Jordan." And ultimately, "Let My People Go," the shared rallying cry of both Jews and blacks in their struggles against oppression.

The connection between Jews and blues, though, was still more complex, shaped by external social forces. "Often barred by anti-Semitism from core sectors of the economy," writes journalist Mark Lisheron, "Jews had long gravitated to the lucrative if risky field of entertainment. Vaudeville, nickelodeons, motion pictures and records at their starts were all shunned by the genteel as tawdry enterprises. Jews already had a foothold in ghetto retail, owning nightclubs, movie theaters and record stores."[19] Jews and blacks were often lumped together, consigned by some to the same bottom rung of the social ladder, viewed as outsiders, fitting partners in a distasteful realm of show business that no self-respecting aspirant would take part in.

As partners in the music business, many Jews and blacks provided a model for healthy race relations. For example, by 1949, Syd Nathan's Cincinnati-based King Records had become a giant among the independents, a "completely self-contained and self-sufficient unit ... in a position to compete on equal terms with the major record companies, at least within its chosen fields of black music and country music."[20] That year, the *Cincinnati Post* published a report on how Nathan's business policies were "smashing Jim Crow."

Two years ago they told ... the King Record Co. .... that it couldn't be done.

"Cincinnati is a border town," said the skeptics. "You can't get Negroes and white people to work together. It's too close to the south. ...

The skeptics were wrong. King hires 400 employees, and the nondiscrimination policies have needed no "backing." ...The musical director, assistant office manager, foreman of the mill room, set up man on the production line, assistant promotion director, legal secretary, a dozen stenographers and 20 per cent of the factory workers are Negroes. ...

The plant sponsors a Negro and white team in a city industrial league. "We pay for ability," says [operations manager] Mr. Siegel, "and ability has no color, no race, and no religion. Our hiring policy and our promotion system are based only on the question of the individual's capacity to fill a given job."[21]

A radical statement and a forward-thinking policy, an ideal model for the future, but a rare state of affairs in 1949.

But in direct opposition to the sunny side, there were also dark clouds that marred the climate of cooperation between Jews and blacks in the music business. In the world of the independents, label owners—Jewish or otherwise—were notorious for short-changing artists, doing what they could to keep as much as they could.

Ira Tucker Jr., longtime publicist for Stevie Wonder and a veteran of the music business, describes the bittersweet relationship between Jews and blacks this way. "No question Jewish people worked closely with blacks in the music business." For the artists, who knew little about the business side, "it was a blessing. They didn't think about was it a Jewish person or not. To them," says Tucker, Jr., "it was a white person in a position to help. Yes," he acknowledges, "Jews knew what it was like to be society's 'whipping boy.' They'd been through that and there was the empathy. They also had a talent for recognizing who was good and who was not." At the same time, due to an acute lack of experience about the business of music, many African American artists were vulnerable to exploitation by label owners.

Relatively speaking, the Dixie Hummingbirds fared well in the late 1940s and early 1950s, considering they had little choice but to rely on independent label owners, many of whom were Jewish. The Birds got a fair shake from Ivin Ballen. "Mr. Ballen was a nice guy," says Tucker, Jr. "He knew talent. His relationship with his artists went beyond recording their music. He branched out, publishing, booking, lending money when they needed it, even renting sound equipment. When a group needed microphones and amplifiers and speakers, Mr. Ballen rented equipment to them. But it was the work of my father and the Dixie Hummingbirds and other black artists who put Gotham on the road to the big time success the company still enjoys today."[22]

No doubt, the success stories associated back then with Gotham and other independents enticed others to try their hand in the recording enterprise. The music business after the war was an exciting and wide-open arena, a venture in which a person with gumption and foresight could establish a niche and, while not necessarily striking it rich, make enough to keep it interesting. Anything could happen. Public tastes in music were in flux, broadening in scope, and the major record companies were sluggish in picking up on the latest trends, leaving a wide-open hole for independents to fill.

Another factor in the rise of the independent label was improved technology, from studio electronics to record pressing to the format and actual materials used to make records. These and other innovations made it more economically feasible for small-time operators to produce hit records. The right combination could spark a rocket ride to the top with a generous payoff at the peak. A "million-seller"—in those days a record that actually sold in the middle hundreds of thousands—could generate a hefty income for company coffers. Not that every record was a million-seller, but hit records did and could happen. This great potential combined with the glamour of the enterprise and a genuine love for the music drew people of all ethnic backgrounds, including an exceptional number of Jews, to the business of recording blues, jazz, and gospel.

The early career of Ivin Ballen reveals a great deal about the struggles and operation of the postwar independent labels on which the Dixie Hummingbirds and so many other African American groups were dependent. Ballen, like many of his counterparts, began his odyssey into the business as a fan and record collector. His tastes were eclectic but tended toward swing and dance bands. Ballen, though, kept his ears open and was in touch with the music scene unfolding around him in Philadelphia's African American community.

In school, Ballen enjoyed working with audio technology and was a member of the radio club. When his father died, Ballen left school and took a job in audio technology to help support the family. "There was no commercial P.A. equipment at that time," says his son Morris Ballen, "so he learned how to build it himself." By World War II, Ballen was fully immersed in the sound amplification business, setting up and running amplifiers, speakers, and microphones for carnivals, pep rallies, bond rallies, any place where audio projection was required. Quite possibly, Ballen's first encounters with the Dixie Hummingbirds might have been when they were performing for the wartime shellac drives.

Eventually Ballen used his technological knowledge to start up a record company. "He was a good engineer," says Morris Ballen. "It was his dream to get into a studio and make his own records, so he built his own recording studio. Then built his own factory to make the records.

He even printed his own labels. That was his way of doing things. Build a studio, build a plant, and then find the artists."

The business relocated a few times in the early years, finally settling in at 1416 Wood Street behind the Broadwood Hotel near Vine Street. For a time, there were two Ballen imprints, 20th Century and Apex. Most of Ballen's acts were culled from local Philadelphia talent and he publicized his labels by news releases and advertisements in trade magazines. In the summer of 1946, Ballen took out an ad in *Billboard* promoting the release on 20th Century label of "Margie" b/w "We Laughed Together," pop fare by Henry Patrick and the Marty Kramer Sextet. The ad also touted two sides by veteran swingster Slim Gaillard, "Tutti Frutti" b/w "Slim's Cement Boogie," a release more indicative of the direction the Ballen labels would take in the future. The record was priced at 49 cents, with distributors listed in Philadelphia, Pittsburgh, New York, and Chicago.[23]

Billboard also ran a story that summer about Ballen's establishment of a music publishing company, Andrea Music.

> *Ballen Diskery's Pub Co. Up Phila. Count*
>
> Ballen Record Company here, which produces the 20th Century platter label, is latest of the indie waxworks to enter the music publishing field. Ivin Ballen, who heads the firm, is setting up a subsidiary, Andrea Music Company, to publish the tunes he introduces and discovers on his disk label. First one is expected to be *I Said It and I'm Glad*, by the local team of Billy Hays and Mike Francis. Andrea swells the ranks of local pub firms, now nearing a dozen.[24]

In addition to creating a secondary revenue stream, the label's publishing arm allowed Ballen to share profits from original material with his artists. The promise of writer's royalties and a ready publisher may have encouraged some of Ballen's gospel artists to try their hands at songwriting. Like both James Davis and Ira Tucker, many postwar gospel artists relied less on reworked spirituals and instead penned gospel originals in the tradition of Dorsey, Brewster, Charles Tindley, and others.

In those first years following the war, Ballen Records failed to produce a hit but managed to stay afloat. In 1948, however, Ivin Ballen deepened his investment in the industry by acquiring the New York label, Gotham Records. Sam Goody, founder of the retail music store chain that today still bears his name, was then a budding mogul; among his other enterprises, he had established this moderately successful independent blues, jazz, and gospel label, using his connections within the entertainment industry to market his records nationwide. Goody had decided to sell off Gotham so that he could focus on distribution and retail.

"Sam Goody was an entrepreneur," says Paul Fine, Ballen's financial controller in those days. "He dealt mainly in New York City. He had what is known as a distributorship, but it wasn't exclusive. He handled most of the different labels. I would say that he was the beginning of the 'one-stop' arrangement."[25] In other words, before Sam Goody, record sellers went to different wholesale distributors to stock each "family" of labels. Goody revolutionized the process by bringing together all labels for sale under one roof, hence the term "one-stop." By divesting himself of Gotham, Goody was free to move in that innovative marketing direction.

Goody had launched Gotham back in 1946 with releases by artists like saxophonist Earl Bostic and New Orleans pianist/singer/song-writer Pleasant Joseph. Joseph had just recorded for the first time under his own name the year before on the Savoy label. Jumping over to Gotham, he broadened his base by recording rhythm and blues as "Cousin Joe" and gospel as "Brother Joshua." Among his gospel tracks were "If You Just Keep Still," "When Your Mother's Gone," "When the Roll Be Called in Heaven," and "Make Me Just as Strong as Sampson."

Whether recording R&B or gospel, on his Gotham sides Pleasant Joseph used essentially the same band—the Earl Bostic Orchestra with Tyree Glen, trombone; Tony Scott, clarinet; John Hardee, tenor sax; Hank Jones, piano; Jimmy Jones, bass; and Eddie Nicholson, drums. His brand of gospel, as the jazz-oriented band suggests, differed markedly from the Dixie Hummingbirds. His was *not* vocal harmony-based but was rather a hot New Orleans style of gospel, solo voice backed by a horn band rooted in the jazz traditions of that city. Cousin Joe brought the same feel to both his Gotham gospel and R&B sides; among the secular titles were "My Tight Woman" and "Lightnin' Struck the Poorhouse." The only difference was in lyrical content.

In his autobiography, Pleasant Joseph provides some insight into the state of gospel recording in the postwar 1940s, his association with Sam Goody and Gotham Records, and the rise of another budding talent, Earl Bostic. In 1946, Joseph had been in Boston on tour with New Orleans clarinetist Sidney Bechet. Bill Simon, an artist and repertoire man, or "A&R man" as they were called, sent him a telegram. "He told me when I got back to New York, he had a recording date for me with Gotham Records, which was owned by Sam Goody."

Well, when they found out I could sing spirituals, I did a spiritual album. . . . I did the tunes, and I got Earl Bostic to write the introductions and endings. Earl Bostic was writing and arranging for different bands. He had records by the Golden Gate Quartet. They were the greatest at that time, but they weren't doing it the way I was going to do it. So I had to go to his house. He'd pick up his guitar and I'd sing it the way I was going to sing it. I gave Earl the privilege of being the leader of the session, and I got the man to pay him a hundred dollars extra for writing the introductions and endings.

Earl Bostic had a job working down at the Rendezvous, down in the basement on Seventh Avenue, when I went down and got him. He played so much horn, he was making nine thousand notes a second. When the record company heard Earl Bostic playing such great alto, they spent ten thousand dollars to build him up in advertisements and write-ups and all that kind of stuff. Earl Bostic won the *Pittsburgh Courier's* poll as the number one alto player of the year. Then he formed his own band and hit the road. Then, he got big."[26]

In his acquisition of Gotham, Ivin Ballen was primarily interested in acquiring Earl Bostic, an artist with an established reputation. "He bought the label for the act, " says Morris Ballen. "Earl Bostic. My father had a hard time getting records to sell so he bought a label for the act. Right down to the label design. When he bought Gotham, he got to thinking about marketing records by black performers to black record buyers. Bostic's contract was part of the deal."[27]

In addition to a name label and artist, Ballen also bought into Goody's distribution network. As Morris Ballen recollects, Sam Goody had no distribution outside New York City, and so he had an arrangement with Syd Nathan of King Records in Cincinnati to simultaneously release all Gotham sides on King, a label that *did* have national distribution. That pact remained intact when Gotham passed into Ballen's hands. Paul Fine also remembers a business relationship with the "diligent and systematic" John Richbourg, a Nashville-based disk jockey and gospel producer/promoter. In exchange for consideration for his acts in the Northeast, Richbourg would push radio play and sales of Gotham product in Nashville. This sort of business relationship was an absolute necessity if independent labels hoped to launch a record or break an act outside their home turf. Loyalties and limited reciprocal partnerships kept the independent labels competitive.

Gotham became Ballen's primary imprint, and as the demand for Gotham artists escalated, Ballen started his own booking agency, Gotham Attractions, which further enhanced business. Groups would make records and be booked for appearances so that they would gain exposure and sell more records and sheet music. That would in turn lead to more recording sessions, more releases, more bookings, and ultimately the acquisition of more acts. "And the whole operation," emphasizes Morris Ballen, "was fueled by the sale of gospel records."

Ivin Ballen also stayed competitive by making use of developing technology. "Early on, he recorded right into wax," says Morris Ballen, "but he was an early convert to tape recorders." Tape paved the way for lower costs, multitrack recording, and better sound quality.

Ballen's technical innovations, however, were sometimes premature. Before consumers were prepared, he adopted 45-rpm records, the 7-inch

1949 Gotham label.

vinyl disks with large center holes that later became the standard format of rock 'n' roll record sales. "My dad had gone to a show in 1948 where RCA was introducing the 45. He thought this was the greatest thing since sliced bread. He said, 'Look, it's microgroove, it's small, it's light.' He immediately began putting out all his stuff on 45. He was ahead of the market. This particular market, the 'race' market, was kind of a retro market, the last to change over to 45. And they *did not* sell. And he walked into a record store in New York, and the owner said, 'Ivin, I finally found a use for these 45s you sent me.' He said, 'I'm using them for pull chains!' He had the records tied to the ends of strings hanging down from his light fixtures and was using them to switch his electric lights on and off!"

Eventually, Ballen abandoned recording to focus on manufacturing. "Ballen became a presser," says Paul Fine, "pressing records for other manufacturers." The operation still exists today as DiscMakers, but in the late 1940s and early 1950s, Gotham was at the center of an artistically exciting period of hit records by the Ward Singers, the Davis Sisters, the Angelics, and, of course, the Dixie Hummingbirds.

"It changed our lives because people started calling."

Ballen had hoped that the Gotham imprint with Earl Bostic and its preexisting roster of R&B and jazz talent would gain him ready entrée into radio play and a leg up on future signings. Ironically, though, neither Bostic nor *any* of the label's other secular artists created much buzz. Instead, gospel records were the label's biggest success. Once he acquired Gotham, Ballen showed sound judgment in the caliber of the musicians he chose to record. "He was a good A&R man," says Morris Ballen. The Gotham roster of the late 1940s and early 1950s stands as representative of the range of African American musical artists who relied on independent labels to reach the marketplace.

Among the jazz-oriented performers were guitarist Lloyd "Tiny" Grimes, sax men Red Prysock and Jimmy Preston, and Kansas City vocalist Jimmy Rushing. The label's blues artists included Sonny Terry and Brownie McGhee, Nathaniel "Stick Horse" Hammond, John Lee Hooker as "Johnny Williams," and New Orleans pianist Champion Jack DuPree as "Meat Head Johnson."

In gospel, Ballen released numerous sides by artists at every level of accomplishment. Some were popular locally or regionally, like trumpet-playing Elder Charles Beck and his Religion in Rhythm, or vocalists like the Sacred Four, the Gospel Messengers, the Gospel Twins, Brother Rodney, and the Evening Stars featuring Joe Cook, who would later cross over to R&B fame as Little Joe of the Thrillers.

Others were established but would achieve greater fame down the line. Before he recorded for Chicago's Chess label, for example, Aretha's father, the Reverend C. L. Franklin, in 1950 released his first sides on Gotham—a Clara Ward composition, "I Am Climbing Up High Mountains Trying to Get Home" b/w "The Lord Will Make a Way, Yes, He Will," and "Wings of Faith" b/w "Your Mother Loves Her Children." Professor Alex Bradford, later famous on Specialty, made his debut on Gotham as one of the Willie Webb Singers. Composer W. Herbert Brewster also recorded for Gotham, performing narratives over compositions written by him for his performing groups, the Brewster Singers and the Brewsteraires.

Gotham also recorded one-time Dixie Hummingbird Otis Jackson, then working primarily as a promoter in Philadelphia. Back in 1946, the year after President Roosevelt died, Jackson had written a tribute titled "Tell Me Why You Like Roosevelt?"[28] The arrangement, a recitation with background vocals by the Evangelist Singers, later the Detroiters, was released on the Chicago-based Hub label and was rerecorded for Gotham in 1949 with the backing of another Gotham act, the National Clouds of Joy.

Gotham also released more than forty sides of the Harmonizing Four—Thomas Johnson, Joseph Williams, Lonnie Smith, and Levi Hansley—of Richmond, Virginia, one of the genre's most respected quartets. Together since the late 1920s, the Harmonizing Four brought on a new young singer, James Walker, who carried the lead on at least two of the group's early 1950s Gotham sides—"Working for the Lord" and "Watch over Me." Walker was a jewel of a performer, charming, dramatic on stage, outstanding as a lead singer. He impressed James Davis, for one, who kept Walker in mind as a singer who someday might fit nicely into the Hummingbirds' vocal blend.

While Ballen was having success with African American gospel, he also decided to venture into its white counterpart, southern gospel. The most important group he contracted, the Blue Ridge Quartet, was coincidentally from Tucker's hometown, though Tucker did not know them nor did they the Dixie Hummingbirds. Instead, the coexistence of the two groups on Gotham facililated the infusion of black gospel into white.

Ed Sprouse, who sang with the Blue Ridge Quartet in their Gotham days, recalls how Ivin Ballen would send them sheet music of songs by the Dixie Hummingbirds and other African American writers published by Gotham's Andrea Music. Ballen would also send along records, encouraging the Blue Ridgers to learn and record the material. Although Ballen was only trying to increase his profit margin by extending the market for original material in his publishing catalog, he inadvertently helped spread black gospel style and repertoire to a white audience.[29]

Yet with black gospel, Ballen enjoyed speedier successes with his start-up Gotham "600" series. Gotham 605 was "Touch Me, Lord Jesus," the runaway hit by the Angelic Gospel Singers. "Huge seller," says Morris Ballen. "It never stopped. This record made the label for a while and it attracted others," like the Wards, the Harmonizing Four, and indeed, the Dixie Hummingbirds. These were times, reminds Morris Ballen, when label affiliations could be very fluid. Performers on their way up constantly shifted to where they thought they might catch a break. "Also, different labels tried to steal each other's acts. Or the group managers would try to shop the acts when the contract was up." In this open market and through the Angelics, Gotham suddenly became hot and other groups were attracted to the light.

Sometimes, like the Angelics, they literally walked in off the street. "Acts would come in sometimes even unannounced," says Morris Ballen. "My dad would take them up in this old industrial elevator to the third floor where the studio was. He'd take them in the studio and if he liked them he signed them on the spot."[30] In 1949, after years of singing locally and on a limited church circuit, Margaret Allison, with her sister and their two friends, knocked on Ivin Ballen's office door.

The Angelics were stylistically quite different from the male quartets of the day. "The female groups sang different from the males," says Allison. "I never even referred to my group as a quartet. I would always just say we were the Angelic Singers and I didn't really want to be a quartet. With the quartets back in that time, they weren't usually into having music—instruments—and see, I was using music. I was playing piano."[31]

The use of musical instruments was not the only difference between male and female gospel performers. Male quartets like the Dixie Hummingbirds tended to be a cappella harmony teams with complex vocal weaves, rhythm-popping bass, and alternating leads. Female groups like the Angelics tended to be piano-driven church-style parallel harmony ensembles with call and response between lead and group. In the early 1950s, the women of gospel dominated the popularity polls and sold the most records.

Margaret Allison was eager to get on board. "I had been to the Coleman Brothers in New Jersey," she says, "to see if we could get recorded with them, but they said they weren't interested. They wasn't interested in no female singers." Allison was bemoaning that rejection to Otis Jackson when he suggested they contact Ivin Ballen. "He said to me 'I know somebody and I'm most sure he'll record you.'"

And I thought I'd have to pay and I said, "How much would he charge?" And Otis said, "I don't know. We'll go down there and see." So Otis carried me to Gotham to see Ivin Ballen. Mr. Ballen, he said to me, "Now, first of all, let me tell you what I want. I want something that you wrote, or even if you didn't write the song, if you arranged it, because I want you to establish your own sound. I don't want you copying off nobody else and I don't want you to record something somebody else has recorded." Then, he said, "Let me hear what you got."

I said, "Well, we've got one song that I sing, I arranged it, but I didn't write it." And I told him I hadn't heard it on a record by anybody. The title is "Touch Me, Lord Jesus."

So, I went and sat down to the piano, we went and got around the piano, the girls did, and we started singing. And he stopped us. And my heart skipped a beat. I thought, "Uh oh, he don't want that." And he said, "That's the song I want!"

Well, we all looked at each other and I said, "You liked that one?" And he said, "Yeah. You arranged that?" I said I did but that Lucie Campbell wrote the song. I heard a young lady at our church sing it for a solo, and because of the written arrangement for music, the way she was singing it, I didn't like it. [Allison sings a sample, slow moving and spiritless.] I didn't like that. I liked the words, but I thought I'm going to change that. Now, I don't read music, to my sorrow, so I just played it on the piano. And that was the song Mr. Ballen wanted.

Ballen signed them on the spot. "He had us sign a contract, I think it was for about six months. And he said, 'If this sells, then we can take it from there.'" Allison recollects that the group was paid about a hundred dollars a side for their initial recordings and arrangements for future royalty payments were made.

Perhaps typical of the sort of business arrangements Ballen made with gospel groups is a surviving one-page contract with the Royal

The Angelic Gospel Singers in the late 1940s. Clockwise from left: Bernice Cole (with pearls), Lucille Shird, Josephine McDowell, Ella Mae Norris in center, Margaret Allison seated at the piano.

Harmony Singers dated July 2, 1949. The deal was for a single record, "Am I Born to Die," and "Dear Lord, Look Down upon Me," released as Apex 1119. "The Ballen Record Company," reads the document, "agrees to ... pay to the Royal Harmony Singers a royalty of one cent per ... record on 90 percent of all records manufactured and sold from the above master. Royalties shall be payable quarterly, 45 days following the close of each calendar quarter. The Royal Harmony Singers hereby agree not to record the above songs for any other company for a period of 5 years from this date." Ballen and the four members and manager of the Royal Harmony Singers signed the contract.[32]

The initial Angelic Singers session took place within a week of the signing. "It was our first time in the recording studio," says Allison. "I was more excited than afraid. I was excited over it."

The techniques they used to record that day were simple by later standards: no multitracking, no overdubbing, no headphones. The Angelics had done their homework before they ever entered the studio, and other than a warm-up, they were ready to record. Josephine McDowell, Lucille Shird, and Ella Mae Morris gathered in semicircle around a microphone. Margaret Allison sat at the piano a short distance away with her own vocal mike. The piano was recorded from the vocal mikes. All the songs were between two and three minutes long, close to the most a 78-rpm shellac recording could hold.

"Touch Me, Lord Jesus" established the signature sound of the Angelic Gospel Singers. Allison built the song's arrangement around her piano style, rhythmic bass note runs accentuated by bright chord splashes on the high end of the keyboard, functioning as fills between the vocal lines. The words were laid out in impeccably timed staccato phrases sung in parallel harmony. No screaming. No shouting. Only a gentle waxing and waning of intensity as the song flowed through to conclusion.

> Touch, Touch me Lord Jesus,
> Mmm Mmm Mmm Mmm,
> With, Thy hand of mercy,
> Make, Each throbbing heartbeat,
> Mmm Mmm Mmm Mmm,
> Feel, Thy power divine Whooaa!

"Touch Me, Lord Jesus" was issued in the spring of 1949 on a 78-rpm disk with a darkish maroon label, silver print, and the squared letters G-O-T-H-A-M standing tall against a skyline that looked more New York City than Philadelphia, a holdover from the Sam Goody days. Along with "The Angelic Gospel Singers," each member was credited by name, but no mention of song authorship or publishing.

Margaret Allison remembers how quickly "Touch Me" caught on. "There was a deejay in Philadelphia—I can't remember his name—he played that song every night." His name was Ramon Bruce, at the time the only gospel radio show host in Philadelphia, broadcasting Tuesday through Sunday over WHAT, 1340 on the dial. Allison remembers being in the Gotham offices one day when a phone call came in from the West Coast. "We had been talking when Mr. Ballen got all excited talking to this deejay on the phone."

> And Mr. Ballen said, "What do you mean am I trying to pave the streets of California with 'Touch Me!'" The deejay was telling him that's all you hear. They just playing it, playing it, playing it. And Mr. Ballen at his place couldn't press the records fast enough, so he had to get another company to help press the record because the sales were going so fast.
>
> It changed our lives because people started calling. At that time, we didn't have a manager or anything. What they did was, Gotham, Mr. Ballen, he started booking us. And he had two guys, Harry and Lou. They were white. Harry would go on the road ahead of us and book the program. And the other young fellow, Lou, he would send along with us to take care of the door and see that we got paid.
>
> We would travel by car, head out of Philly on our way going South. We would have three or four uniforms and we took them along. We'd do Baltimore or D.C., maybe North Carolina on down to South Carolina, Georgia, Alabama, and then we just made jumps. Wichita, Kansas. Never did go to California, though. Most of the work was in the South.

Gotham 605 would be the first of a dozen releases by the Angelics over the course of 1949 and into 1950. As their popularity grew, Ivin Ballen encouraged them to embellish their instrumental mix. "In the beginning when I first started," says Allison, "we didn't have anything but the piano, but Mr. Ballen wanted to add on organ." Margaret Allison acquiesced. "I felt like he was the man spending the money, and if it didn't sound right, he was going to be the one who would pay the price. And the young man who played organ at that time was a jazz pianist and he was learning how to play the organ. He was learning on us. His name was Doc Bagby." Bagby had been active as an orchestra leader in Philly and the Northeast since war's end and would be an A&R man, producer, and session musician at Gotham for years to come.

"They were all friendly guys. . . . We did well together."

The success of the Angelics brought standing to Gotham and increased the odds that disk jockeys would pay attention to and play subsequent releases on the label. The Angelics hit in the spring of 1949, and by that summer, two Hummingbirds disks—Gotham 614, "Lord Come See about Me" b/w "I'll Be Satisfied," and 628, "Move On Up a Little Higher" b/w "We Shall Walk Through the Valley"—were on the market.

At this point in their career, the Hummingbirds were consummate professionals, their recordings of consistently high caliber and often masterwork in quality. Ira Tucker, now twenty-four years old and clearly the shining light, sang lead on all four tracks. James Davis, Beachey Thompson, and William Bobo had also progressed as a backing unit, turning in tightly knit harmonies that were intricate, distinctive, and unconventional compared to those of the mainstream pop vocal groups of the day. The Hummingbirds were creating complex vocal rhythms, unusual chords, and arrangements that followed their own rules. They were inventing as they went along.

"I'll Be Satisfied" was sweet and crisp in the up-tempo jubilee style of the Golden Gates, light handclaps marking the beat. Tucker sang on the mellow side, Bobo lacing in and out behind him as needed.

"Come See about Me" rode on a repeated pulsing phrase, "See about me . . . See about me . . . C'mon see about me." Tucker soared over top in a sharp timbre, stretching words, playing with sound, sometimes squeezing in ten notes to a syllable. Just as the arrangement set in, the Birds broke from it, moving into an offbeat interlude before returning seamlessly to the original rhythm pattern. Bobo's close was memorable, like nothing heard on record before. He sings, "Lord, come see about . . . ," stops dead without completing the phrase, pulls in a long audible breath, and reaches down to the lowest part of his voice, plunging into the final word "Me-e-e-e-e," savoring it in an astonishingly profound register. Tucker comes in behind him, gently resolving the piece in a shimmering falsetto glissando.

"We Shall Walk Through the Valley" was the Hummingbirds' take on a composition that Thomas Dorsey based on a traditional spiritual. Sam Cooke and the Soul Stirrers would record the song in 1951 as "Peace in the Valley," and Elvis Presley would record it as pop fare in the middle 1950s. The 1949 version by the Dixie Hummingbirds was performed in a reverent style closer to the intentions of composer Thomas Dorsey.

There will be peace in the valley for me someday,
There will be peace in the valley for me I pray,
No more sadness, no sorrow, no trouble I'll see,
There will be peace in the valley for me.

Of the four Gotham tracks released by the Hummingbirds, the earth shaker was W. Herbert Brewster's "Move On Up a Little Higher," a hit a few years earlier in 1947 for Mahalia Jackson on Apollo. The Birds, of course, changed it all around in their version. "'Move On Up' was a song we heard Mahalia do," recalls James Davis, "but that we rearranged in the studio. We were doing it the way Mr. Ballen thought it would sound the best, singing it a little higher than we usually pitched a song."

The performance was a tour de force, a foretaste of the fiery side that would become a hallmark of Dixie Hummingbirds presentations in years to come. In fact, compared to the serenity of their other Gotham releases, on this track, the Birds sounded almost like another group. In these years, singers like Claude Jeter, Archie Brownlee, and June Cheeks were beginning to emerge, transforming gospel style with the pyrotechnics of their lead vocals. The Hummingbirds had to stay competitive, and with "Move On Up," Ira Tucker showed that he could burn with the best.

The arrangement begins with a call and response between Tucker and the group. He sings each line with forceful deliberation, pushing his voice to its upper limits, crying and wailing as he goes, the group witnessing in close harmony.

TUCKER: Just as soon as my feet strike Zion,
GROUP: Ye-e-a-a-a-h
TUCKER: I'm gonna lay down my heavy burden,
GROUP: Oo-o-o-o-o-h
TUCKER: Try on my robe in glory,
GROUP: Ye-e-a-a-a-h
TUCKER: And I'm gonna Shout Shout Shout Shout
GROUP: Shout Shout Shout Shout
TUCKER: Shout and tell the story.

The background voices enter on a recurring phrase—"Gonna moo-hoo-oove. Gonna moo-hoo-oove"—kicking the song into gear. With the rhythm established, Tucker begins his vocal dance, singing his lead lines in contra-time to the beat of the harmony backdrop. He is masterful in his vocals, employing all the devices—growls, moans, inflections, melismas, impeccable timing—that would become the trademarks of his lead style.

> Then I'm gonna move on up a little higher,
>   Gonna moo-hoo-oove Gonna moo-hoo-oove
> Gonna meet with Old man Daniel,
>   Gonna moo-hoo-oove Gonna moo-hoo-ove
> Gonna move on up a little higher,
>   Gonna moo-hoo-oove Gonna moo-hoo-oove
> Gonna meet the with Hebrew children,
>   Gonna moo-hoo-oove Gonna moo-hoo-oove
> Gonna move on up a little higher,
>   Gonna moo-hoo-oove Gonna moo-hoo-oove
> Gonna meet Paul and Silas,
>   Gonna moo-hoo-oove Gonna moo-hoo-oove
> Then, I'm gonna live on up in glory.

On the second verse the tempo picks up. Tucker raps out the lyric, each word perfectly placed within the rhythm. The group comes together sweetly on the final line, "I'm gonna live up in glory after while."

Though the Dixie Hummingbirds debuted strongly on Gotham, neither record was a million-seller but both did sell steadily and fueled demand for personal appearances, encouraging Ballen to arrange further sessions with the Hummingbirds in months to come. Through-out 1949 and into 1950, the Birds toured extensively in support of their Gotham releases. They also undertook a novel collaboration that ulti-mately linked them in gospel history with Margaret Allison and the Angelic Gospel Singers.

The Hummingbirds had an established and sizable fan base but had never scored a megahit as had the Angelics. In the wake of their hit, the Angelics had accrued within a matter of months more national fame than the Hummingbirds in more than a decade of recording and relent-less touring. On the other hand, however, the Birds were far more roadwise than the Angelics and masters of live performance. Both groups stood to gain from a limited musical partnership. The rather daring idea to team up originated with Otis Jackson.

"When I started my group in 1944," recalls Allison, "I really didn't know the Dixie Hummingbirds. I had never met them, but I had heard all about them. They had a good reputation around town. Then, Otis Jackson was talking to me one day, asking me about doing some work with the Dixie Hummingbirds. And I thought they probably wouldn't want to record with us. So he said, 'No, I think it would go over great if you two groups would record.' During that time, no groups were working together like that. So I said, 'Well, if they are willing to try, I'll be willing to try.'"[33]

In late 1950, early 1951, Gotham Records released six sides that paired the Dixie Hummingbirds with the Angelic Gospel Singers. Not only a radical musical departure for each group, this combination of a male harmony quartet with a piano-based female ensemble had rarely, if ever, been done before on record.

In choosing what to record and developing arrangements, the Angelics, according to Allison, deferred to the Hummingbirds. "James Davis and the Hummingbirds," says Allison, "they seemed to have all the say so of everything, so we just left it up to them. In the studio, whatever they wanted to record. They chose the material." Tucker was in charge of arrangements. "Whatever Tucker wanted us to do," she says, "we would do it." Nonetheless, the working relationship between the two groups remained upbeat and affable. "They were all friendly guys. Davis was the most reserved. Tucker and Beachey were the clowns. They were always kidding and carrying on. Bobo was also a real gone guy. We did well together."[34]

The melding of the two groups required both the Hummingbirds and the Angelics to break from their usual way of vocalizing. There would be more trading off on leads, less reliance on precision harmony back-drops, and with all those voices, not everyone singing at the same time. In addition, the Birds had to accommodate instrumental accompaniment as during their days at Café Society with Lester Young's band and their recordings for Regis/Manor with Sister Ernestine Washington. The Gotham tracks would make use of Margaret Allison on piano, Doc Bagby on organ, and a session drummer as well.

In that interval between 1949 and the first years of the 1950s, a cappella was still the reigning fashion, at least for male quartets, but tastes were clearly changing. During their stay at Gotham, the Hummingbirds experimented with instrumentation. James Davis, ever the conservative in matters of presentation, had no objections to the instrumentation. The Hummingbirds noticed how audiences were responding, whose records were selling and getting radio play, and how younger people seemed to be looking for more spiritual wallop than a cappella seemed capable of delivering. "It was new for us, but we could do about anything. My only concern was, I just didn't want things overdone." Davis worried that Tucker, singing over instruments, might have to sing even louder and might burn out his voice. Screaming and shouting had already taken a toll on many lead singers.

To ease the strain on Tucker, Davis decided to try out a second lead. He invited Ernest James, a veteran of the Philadelphia gospel scene, to join the lineup. James had never recorded before, but he was a compelling singer, and his job was to work over the crowd until Tucker came in for the final knockout.

Ernest James had his first taste of the studio with the Hummingbirds/Angelics collaborations, taking occasional lead on a couple of numbers. He also split the lead with Tucker on "What Then," one of the tracks the Birds cut on their own for Gotham. James, however, stayed only a short time with the Hummingbirds. "About six months or so," says Tucker. "He didn't sing with us but a little while. But he could sing real high–and naturally, not false."

"He really was a nice fellow," says Davis with genuine affection, "but he wasn't used to singing as low as we sing."

> Most everything we sang was too low for him to lead. Tucker, now, could sing real high *and* real low. And so many of our songs, well, we were just singing out of this boy's range. Tuck would build something up and he would tear it down trying to sing as low as we sung. If you pitch him up high enough, he could squeal up a blue streak! But you'd have to kill a tenor singer. Ernest James was a good singer in his range, but we had to let him go.

"He went to the Nightingales," says Tucker. "He did better with the 'Gales than he did with us."[35]

The 1950 Hummingbirds/Angelics sessions yielded inspired performances by both groups. In his arrangements, Tucker managed to combine the jubilant freedom of a rocking country church service with the complexity of a seasoned urban gospel choir.

Almost all the selections were public domain, "old church songs," says Margaret Allison. Among the selections, "In the Morning," "I'm on My Way to Heaven Anyhow," "Glory, Glory, Hallelujah," and "Standing Out on the Highway," the latter a classic from Silas Steele and the Famous Blue Jay Singers. The most successful sides to come out of those sessions, however, were Thomas Dorsey's "Dear Lord, Look Down upon Me," and one of Ira Tucker's early originals, "Jesus Will Answer Prayer."

"Dear Lord, Look Down upon Me," like the others, was skillfully arranged to take full advantage of the talent gathered in the studio. Doc Bagby opens with an organ arpeggio. The Angelics begin chanting "Look Down upon Me Lord." The organ establishes the beat, and both groups enter on a harmony backdrop. What at first sounds like a string bass turns out to be William Bobo pumping out single notes in tandem with the foot drum. Tucker comes in mellow voiced, jumping occasionally on key phrase endings into a high tenor trill.

> In my heart, sometimes I ponder,
> Going down life's road I wonder,
> To a city over yonder,
> Where there is peace, peace and joy I'm told,
> Where my loved ones are gone forever,
> Where no tears will find me, never,
> We'll have peace and joy and love that will be,
> When I reach the other side.

The mood is peaceful, the lyrics conjuring up a reassuring vision of heaven. The Hummingbirds are "ooh-ing" and "aah-ing," and then quite unexpectedly, the Angelics break in on an urgent march-time phrase, "Mer-cy Lord—Mer-cy Lord—Mer-cy Lord."

For a few measures, the intensity builds, and then the female voices drop out as quickly as they entered, Tucker resuming his calming lead. Throughout, the arrangement plays on contrasts—male/female, fast/slow, long/short, mellow/sharp. The song finally closes on a retard with Allison singing, "And . . . take . . . me . . . safely . . . home," the ensemble echoing in close harmony.

The other breakout track, "Jesus Will Answer Prayer," was one of Ira Tucker's first songwriting credits. The message was a straightforward testimony on Christian ideals as well as a paean to the power of prayer. Margaret Allison sang the lead.

She sets the tone with a piano introduction, drums and organ coming in behind her a measure or two later. The Birds hum in the background as Allison and the Angelics alternate on the lead lines.

> ALLISON: Oh, blessed is he that loves the Lord,
> ANGELICS: Blessed is he that harkens to his word,
> ALLISON: Well, my Savior is your Savior,

ANGELICS: And on Him you can depend,
ALLISON: Blessed is he that gives to the poor,
ANGELICS: Trust in Jesus and He'll restore,
ALLISON: When your burdens get hard to bear,
ANGELICS: Jesus will answer prayer!

Tucker's words had the ring of biblical verse and spoke in simple comforting terms to African Americans acutely mindful of the double standards of the day—prosperity, but less so for African Americans; opportunity, but limited for African Americans; tranquility, but threats and violence for African Americans; justice, but inequitable for African Americans.

In the best tradition of gospel, Tucker's song was medicine for the mind. The record sold well because it offered an appealing message within a compelling package of sound.

ALLISON: Yes, I know that bright day is nigh,
ANGELICS: When I'll walk through that truly heav'nly door,
ALLISON: I'll talk with my dear Savior,
ANGELICS: In my home up above,
ALLISON: He'll be my shelter in that black storm,
ANGELICS: Ever present when things go wrong,
ALLISON: If you take Him for your own,
ANGELICS: Jesus will answer prayer,
Yes, Jesus will answer prayer.

Sales of "Jesus Will Answer Prayer" were sufficient to persuade Ivin Ballen to release it in sheet music form. Dated 1950, the 7 x 10 four-page foldout pictured both groups in separate photos on the cover. "Featured and Sung by the Angelic Gospel Singers and the Dixie Humming Birds [*sic*]. Words and Music by Ira Tucker. Price 15¢. For Quartets, Choirs, and Choruses. Recorded on GOTHAM Record 663." At the bottom of the cover, a logo in the form of a "shadow-box" cross, lines radiating out like rays from the sun. "Andrea Music Company, 1626 Federal Street, Philadelphia 46, PA."

"We had a hot number and people just went for it."

The Hummingbirds/Angelics sides sold well, collectively in the multi-thousands, as did four other records released in the Gotham 600 series by the Birds under their own name during the same period. The solo

Birds tracks included reworked spirituals, covers of songs made popular by other groups, and originals. The Birds also continued to experiment with instrumentation, working on many of their solo tracks with the organist and drummer who had backed them on their Angelics collaborations.

Gotham 632 paired "Search Me Lord," a cover of Brother Joe May's 1949 Specialty debut, with "Two Little Fishes and Five Loaves of Bread," the Birds' version of Sister Rosetta Tharpe's popular 1944 novelty about Jesus feeding a multitude on a miniscule amount of fish and bread. In place of Tharpe's driving guitar, the Birds used a theater-sounding organ. Tucker made a few word changes and by then had absorbed Tharpe's rapid-fire singing style into his own. "Tucker's my baby," Sister Rosetta liked to say. "He sing just like me."[36]

> A crowd of people went into the desert,
> To listen to what the good Lord said,
> All day long they heard the good Lord's word,
> But they got hungry and had to be fed,
> On only two little fishes and five loaves of bread.
>
> They broke the bread up, and also the fishes,
> And each of them had to scratch their heads,
> Yes, it was true, and everybody knew,
> There was a big crowd that had to be fed,
> With only two little fishes and five loaves of bread.
>
> Jesus said, "Just pass me the fishes.
> "No, pass me the bread instead.
> "Pass it all by and let me try,
> A little idea I have in my head.
> About them two little fishes and five loaves of bread."
>
> They blessed the fishes, they blessed the bread,
> And began to pass it around,
> The more they passed around, the more they found,
> Lots left over when all had been fed,
> With those two little fishes and five loaves of bread.

Gotham 641 was "I Must Have Jesus," a traditional song led by Tucker, and "Is There Anyone in Heaven That You Know," an original learned by Beachey Thompson during a previous quartet affiliation.

With an organ backdrop and support from William Bobo, this was one of the few sides featuring Thompson on lead.

Tucker credits "You've Got to Live So God Can Use You" and "Beaming from Heaven," Gotham 686, to two of his favorite groups. "You've Got to Live," recorded by the Birds with light drums underscoring the tempo, was taken from the singing of his early idol, Norman "Crip" Harris of the Norfolk Jubilees. "Beaming from Heaven" came from Thurman Ruth and the Selah Jubilee Singers. The performance was serene and elegant, sung a cappella in striking parallel harmony with jazzy chord changes.

Finally, two more a cappella performances released as Gotham 697. "What Then" featured Ernest James and Ira Tucker splitting the lead. "Down On Me" was a somber performance brought in and led by James Davis. The highlight was William Bobo singing his answering line at the end of each verse, "Lordy, Lordy, it seems like everybody in the whole wide world is down on me."

The Birds recorded other tracks at those sessions that were not released at the time. "Cool Down Yonder" was their take on a tune recorded by Norman Harris with backing by the Selahs. They also recorded the classic spiritual, "Get Away Jordan"; another Davis original, "Young Man"; and "Born to Die," the Birds' spin on "Lord, Am I Born to Die?" recorded in 1938 by the Golden Gates.

The Hummingbirds' Gotham sides were issued as ten-inch 78-rpm shellac disks. Later, they would be reissued as vinyl 45-rpms with a "7" added as a prefix to the serial number. Retail price, 79¢.[37] In that way, Gotham, like most independent labels at the time, was able to further capitalize on bought-and-paid-for masters already in their back catalogs.

Record sales, of course, piqued demand for personal appearances. In 1950, the Dixie Hummingbirds had a national constituency but were still best known in the Northeast and along the southeastern coast. The Angelics, on the other hand, riding the crest of their hit record, had overtaken the Birds in popularity. On the basis of "Touch Me, Lord Jesus," calls for the Angelics had been coming in from across the country. Now, with the flurry of new Dixie Hummingbirds releases and the tracks pairing the two groups, requests for appearances by both began pouring in. "After we started recording together," says Margaret Allison, "we had to make tours together because the people were demanding it!"

The first time the Birds and Angelics performed together in Philadelphia was in early December 1950 at Turner's Hall. The event, sponsored by Paul Owens' group, the National Bay State Gospel Singers, "artists of W-H-A-T," was billed as a "welcoming recital for the famous Dixie Hummingbirds and the Angelic Gospel Singers." The two groups had returned home in triumph.[38]

As to the road trips, Horace Boyer, noted gospel performer and historian, remembers seeing the Angelics first alone and then during their touring heyday with the Dixie Hummingbirds. The year was 1948. "The Angelic Gospel Singers were in Orlando, Florida."

Now, they didn't have a recording contract in 1948, but they were doing the circuit through churches. They stayed with Sister Willie Mae Pope. She was a friend of ours. The Boyer Brothers [Horace and James] were just beginning to sing and at that time, we had never heard anybody who could eat that piano up like Margaret Allison! We went to that concert that night, the first time we saw the Angelics.

The next time was about two years later and with them, the Dixie Hummingbirds.

Well, the next thing we know, the Angelics have a record contract, and then they come through with the Dixie Hummingbirds. Oh, my lord! What excitement. It was still a quartet world back in those days, but "Touch Me, Lord Jesus," of course, was extremely popular. The Angelics sang first, then the Dixie Hummingbirds. And, oh, when they got together! It was unbelievable. I mean, we had just never seen anything like it. It was one of the most successful ventures I'd ever heard.[39]

"At that time," says Margaret Allison, "there were certain places where the Dixie Hummingbirds had been and done well, but there were a lot of places they had never been. Until they started working with us, a lot of people didn't know them."[40]

The tours could be grueling. "We'd be out there maybe two or three weeks doing one-nighters wherever the promoters had us," says Allison. The two groups traveled each in their own automobile. "When we got to town, we'd stay in different homes. Someone would say, 'I'll take the girls at my house,' and the Birds would stay at other homes."

The shows typically opened with about thirty to forty-five minutes of local talent followed by an intermission, during which an offering would be taken up. Then the Angelics would come on and perform about five or six songs.

We would sing our songs about as long as the record, two or three minutes, because that's the way people wanted to hear them. Then the Dixie Hummingbirds would come out and do some of their songs.

The last part of the program would feature both groups together. We would come back up and sing two or three more songs as a grand finale. Something like "When the Dark Clouds Roll Away" or "Glory Glory Hallelujah, Since I Laid My Burden Down."[41]

Horace Boyer is ecstatic remembering the Angelics and Birds on stage together. "They were at Jones High School, the largest venue for black performers in Orlando during that time. It was on a Sunday afternoon and the place was absolutely packed. Margaret Allison and Ira Tucker would alternate on things and, oh, it was just gorgeous!"

Boyer remembers the Angelics' hair attachments, "just enough to enhance their beauty." The style of hair stacked up high had been popularized by the Famous Ward Singers. "And, of course," says Boyer, "there were the uniforms! Both groups. But then the Birds, they *always* liked to dress. It was very exciting. The people just went crazy over it!"[42]

The Birds and Angelics were a powerful double attraction, but their teaming did not preclude either group touring alone. In fact, the Birds continued to tour on their own throughout the East and South during this same period. In effect, they were on the road most of every month, literally more than three hundred days out of the year. When they did appear with the Angelics, the shows were usually block-booked, a short run of one-nighters set up at reasonably distanced venues.

Although touring was as arduous as it had been earlier in their career, traveling was a welcome reminder that they were a respected and vital part of a community. The hospitality, the reunions, the admiring fans, the audiences moved to spiritual bliss constantly buoyed them. The Dixie Hummingbirds were becoming stars and Ira Tucker a celebrity in his own right. They felt blessed with the knowledge that they were making people feel good.

Their new renown made travel easier. Some small-town sheriff might still pull them over or, as had happened, even jail them, but someone was more likely to come forward, black or white, and say, "Hey, that's the Dixie Hummingbirds!"

Camaraderie with other performers also sweetened the journeys. Ira Tucker still remembers the night in Norfolk, Virginia, when the Dixie Hummingbirds stayed in the same "colored" hotel with Big Joe Turner, Ray Charles, Teddy Wilson, Duke Ellington, and Louis Armstrong. "We *all* was in Norfolk at the same hotel," says Tucker. "That was back when you couldn't stay in white hotels. I remember most talking to Louis." Tucker admired Armstrong for his "rags to riches" climb to success. "He had to walk out of New Orleans, but he came back a millionaire."

> I talked with Louis seven hours that night. We talked all night and he missed the bus. So he said, "What the heck." Got him a cab from Norfolk to Reading, Pennsylvania.
>
> Me and Duke had breakfast together. I was down there. Duke come in and saw me. I had two spot fish. Old man Mack [the hotel proprietor] had gone fishing that morning. I had those nice spots and some grits. And Duke said, "I want what this M.F.'er got!" [Tucker laughs] That's the day that I met him. And he told me, "Man, I've been listening to you guys." He said, "I've been stealing from some of you all's stuff." He told me! And after that, he said, "Hey, do you all know who this is? This is Ira Tucker of the Dixie Hummingbirds!"

In the early 1950s, this mix of black entertainment was common on the road—Armstrong and Ellington of the old school, Big Joe Turner and Ray Charles on the ascendance, the Dixie Hummingbirds themselves now celebrated within the African American community and among those open-minded enough to appreciate their music purely for its brilliance.

"We just thought that Okeh could do more for us."

The early 1950s were exciting times for gospel and for African American musical performers of all kinds. Record sales were healthy. Radio stations were spreading the music beyond color lines. Artists like Nat Cole, Louis Armstrong, Ella Fitzgerald, Lionel Hampton, and Louis Jordan were enjoying crossover appeal like never before. At the same time, African Americans were gaining power as consumers of entertainment.

In 1951, black Philadelphians ushered in the gospel season with a New Year's Day extravaganza at Turner's Hall. Headlining was Elder Charles Beck, "Gotham and King Recording Artist," hailed in the papers as "The Trumpet King of the Religious World." "Blow-Gabriel-Blow" read the ad banner, and beneath it, a picture of Elder Beck, trumpet raised heavenward. "The world's greatest faith man according to testimonies heard over his broadcast from Buffalo. His prayers have helped thousands in financial distress. Also the sick with long standing illness."

Earlier that day, Elder Beck would be heard in a live broadcast over Philadelphia's then-premier gospel station, WHAT, a teaser for the evening's program.[43]

Later that fall, two other Gotham acts, the Davis Sisters and the Harmonizing Four, headlined a "charity gospel festival" at the Met. Sponsored by the *Philadelphia Tribune*, now positioned as the primary voice of Philadelphia's African American community, the paper ran a series of pre-concert promotional articles. Calling the event "the musical highlight of the fall season," the *Tribune* predicted, "the program will be unequaled in the city's history, both from the viewpoint of sheer size and talent."

The articles published in the *Tribune* about the two groups offer insight into gospel promotion and the healthy state of the industry at the time. About the Davis Sisters, wrote the *Tribune*, "In their five years as professionals," they have "established themselves as one of the leading groups in the country," and have "toured 20 states." On the program they would perform "record favorites," like "Footprints of Jesus," "It's Real," and "Walk in the Sunlight of the Lord." About themselves, said the Sisters, "We have never been interested in the money or mercenary angle of gospel singing. We sing because we get joy in singing. That is why we have not gone in for professional promoters. We always sing through churches or through groups like the [*Tribune*] Charities. We believe that our singing brings folks closer to God," Miss Thelma Davis explained.[44]

In a later article, the Harmonizing Four were portrayed as revered stalwarts in the field. They would perform "classics, folk songs, gospel songs, and spirituals," and had "appeared in 46 states of the Union as well as Canada and Mexico." And, attesting to their draw, "at what is believed to have been the largest Gospel festival audience anywhere, the Harmonizing Four sang before 25,000 in Griffith Stadium in Washington, D.C."[45] The Four, noted the *Tribune*, were heard regularly over WRNL, Richmond, Virginia, their home base, and speaking to "their popularity in Philadelphia," they sell "more records here than anywhere else in the United States."[46]

That summer of 1951, the Harmonizing Four would once again appear at Griffith Stadium in Washington, D.C., this time as part of an unprecedented gospel event—the wedding of Sister Rosetta Tharpe to Russell Morrison, an executive at the famous Savoy Ballroom in New York City. That such an event could occur and draw multithousands was a testament to the popularity of black gospel and its brightest stars at that time. The entire program, including wedding ceremony and musical performances, was recorded and released by Decca Records.[47]

Gospel was at the moment perhaps the only genre of African American music that could fill stadiums with black audiences, but black secular music now had the capability of pulling similarly sized audiences across color lines. The "Biggest Show of 1951," for example, was an assemblage of superlative "Negro talent" designed specifically to appeal to multiracial audiences. The revue included Nat "King" Cole, Duke Ellington, and Sarah Vaughan with comedian Dusty Fletcher, dancer Peg Leg Bates, chorus girls, dancers, and a host of other lesser-known acts. The tour started out in September at the Boston Arena and, after a short run, moved on, first to Philadelphia, then Pittsburgh and cities further west.

The nation's African American community looked upon shows of this sort with pride. Performers were presented with dignity and were well paid. Yet racist programming also proliferated, such as Blatz Beer's 1951 television version of *Amos 'n' Andy* featuring African American actors. The NAACP immediately responded in protest, launching a campaign to shut down the broadcasts. As one protester wrote to the show's sponsor, "We are in full sympathy with the NAACP, which condemns presentation of such radio and television programs as . . . cater to prejudices and tend to ridicule 15 million Negro Americans, and obviously perpetuate racial misunderstandings and race conflicts."[48] In spite of protests, *Amos 'n' Andy* remained on television for a dozen years.

In the early 1950s, African American artists had the best opportunity to perform with dignity in the music industry, particularly through radio, as the medium was well suited to targeting specialized audiences—like those who enjoyed jazz, rhythm and blues, and gospel.

Billboard ran an article in 1951 saluting station WERD in Atlanta, Georgia, on the occasion of its anniversary as the nation's first "Negro-owned" radio station. The article noted, "According to music distributors, retail houses, and those generally connected with the trade, station WERD has done more for the increasing sales of 'Negro artists' recordings' in the Greater Atlanta area than any other factor."

In addition, Atlanta "coin machine [jukebox] operators," reported *Billboard*, "noticed an increase in the playing of blues and spiritual records in their boxes, and are attributing this increase to the constant playing of these tunes on the station." The year was also notable, reported *Billboard*, for an "upsurge in . . . radio stations airing programs for Negro listeners" and the hiring of "added Negro personnel."[49]

The strength of the African American record-buying market and radio play plus an expanded, multiracial fan base helped to make African American musical styles more commercially viable in the early 1950s than ever before. As a result, old-line major record labels were taking a second look.

In 1951, Columbia Records revived their Okeh imprint, a subsidiary that had been dormant for a number of years. Okeh, first established in 1918 as an American offshoot of a Franco-European recording corporation, had made history in 1920 with Mamie Smith's "You Can't Keep a Good Man Down" b/w "That Thing Called Love," the first blues recording by an African American artist. Columbia Records acquired the Okeh imprint in 1926 and maintained the label's continuity through the middle 1930s.[50] But the imprint was used inconsistently and ground to a halt during the war years–until the rekindling of interest in 1951.

"Columbia Revives Okeh Label for Renowned R&B Push," read the *Billboard* headline in May of that year. "The move, which is viewed as a heavy bid by the major firm to grab a heftier share of the rhythm and blues market, will designate Okeh as an exclusively rhythm and blues disk tag.... The reasoning behind the activation ... is that the label change would give Columbia a fresh start in a field which is dominated by independent companies."

Picked to head the new subsidiary, Danny Kessler, in charge of Columbia's fledgling R&B department at the time, would ultimately record gospel as well as R&B sides. "Kessler has been on an intensive talent drive for the past two months and has rounded up quite an extensive stable to complement those artists who already were pacted to Columbia."[51]

The new Okeh imprint signed the Ravens, Red Saunders, the Treniers, Maurice King and the Wolverines, and the Big Three Trio with Willie Dixon. Rhythm and blues historian Arnold Shaw talked to Danny Kessler about his role in reviving the Okeh label. Kessler had been headquartered in Philadelphia working in promotions. At that time, said Kessler, "Philadelphia was what was known as a breakout market." If the local deejays could break a record in Philly, "then you could spread it to other big record cities like Detroit, Chicago, etc."

> I had always a great feeling for black records. I promoted the few black artists who were on the Columbia label. When Columbia decided to reactivate Okeh Records as a black label ... it was a super thrill, particularly when I was given the green light to go out and sign new black artists.

At that time we began to cover stations that Columbia Records had never heard of in the South as well as in the North—you know, stations at the top of the dial. Like WHAT in Philadelphia, basically a gospel station that devoted two hours a day to R&B records.[52]

Kessler's gospel signings included the R. S. B. Gospel Singers, Brother Rodney, the Bailey Gospel Singers—and most important, the Dixie Hummingbirds. With their high profile in Philadelphia and their successes on the Gotham label, the Dixie Hummingbirds were well known to Kessler. In late 1951, he pursued the Birds and contracted them for one Okeh release on their own and another in a reprise of their collaboration with the Angelic Gospel Singers. "Okeh Records' . . . boss Danny Kessler," reported *Billboard*, "inked a pair of top spiritual groups, the Angelic Singers and the Dixie Humming Birds, to Okeh papers. He went whole hog with these groups."[53] Session logs indicate that the recording sessions took place on December 27 in New York City,[54] with an anticipated mid-February 1952 release date.

The Dixie Hummingbirds had done well with Gotham, but Okeh had ties to the far-reaching promotion and distribution machinery of Columbia Records and the prestige of the association. "We just thought that Okeh could do more for us," says James Davis. A handful of other gospel quartets—the Golden Gates, the Deep River Boys, and the Charioteers, among others—had broken through to the mass market on the strength of major label affiliations. These groups were nationally syndicated on radio and recorded with the most popular singing stars of the day—Bing Crosby, Frank Sinatra. The Dixie Hummingbirds, as long as their style was not compromised, were hoping for the same mainstream success. They felt justified in switching their allegiances because at the time, they had gone as far as they could go with Gotham, and Ivin Ballen had already begun the move away from recording to the manufacturing side of the business. Not since they had recorded for Decca had the Birds been signed to a major label, and now they would once again have that opportunity.

The sessions took place in a state-of-the-art New York City studio, technically more advanced, recalls Tucker, than any the Hummingbirds had ever worked in before. They recorded in late December and the releases were announced in the March issue of *Billboard*. The two sides by the Hummingbirds alone were "I'll Never Forget" b/w "I'll Live Again" [Okeh 6864], and the two with the Angelics, "Today" b/w "One Day" [Okeh 6858].

The Dixie Hummingbirds recorded as a quintet with, for the first time, Paul Owens who had quit the Sensational Nightingales. The Birds had been trying Ernest James in the fifth spot, but when he did not work out, Davis offered Owens the position. He brought considerable studio experience to the Birds' Okeh sessions. Owens had recorded in 1949 with the Nightingales for the Coleman label and later for King. In January 1951, Marie Knight invited the 'Gales with Owens to back her on tracks she cut for the Decca label,[55] and a month later, the 'Gales would record for Decca on their own.

Owens, with his Carolina roots and Philadelphia upbringing, felt at home with the Birds. Born on July 27, 1924, in Greensboro, North Carolina, his first experiences as a gospel singer were in Philadelphia churches. Owens was thirteen when he first sang publicly at the Mt. Carmel Baptist Church in Philadelphia. "That's where I started, in the junior choir, and then I moved on up, got baptized, and that's still my home church." In the mid-1940s, Owens, in his early twenties, sang with the Bay State Gospel Singers on WHAT's Sunday morning gospel broadcast. "The station," says Owens, "would also bring in every out-of-town group that was going to appear in Philadelphia to broadcast on those Sunday mornings."

One particular morning, the Evangelist Singers were in the studio visiting from Detroit and waiting to go on the air.[56] Paul Owens remembers their lineup as Oliver Green, LeRoy Baines, LeRoy Lewis, and "a fellow called Big Jesse." The studio was crowded and the Bay States were performing their segment.

> And the Evangelists, they was standing back there listening to us singing. We got through, and then *we* was listening to them. When *they* got through, Oliver Green—he was the Evangelists' manager—came up to me and said, "We need another lead singer. We listened to you and you got a pretty good voice. Think you'd like to travel?"
>
> I jumped at the chance. That was on a Sunday and I left with them on Monday.

Owens, anxious to perform for fresh audiences, took to the road, but his association with the Evangelists did not last. "There were just some things that went on in the group," says Owens. "Personalities, so to speak. . . . Things just didn't turn out like I thought they would."

Owens returned to Philadelphia in 1949 and began working outside gospel. "At that time, I was fooling around playing piano, singing a

The Swan Silvertones in the 1950s. Paul Owens is in the upper right;
Claude Jeter is front center

little blues. I had a group, a bass player, a sax man, and a drummer. We were doing Friday and Saturday nights at a nightclub on 42nd and Lancaster."

> Around that time, a friend of mine came and told me Howard Carroll [of the Sensational Nightingales] was looking for me. I knew Howard because me and him had done some gigs together. Howard came to me, told me, "Man, we want you to come with us in the group!"

That invitation was Paul Owens's entrée into the Nightingales. With the involvement of Barney Parks, their career progressed rapidly. Parks made the connection to Marie Knight that got the 'Gales into the Decca studios. The group recorded six sides for Decca at the Beltone Studios in New York City. June Cheeks led on "There's a Vacant Room in Heaven" [Decca 48238] and "Our Father" [Decca 48205]. He and Owens split the lead on "Live So God Can Use You" [Decca 48238]. Paul Owens would be the featured lead on the remaining three tracks, "My Rock" b/w "Guide My Mind" [Decca 48225], and "In a Land Where We Never Grow Old" [Decca 48205].

"I stayed with the Nightingales for quite a while," says Owens, "but then things started pulling apart. That's when the Birds got me. It was Beachey, Bobo, Davis, and Tuck. They had been on the road with the Angelics, and that's when I joined the Dixie Hummingbirds."

Owens was a forceful addition to the Birds' vocal arsenal. He could sing pop-ballad smooth, shout, or growl it out as needed. "What we called 'trickeration,'" Tucker once explained to Tony Heilbut. "Their kind of 'trickeration,'" wrote Heilbut, "meant note-bending of a dazzling complexity executed with a lyrical skill bordering on the erotic." As Tucker told him, "We knew the range of each other so good until I could always depend on him to pick a note up where I left off. A split second before I finished, he got it. We understood each other just that close."[57] The musical compatibility between Tucker and Owens was apparent from their initial teaming on the Okeh releases, and again on the sides the Birds cut with the Angelics.

Of the sides cut with the Angelics, Thomas Dorsey's "Today" was the more down tempo of the two. The lyric extolled the virtues of charity and giving. Margaret Allison began with a spoken word question. "Have I given ... anything ... today?" The song then gently unfolded, chiding as it went.

Have I helped some needy soul on the way,
From the dawn till setting sun,
Lord, have I wounded anyone,
And shall I weep for what I've done today?

At the second go-round, though, the song exploded into double time as Tucker ignited on the chorus.

TUCKER: Oh, Lord, today,
GROUP: Oh, today,
TUCKER: Oh, Lord, today,
GROUP: Oh, today,
TUCKER: Oh, have I helped some needy soul on the way,

He then passed the lead to Owens who picked up the cry:

Did I counsel with the sad,
Try to make some poor heart glad,
And share with them what I had today?

Tucker and Owens eventually took the song out in glory, working in tandem as Margaret Allison and the newest member of the Angelics, Bernice Cole, added their own flourishes along the way.

The rapport and split-second timing between Tucker and Owens was even more evident on "One Day." The song came to the group via Bernice Cole. "She had a group called the Four Believers," says Tucker.

Then, they added a fifth singer, Lenace Washington. She was Denzel Washington's mother. When they added Lenace, they called it the Four and One Believers.

Oh, they had harmonies out of sight!

Anyway, Lenace did that song "One Day" with the Believers. When the Believers broke up, we put Bernice Cole with the Angelics and she brought that song with her to the Okeh sessions.

The song "One Day" was an adaptation of a Thomas Dorsey song titled "Living, He Loved Me."

Living, He loved me, Dying, He saved me,
He carried my sins far away.

Rise and be justified, Free me forever,
One day He's coming, On that glorious day.

The performance by the Birds/Angelics rides along on Allison's rocking piano and the rousing exchange between male and female units, by then a hallmark of their collaborations. "One Day," however, transcends the ordinary when it closes with Tucker and Owens shifting into overdrive, pumping rapid-fire like alternating pistons on the single word, "one."

TUCKER: One!   One!   One!   One!   One!   One!

OWENS: One!   One!   One!   One!   One!

The device was startling, exhilarating, projecting all the energy of sanctified church. The technique would be heard in one form or another over the years as the younger generation of African American performers absorbed it into rhythm and blues and soul. The Isley Brothers rocked back and forth on the word "shout" in their 1959 R&B masterpiece of the same name. Sam Cooke and Lou Rawls traded "Yahs" in their 1962 classic, "Bring It On Home to Me." Sam & Dave tossed around "hold on" in their 1966 soul hit, "Hold On, I'm Comin.'" Tucker and Owens had burned their way to a definitive soul moment, showing the world what raw power could be captured in the groove of an ordinary 78-rpm phonograph record.

The duo continued their inspired interplay on the two Okeh sides released by the Hummingbirds alone. The improved sound quality is immediately noticeable as is a reverb uncharacteristic of previous Birds recordings. Also, on both tracks, the Birds revert back to their earlier unadorned a cappella style.

Tucker opens "I'll Live Again" with calm sweeping phrases, the group echoing him on each line. "I'm a servant . . . Of the King . . . Whoa, praising His . . . Oooh, Holy name . . . And if I live . . . This life and die . . . I'll live again . . ."

With the second verse, Tucker occasionally screams, singing full voiced. The tempo breaks into double time and Owens takes the pass, pressing forward in high voice, his singing rough edged. The Birds provide a backdrop of crisp clipped phrases as Tucker and Owens fall into their vocal dance, eventually taking the song out in classic slow-down mode adorned with jazzy-sounding chords.

The flip side, "I'll Never Forget," has all the qualities of a pleading ballad. Tucker in sotto voce, cries out the words: "I know the time . . . I know the place . . . Jesus saved me . . . By his grace . . . I'll never forget . . ." The group takes up a mantra-like repetition of the line "Brought Me Through" as Tucker lays out his message of praise and salvation, Owens deftly interlacing a subtle underscore. The performance closes down gently on Tucker's final line, "Oh, Lord, how he brought me through."

The four sides recorded for Okeh by the Hummingbirds, with Tucker and Owens bringing out the best in each other, were masterful and engaging. With the clout and prestige of a major label like Okeh, there seemed every chance that the Birds would finally be launched into the upper echelons of gospel show business. But the Okeh sides sold only moderately. "Okeh didn't even push it," says Tucker, who still bristles thinking of the missed opportunity. "Everything was changing back then. They was so deep into this rhythm and blues and stuff . . ." His voice trails off into silence.

Feeling that Okeh Records had let them down, by late winter 1952, the Dixie Hummingbirds were already looking for another record deal. Okeh had not promoted them heavily, but even more important, label execs had cast the Birds in the old a cappella mold, a sound that was rapidly losing favor with younger gospel fans. Instrumentation was taking over and new rhythms were finding their way into the music. The Hummingbirds were eager to move forward and advance their sound, ultimately pursuing that new sound with another label.

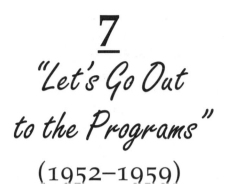

7
"Let's Go Out
to the Programs"
(1952–1959)

If you want to hear singing,
Good old gospel singing,
Go out to the programs,
Whenever they're in your town,

—"Let's Go Out to the Programs"
The Dixie Hummingbirds, 1953

The seven years between 1952 and 1959 were an extraordinarily rich period for the Dixie Hummingbirds and also for African American cultural history. African American artists of every kind continued to the forefront of popular entertainment, particularly in the field of music. Although rhythm and blues especially succeeded in the pop mainstream and influenced more popular genres such as rock 'n' roll, gospel remained primarily "insider" music, culture bound, and still celebrated mostly within the African American community.

For many white Americans, Elvis Presley served as a gateway to the world of black rhythm and blues. Presley's "Hound Dog" was originally released by "Big Mama" Willie Mae Thornton in 1953 on Don Robey's Texas-based Peacock label. Declared the "biggest tune of the year" by the National Rhythm and Blues Juke Box Jury,[1] Presley's 1956 version, though a far cry from the original, bore traces of the sound and style of music by black artists.

Black gospel occasionally did reach multiracial audiences via radio, records, television, and news stories, but throughout the 1950s, the stars of gospel were for the most part stars within the sphere of African American entertainment. In gospel music, "almost every song," observes pioneering soul singer Jerry Butler, "had some connection to the plight of African Americans in America."[2]

In 1954, the Supreme Court ruled segregation in public schools unconstitutional. In 1955, Emmett Till, a fourteen-year-old African American from Chicago, was lynched while visiting family in Mississippi, his mutilated body dumped in the Tallahatchie River. Governor Hugh White denied the incident had anything to do with the recent court-ordered desegregation of public schools. The perpetrators were acquitted.[3]

That year in Montgomery, Alabama, Rosa Parks was arrested for refusing to give up her seat to a white man on a city bus. The Reverend Martin Luther King, Jr., organized a boycott in her support, ending it only when the Supreme Court ruled the city ordinance unconstitutional. The boycott marked the beginning of organized civil rights activism and the emergence of Dr. King as an effective and inspiring leader.

A story in a 1955 issue of the *Philadelphia Tribune* trumpeted, "Fear of Ku Klux Klan spreading from South and on up to Philly."[4] Blues singer Big Bill Broonzy summed up African American sentiments in an early folk protest song. "If you're white, you're right, and if you're brown, stick around, but if you're black, O brother, get back, get back, get back."[5]

In the Deep South, white supremacists condemned rock 'n' roll as "vulgar and animalistic . . . nigger music."[6] In April 1956, pop crooner Nat "King" Cole was attacked on the stage of Birmingham's Municipal Auditorium by members of the North Alabama Citizens' Council. "Down the aisles, feet thumping the wooden floor, bounded five men," reported *Time* magazine. "They . . . crossed the ten feet between front row and stage and jumped the four-foot parapet. One swung on Cole and sent him reeling onto the piano bench, which split under him. . . . One attacker, twisting Cole's foot, was wrestled until he let go. . . . Cole limped off stage . . . 'Man, I love show business,' Cole later said to reporters, 'but I don't want to die for it.'"[7]

In the face of developments like these, black gospel offered an unwavering message of hope, fortitude, nonviolence, and faith in God. "The music gave us a spiritual lift," says the Reverend Gadson Graham, pastor of the Canaan Baptist Church in Paterson, New Jersey, and a longtime friend of the Dixie Hummingbirds. "When they sang their songs, the Birds just made us feel like we could deal more with what we had to deal with."[8] Gospel songs evolved into rallying cries for the civil rights movement. "Freedom songs," they would be called; the best known of these was "We Shall Overcome," adapted from

"I'll Overcome Some Day," composed in 1901 by Philadelphia minister C. A. Tindley.

Reverend W. Herbert Brewster started his gospel songwriting career in Memphis, Tennessee. In 1946, he wrote "Move On Up a Little Higher" with the intention of setting people astir. Both Mahalia Jackson and the Dixie Hummingbirds would record it for the same reasons. "The fight for rights here in Memphis," said Brewster, "was pretty rough on the black church. The lily white, the black, and the tan were locking horns; and the idea struck me and I wrote that song. . . .That was a protest idea and an inspiration. I was trying to inspire black people to move up higher."[9] In 1953, on the occasion of his signing an exclusive writing contract with the Philadelphia-based Clara Ward House of Music, Brewster was hailed by the *Pittsburgh Courier* as the "top gospel song writer in the country."[10]

By the middle 1950s, black gospel began realizing its potential as a "big money" enterprise. A theatrical poll conducted in 1953 by the *Pittsburgh Courier* rated among the top favorites Clara Ward and the Ward Singers, Mahalia Jackson, Rosetta Tharpe, the Angelic Gospel Singers, the Boyer Brothers, the Five Blind Boys, Brother Joe May, the Pilgrim Travelers, and the Golden Gate Quartet.[11]

In May, the Ward Singers launched a nationwide tour starting in Philadelphia. The "Ward Gospel Cavalcade" showcased an array of gospel talent with the Ward Singers, of course, headlining. The initial concert, staged at Philadelphia's Convention Hall, drew 15,000 and grossed over $40,000.[12] That summer, reported the *Courier*, the Ward Singers, drawing 3,000 to 12,000 people per concert, had purchased a "two-tone green Cadillac limousine for the trifling sum of $7000," with a matching luggage trailer for an additional $800. "It makes a very foxy picture as . . . the Ward Singers hit the road in first-class fashion."[13]

The Wards were among the first to bring professional promotion and management into gospel. Articles about the Wards appeared frequently in the African American press. "We had a publicist," says Willa Ward Royster, "who did an excellent job of placing stories."[14] By 1955, mother Gertrude Ward had opened the Ward's Booking Agency in Philadelphia. She proactively pursued gospel acts to participate in package tours. As she wrote to James S. Hill, formerly of the Fairfield Four but then heading up the Skylarks, "I would like to include your group in the new package, which will consist of six groups. . . . I'M DETERMINED . . . This will not stop you from singing in your own usual way, but your contract will not permit you to go to other Bookers like Herman Nash, Ronnie

Williams, Lillian Cumber of California, or Romans of Detroit, Pope in Birmingham, or Chicago without my consent; you will be my artist." In exchange for exclusivity and a 15 percent commission, Ms. Ward offered nationwide contacts, work almost every night of the week, and publicity.[15]

"Gospel Singing! ... It's Big Business," read the headline over a 1955 front-page story in the *Courier*.

> The effect is electrifying ... soul-stirring ... deeply spiritual and highly emotional! ... You get it in the voices of the incomparable Mahalia Jackson ... the dynamic Ward Singers ... the shouting Rosetta Tharpe ... the muted voices of the Harmonizing Four ... the silver voices of the Swan Silvertones ... the humming of the Hummingbirds.
>
> It's gospel music ... the kind that has filled Chicago's Coliseum, Philadelphia's Convention Hall, and baseball parks in Richmond, Va., and numerous places in Georgia and Alabama!
>
> For years, gospel singing has been popular.... But it has been left to a small band of pioneers to combine musical ecstasy with superb salesmanship to give it economic value and stature.[16]

By the late 1950s, even mainstream media was taking notice of black gospel's successes. "Singing for Sinners," read the *Newsweek* banner. "Borne along in a cream-colored limousine with eight doors, costumed from a richly colored wardrobe worth $50,000, flanked by the five other 'Famous Ward Singers,' 34-year old Clara Mae Ward led the 'Big Gospel Cavalcade of 1957' deeper into the South this week."

Asked why gospel was so popular, Clara Ward replied, "I think it fills a vacuum in people's lives.... For people who work hard and make little money it offers a promise that things will be better in the life to come. It's like in slavery times, it cheers the downtrodden."

The article went on to note that black gospel had become a money-making industry, pointing out that the previous year, the Ward Singers had grossed more than half a million dollars. The music was now also reaching a broader market as gospel artists like the Wards and Mahalia Jackson were agreeing to appear in the context of jazz festivals. Said Willard Alexander, jazz booking agent, "Gospel has always been big and it's going to get bigger. It's not so much a trend as a penetration into the white market. We are getting a public for gospel that has never accepted or known about it. Good gospel really swings!"[17]

The boom in gospel music continued throughout the 1950s, and the Dixie Hummingbirds rode along with it, emerging at decade's end as indisputable champions of the genre, the "boss" group, as their peers called them.

" . . . shows promise of creating new singing stars in the gospel realm."

By 1952, the Dixie Hummingbirds had recorded on Gotham and Okeh without a hit or an appreciable difference in their career. Requests for personal appearances remained strong and the Birds maintained an intense tour schedule, but they continued to seek a better record deal The genre of black gospel itself was thriving and "package shows" were especially catching on, boosting fan and label excitement about the music nationwide.[18]

The leading package show on the national circuit that year was Mahalia Jackson's "Gospel Train." The tour kicked off in Philadelphia at the Met on Thursday, February 21, "a gospel and spiritual extravaganza in concert," declared the program booklet. Featured were the Clara Ward Specials—the Ward Singers without Clara—Thermon Ruth's Selah Jubilee Singers, and, of course, "the inimitable Mahalia Jackson." "Still moving up," noted the program, adding that on Sunday, January 27, Jackson had "made her coast to coast Television debut on Ed Sullivan's 'Toast of the Town.'"[19]

The "Gospel Train" would roll into Trenton's War Memorial the next day, then to the Mosque Theater in Newark, and on February 24 to the famed Golden Gate Auditorium in New York City. Program sponsor, the *Amsterdam News*, described the event as an "unusual $100,000 religious entertainment package . . . slated for a coast-to-coast tour."

A professional New York City-based management company, William B. Graham Associates, coordinated the entire "Gospel Train" tour. Ticket prices for the Golden Gate show ranged from one to three dollars and readers were reminded "when Miss Jackson appeared last year at Carnegie Hall, people were turned away because the Hall could not accommodate the crowd."[20]

In the wake of the tour's success, Don Robey, owner of Peacock Records in Houston, coordinated the Texas–Louisiana leg of a national Rosetta Tharpe tour featuring former Soul Stirrer R. H. Harris and his new group, the Christland Singers, recently signed to Robey's Peacock label.[21] The Soul Stirrers, now with Sam Cooke, announced their own cross-country tour that would "embrace 101 cities" and be seen by

Souvenir program from Mahalia Jackson's 1952 "Gospel Train" tour.

"50,000 people before" it was finished. Traveling with them, the Blind Boys of Alabama and the Pilgrim Travelers—Houston-based protégés of the Soul Stirrers and, like them, recently signed to Specialty Records in Los Angeles.[22]

In addition to high-profile package shows and the relentless touring of popular groups like the Dixie Hummingbirds, black gospel grew in the early 1950s through improvements in recording technology. "High fidelity" allowed a broader range of frequencies to be captured in the groove and reproduced by record players. The new 45-rpm disks, available since the late 1940s but only now seriously displacing 78 rpms, were inexpensive, easy to handle, and more durable than the brittle old ten-inch 78s. Consumers quickly took to these inexpensive, better-sounding single records by their favorite gospel groups.

Billboard reported that in 1952, fifteen million 45s had been pressed for jukebox use.[23] Independent labels reissued on 45-rpm sides that had originally been released on 78-rpm disks, extending the shelf life of artists whose records had already run their course. Throughout the early 1950s, Ivin Ballen issued 45-rpm recordings from the Dixie Hummingbirds back catalog, publicizing the releases as if they had been cut just recently.

With the fans energized by recording technology and cross-country performance activity, independent labels were innovating the sound and style of gospel music—labels such as Nashboro in Nashville, King in Cincinnati, Savoy in Newark, but especially Vee Jay in Chicago, Specialty in Los Angeles, and Peacock in Houston. Having recorded gospel since just after World War II, these labels now sought a fresh brand of soul-rending gospel that played up the male group sound, intense angst-driven leads with equally intense call and response backup, forays into shouting and startling falsetto, and an instrumentation—drums, bass, electric guitar, piano—that sounded more barrelhouse than praise house. At times, the line between their R&B and gospel releases seemed thin. The beat, the instrumentation, and the chord changes were essentially the same but the words and the performance style differed. This new-style gospel—the inheritance from Dorsey, Sister Rosetta, and southern country and urban storefront churches—burned with a passion simply not heard in R&B.

The innovative groups with far less vocal sophistication and performance experience than the Dixie Hummingbirds were signing with the "hot" labels and winning thousands of fans that by now the Hummingbirds had hoped would be in their column. Some of their toughest competition was signed to Art Rupe's Los Angeles-based Specialty label. Sam Cooke and the Soul Stirrers were tearing up young gospel fans with releases like "Peace in the Valley" and "Jesus Gave Me Water." In addition to the Soul Stirrers, the Specialty label had arguably the most formidable roster of male quartets in gospel at the time, including the Swan Silvertones, the Pilgrim Travelers, and the Alabama Blind Boys.

The Silvertones, headed by old Hummingbirds' friend Claude Jeter, had like the Hummingbirds been gentle masters of a cappella spiritual and jubilee singing. Now, on the Specialty label with Jeter and support tenor Reverend Robert Crenshaw, baritones Solomon Womack and John Myles, and Henry Brossard, one of the genre's important bass singers, the Silvertones had fortified their sound with the instrumental backing of drums, piano, organ, and later guitar, with tight group harmonies and Jeter soaring over top in breathtaking falsetto. The Silvertones, now based in Pittsburgh, had become formidable competitors in the gospel field.

The Pilgrim Travelers, another mighty presence in Specialty's lineup of male quartets, with lead tenors Kylo Turner and James "Woodie" Alexander, had been charting a course toward soul gospel since late 1948 with lithe vocals and the jubilee rhythms of Specialty releases like "I'm Standing on the Highway," "Stretch Out," and "Jesus Hits Like the Atom Bomb." Kylo Turner, observes Horace Boyer, was the source of a vocal device that by the early 1950s was identified more with the ever-absorbent Ira Tucker. With the group laying down a harmony bed, Turner would come in an octave above the group, then "shimmer down an octave," finishing out at the lower end of the scale.[24]

Specialty's Five Blind Boys of Alabama featuring Clarence Fountain were of the fiery Birmingham tradition, having developed their style as students at the Talladega School for the Blind. They had been making records since 1948, but they hit their stride on Specialty in the early 1950s with principals George Scott, tenor and guitarist; Reverend Samuel Lewis, baritone; and Johnny Fields singing bass. The Blind Boys offered pulsing drums behind rich electric rhythm guitar and solid harmonies with Fountain and Lewis using frenzied screaming and crying. Blind Boys' later hits like "This May Be the Last Time" and "Oh Lord—Stand by Me" would inspire 1960s rock 'n' roll hits by the Rolling Stones and Ben E. King, respectively.

The other Five Blind Boys, from the Piney Woods School for the Blind in Mississippi, recorded for Specialty's chief west coast rival, Peacock Records. Archie Brownlee, the Blind Boys' lead tenor, idolized R. H. Harris and was the trendsetter when it came to soul gospel shouting. The Mississippi Blind Boys—Brownlee, Vance Powell, Lawrence Abrams, Lloyd Woodard, and J. T. Clinkscales—with their 1951 hit, "Our Father," established their signature sound: heavy drum back beat, group in harmony, Brownlee pleading over top, his sweepingly emotive voice leaping into sudden shrieks and moans. The Mississippi Blind Boys set the tone for Peacock's distinctive approach to gospel and were a mainstay of the label for almost two decades. When Archie Brownlee

Peacock label-mates, the Five Blind Boys of Mississippi with formidable lead singer Archie Brownlee.

died at the height of his fame in 1960, his funeral program read, "Many souls were converted through his songs. He sang to both white and colored and was loved dearly by all."[25]

Peacock's Bells of Joy, with lead vocalist A. C. Littlefield supported by Ester Littlefield, Clem Reed, Vernon Maynor, A. D. Watson, and vocalist/guitarist Namon Brown, recorded "Let's Talk about Jesus" in October 1951. The label boasted in a February 1952 *Billboard* ad that the record had sold 26,000 copies in its first eight days, and in May, the group was honored with a *Cash Box* "outstanding achievement award."[26]

The Bells' performance on "Talk" alternated "between jubilee and hard gospel techniques," notes Horace Boyer. Black gospel was at a juncture at that time and in Boyer's view, the Bells of Joy "personified the changing quartet" sound. "The jubilee style, with its emphasis on harmony, attacks, and releases, and time and tune, was replaced by much louder singing, extreme range investigation, and faster tempos."[27]

These emerging groups were dubbed "hard" or "soul" gospel artists. The distinctions between the two styles are subtle. According to Boyer, "hard" gospel was "first introduced by the saints of the sanctified church," and "characterized by straining the voice during periods of spiritual ecstasy for spiritual and dramatic expression, singing in the extremes of the range, delivering perpetual text, in some cases repeating words or syllables or developing the text through the employment of wandering couplets or quatrains or stock interjections ('Yes, Lord,' 'Don't You Know,' 'Listen to Me,' and so on), and 'acting out' songs with physical motions like hand movements, dance steps, and posturing."[28]

"Soul" gospel came later and was further characterized by that abstract quality called by the singers "feel," a soulfulness that emerged in the nuances of tempo. Soul gospel played on off-beats, hesitancies, pacing, and the tactical placement of words relative to the rhythmic pulse, the very qualities that Ray Charles would extract to create secular soul music in the late 1950s. As a result, although female gospel groups were still the genre's biggest stars, in the early 1950s, male quartets and the soul gospel sound were increasing in popularity and influence.

"Spirituals with Feelings. Blues with the Zip."

In the early months of 1952, the Dixie Hummingbirds had made the decision to put Okeh behind them. They had made a connection with Don Robey and were down in Texas recording their first sides for Peacock.

On Peacock, the group revamped their sound to make a place for themselves on the cutting edge of soul gospel. Don Robey was precisely the right partner for them. Up to this time, the Birds' associations had been with label owners outside the culture. Don Robey was an African American with Deep South sensibilities. He knew and loved gospel music and understood the black gospel-buying public. At the time they met, James Davis at thirty-six was the "old man" of the group, and Tucker at twenty-seven still the baby. Robey, close to fifty years of age, had the experience and authority to guide them. Robey had a clear vision of how his gospel records should sound and did not hold back in voicing his opinions.

The Dixie Hummingbirds signed with Peacock on the recommendation of the Reverend I. H. Gordon, the host of a Cleveland gospel program that aired over station WABQ. Gordon, originally from Texas, had released "Doctor Jesus" b/w "Seek the Lord" with Archie Brownlee and the Gordonaires, and "In the Upper Room" b/w "Dry Bones" backed by the Blind Boys on Peacock in 1951.

"We went to Cleveland one time," says Tucker, "and he came out to see the program. Reverend Gordon was a very popular DJ and he had the best show in Cleveland. He said, 'Man, look. You wanna be on Peacock?' We said, 'Yeah, yeah!' He said, 'Well, I'll get you on there.' Don Robey called three days after we got home!"

Don Robey is remembered as one of the legends of early independent label gospel and rhythm and blues. A rough-and-tumble man from Houston's Fifth Ward, Robey was also a "debonair and astute impresario ... willing to wager his intelligence against the opposition in any field of endeavor."[29] Before the war, Robey promoted local dance hall appearances by touring territorial jazz bands, in time, dealing with big names like Ellington, Calloway, Basie, and Armstrong. In the wake of postwar prosperity, Robey opened the Bronze Peacock Dinner Club in the heart of Houston's Fifth Ward. Gambling was a backroom staple, and that led to the club being shut down. Robey responded by diversifying, opening a record shop in the city's northeast business section. The move into recording was a natural progression.[30]

Robey launched his recording venture on the potential in Clarence "Gatemouth" Brown, an exciting electric blues guitarist. According to Evelyn Johnson, Robey's right hand at the label, "Gatemouth signed with Peacock Records based upon the recommendation of T-Bone Walker. And," she adds, "Gatemouth was signed for four cents a side. Even Nat Cole wasn't getting four cents at that time."[31] Robey's first release came out in 1949, Peacock 1500, Gatemouth Brown and the Jack McVea Orchestra, "Didn't Reach My Goal" b/w "Atomic Drive." The record sold well enough to get the Robey show on the road.

Over the next few years, Robey signed some of the most important artists in African American blues, rhythm and blues, and gospel, making Peacock a prime force in the business of recording American roots music. His first gospel signing was the Mississippi Blind Boys, and from the start he saw soul gospel's potential to cross over into the R&B market. "This first rate spiritual group," Robey put in one of his ads, "really ups the pulse beats with a rock-and-roll-'em go. . . . Could also pick up a slice of the regular R&B market."[32] Within a short time, Robey would initiate an exclusively gospel Peacock series numbered in the 1700s. "We had so many gospel records," says Evelyn Johnson, "until we were releasing them so fast, we had one heck of a catalog! It was unreal."

The Dixie Hummingbirds would travel to Houston to cut their first Peacock sides: C. A. Tindley's "What Are They Doing in Heaven Today"; "I Know I've Been Changed," a public domain spiritual; "Wading Through Blood and Water," a Tucker original, and "Trouble in My Way," written by Paul Owens's brother-in-law, Billy Mickens of the Bay State Gospel Singers.

The Birds cut their new records for Peacock in February; in late March, Okeh finally released the Birds and Angelics duets [Okeh 6858], and in early April, the Birds' solo single [Okeh 6864]. *Billboard* magazine, in its "Record Roundup" column, awarded each of the Okeh sides three stars out of four. Peacock, meanwhile, took out a quarter-page ad later that April heralding the pending release of "Wading Through Blood and Water" and "What Are They Doing in Heaven Today" [Peacock 1594]. The Birds were pictured along with two other recently signed Peacock acts, Marie Adams and the Golden Harp Singers. "Spirituals with Feelings. Blues with the Zip. Available on 45-RPM," read the ad copy.[33] By mid-April, the Birds' first Peacock sides were out. *Billboard*'s "Record Roundup" rated both three stars out of four. The following week, the *Philadelphia Tribune* ran a photo promoting the hometown group. "Among the top recording artists of religious music are the Dixie Humming Birds," noting that their new record on Peacock had "reached the top register."[34] For the Dixie Hummingbirds, the spring of 1952 could not have looked better—three new disks on two different labels all on the market simultaneously. The group would spend the remainder of the year touring behind their new releases.

Robey, meanwhile, busied himself expanding the Peacock roster, further strengthening the label's presence in the independent market. At Peacock, as at other independents, gospel records tended to provide long, steady sales runs rather than the immediate big success of R&B sides. "Our sales count was far different then," says Evelyn Johnson. "There was no platinum and those kinds of things at that time. You didn't sell a million records. You were lucky if you sold a hundred thousand in your career."[35] That was true of the Dixie Hummingbirds. "Our records," says James Davis, "were solid sellers. They were not records where people bought them the first month they came out. But they just continued to be good sellers."

In those few years between Peacock's first release in 1949 and the start of the "1700" series in 1952, Robey turned the label into a national success. By then, he had built a roster of gospel artists that included the Blind Boys, Oklahoman Sister Jessie Mae Renfro, the Christland Singers, the Bells of Joy, the Southern Wonders, the Stars of Hope, and the Dixie Hummingbirds. Robey also signed the Birds' hometown rivals, the Sensational Nightingales. Ira Tucker helped produce their first Peacock release, "Will He Welcome Me There" b/w "A Soldier Not in Uniform," featuring June Cheeks in the resonant dark baritone voice that he could make sound like an overdriven guitar amp.

Robey complemented his gospel roster with a stellar lineup of blues and R&B talent, further bolstering his holdings in the summer of 1952 with the acquisition of the Memphis-based Duke label.[36] By year's end, Robey's nongospel stable included Gatemouth Brown, Big Mama "Hound Dog" Thornton, Little Richard, Johnny Ace, Roscoe Gordon, Junior Parker, and Bobby "Blue" Bland. "Lots of work," Robey told the *Chicago Defender*. "But it looks like it will develop into the best business I've ever had. Of course, I must spend from 12 to 14 hours each day with the business. But I think it is worth the efforts."[37]

"If you leave Duke Peacock, I've got five black boxes for all of you."

Robey was a hands-on operator, but from the stories that abound, more "hands-on" than some of his artists would have liked. He and Little Richard, for example, "clashed like a prairie chicken and a rattlesnake." As Richard told his biographer, Charles White, "He jumped on me, knocked me down, and kicked me in the stomach. . . . Right there in the office he beat me up. Knocked me out in one round. Wasn't any second or third round—he just come around that desk and I was down! He was known for beating people up, though. He would beat everybody up but Big Mama Thornton. He was scared of her. She was built like a big bull."[38]

Robey's hot temper apparently surfaced most often when the subject turned to royalties or loyalty to the label. The Pilgrim Jubilee Singers with Major Roberson and brothers Cleve and Clay Graham signed with Robey in 1959. The Jubes came to Robey through Dave Clark, one of Peacock's key talent scouts and producers. When the contract came, "Everybody's rejoicing," said Roberson to interviewer Alan Young. "We didn't read anything. We didn't think about an attorney. Lordy, if you could record for Peacock, you were top stuff."

The Pilgrim Jubilees, in their rush to sign, had missed the part of the contract that stipulated a lifetime commitment with no options to terminate or renegotiate. The situation came to a head with the success of their breakthrough hit, "Stretch Out." Don Robey had been boasting to the Dixie Hummingbirds about the phenomenal sales of "Stretch Out," showing them an invoice that indicated sales of over 85,000 copies in three weeks. When Ira Tucker ran into the Jubes a few weeks later, he told them, "Y'all got the biggest record Don Robey had in a long time." The Jubes at that point had not been paid any royalties, so Major Roberson made the trip to Houston. When he got there, Robey showed him "something that said we had sold eighteen hundred records."

> And he said, "Y'all got to do something a bit better than this." Eighteen hundred was all he gave us credit for. That thing was on fire! . . . Like an R&B record, it just went. All the jukeboxes across the country was playing it. He told us we had to sell fifty thousand copies before we'd be eligible for a royalty. But we had no way of knowing if we'd sold fifty thousand. It was whatever he said. If he said we didn't, we didn't.

And when the Pilgrim Jubilees told Robey they were planning to leave the label, Robey said, as Cleve Graham remembers, "I made you, and now you want to go over to those people? . . . I'll see you dead in the street." Robey refused to record the group but would not let them go. Each time Roberson pleaded to either be recorded or released, Robey responded by pulling out a .357 Magnum. "We knew we were being mistreated. But we didn't look at the dotted line before we signed." Embittered by their experience, when Robey died in 1975, the Jubes declined an invitation to sing at his funeral.[39]

Don Robey could be "as good as he was bad . . . a Dr. Jekyll and Mr. Hyde," says Evelyn Johnson. She remembers him as "fair . . . with his musicians,"[40] and yet recalls how with a "rubber stamp replica" of his signature she was instructed to shift money between accounts to hide debt and create the illusion of solvency. Robey, says Johnson, made her a "crook," but because she "was just a young girl," she did not realize it at the time.[41]

Joe Ligon and the Mighty Clouds of Joy also experienced Robey's extremes. They knew his reputation going in. "We had heard that he was a crook."

> We knew all that, but going down there as young boys, first time making a record, we were excited. . . . Our manager now looks at the contract we signed, he said, "Man, the contract . . . was terrible!" . . .

When we should have been making a quarter, we was making a nickel. When we should have been making a nickel, we was making a penny.... If he wanted to hold us for life, he could have."

On one occasion when the group threatened to walk out, Robey sent them a letter. "If you leave Duke Peacock, I've got five black boxes for all of you." Apparently, though, the benefits outweighed the threats and even the short-changing.

We didn't care.... We wanted to get started, and if we had to do it all over again, we would... Anything that we wanted, ... a van, ... records, ... uniforms, he would buy them. He was real good to us.... He made us known to America. To the world. Don Robey did that."[42]

Label stalwart Bobby "Bluc" Bland corroborates that position. "Robey gave every artist the benefit of the doubt starting out. He was a hell of a man, and he was a help to a lot of black entertainers who would never have gotten a record label at all."[43]

The Dixie Hummingbirds never regretted working for Don Robey. "We liked Don Robey and he seemed to like us," says James Davis. "He called me 'Pappy.' We had a great rapport." Nonetheless, the Hummingbirds entered the association with skepticism, never expecting to get all that was due them. "But," says Davis, "we did get nice change from him. Making records back when we were with Robey, let's just say we knew we were behind the eight-ball in the first place." The Birds understood that they would have to bear all the production costs up front. "*We* had to pay the operators in the studio, *we* had to pay for the room to record in, the engineers—everything," says Davis. "They tell me Michael Jackson once took eighteen hours to record a particular song. But us, we couldn't afford that. We would go in and do our whole record in an hour."

At the beginning of the Hummingbirds' recording career, they made almost nothing from their records. "When we got with Robey," says Davis, "we were getting ten per cent. We were his top artists for a long time.... Our best selling numbers, though, they sold enough for us to get a little money and helped to popularize us enough to make a living. But then, as far as gospel, it never paid off as much as rock or blues."

Davis also appreciated that Robey had to grease palms to get records played on the radio. Payola was de rigueur. "Now I'll tell you," says Davis, "a lot of disk jockeys felt like they're the greatest thing that ever happened to groups—but the groups made them! Without something to play, they didn't have a shot." Davis brings up a conversation he had with a record promoter in Miami. "The man said, 'Davis, if you could get out there in that water and have on a scuba diver's uniform, you could get enough records to go in business!' I said, 'What do you mean?' I knew what he was talking about, but I wanted to make him say it. 'Errr, what all . . . , ah, *new* records?' He said, 'Yeah. Brand new. Never been played.' I say, 'Why are they there?' He say, 'Ain't no use fattenin' the frog for the snake.'" In other words, if the label failed to pay, the disk jockeys dumped the records en masse into the ocean waters.

Moreover, Davis believes that Robey faced higher payola fees than white label owners. Davis remembers a time he advised Robey *not* to attend an awards show out of concern that disk jockeys would discover Robey was black. Robey attended anyway and in due course found himself hit up for higher fees. "That's what they did to him," says Davis, "after they found out he was black. Robey called me back about six months after that. He said, 'Pappy, I'm sorry I didn't listen to you.'"

Like Davis, Ira Tucker also looks back favorably on the Birds' relationship with Robey. "At one time, Peacock was the biggest label that was going," he says. "During the time when Peacock was at its best, you couldn't hardly find a gospel label. See, those rock 'n' roll people, they wasn't interested in spirituals and gospel too much then. They didn't want nothing like that, the likes of Columbia [parent company of Okeh] and . . . Atlantic wouldn't touch it with a ten foot pole." As far as Tucker was concerned, Robey was "a nice fellow."

> Tell you why I say that. When you are in business, you look back at a guy and say he's got his faults. Well, the one thing you had to watch was, if you made a deal with Don, you had to keep him with the deal, and if he could take you out of the deal, he would. If he could scare you down $100 or whatever, he would. But on the other hand, . . . what businessman won't![44]

Seasoned veterans of the music business like the Hummingbirds and Robey understood each other and needed each other to succeed.

Tucker especially appreciates that Robey allowed him to evolve as a producer. At Peacock, Tucker and the Birds worked with a variety of producers, including Larry Gold and Richard Simpson. "We had a whole lot of producers," says Tucker. "When I started giving ideas about things, that's when they started in on 'this guy's on his way to being a producer.' I've been producing records for a long time now . . . Robey gave me my first break into that."

"They going to have an entire orchestra playing behind gospel singers."

"Wading Through Blood and Water" and "What Are They Doing In Heaven" were the first sides released by the Dixie Hummingbirds on Peacock. Already, changes in their style were evident. "Wading" was a Tucker tour de force with the same political overtones as the material they had sung a decade earlier at Café Society. Now, though, Tucker was responding to the Korean War. He began somberly, building as the group filled in behind, anguish coming through in Tucker's growling moans and cries.

> Our boys are wading,
> Through blood and water,
> Trying to come home,
> Oh, yeah.
>
> Some are fighting on land and sea,
> Yeah, they're fighting for you and me,
> And I know they are wading,
> Through blood and water,
> Trying to come home.

"It was a real tearjerker," says Tucker, "because so many people was getting killed at the time." This Hummingbirds recording possessed a different sound from any previous side, an underlying urgency, a "soulfulness"—the distinctive Peacock sound—that came through in the rhythmic feel.

The reverse, "What Are They Doing in Heaven Today," was Paul Owens's joyful take on a Tindley composition. The Birds performed it up tempo with responsive group harmonies over Bobo's pulsing bass, occasional bursts of echo provided by studio engineers.

> Well, you know I'm thinking of friends,
> Whom I used to know,
> Who lived and suffered in this world below,
> Gone on to glory, and I want to know,

What are . . . ,
Hmmm,
What are . . . ,
Hmmm,
What are . . . ,
Yes,
What are they doing in heaven today?

"I remember doing 'What Are They Doing in Heaven Today,'" says James Davis. "It was a nice studio. We worked with four mikes. No earphones or anything like that. They didn't have no drum. Robey had us standing, stomping our feet on a heavy wooden plaque on the floor. We slammed on it and it sounded like a bass drum. No big thing. Once they got us settled down to how the sound come out—boom—it was done!"

Later, the Dixie Hummingbirds and virtually every gospel group would record with drums. That was one of Robey's most important contributions to the genre. As early as 1950, he had pioneered the use of drums on tracks with the Blind Boys, and from then on he urged his artists to record with them. Cleve Graham remembers when the Pilgrim Jubilees auditioned a cappella for Robey. "We sang right there in his office. After a while, he took his hands from behind his head and said, 'I'll record you. But . . . I would like to get y'all to rehearse a couple of days with my drummer.'"[45]

Leroy Crume, guitarist with the Christland Singers and the Soul Stirrers, remembers that Robey sometimes added drums after the fact, much to the surprise of the group. "Robey," he says, "played a big part in the production of his records. Instruments was new during that time, and I was playing with R. H. Harris. And after we put the music on the records, Robey would dub drums on it. After we left town! At the time, I thought it was awful because mostly it was off time. But then I thought it was good because it was new. The ones that was pretty close to the timing, it sounded great to me."

At Peacock, with Robey's encouragement, drums, guitars, keyboards, and other instrumentation became standard. In Crume's estimation, Robey helped shape the sound of modern gospel. "Back in 1951, I remember the ex-baritone of the Soul Stirrers, T. L. Bruster, saying to me, 'You know, Leroy, one of these days they going to have an entire orchestra playing behind gospel singers.' And I thought that was so far out. I said, 'No way.' He said, 'Just wait!' I said, 'I can see couple of guitars, drums, and stuff like that, but an entire orchestra!?' He said, 'Yes. And it won't be long.'"[46] As it transpired, at least for the near future, Leroy Crume's vision of guitars, bass, and drums was accurate.

Indeed, shortly after Peacock released their essentially a cappella debut single, the Dixie Hummingbirds would take a step in that direction. The move was precipitated by the departure of Paul Owens, who left the group under disputed circumstances. (Owens claims to have left the Birds for the Swan Silvertones after filling in for the Reverend Crenshaw in an emergency; Tucker, on the other hand, remembers that Owens was fired for racetrack gambling.)

Even though Owens had been a tremendous asset to the Birds, James Davis, ever vigilant about the rules and with the support of the group, let him go. The Birds invited longtime friend Howard Carroll, fellow Philadelphian and superlative guitarist, to join in his place. Carroll had recently dropped out of the Sensational Nightingales, the group he had founded, and was working outside of music. The Nightingales, he says, "were climbing the ladder and making a name for ourselves—but there is such a thing as making a living too, you know [laughs]."

> Everything was going well except the money. I was raising a family, so I had to make a choice. So, my choice was to get me a job. That's what I did, and I worked for a while. And when the Hummingbirds decided to use an instrument, I was nominated for the job.[47]

Although he could sing, Carroll preferred to stick to electric guitar accompaniment, while Beachey Thompson stepped back into his role as Tucker's vocal foil. Howard Carroll's guitar style was perfectly suited to the soul gospel trend of the day and, in fact, his pioneering use of electric guitar would influence others in the genre and would further infuse black gospel with jazzy chords and the feel of swing blues. "Howard is one of the best there is," says Leroy Crume, "and he helped me a lot on the guitar."

Howard Carroll's approach to playing evolved out of an urban scene and an unusual mix of musical styles. He was drawn to the guitar at an early age, impressed with the instrument's role in the country, blues, and jazz of the day. Born in North Philadelphia on April 27, 1924, Carroll was raised by his father following the death of his mother. "He was strict and meant what he said. But my father was also my teacher. He was a musician and he had a group called the North Union String Band."

Howard Carroll (right) and Rudolf King of "Ace, Deuce, and Trey"
(Trey not pictured). Philadelphia, 1930s.

The elder Carroll, from Baltimore, loved gospel and blues. Howard remembers hearing Victrola records by Amos "Bumble Bee Slim" Easton, Big Bill Broonzy, Blind Boy Fuller, Big Maceo, and Blind Lemon Jefferson. On the other hand, Horace Carroll also loved country music, "bluegrass," says Howard, "and I love it, too. Very good sounds. My dad, he lived for the 'Grand Ole Opry!'"

His group, the North Union String Band, reflected this amalgam of black and white musical styles, and apparently Horace Carroll was not the only African American in town with these cross-cultural tastes. "The North Union String Band," says Howard Carroll, "was all strings, about fifteen of them in the group."

> Guitars and banjos and violins—and there was one who played the mandolin. Two violins. About four banjos. And the rest guitars. My father played the five-string banjo. All they played was hymns like "Precious Lord" and "Amazing Grace."
>
> The lady that organized the group was Ms. Johnson. She was in the Holiness Church and the Holiness Church was the one that had all of the music, usually brass bands, but this was all strings. And each member belonged to different churches. Ms. Johnson got them all together and it was a union, and that's how they got their name.

The tradition of stringed instrument players went back a long way in the Carroll family. "Way back," says Carroll. "I had uncles who played banjoes and ukuleles, tipples, mandolins and violins. All instruments you don't see too much now." Horace Carroll played in church, but his livelihood came from performing at parties, clubs, and speakeasies.

Like his father, Howard was also attracted to stringed instruments and performance. He disliked the classical music he was compelled to listen to in school. "Beethoven and Chopin were putting me to sleep. I had other ideas in my head. I just wanted to finger pop, so to speak." Cab Calloway and Jimmy Lunceford were more to his liking. "Those guys were kicking it up. Whenever I heard a jazz band, I was picturing myself up there." Radio and records were most often his musical sources in those days. "Different shows would come on and I would listen."

> And each one would feature a different artist. That's how I knew about Jimmy Lunceford. And then, all the boys I hung out with, they were music fanatics anyway. They would bring in these great big 78-rpm records. We'd work all week for fifty cents to go buy a record.

Those were his first exposures to guitarists like Nick Lucas, Eddie Lang, and his particular favorite, Django Reinhardt. But Carroll was most impressed with Charlie Christian, the pioneer of electric guitar from Kansas City and one of the first African Americans integrated into the Benny Goodman Band and Sextet. "Charlie Christian was hot, hot, hot!"

Carroll started fooling with the guitar as a child. "I didn't like the way the banjo looked, all them clamps all around."

> I liked the look of a guitar. I could just see myself setting behind it. My father used to have a guitar hanging on the wall and he would tell me not to touch it. But every time he turned his back, I had me a chair and I'd climb up, get the guitar, and fool with it. Then, when I heard him coming, I'd get the chair and put it back up. He would come in, pick it back up, and say, "Who had my guitar?" I wouldn't say a thing because I was afraid I'd get a licking for it.

In time, though, Carroll's father showed him how to tune the guitar and moved him in the direction of committing to it.

> He would wait until I was good and ready to do one of my favorite sports, pitch horseshoes or play softball, and he would stop me at the door. He was finding out what choice I was going to make. He would cut me off from what I was going to do and five minutes into practicing on the guitar, I would forget all about ball or horseshoes. It worked.

Carroll soon began playing publicly, initially alongside his father in the North Union String Band and later in the city's small clubs and cabarets and at parties. As a young man, he had a "day job" working for the railroad in what they called "woolen waste." "There was a lot of wool factories around here," says Carroll. "They would pack wool on the trains for oil clean up, and I used to bale wool out of the baler." He kept a cheap acoustic guitar—brand name "Keystone State"—in his work locker and played on breaks or whenever he could. By the late 1930s, he formed his own group with friends Bob King and Shorty Scott, calling themselves Ace, Deuce, and Trey. "I was Deuce," says Carroll.

> Then we changed our name to the Hot Dog Rhythm Boys. Two guitars and a washtub. We did all of the songs the bands played. Louis

Jordan. Nat King Cole. Lonnie Johnson. The Three Blazes. Cats and the Fiddle. They were my boys. We did a lot of their material.

We used to go to a nightclub—Palumbo's—downtown. Just walk in. And when the band takes a break, the man would announce, "and now we have a special treat. Ace, Deuce, and Trey!" My man starts bumping up there with that washtub. White audiences. Yeah, man, they loved it!

Howard joined the military during World War II. While working off-duty in the base's wood shop one day, a table saw took off the top of the second finger on his left hand. "Luckily, the ball grew back," he says, and although that one finger was debilitating in its shortness, Carroll adapted and developed a percussive chord style tailored to his handicap.

I mainly fell in love with chords for backgrounding singers—like the piano supports the choir. I felt like the guitar could do the same for the quartet. I was also fascinated with the blues players because I liked to hear certain runs. Where if a song is built around a certain subject, there's a sound that really punctuates the story. I can hear it in my imagination.

These were the musical sensibilities and skills Howard Carroll brought to the Dixie Hummingbirds when he joined in 1952. The group gave him free rein to play what he liked. "That's one thing about my fellows," he says. "Whatever decision that I make as far as the music is concerned, they leave that strictly to me. If I think it sounds good and it fits, then it works okay with them."

Carroll came into the Hummingbirds just as electric guitar was emerging as a defining hallmark of black quartet gospel. Certainly, the instrument had been a part of gospel for years, initially in its acoustic form as heard in the 1920s recordings of guitar evangelists like Blind Willie Johnson and blues singers like Charlie Patton who included gospel in their repertoires. Then later, the tradition was carried forward by guitar wizards like Blind Gary Davis and the ever-popular Sister Rosetta Tharpe, who would ultimately trade in her acoustic metal-bodied Dobro for a new-fangled electric.

Leroy and Arthur Crume, themselves gospel guitar trailblazers, reflect on the advent of electrification. The Crumes, like the Carroll family, were raised on country and Western. "That's all we knew growing up in Missouri," says Arthur Crume. "Roy Acuff and Hank Williams. That's why I first played acoustic guitar. That would have been around 1947. But," he adds, "they were not letting the guitar inside the church." Says brother Leroy, "They said it was the instrument of the devil. Before we went to church, we had to go find the pastor and ask him would it be okay for us to bring the guitar in and play."

"Then the electric guitar came out," says Arthur. "My brother heard it and told us about it. We were kind of skeptical of getting it. He said, 'Now, if you get this electric guitar, we're going to hear what you're doing and what you are not doing.' I thought, well, I'll get it anyway. I bought one and it went from there. Then came the Dixie Hummingbirds with electric guitar," says Arthur, and all the Crume brothers learned the instrument and hired themselves out as guitarists for some of the best gospel groups.[48]

When he was with the Christland Singers and later the Soul Stirrers, Leroy Crume played a Gibson guitar through a Gibson amplifier. Did the brashness and audibility of the instrument affect the way the quartets sang? "We tried not to let it affect our harmonies," says Leroy, "but I think it did. You kind of get lax when your guitar is playing. But the Soul Stirrers, I have to say, held theirs together. We really paid attention to our harmonies. What we would do, we rehearsed our harmonies first, and then later on rehearsed with the guitar."

When Howard Carroll joined the Dixie Hummingbirds, their vocal equilibrium was also momentarily jolted by the presence of the electric guitar. Carroll was playing a large-bodied f-hole Epiphone rigged with a D'Armand pickup and a "little old cheesebox of an amplifier" picked up at a pawnshop. "It took us a little while to sing so we could get in time with him," says James Davis. "We'd been following the lead singer. Wherever he would go, that's where we would go. And with the guitar in there destabilizing everything, it made things a little awkward for a little while." Tucker corroborates that. "Man, that first week we decided to go out on the highway, we had the worst showing that I ever think we made against the Nightingales."

> We were used to singing a cappella and Howard didn't know us well enough to know our moods and the way we were singing. And when you are singing a cappella, then half the time you're singing out of synch.
>
>   Anyway, we really didn't make any kind of show that Sunday.... Julius Cheeks walked all over us, but I guess during a changeover,

you've got to start somewhere. But once we got to know him good, anything we would come up with he could do. After that, when we got to kicking, we wiped out most of them. It was really devastating at one time, but we finally put it together.[49]

Once the Hummingbirds adjusted to Howard Carroll, they would return to the studio and record a track that became their first big hit on Peacock, maybe their biggest record on any label to date.

"This is to inform you that we have available a wonderful spiritual attraction."

The Hummingbirds had recorded their initial sides in Houston, but later sessions took place in a variety of locations, usually Chicago or Tennessee where more side musicians were available. "They recorded wherever it was convenient," recalls Evelyn Johnson. The Tennessee sessions took place in Nashville at a Quonset-hut country-and-Western studio built by pianist and producer Owen Bradley. "Most of the time, though," says James Davis, "we recorded in Chicago."

> There were three guys in Chicago that Don Robey knew and he would send us out there. They were the fastest bunch of guys. They just picked up on your song and played it. I don't care how you wanted to sing or how high or low or how fast or slow. They were good. One was Big Will. That's the only one I remember. He was really something!

"Big Will" was Chicago blues master Willie Dixon, an accomplished bassist, composer, and producer. "Robey would send me a letter to get the spiritual groups together and record 'em," wrote Dixon in his auto-biography, "and I would." The sessions supervised by Dixon further contributed to the infusion of urban blues into black gospel. Dixon used the backing of some of Chicago's finest blues sidemen. "Clifton James would be on drums, Lafayette Leake on piano, and I'd be on bass.... We added the bass and piano and that gave it a drive."[50]

When Dixon recorded the Dixie Hummingbirds, though, William Bobo's remarkable bass vocal skills made string bass superfluous. The combination of Bobo's bass and Howard Carroll's guitar would be all the instrumentation the Birds needed to stay competitive in the changing world of black gospel.

With Paul Owens out of the group and Howard Carroll in, the Birds were anxious to get back into the studio and capitalize on their new sound. Ira Tucker was particularly urgent about it when he learned that Owens had joined the Swan Silvertones. He was concerned that the Silvertones would get the jump on a tune the Birds had already recorded at their first Peacock session with Owens still in the lineup. Owens's brother-in-law, Billy Mickens of the Baystate Gospel Singers, had written the song, "Trouble in My Way," and Owens had brought it to the Birds. Peacock had not released the track, and now Tucker wanted to record it again as quickly as possible.

"I knew by the time Paul got with the Silvertones, they were going to come up with it," says Tucker. Both groups recorded the song in August 1952; the Birds on Peacock with Carroll on guitar and Tucker and Thompson trading leads; the Silvertones on Specialty with Paul Owens in the background and Jeter and Crenshaw on leads.

The Birds' "Trouble in My Way," paired with "I Know I've Been Changed," recorded at their first session, was released as Peacock 1705 in December 1952. It would be their second Peacock single and their first in the "1700" series. "We got out with it about a month before they did," says Tucker, the timing helping them eclipse the Silvertones' version.

"Trouble in My Way" opened with a guitar arpeggio from Howard Carroll, but on this, his first outing with the Birds, his presence is otherwise hardly noticeable. The appeal of "Trouble" was in the sheer energy of the performance. There was a drum track, and Tucker, inventing as he went, soared over Bobo's pumping bass and the group's mantra-like repetition of the phrase "Father of Abraham." "A Hummingbirds masterpiece," wrote Anthony Heilbut, in which the "resemblance to jazz improvisation is obvious." With this sort of performance, contends Heilbut, "Tucker expanded the freedoms available to quartet singers."[51]

The Birds swing on "Trouble in My Way," and the groove carries the song to spiritual heights. Tucker reaches deeply into his vocal bag of tricks, making particularly effective use of a guttural "AaahAaahAaah" that sounds like the cranking over of a stubborn automobile.

> Trouble's in my way,
> I've got to cry sometime.
> Trouble's in my way,
> I've got to cry sometime.
> Trouble's in my way,
> I've got to cry sometime,
> Jesus will take me,
> By and by.

"Trouble" sold well, and by the end of 1952, the Birds were riding high on the combined momentum of their Peacock and Okeh releases along with tracks being reissued on 45-rpm from their back catalog at Gotham and Apollo. Each label represented a different stage in the Hummingbirds' evolution. The Okeh, Gotham, and Apollo sides were "old school," a cappella spirituals, performed brilliantly, but more appealing to the "Sister Flute" generation and to cultural outsiders who were fans of "Negro" religious music. The Peacock tracks, by comparison, were hot and getting progressively hotter, geared to the younger generation of African American record-buyers.

The Birds were increasingly in demand as their records received radio play and reached the stores. They established a touring pattern that they would maintain for decades to come. From January to March, the Birds stayed warm by touring the South, sometimes with the Angelics and occasionally on package shows. From April through the onset of winter, the Birds returned to Philadelphia and the northeast.

The logistics of touring were an increasing burden for James Davis who handled requests for personal appearances and worked out the details. Gospel had become a "growth industry," and with that status, a number of professional booking agencies had sprouted up around the country.

The year before the Birds signed with Peacock, they were listed with International Artists Corporation (IAC) located on Madison Avenue in New York City. In their catalog, IAC claimed that "through its influences and resources," they had "discovered and carefully developed many talented and aspiring artists, immeasurably aiding them in blazing a path of glory in the Religious and 'Pop' Concert field." Among the gospel artists they handled were the Angelics, the Wards, the Fairfield Four, the Harmonizing Four, the Selahs, the CBS Trumpeteers, the Deep River Singers, the Golden Gate Quartet, Josh White, and of course, the Dixie Hummingbirds. The caption under their picture read, "Acknowledged leader among today's outstanding Gospel-singing interpreters, this brilliant group of musical personalities enjoy tremendous popularity among religious concert audiences everywhere, coast-to-coast."

By 1953, most of the leading independents had established their own booking agencies. Specialty Records, for example, relied on Lillian Cumber and Herald Attractions to book their acts in gospel: the Soul Stirrers, Pilgrim Travelers, Swan Silvertones, Mississippi Blind Boys, Original Gospel Harmonettes, Sally Martin Singers, Brother Joe May, and Sister Wynona Carr.

Peacock also started its own booking operation with Evelyn Johnson at the helm. In the beginning, the Buffalo Booking Agency (BBA) handled the label's secular acts. "BBA was created," says Johnson, "because those [Peacock] artists didn't have anybody to represent them.... So, I applied for a franchise from the American Federation of Musicians. And that's how it all got started. I didn't know up from down."[52] With innate savvy, though, Johnson got the job done.

By the time the Dixie Hummingbirds arrived at Peacock, Johnson had set up a parallel agency to handle gospel. "The Spiritual Artists Agency was mine," says Johnson. "I went downtown and I got every permit and license, labor law, and this and that to operate an agency. I booked those gospel groups in the South."[53]

In the process, Johnson laid the groundwork for the southern extension of the "Chitlin' Circuit," that network of venues that catered to African American tastes, providing black artists the means to crisscross the country and earn a living wage. "For artists signed to the Duke and Peacock labels," writes James Salem, Johnny Ace biographer, "Evelyn Johnson had created by 1952 perhaps the most efficient system for arranging personal appearances of any independent label in America."[54]

Johnson proactively booked Peacock gospel acts, sending out advance notice to promoters about future tours and open dates and rates. Typical was a Bells of Joy flyer mailed in the fall of 1952 following their *Cash Box* award for best-selling spiritual record of the year, "Let's Talk About Jesus."

> This is to inform you that we have available a wonderful spiritual attraction, namely: The Bells of Joy.
>
>   You may select either of the following terms on the Group $250.00 Guarantee with 50% Privilege or $200.00 Guarantee with 60% Privilege for week days, and the Sunday dates are: $350.00 Guarantee with 50% Privilege or $300.00 Guarantee with 60% Privilege.

Johnson required a $50.00 per date deposit and offered "window card" advertisements at $10.00 per hundred. "Lobby pictures" and "news mats" would be provided free. The date—in this instance, November 4, 1952—was not flexible. "If we do not receive affirmation . . . within 10 days from the date of this letter, we shall consider this offer disaffirmed." The letter was mimeo-signed "Evelyn J. Johnson" with a P.S. "Let us know the *number* of Window cards you desire."

Johnson sent out a similar pitch in December of 1952 regarding the

Dixie Hummingbirds and the Angelic Gospel Singers, the latter at the time a Gotham recording act.

> We are promoting a series of dates on two of the best known spiritual groups in the field today, namely, THE DIXIE HUMMING BIRDS & THE ANGELIC GOSPEL SINGERS. We are positive that this is one of the best packages that you have had the opportunity to book in quite some time, and we feel that you will be passing up the opportunity of your life if you fail to take a date or a group of dates on this package.

The letter mentions both Peacock and Gotham titles by the Hummingbirds and the two groups together. The terms:

> SUNDAY DATES $500.00 guarantee with 50% privilege
> WEEK DATES $400.00 guarantee with 60% privilege
> DEPOSIT $100.00 on each date.

"Window cards" were $12.00 per hundred and the date offered was May 2, 1953, five months from the date of the letter's postmark.

With Peacock, the Dixie Hummingbirds had clearly signed on to an operation willing to work the group, their recorded output, and their personal appearances. It was an arrangement that lasted almost twenty-five years, spanning the glory years of both the label and the Dixie Hummingbirds.

"These guys have another kind of vision about this music . . ."

The Birds toured incessantly throughout 1952 and into 1953, endearing themselves to both fans and promoters by always putting commitment ahead of monetary gain, this at a time when they were beginning to command top dollar for personal appearances.

"The bookers really came to appreciate us," says Davis. "If the Hummingbirds give you a date for fifty dollars, don't care what they were offered, they will come to you for that amount." Davis underscores the point with a story about Roney Williams, a promoter who tripled an offer trying to get the Birds to cancel a Detroit date and come instead to Newark. The Birds turned him down. Those kinds of hard choices, agree both Davis and Tucker, helped them establish a reputation for integrity that stood them well over the years. "And Roney Williams," says Davis, "would always be preaching to other singers that he wished their group could be more like us—and some of those groups didn't like us because of it." In the end, though, the payoff for the Birds was a fierce fan loyalty and the trust of promoters.

One of the highlights for the Birds during this period was their annual homecoming trek to Greenville and Spartanburg, always a grand event. "Everybody went to see them," recollects William Bobo's cousin, Lula Mae Watts. "Bobo used to come and spend some time at my mother and father's house. They were real close." She remembers Bobo as "a lively person. And he could eat! His great food was buttermilk and corn bread."

And when the Birds were in town, they performed at the largest churches and auditoriums. "Any time they come back, they would draw a crowd. And a lot of white people went to see them. All in the same space."

> And if you didn't get a ticket early, you probably wouldn't find a seat. Sometimes it got so hot, doors would be open and there would be folks in there with fans fanning. . . . And when they would call up the Hummingbirds, everybody would stand and applaud.[55]

The Birds had also established a tradition of returning to Philadelphia each spring and marking their arrival with an Easter Monday concert at the Met. But thanks to their Peacock sides, their newfound stature as one of the leading acts in contemporary gospel also earned them invitations to perform at New York City's prestigious Carnegie Hall.

The first opportunity came in September 1952 when the Birds appeared there as part of Clara Ward's "Gospel Caravan." They would return in October of the following year to perform at the Fourth Annual Negro Gospel and Religious Music Festival headlined by Mahalia Jackson. A reviewer noted that the Dixie Hummingbirds had "stirred the crowd" and that "several nurses were on hand to revive those who passed out from sheer enthusiasm."[56]

A testament to their rising star, the Hummingbirds were also frequently asked to perform at anniversary programs in honor of other venerated groups. In September 1952, they traveled to Richmond to participate in a tribute to the Harmonizing Four on that group's twenty-fifth anniversary.[57] The event, staged in Richmond's City Stadium, featured three groups in the first half: the Sensational Nightingales, the Selah Jubilee Singers, and the Ward Singers. Then, following an intermission complete with fireworks came the Bells of Joy and the Angelic Gospel Singers—and in the prestigious closing spot, the Dixie Hummingbirds.

As the Birds crisscrossed the country, Don Robey strategically released Hummingbirds singles. As soon as sales slowed on one, Robey would release another. In June 1953, the third Peacock single, 1713, "Lord If I Go" b/w "Eternal Life," recorded the year before, was issued. That same month, the Birds returned to the studio to record six new tracks for future release. Two would be released as the fourth single the week of November 7, 1953. Peacock 1722 paired "I'll Keep on Living After I Die" with "Let's Go Out to the Programs," a track that would prove to be one of their most popular and enduring.

"I'll Keep on Living After I Die," an easygoing ballad seasoned with Tucker's gritty moans and falsetto crescendos and Howard Carroll's jazzy chords and blues fills, was the first of many tunes composed by Roxie Moore for the Dixie Hummingbirds. Moore and her husband Roosevelt were close friends of Ira Tucker and his wife Louise. Roosevelt Moore traveled regularly with the Birds; his primary job was "looking out for the door." He had earned the group's lasting trust by uncovering a counterfeit ticket scam at a concert in North Carolina. "They had to shut down everything until they straightened it out," says Roxie Moore.

Roxie had only the slightest musical training and no intention of becoming a professional songwriter. She thought of herself more as a poet. Living in Baltimore at the time, Moore had put a melody to a poem called "Jesus, He Looked On Me." She performed it in church, and it became a favorite with the congregation. "My husband told Ira that I had one song that everybody was singing, and so Ira asked me, how would I like to write for them."

Her approach was to "just walk around and start singing." If it sounded good, she wrote out the words, worked up a piano part, and recorded herself on tape. "'I'll Keep on Living After I Die' was a hit for the Birds, so they asked me to write more." Songwriting was never a big moneymaker for Moore. The royalty checks, always modest, came twice a year. "You might get six hundred dollars one time and three or four hundred the next time."[58]

While "Keep on Living" was popular, the firecracker proved to be "Let's Go Out to the Programs," a Tucker original. Literally, nothing like it had ever been done before in gospel. "We were in Chicago getting ready to do a broadcast one Sunday morning," says Tucker, "sitting back at the station. I heard them play this 'Juke Box Saturday Night,' and I said 'Hey, let me try something just like that.'" "Juke Box" had originally been a hit for the Modernaires in the early 1940s. In it, they imitated the top pop vocal groups of the day. That Sunday morning, Tucker was hearing the Modernaire's updated version, "New Juke Box Saturday Night," released in 1953 on the Coral label. Tucker wrote his version—a string of dead-on gospel quartet impressions—that same morning.[59]

The track kicked off with bright vocal harmony chords over drums, handclapping, and guitar:

> Oh, preachers and friends, If you want to hear singing,
> Good old gospel singing,
> Go out to the programs, Whenever they're in your town.
>
> Well, today they have the Blind Boys, the Soul Stirrers,
> The Pilgrim Travelers, and the Bells of Joy,
> They're gonna sing God's praises, Word for word,
> And now we present [pause]
> THE SOUL STIRRERS . . .

With that, Tucker and the Birds launched into their impression of the Soul Stirrers, and in turn each of the other named quartets. They closed the medley with their own "Trouble in My Way" and the invitation to "go out to the programs whenever they're in your town." A masterpiece of homage and marketing in one three-minute musical package.

"At first," says Tucker, "some people at different record companies, when they heard it said, we going to see you in court." They thought Robey had without permission spliced together actual samples from these hit recordings. "But Robey finally said, 'No, no. That's *my* artists," meaning Tucker and the Hummingbirds, "doing all of that."

"Let's Go Out to the Programs" caught the full attention of the gospel world. Larry Fuller, host of Harlem's WLIB "Gospel Train," told *Billboard* that "with each hearing, . . . he finds himself loving it more and more."[60] Says Jerry Butler of the Impressions, "My favorite recollection of the Birds was that they had the audacity to imitate all the other great gospel groups."

"Let's Go Out to the Programs," I must've been twelve, thirteen years old when I heard that. Now, Archie Brownlee was one of the greatest gospel singers of the time—and *nobody* sounded like Archie Brownlee. And there was Sam Cooke. And then here comes Ira Tucker saying, "I'm good enough to sing like that guy!" They say imitation is the greatest form of flattery, so, here they were imitating the giants!

But, you know, aside from all that, "Let's Go Out to the Programs" was not *just* a gospel piece. I remember thinking at the time, "These guys have another kind of vision about this music that transcends the spirituality of the church."[61]

"The thing about 'Let's Go Out to the Programs,'" says James Davis, "is that we showed people we could sing like anybody."

"They joined forces and twinned up on him!"

For the Birds and for gospel, 1953 was a stellar year. A year-end retrospective in the *Chicago Defender* decried the absence of African Americans in mainstream entertainment, especially the "newest media, television," which "seems to exclude the Negro entirely." The one exception, noted the *Defender*, was a recent "trend" of the "acceptance of gospel singers by audiences throughout the country." Gospel, of all genres, was garnering national attention. Mahalia Jackson and the Pilgrim Travelers were singled out with the observation that their concert hall and theater appearances were "broadening their scope from the church alone."[62]

That year, according to figures compiled by *Billboard*, the Soul Stirrers had earned $78,000, the Pilgrim Travelers $100,000 on 173 dates, and Clarence Fountain's Alabama Blind Boys, $130,000 in 40 weeks. Gospel record sales were averaging about 10,000 per single.[63] Don Robey also had a lucrative year. In early 1954, the entire Duke/Peacock operation moved to larger quarters. Robey reported a million and a half records sold in 1953, most of them Willie Mae Thornton's "Hound Dog," but 500,000, "Let's Go Out to the Programs" by the Dixie Hummingbirds, an exceptional tally for a record in any genre.[64]

The Hummingbirds, and Ira Tucker in particular, had become true gospel stars. And their impact derived not only from their music but also from their appearance. "A lot of people would come out just to see what we were wearing," says James Davis. It was in about 1953 that the Hummingbirds donned white tailed tuxedos and struck an art deco pose for a Peacock publicity shot. "The idea for the white tuxedos," says Ira Tucker, "came from the Soul Stirrers."

R. H. Harris and the Stirrers came to Turner Hall in Philadelphia and that's what they had on. And I said, "Gentlemen, that's what we need!" I was judging from the applause they got when they walked in. They had a different look and it had a lot of assurance to it—like the house is mine. They didn't have to sing so hard. They looked so much better than everybody else until it was easy.

The Hummingbirds had their white tuxes custom tailored at Wool-muth's in Philadelphia. "And when we first came out in them," remembers Tucker, "I was so hoarse, I couldn't hardly talk. But, man, we took the show. Because of the tuxedos. And we got to be known as the dressing-est group on the road."

One of the audience members impressed by the Birds that night was James Williams, then a teenager. He remembers thinking when the Birds came out, "Now, that's my style! I liked the way they looked. . . . I knew then I wanted to be a quartet singer."[65] Not long after, the sons of James Davis and William Bobo—James, Jr., and William, Jr.—would recruit Williams to sing in a group called the Varietyaires. Under the tutelage of the Hummingbirds, the Varietyaires would become the Sons of the Birds and tour as openers for their mentors/fathers, their ambition fueled by the elegant vision they all had of the Dixie Hummingbirds and the magnetic Ira Tucker.

In the wake of this burst of popularity, James Davis was having concerns that gospel shouting was taking a toll on Tucker's voice. It was in the studio in 1954 that Davis began taking notice. "I remember one song we did in Chicago. We hollered so *loud* on it. But the guys we had backing us said, 'Oh boy, the people going to eat this up.' And the people *did* like the song, but I never did because we were hollering too loud." Howard Carroll's amplified electric guitar only exacerbated the problem onstage. Tucker was pushing his voice harder than ever. "You're screaming," Tucker told interviewer Seamus McGarvey, "trying to be heard, and pretty soon you'll have a . . . problem."[66]

Davis decided to bring an alternate lead singer into the group to ease the pressure on Tucker. Rumor had it, though, that Davis was actually looking for someone to put Tucker in his place. As Barney Parks recalls, "I heard Davis got another singer because he was trying to hold Tucker down. Tucker knew he had weight in the group. Wouldn't have no Birds without Tucker. Back then, he could be a little contrary at times, so Davis wanted to let Tucker know somebody else could step in."

Davis brought James Emerdia Walker into the group in early 1954. Born in Mileston, Mississippi, on May 24, 1926, Walker was an experienced gospel singer and, like so many of his contemporaries, was raised on gospel singing. "My family was very religious and naturally, I grew up in the church. Every Sunday we had to go to church whether we wanted to or not."[67] In 1941, Walker moved to Missouri and began singing professionally around St. Louis. During the war, he joined the Navy, returning afterward to St. Louis where he began singing with a quartet called the Union Melody Men. Walker was traveling with them when he crossed paths with Clifford Givens, bass singer and leader of the Southern Sons.[68]

James Walker became the lead singer in Givens's third incarnation of the Southern Sons. Based in Jackson, Mississippi, the Sons recorded for Trumpet Records and soon emerged as the hottest group in town, often, according to Givens, beating out the other hometown heavies, Archie Brownlee and the Five Blind Boys.[69]

Walker left the Southern Sons in 1953 to join the famous Harmonizing Four. He traveled with the Four and recorded at least two tracks with them on Gotham where he caught the attention of James Davis. Walker's versatility suited the Birds who still loved to mix it up, shifting voices and switching parts when they sang. "Walker could do just about any voice in the quartet," says Tucker.

But Walker also brought to the Dixie Hummingbirds a gift for song-writing. One of his best, "A Prayer for Tomorrow," was written in 1953 for the Southern Sons. In the tradition of Paul Robeson and the Golden Gate Quartet, the song had a political message. "Prayer" was a sincere reflection of Walker's thinking at the time, and it expressed the sensibilities of the growing civil rights movement. "I always wanted to sing songs I could get a feeling from," says Walker. "Not just a beat. I like to sing songs with a message."[70] Released on Trumpet, "A Prayer for Tomorrow" would one day be rewritten by Walker for the Dixie Hummingbirds.

> Lord, help us to love one another,
> Every creed and every color
> Help us to honor father and mother
> Help us to know we are sister and brother . . .
>
> I long to see that great day come,
> When everybody will be as one,
> When there will be no separating,
> When there will be no discriminating . . .
>
> This is my prayer for tomorrow . . .

By April of 1954, the Birds had assimilated Walker into their vocal blend and were ready to return to the studio.

At the April Peacock sessions, the Birds recorded for the first time as a sextet in what would be the quintessential lineup of the Dixie Hummingbirds: James Davis, Ira Tucker, James Walker, Beachey Thompson, William Bobo, and Howard Carroll. Six tracks were recorded—two traditional, "Sinner, Sin No More" and "Poor Pilgrim of Sorrow," Roxie Moore's "Will the Lord Be with Me," Tucker's "Christian Testimonial" and "Devil Can't Harm a Praying Man," and Walker's "Take Care of Me."

All six were put aside for later release and instead two more tracks from the year before were issued in mid-July. Peacock 1727 featured Tucker leads on "Prayer Wheel" and Roxie Moore's "Live Right, Die Right." Both were given a four-star rating by *Billboard*.

Hummingbirds 1950s-era Peacock 45-rpm in its paper sleeve.

"Live Right" was a mellow swing jubilee, Bobo popping out the bass with Howard Carroll contributing guitar chords and fills unconventional in gospel.

> I fully decided, I counted the cost,
> I made it up in my mind,
> To live right, to die right,
> Cross Jordan at a calm time.

"Prayer Wheel" was inspired by the Heavenly Gospel Singers, who recorded their version in 1936. Tucker's melody and arrangement, though, were completely different. The song begins dirge-like with a heavy drum backbeat reminiscent of the Mississippi Blind Boys. The performance takes off from there, kicking into high gear on the rhythm of the phrase, "Prayer Wheel Keep on Turning in My Heart."

The record was a double-sided seller for Peacock and the Dixie Hummingbirds. The group's stock in the gospel market continued to rise. The follow-up, Peacock 1736, issued four months later in October, coupled two of the sides cut earlier that spring with James Walker in the lineup.

Side one, Walker's recording debut as a lead singer with the Birds, was Roxie Moore's "Will the Lord Be with Me," in which he and Tucker traded off on leads. Side two was "Christian Testimonial," a Tucker composition with Walker and group "backgrounding," Tucker delivering a soulful lead in his pleading ballad style.

> I've tried everything, but I couldn't find nothing,
> Like serving the Lord, Oh Yeah.
> I tried gambling,
> Lying,
> Midnight riding,
> Backsliding,
> But I couldn't find nothing, like serving the Lord.

The record was a powerful year-end release for the Birds, their sixth in a string of well-received singles, and sales were brisk. "Christian Testimonial" became a Birds standard, and "Will the Lord Be with Me" was Roxie Moore's best-selling Birds song ever.

That fall, on Thanksgiving Day 1954, the Birds returned to Philadelphia to perform at the Met with the Angelics, the Davis Sisters, and

Edna Galmon Cooke, now married to and managed by Barney Parks. Turkeys were offered as door prizes and anyone over the age of seventy was "admitted for half price and will sit on stage as Guests of the Evening." Throughout that holiday season, the *Philadelphia Tribune* ran a promotion offering with every new subscription a free record by either the Birds, the Angelics, the Davis Sisters, or Clara Ward. "All new Gotham releases," read the ads, although the Hummingbirds' sides, "What Then" b/w "Down On Me," were already almost four years old. Toward the end of the year, Robey announced the release of Peacock 1740, "I'm Not Uneasy," another from the June 1953 sessions, paired with "Sinner, Sin No More," recorded that past April with Walker and Tucker sharing lead. It would be the seventh Dixie Hummingbirds single.

If the intention in hiring Walker was to put Tucker in his place, it had backfired. "James Davis was a hard taskmaster," said Evelyn Johnson, "and he ruled that group. Make no mistake. He brought Walker in as competition for Tucker, but they did just the opposite. Ira and James would do a lot of back and forth as they built the show. They joined forces and twinned up on him!"

"If anyone is guilty of taking a beat, then it's the current rhythm and blues artists."

By 1955, gospel's commercial rise had bottomed out, with record sales down 25 percent from the previous year's levels. *Billboard* attributed the slump to fans of traditional gospel who felt a "strong resentment . . . against the commercialization of religion." These "gospel devotees," reported the magazine, believed there should be "no connection between their music and any other kind of music, even classical, and, furthermore, want no association with these other fields."

Even more controversial was soul gospel's close relationship with rhythm and blues and the newly emerging rock 'n' roll. "The artists, their recording companies, and the churches, . . . these people, the core of the business, claim that gospel or spiritual music should not be classed in the rhythm and blues category, as it has been for quite some time. The claim is that R&B actually was an outcropping of the gospel field."[71]

Indeed, the debate cropped up often that year in the black press. Specialty recording artist Brother Joe May told the *Chicago Defender*, "This so-called rhythm and blues is nothing more than an off-shoot of good gospel song." May cautioned that "failure to recognize R and B for what it really is may cause a general undermining of all true gospel singing everywhere."[72]

Clara Ward "heatedly" denied remarks by "blues singer Lavern Baker that she was injecting a Rock and Roll beat into her religious tunes." Baker had complained that the "nation's gospel quartets were copying rhythm and blues songs." Ward responded, "If anyone is guilty of taking a beat, then it's the current rhythm and blues artists, because most of them are former choir singers."[73] Philadelphia disk jockey Kae Williams concurred, telling the *Tribune* that "spiritual copy-cats" included Ray Charles whose "I've Got a Woman" and "This Little Girl of Mine" were "direct copies of spiritual songs."[74]

All of this, reported *Billboard,* added up to gospel record buyers not being willing to "enter a retail store to purchase records" because of the unholy mix of blues, R&B, jazz, pop, and classical available on the same shelves. By mid-decade, mail order had become the prime source for purchasing gospel recordings, as sales between 7,500 and 12,500 remained the average and 20,000 signified a "hit."

The Birds by then were in a category that left them unaffected by the slumping sales and the debates. Don Robey called them members of his "100 percent club" because every record he had released by them had been a hit.[75] In their recordings, they managed to toe a fine line between traditional and modern; their reliance remained primarily on vocals and their only concession to trend occasional drums and Howard Carroll's electric guitar. Their records sold respectably and steadily. As to their colleagues in the field, the Birds were nonjudgmental. For them, the value of the music was in the message and the instrumental trappings were only a means of delivery.

Along with the Dixie Hummingbirds and label-mates the Five Blind Boys, *Billboard* listed top-selling gospel artists at mid-decade as Mahalia Jackson, the Soul Stirrers, the Pilgrim Travelers, Professor Alex Bradford, Brother Joe May, the Gospel Harmonettes, the Angelics, the Caravans, the Roberta Martin Singers, the Wards, the Swan Silvertones, the Spirit of Memphis, and the Trumpeteers. "Major markets" for black gospel were Birmingham, Baltimore, Detroit, Pittsburgh, New York, Los Angeles, Cleveland, Philadelphia, Cincinnati, and St. Louis. Concert bookings and performance fees were up, and though gospel record sales were down, the disks continued to sell steadily. As one retailer put it, "I never have to return my spiritual records. I can keep them for years, that's true, but eventually, somebody will come in and buy them."[76]

Because of the decline in gospel record sales, Peacock slowed the output of Dixie Hummingbirds releases over the next two years. The Birds were maximizing their time on the road—their major source of income—and they now had a substantial backlog of singles for release as needed.

Peacock 1742, "It Must Have Been the Lord That Touched Me" b/w "Take Care of Me" was issued in July 1955. "It Must Have Been the Lord" had been recorded two years earlier. Walker's "Take Care of Me," on the other hand, was cut the year before. It was his first solo outing as a Birds lead singer, and, in later years, Walker would call it his favorite. Walker's presentation was easygoing, the Birds in parallel harmony as Walker accented with facile leaps into falsetto. Brushed drums and guitar provided the rhythmic backdrop.

> Well, mother and father, they are both gone,
> They left me in this world all alone,
> You know I'm trusting in you Jesus,
> I want you to take care of me.

The Birds only other single release in 1955, Peacock 1753, was as background to Otis Jackson's "The Life Story of Madame Bethune, Parts 1 & 2," a tribute to the founder/president emeritus of Bethune-Cookman College in Daytona Beach, Florida. "A sure-fire hit and collector's item," reported the *Philadelphia Tribune.* "[77]

> I shall attempt to recite,
> The life story of Madame Mary McCleod Bethune,
> It was in the year of eighteen seventy-five,
> Another gift to America became alive,
> Then I said to myself,
> That it wasn't too soon,
> Because we need more true Americans,
> Like Madame Mary McCleod Bethune.

The song, though maudlin to some tastes, fit squarely into the ballad tradition—story-songs about important events of the day—the most common way to honor African American heroes. Gospel was the fitting milieu for such a tribute.

The Dixie Hummingbirds sang tribute again in 1955, this time for twenty-six-year-old Thelma Davis of the famous Davis Sisters. "10,000

Mourners Jam Davis Rites," blared the *Tribune* headline. "At least a half dozen persons fainted during the seven hour long emotion-charged services." Police guarded the sanctuary doors of the Cornerstone Baptist Church where benches had been broken from "the crush of spectators trying to get one last look." The Dixie Hummingbirds sang in homage at the funeral, as did the Daniel Singers, Alex Bradford, the Roberta Martin Singers, and the Wards.[78]

The season had been sad, but by spring, the Dixie Hummingbirds would have two more singles on the market and a primary role in the inauguration of a tradition at the nation's premier showplace for African American talent, the Apollo Theater.

"Devil can't harm a praying man!"

Robey launched 1956 with a ninth Hummingbirds single, Peacock 1757, "Devil Can't Harm a Praying Man" b/w "Poor Pilgrim of Sorrow." "Pilgrim" was a gospel standard, but "Devil Can't Harm a Praying Man" was a rollicking Tucker original with a novelty edge that made it one of the Birds' best loved hits.

Howard Carroll opened with a flurry of jazzy guitar chords followed by a bravura vocal intro. "Devil can't harm a praying ma-a-a-an." Tucker picked it up from there and over Bobo's pumping bass, engaged the group in brisk dialogue.

> IRA: Brothers and sisters, if you want to see my Jesus,
> GROUP: Let me tell you what to do,
> IRA: Fall down on your knees, and get good religion, now,
> GROUP: That's just what you've got to do.
> IRA: You've got to ...   GROUP: Pray!
> IRA: In the morning ...   GROUP: Pray!
> IRA: In the evening ...   GROUP: Pray!
> IRA: Way over in the midnight hour!   GROUP: Pra-a-a-ay!
> IRA: Somebody needs to pray now,
> ALL: Devil can't harm a praying man!

Then, in the middle, Tucker broke into a rap, Howard Carroll riffing rapid fire behind him on single-note guitar runs.

> Now, here's one thing, boys,
> You know, I can't understand,
> The devil told God,

> That he could make a man,
> But the Lord caught the devil,
> In a great big lie,
> He kicked him out of heaven . . .

Bobo picked it up there, moving deeper down the scale with each word.

> And . . . ga-a-ve . . . him . . . the . . . FIRE.

The group comes back in and finishes with a final admonition: "Devil can't harm a praying man," Howard Carroll capping it with two quick-slash guitar chords.

"Devil Can't Harm a Praying Man" propelled an entire year's worth of appearances by the Hummingbirds. That winter, on the strength of that and their other Peacock hits, the Dixie Hummingbirds were invited to headline the second all-gospel show ever staged at the Apollo Theater.

The Apollo booking was extremely important to the Birds, a true measure of their stature in the gospel field. They were tops in the genre. Meanwhile, other quartets and singers like the Golden Gates, Mahalia Jackson, and Clara Ward had managed to appeal to broader audiences by tempering style or presenting themselves "in the tradition" as folk performers. For the Dixie Hummingbirds, cross-cultural appeal remained elusive. Instead, the Birds had committed to gospel Peacock-style, making music *their* way for *their* people.

The Apollo at 253 West 125th Street in Harlem was black America's leading showplace for African American artists to perform exclusively for African American audiences. The theater, initially a music hall in 1913, then a vaudeville house, became the Mecca for black entertainment in 1934. The first show under the Apollo rubric was "Jazz à la Carte" starring the Benny Carter big band. Over the years, Armstrong, Calloway, Ellington, Bessie Smith, Bojangles Robinson, the Nicholas Brothers, Butterbeans and Susie, Moms Mabley, Pigmeat Markham, and many others played the Apollo.

By the time of the Birds' booking in the middle 1950s, the Apollo offered top-quality jazz along with rhythm and blues and rock 'n' roll revues, especially blues shouters and doo-wop groups including Big Joe Turner, Wynonie Harris, the Spaniels, Hank Ballard and the Midnighters, the Flamingos, the Orioles, and the Ravens.

Thermon "T" Ruth of the Selah Jubilees, longtime friend to the Dixie Hummingbirds, at the time was hosting *Ship of Zion*, a popular radio show airing on Harlem's WOV. Ruth approached Frank Schiffman, the owner of the Apollo, about, as Ruth tells it, "putting gospel in like the rock-and-roll shows. . . . It had never been done. Nobody had gone into the Apollo Theater with gospel." The Apollo's R&B programs had occasionally included gospel acts; for example, the previous May, Sister Rosetta Tharpe and Marie Knight had headlined a bill that also included the R&B group the Cardinals and the comedy team of Flournoy Miller and Mantan Moreland. But the Apollo had *never* staged an exclusively gospel show.

Thermon Ruth went to Schiffman, "who said, 'I don't think gospel will go here. They'll probably just throw eggs at you.' But he gave me a chance and told me to come back in two weeks." Ruth also had a problem with the local clergy, many of whom thought "to take God's music out of his holy place was one of the biggest unforgivable sins." One elderly Harlem resident declared to Ruth that "the Apollo is the devil's house; . . . righteous folks don't go in there and sinners can't hardly find their way out."[79]

Schiffman's son, Jack, explains that his father called together a group of ministers and told them about the plan: "an all-gospel program, presented with taste, dignity, and sincerity."[80] Thermon Ruth did the same on his end, conferring with prominent clergyman Bishop F. D. Washington, husband of Sister Ernestine Washington. Bishop Washington's response: "If you want to catch some fish, you must go out to the river."[81]

For Schiffman, there was another distinct advantage. Gospel historian Horace Boyer notes that the Apollo was losing money at the time. A sameness had befallen the shows and audiences were losing interest. Second, numerous integrated clubs opening up around the city were drawing African American performers and audiences away from the Apollo. Schiffman's choice was to move in a direction still "left untouched by white entrepreneurs: gospel."[82]

Performers, too, had to be convinced to play the Apollo. Although the blessings of religious leaders helped, the prestige of the venue and the sizable performance fees tipped the balance. "Mr. Schiffman guaranteed the money," says Ruth. "The groups were paid nice money. One group in those days could make $3000 for a week's engagement."[83]

The first "Gospel Caravan," as Ruth called his program, took place over the weekend of December 15, 1955. The opening was feted in the

African American press nationwide. There would be "four shows daily," reported the *Chicago Defender*, and "the idea of using gospel groups via this means in a regular vaudeville house is unprecedented in the annals of show business."[84] The inaugural program featured the Pilgrim Travelers, the Mississippi Blind Boys, the Caravans with Albertina Walker and James Cleveland on piano, Brother Joe May, the Sensational Nightingales, and the Harmonizing Four.

The Apollo shows were set up so that all the performers were on stage throughout. "We had chairs out on the stage with that church atmosphere," explains Ruth.

> Everybody would be singing that opening song, "Glory Hallelujah" or "Since I Laid My Burdens Down." After that, they introduced me as master of ceremonies, and I'd bring the first act on. Each group used to push one another. If one group was singing, the other group was clapping or they would help you amen or something to help you out. This was cooperative. Everybody wanted to see everybody go big.[85]

The first all-gospel event at the Apollo was a winner for all concerned. Thermon Ruth, reported *Billboard*, "had a successful week with his Gospel Caravan at NY's Apollo Theater. . . . Good crowds attended the day-time shows, but the evening hours filled the house to overflowing."[86]

Frank Schiffman ordered up more "Gospel Caravans," and Thermon Ruth scheduled the next one for the week of March 23 with the Dixie Hummingbirds headlining. Booked to appear with them were the Davis Sisters and the Wards. The *Defender* reported that Clara Ward had cleared her participation with "ministers and civic leaders" and cut short a southern tour "to return to Philadelphia to prepare for their Apollo debut."[87] The bill also featured a number of local acts, the Charles Taylor All-Stars, the Skylights, and soloist Christine Clark, who had recently been discovered at an Apollo amateur night.[88]

Like the premiere, the second "Gospel Caravan" was a critical and financial success, ensuring that the event would continue at the Apollo for decades to come. The Dixie Hummingbirds would return often, sometimes twice a year. Gospel at the Apollo would be an experience they would never forget.

Dionne Warwick, whose mother sang with the Drinkard Singers, recalls people "falling out all over the place," including the balconies. "Brothers with shark skinned suits and alligator shoes," remembers

Thermon Ruth, "rolling down the aisles, sisters . . . jumping up and down, . . . Every seat . . . filled and . . . others waiting to get inside to see some of the best gospel singers of all time performing outside the church."[89]

Beverly Lee of the Shirelles remembers "such a spirit in the building . . . People would faint. . . . The gospel acts . . . sang from the bottom of their shoes . . . and the notes they hit were incredible."

"Somebody would jump up and scream and take off like a shot," recalls Schiffman's youngest son, Bobby, "but what you had to be careful of was that they didn't go into a spastic convulsion." Nurses were always on duty at the Apollo gospel shows.[90]

Ira Tucker, Jr., loved to go to the Apollo shows to see his father perform. When not in the wings, he sat in the front row taking it all in. Indelibly etched in his memory, proud performers like Little Baldhead Johnny and the Mule Man who in lieu of a handout sang for a pass of the hat. "Little Baldhead Johnny had no tongue and would come up and pray for everybody, and the 'Mule Man'—we never did know his name—had buck teeth and a face like a mule. He would work the audience with the collection plate while Little Johnny prayed." Most of all, Tucker remembers Yvonne and Yvette, joined-at-the-head gospel-singing Siamese twins. "Yvonne and Yvette would give it a try," says Tucker, "but the sad fact was they couldn't sing a note!" All of these elements made up the charged atmosphere that was gospel at the Apollo.

For the performers, the experience was a mix of glory and grueling routine. There were four shows a day with an extra midnight show on Saturdays. Each group was allotted ten minutes, but they "never came off on time," says Thermon Ruth. The "spirit would get them, and instead of singing ten minutes, they'd sing twenty-five minutes, thirty-five minutes. Some . . . would stay almost an hour."[91]

Willa Ward-Royster remembers that she and sister Clara dreaded the experience. "Even when not performing we had to sit on stage for the duration of each show. . . . I was so exhausted, I sometimes skipped a show. . . . Poor Clara was beat, too, but dared not miss a performance. . . . She dipped heavily into the bottle to make it through. She would sit on stage completely dropped out until it was time for her to sing herself back to consciousness. Most of the time I was her 'bag lady,' carrying Clara's booze in my handbag to keep Mom [Gertrude Ward] from finding it in hers."[92]

Leroy Crume played the Apollo with the Soul Stirrers. "Working at the Apollo," says Crume, "was just like going to the steel mill everyday."

But we did it because the Apollo was such a hot spot. And people that came to the Apollo would see us that didn't come to our concerts—which would mean the young people. The Apollo was a hot spot for young kids. And although we had a young audience when Sam Cooke came to the group, there were some rock 'n' rollers who didn't want to dress up to come to our concerts—at that time, people dressed up to come to gospel concerts—but would go to the Apollo, dress any way they want to dress. There were people at the Apollo who wouldn't ordinarily come to our concerts in church and other auditoriums. It was a hot spot, and so we did it. That could increase our popularity.[93]

As it did with the Dixie Hummingbirds. "The Dixie Hummingbirds were one of my favorites," wrote Thermon Ruth in his biography. "Ira Tucker was one of the greatest lead singers. To me, the Dixie Hummingbirds were real pure gospel singers."[94]

"We played at the Apollo a lot," says Ira Tucker. "The money was good. Better than anything we had been doing in the churches. Gospel was really the rage then. The rafters were really ringing. First show was about twelve something. Last show was about twelve something. We were really a big name. And the backstage atmosphere was great!" The backstage camaraderie, in fact, was a saving grace that made the routine tolerable. There, performers had a chance to stay put for a time and form lasting friendships. Leroy Crume remembers the card games. "Everybody would join in. We'd play what we called 'rise and fly.' When you lose, you get up and leave! We were stuck there all day! We were so tired we couldn't go out anyway."[95]

At the Apollo doing four shows a day, the Birds perfected material and performance style. There were rivalries, and groups tried to get over on one another. The Hummingbirds learned from the competition, and the competition learned from them. "They were great," says Leroy Crume.

The Birds was star material. You gotta watch the Birds. Keep your eye on Ira Tucker and James Walker. When Walker and Tuck get in their stride, man, they was something else. They started chanting back to each other with the mikes. Tuck would have the mike and then shove it over to Walker, then back to himself, over to Walker. They'd get down on their knees and they start prancing around on the stage. It's hard to describe. You just have to see it.

Occasionally, the Birds and the Soul Stirrers were booked together at the Apollo. Ira Tucker, Jr., has vivid memories of those performances. He talked about them as James Davis sat nearby listening. "Sam Cooke and the Stirrers would take the house," he said. "Then the Hummingbirds would have to come behind them. The people would still be into the Soul Stirrers when the Hummingbirds were now walking on to the stage. I would sit there wondering . . ." James Davis cut him off abruptly and finished the sentence. "How are they going to do this?" Tucker smiled and picked it up again. "All of a sudden," he said, "the Birds would bring the house down to almost a whisper." Then Davis again. "That's the way we did it! . . . Don't try to start no fire on their fire. Don't do that or you'll go down in flames!"

"Strategy," Ira Tucker, Sr., called it—entertainment savvy. The Birds were masters at working the audience. Horace Boyer calls Tucker the "model for the 'activity' singer.' He ran up and down the aisles, jumped from the stage, and spun around without sacrificing one iota of the pure musical sound that he first brought to the quartet. Indeed, he served as the model for many of the rhythm and blues and soul singers from Jackie Wilson and Clyde McPhatter to Bobby 'Blue' Bland and the Temptations."[96]

The Gospel Caravan shows brought the best in spiritual entertainment to the Apollo for the remainder of the decade and well beyond. An Italian film director, Nino Falanga, famous for tabloid films like *Mondo Cane*, documented performances by the Dixie Hummingbirds, the Selahs, and the Swanees, subsequently released in a 1960 movie called *The World by Night*. Over time, "T" Ruth would have competition as other producers—most notably Doc Wheeler and Fred Barr of radio station WWRL—brought their own gospel extravaganzas into the Apollo.

"Glad to see him come, but glad to see him go!"

The Dixie Hummingbirds maintained their pace, marking their touring year with high points like the appearances at the Apollo, Easter Sunday shows at the Laurel Gardens in Newark, Easter Monday at the Met, and anniversary concerts in Philly and again in Raleigh for Carolina family and fans.

Davis, Tucker, Walker, Thompson, Bobo, and Carroll were tighter than ever. James Williams, the young fan who went on to sing with the Sons of the Birds, traveled with his mentors during this period and felt like an outsider when he first heard the private lingo the Birds had developed on the road together over the years. "Mr. Tucker would say, 'That group's got sandpaper in their pockets.'"

> I'd say, "What do you mean by that, Mr. Tucker?" He'd say, "That's a rough group." . . . The first time he said, "Slim is here, Joe," I said, "Who is Slim?" He said, "That means a slim crowd." He'd say when a group did pretty good, "That's a sweet singing group." Or, if you "go on the mountain," that means you really bombed out, didn't go over." Suits were called "togs." Shoes are called "kicks." It took me a long time to understand the language.[97]

The Birds, although often on the road, had set down firm roots in Philadelphia. They had nice homes in inner city neighborhoods and sufficient income to pay the bills with a few luxuries. Families remained intact, children joyfully welcomed their fathers' returns, and wives dutifully maintained the home front. There was pride at being part of the Dixie Hummingbirds family and wonderful opportunities to accompany the Birds to performances and meet the fans, fellow performers, celebrities, and dignitaries who attended.

"Beachey was away most of the time," says Carrie Thompson, "but it was a wonderful reunion when he came back." She and her two sons, Beachey, Jr., and Sonny, "were glad to see him come, but glad to see him go." In her case, she did not mind the "solitary lifestyle" and enjoyed staying home with family. Carrie Thompson maintained a friendship with Hortense Davis, wife of James Davis. "We would dress the kids up, get together and take them to play in the park." [98]

Howard Carroll's wife, Mabel tells much the same story. She and Howard met in 1939. "He was singing in the street, he and Carl Meade, the minister he was playing for." As far as the months away from home, "We understood that it's a job that has to be done. I knew that going in. I knew what I had to do," she says. "I was the man and the woman. The father and the mother. I kept a firm hold."[99]

Ira Tucker's wife, Louise, responds with a "hah!" when asked how many days of the year her husband was on the road. "Three hundred and sixty!" she says. "He was in and out, but he was gone most of the time." And like the other spouses, Louise handled it in stride. "At the time they really started to make money, it was fine with him going, staying away. Certainly they didn't get their just dues. But I had the money to pay whatever had to be paid," she says. "And there were times when I would go with them. . . . Ira's mother was living with me at the time and she could take care of the children. But I never stayed too long. I hated the road. I never really liked the road." Ira Tucker breaks in at this point. "And I'll tell you, I never taught my children nothing!" he says with genuine regret. "Louise did. I never saw 'em." He mentions a "little stage" that Louise used to bring out. "But they wouldn't put it up when I was around. Kept it down in the cellar."

Louise continues, "I didn't want him to know what we were really doing when he was away. But we would have a show every Saturday night and the children would sing."

"And I didn't even know my daughters could sing!" says Tucker.

Louise continues, "We called it the 'Saturday Night Late Show.' I got the name from an album by Dakota Staton. Of course, I would have the ice cream and the cookies and all, and of course the children loved that."

And Louise Tucker would have the children sing. "Of course, my son, Ira, Jr., he didn't want to do nothing but beat the drums. He would take his sticks and beat the cotton out of the arm of the chair. And Sundray would sing the soft sweet stuff she always loved. And Linda always loved music that was really jumping and moving. I always had to tell her don't sing so loud because she was that kind who would blast away."

It was Linda's precocious singing that landed her a spot on shows with the Dixie Hummingbirds. Louise Tucker remembers it started with a dream. "I just saw Linda on top of the Empire State Building singing! It just got me until I got up out of the bed." That morning she had Linda sing the "Lord's Prayer." Linda asked if she could stand on the table. Louise lifted her up, "and she sung the 'Lord's Prayer' from the beginning until the living end."

Meanwhile, Ira's still sleeping and she woke him up. Ira came to the top of the stairs and said "Louise. Who is that singing?" I said, "It's just Linda."

He said, "Baby, sing that again for daddy." She started over. Did the same thing. Ira sat down and said, "Will you sing that at daddy's anniversary?" And Linda said, "Yeah, daddy. I'll sing it."

That night at the Met, Roney Williams announced Linda. "Ira Tucker's daughter! And she's going to introduce the show!" "Linda was four at the time," says Louise. "She went through the whole thing, did that note on the end, and the house came down!"

For a few years in the late 1950s, Linda Tucker opened for the Birds— even at the Apollo—until she was old enough to start school. As Linda

Lawrence, she would go on to sing backups for Stevie Wonder and eventually became one of the Supremes with Diana Ross. Sundray Tucker also grew up to work in music. In the 1960s, she sang backup for Patti LaBelle and later, joining her sister, with Stevie Wonder. Later, Sundray would work with producer Leon Huff, eventually forming her own group, the Three Degrees. In recent years, Sundray has made a name for herself in England's "Northern Soul" scene as soul diva Cindy Scott. Ira Tucker, Jr., graduated from the Philadelphia Musical Academy and worked in the music division of the Philadelphia public school system. Through his sisters, he would meet Stevie Wonder and become Wonder's publicist and confidant.

"They had a congregation behind them for concerts."

As the Dixie Hummingbirds forged ahead making gospel history, the world of popular music changed rapidly around them. By 1956, Philadelphia was home to the hottest teen rock 'n' roll show in the nation. Dick Clark, a young white disk jockey, had parlayed a radio program into a nationally syndicated dance party—*American Bandstand*. Local teenagers came after school to the WFIL studios to dance to the latest records, many of them by black artists like Chuck Berry and Little Richard, Ruth Brown and LaVern Baker, the Bobbettes and the Chantels, the Flamingos, Penguins, Moonglows, and Five Satins. Often, black performers appeared as guests on the show.

In the fall of 1956, the *Tribune* ran a story decrying that African American teenagers had been barred from the WFIL studios. The station denied the allegations, but a receptionist acknowledged that there had been complaints.[100] It took a year of protests from black teenagers before the barriers finally came down.

African American artists like the Dixie Hummingbirds, because they worked within a cultural tradition, stood outside and independent of rock 'n' roll and its attendant prejudices. Their popularity base lay primarily within the African American community. That would begin to shift, though, late in the 1950s.

In gospel, some artists continued to extend the music across color and genre lines. In 1957, Mahalia Jackson and Clara Ward, appearing on a bill that also included Count Basie and Sarah Vaughan, became the first gospel artists to play the Newport Jazz Festival, then in its fourth year. Festival organizers justified their choice by describing gospel as "one of the most basic forms of jazz."[101]

The Jackson and Ward festival appearance was so successful that promoters launched an eight-week gospel tour of "ball parks, arenas, and auditoriums with seating over 5000," designed to "hit the general type of audience" like at the Newport Jazz Festival. Billed as "the Biggest Gospel Cavalcade of 1957," the program included the Nightingales, Five Blind Boys, the Caravans, the Harmonizing Four, and the Gospel Harmonettes.[102]

Some gospel artists like Sam Cooke had abandoned the genre completely, hoping to cash in on the expanded interracial market. In December 1957, the Reverend C. L. Franklin appeared in Philadelphia with his daughter Aretha. Within a few years, she too would cross over to the secular side.[103]

The rock 'n' roll dance craze the "Twist" was also a crossover from gospel. "Don't you know," says Ira Tucker, "that 'The Twist' came from the Sensational Nightingales?" Joseph "JoJo" Wallace, the 'Gales guitarist and tenor lead, came up with the idea in 1956. In Atlanta on a gospel show with the Davis Sisters, Wallace offered the song to Little Joe Cook, a former gospel artist now recording rock 'n' roll for Okeh, but label executives passed on it because the lyrics were "too dirty."

A year later, Wallace took the song to Hank Ballard. Cal Green, Ballard's guitarist at the time, remembers the occasion. "We were in Tampa, Florida ... staying at the same hotel as ... the Nightingales." Wallace brought the song to Ballard "scribbled ... on a piece of paper" and told him, "We can't record this, we're a spiritual group, see what you can do with it." Ballard made the song his own, Chubby Checker copied it, and "The Twist" became rock 'n' roll history.[104]

Little Richard, meanwhile, stunned the rock 'n' roll world in 1957 by announcing his switch from rock to gospel. Rattled by the launch of the Russian satellite, Sputnik, Little Richard canceled three appearances in Australia, flew home to Los Angeles, and told reporters at the airport, "the end of the world is coming and I want to get my affairs in order." Told by his manager that he could be sued for the cancellations, Little Richard responded that the "Act of God" clause in his contract covered his actions.[105]

By comparison, the world of the Dixie Hummingbirds was reliable and steady. In the summer of 1956, they performed in Nashville on a program sponsored by Morgan Babb of the Radio Four. Babb was typical of the promoters who kept the Hummingbirds in business back then. He had broadened his position from gospel singer to radio show host and now promoter, and he loved to bring the Dixie Hummingbirds to town. Because they consistently worked the church circuit, "they had a congregation behind them for concerts," says Babb. "It was a guaranteed attendance. Usually around six hundred would come out with ticket prices around a dollar or so."[106]

That summer in July, Peacock released the last Hummingbirds single of the year. Peacock 1763 featured a James Walker lead on "Way Up on High" and an Ira Tucker lead on "Troubles Will Be Over."

"Every child of God, running for Jesus, just like an automobile."

By 1957, the Dixie Hummingbirds had built up a substantial catalog of gospel singles. The consistent quality of their work made it one of the richest periods in their creative lives. James Davis and Beachey Thompson provided the core of solid vocal backing. William Bobo and Howard Carroll comprised a solid rhythm section that also invested the Birds with a unique sound. Ira Tucker and James Walker were the double dynamos that powered the Birds in their immutable move forward.

Tucker found that Walker's presence pushed him even further into writing. "Competition would come up. I had to write because James Walker was a writer. I would go to bed thinking about ideas and I woke up thinking about them. I used to write a song just about every night."

Walker also urged the Birds to pay closer attention to the quality of their stage vocals. "He tape recorded every program we ever did," says Tucker. "And no one could say he sang this, so-and-so was flat on that. Walker had you right on tape. And Davis would say, 'Why you want to go and do all that?' And Walker would say, 'It was *good* for the group.'" Through Walker's tapes, the Birds were able to fine-tune their performance sound.

For his part, James Davis remained vigilant about his singers. "I was always aware of what could happen to a guy's voice." Both Walker and Thompson, he says, had a tendency to bring in songs pitched too high either for them or for the group. "You're going to have to turn the house out every night with that song for me to continue to sing it," Davis once told Walker, "because you're the only one it seems to be made for." With Tucker, Davis worried more about overworking him than straying out of his vocal range. "Tucker comes nearest to singing any song, any range, than anybody I've ever seen."

With his showmanship and charisma, Tucker was always the one to stand out. "Tucker was the ideal singer to me," says Joe Ligon of the Mighty Clouds of Joy. "I thought he could do anything he wanted to with his voice." But while Tucker was a show stopper, Walker held his own on stage and during this period developed a reputation with young singers as a trainer and advisor.

It was Walker who trained James Williams and William Bright when they joined the Sons of the Birds. Joe Ligon too benefited from Walker's tutelage. "I loved his singing and I was closer to Walker than I was to any of the rest of the fellows. He gave me a lot of advice, told me a lot of things because he had been singing professional for a while longer than me."[107]

Between 1957 and 1959, Peacock released fourteen more Dixie Hummingbirds sides including reworked spirituals, old favorites learned from other groups, and striking originals. Peacock 1770, released in February 1957, featured Tucker and Walker in a vocal duel on Roxie Moore's "Loving Hand," while "Cool Down Yonder" was Tucker's take on a song originally recorded by his idol, Norman Harris, with the Norfolk Jubilee Singers. The Birds had previously recorded the tune in 1950 for Gotham, but the track had never been released. Now, it was pressed into service for Peacock.

In June, Peacock 1773 paired two more Roxie Moore tunes, "Just Trusting" b/w "Live on Forever." Then, in November, Peacock 1780 was released. The record was a blockbuster, their biggest since "Let's Go Out to the Programs." The "B" side, "Stop by Here," was an energetic tune with Walker singing lead, but the track was overshadowed by "Christian's Automobile," a tune destined to become a signature song for the Birds.

"Christian's Automobile," according to the label, was written by "J. Archie," in reality, Tucker's sister-in-law. Assigning her the credit was his way of "gifting" a family member. But the song was Tucker's, and it took off on the strength of novelty and a rhythmic feel that presaged the southern soul tunes that followed in its wake a decade later.

The performance was driven by Howard Carroll's blues-inflected guitar and William Bobo's pumping bass, sounding more like an acoustic instrument than a human voice. Adding to the appeal, the urgency of the vocals, the harmonies pushed to the high end of their ranges. Tucker's phrasing is impeccable as he accents with screams and breaks into his gravel voice.

The lyric was an extended automobile metaphor, perfectly in synch with the rocking R&B of the time, the gospel parallel to "Rocket '88" and Chuck Berry's high-octane car songs. "Christian's Automobile" was the perfect vehicle to reach gospel's younger generation of fans.

Every child of God, running for Jesus,
Just like an automobile,
Prayer is your driver's license,
Faith is your steering wheel.

You gotta check on your tires,
You've got a rough road ahead,
And when you are weary from your journey,
God will put you to bed,
You've got to check on your brakes,
And stop your wicked ways,

Man is born of a woman,
He's only got a few days,
You've got to check on your lights,
And see your own faults,
Stop while you can see them, children,
Or your soul will be lost.

You got to check on your generator,
You need more strength and power,
You can't do nothing without the Man,
You need Him every hour,
Christians, whoa, Christians,
Press on your starter and start your automobile.

"'Christian's Automobile'," says Tucker, "now that's a song that will never grow old. We *still* get requests to do that song at every show." If the Birds' record sales had flattened at all during this period, "Automobile" was the single that reinflated them.

"... undoubtedly the finest Gospel group in the world."

In 1958, three more singles were released: 1783, "Walls of Zion" b/w "Just a Little While"; 1788, "I Don't Know Why (I Have to Cry Sometime)," with William Bobo carrying the lead, and "Let's Go Out to the Programs No. 2," the Birds imitating the best female groups in gospel; and late in the year, 1791, "Make One Step" b/w the upbeat "Come On and See About Me."

That February, the Birds would headline a "Gospel Caravan" at the Apollo on a bill that included Thermon Ruth's own Selah Singers and, making their first New York City appearance, the Staple Singers—Roebuck "Pops" Staples, his son Purvis, and daughters Cleotha and Mavis. Tucker had made the connection that prompted Ruth to invite the Staples to New York. Ruth was vacationing in Chicago, and the Dixie Hummingbirds were staying at the same hotel. "Ira Tucker, my good friend, said, 'Brother Ruth, let's go down and hear the Staple Singers.' I had never heard them in person, and ... Mavis, ... man, she tore the church up. I booked them right away for the Apollo."[108]

Sparked by their recent Peacock releases, that edition of the "Gospel Caravan" was a triumph for the Birds. Wrote the *Amsterdam News*:

> The Dixie Hummingbirds are undoubtedly the finest Gospel group in the world. Their current recording "Christian Automobile" is the biggest thing in Gospel music and their "Stop by Here" receives more record requests than any other discs according to disc jockeys.[109]

That summer, the Hummingbirds also appeared on a national radio program called *Sunday Morning*. Hosted by Sid McCoy, the half-hour show was sponsored by Pet Milk and featured "outstanding singing groups in the field of inspirational music." Originating from station WLIB in New York City, the spot provided the Hummingbirds with an opportunity to be heard nationwide.[110]

The Dixie Hummingbirds had only one release in 1959, Peacock 1803, Tucker's moving rendition of "Nobody Knows the Trouble I See" b/w "The Final Edition," a novelty allegory in praise of the Bible.

> Well, I'm a news reporter,
> Of my God's word,
> Jesus came here in time,
> And the good news I'm talking about,
> Will ease your troubled mind,
> The subject of the book is Christianity,
> And it's headlined with religion,
> And I don't care how many books you read,
> The Bible is the final edition.

In June of 1959, Peacock released their first gospel 33 1/3 long-playing record album, PLP-100, "The Dixie Hummingbirds and a Christian Testimonial."[111] The LP concept, on the scene since late 1956, only in late 1957 became viable in the world of R&B and gospel. Among independents, the buzz that year was that LPs would never be more than a "minor side-line attraction," but sales were already beginning to take off. During the winter of 1957, independents like Vee Jay, Atlantic, and Savoy heralded their first LP releases.[112] The cover of the Dixie Hummingbirds long player, against the backdrop of a star-studded sky, showed the white-tuxedoed Birds from the waist up, handsome faces with pencil-thin moustaches smiling up off the cover.

Among the "hits," the title track, "Christian Testimonial," along with "Devil Can't Harm a Praying Man," "Nobody Knows the Trouble I See," "Final Edition," and "Christian's Automobile." The LP also included newly issued tracks, two featuring Ira Tucker, "Are You Ready" and "God Is Now Speaking," a title he had previously cut for Apollo Records in 1949. The remaining tunes, all featuring James Walker and never issued as singles, were "We'll Meet Again," "Oh, How I Love Jesus," "He'll Do the Same for You," and "I Just Want to Tell You."

While the album offered the Hummingbirds a chance to earn additional royalties on previously released material and first-time royalties on songs that might not have done well as singles, live performance remained their primary source of income.

In November 1959, the Hummingbirds again headlined at the Apollo with support from the Swanee Quintette and the Blind Boys. Their biggest show that year, though, was in May at New York City's Madison Square Garden. The program, billed as an "International Festival of Gospel, Religious, Spiritual, and Folk Music," was promoted by WLIB disk jockey Joe Bostic and advertised as a "special salute to Gospeldom's 'First Lady,' Mahalia Jackson." The lineup, as spectacular as the venue, was a showcase of the finest groups in the genre. In addition to the Dixie Hummingbirds, there were the Soul Stirrers, Swan Silvertones, Selahs, Swanees, Rasberry Singers, Caravans, Davis Sisters, Drinkard Singers, and Original Gospel Harmonettes. Sidney Poitier served as a master of ceremonies, and the Ward Singers made a novelty electronic appearance, singing directly from Stockholm via transatlantic wire. This gargantuan five-hour gospel event with ticket prices at four and five dollars apiece was a fitting testament to the commercial heights both gospel and the Dixie Hummingbirds had reached by the end of the 1950s.[113]

The Dixie Hummingbirds, of course, would follow their usual course—top of the world one night, a small country church the next. Now that they had a bit of history behind them, the Hummingbirds were coming to be appreciated not only as spiritual entertainers but also for what they had come to represent over a troubled decade.

The Reverend Gadson Graham, a longtime follower of the Birds, is the pastor of Canaan Baptist Church in Paterson, New Jersey. In the 1950s, he lived in Lake City, South Carolina, about a hundred miles from Greenville and Spartanburg. He remembers what the Birds meant to people living there at that time. "They would come to our town, the Dixie Hummingbirds, they would come and they would sing," says Reverend Graham.

And this would give us inspiration. Whenever they came around, it was a tremendous uplift that helped us cope and deal with all of the negative things that was going on at that time. Racism, social injustice, economic injustice.

The Birds would sing and it would just seem that heaven came open and God had come down. We just felt like we could deal more with what we had to deal with, after hearing them.

And when the Birds came out, they would look different from anybody else. I mean, they were dressed immaculate.

They would start with a low-key number and then they would end with one of their shouts. Mr. Davis would sing and, of course, James Walker would sing. Then, when they got down to business, Ira Tucker would take over. In those days, he had a way, he would pull off his top coat, and, oh boy, when that happened, the place would just go up!

The Birds, you got sincerity from them that you did not get from anybody else. Their singing was like a salve on a wound. Whatever hurt that you had experienced, when you put that hurt up against the singing of the Dixie Hummingbirds, it was like a soothing situation that made it possible for you to deal with whatever you had to deal with. They would sing that, and that's how they would send us home, rejoicing in what we were.[114]

8

"Loves Me Like a Rock"

(1960–1976)

When I was a little boy,
And the Devil would call my name,
I'd say, "Now who do . . .
Who do you think you're fooling?"

I'm a consecrated boy,
I'm a singer in a Sunday choir,
Oh, my mama loves me, she loves me,
She get down on my knees and hugs me,
She loves me like a rock . . .

—Paul Simon, 1973

Black gospel in general and the Dixie Hummingbirds in particular had profoundly influenced rhythm and blues and rock 'n' roll. Bobby Bland struggled early on to find a sound but developed his phrasing and trademark "growl" by listening to Ira Tucker. As a young man in the Mississippi Delta, B. B. King played guitar with the "Famous St. John Gospel Singers," a local group that modeled itself after, among others, the Dixie Hummingbirds.[1] But the Hummingbirds had their broadest impact on the singing of doo-wop vocal groups.

New Yorker "Little" Anthony Gourdine, who with the Imperials scored a hit in 1958 with "Tears on My Pillow," came to the Apollo gospel shows for inspiration. "I was influenced by the gospel singers there. The Imperials needed something to make the audience come up out of their seats." In church, "you . . . reach their sensitivity mark, the emotional thing that they can relate to." Gourdine came up with "I'm

Alright," a gospel-inflected show stopper co-written with Sam Cooke. "I just did a gospel thing, and fell to my knees and started reaching.... I went to my old gospel roots and my emotion went into the audience, and it totally blew the Apollo down.... The Isley Brothers learned from us and did 'Shout'—the record that established their reputation as gospel-in-soul wailers."[2]

James "Pookie" Hudson, best remembered for his hit with the Spaniels, "Goodnight, Sweetheart, Goodnight," first performed as a boy in the Three Bees. "When I first started group singing, we basically did a lot of gospel. We did jubilees." Every time the Dixie Hummingbirds passed through his hometown, Gary, Indiana, Hudson was sure to see them. "The Hummingbirds performed at what was called the neighborhood house, a kind of community center. They were the show all by themselves. One time, we were standing outside when they pulled up, and the thing that really struck me, each one had their own Cadillac." (The show's promoters and local friends of the Birds supplied the Cadillacs.) "The place was packed," remembers Hudson, "three or four hundred people. And the Birds came out wearing good-looking suits. They were professional and they did their job well."

The Spaniels also modeled their harmonies on the Dixie Hummingbirds and other top gospel groups of the day, and Hudson would even write a gospel tune for the Spaniels, the ethereal ballad, "You Gave Me Peace of Mind." "I wrote it as a gospel. But the company [Vee Jay] didn't want to take it gospel-wise. So they made me change a couple words and make it sound contemporary."[3]

Hank Ballard of the Midnighters grew up in Detroit and Bessemer, Alabama, where, he says, "Gospel was my roots. My aunt and uncle, they kept me in church all the time down there in Alabama. I was singing in the Sunday school choir." His Midnighters scored with a string of risqué R&B hits in the mid-1950s—"Sexy Ways," "Work with Me Annie," and "Annie Had a Baby"—and "The Twist." But his heroes were the Dixie Hummingbirds. "Man, I was so crazy about the Dixie Hummingbirds. They sounded like blues singers. Tucker sounds like a s-o-o-o-ulful blues singer. He's got that old gravel sound I love. I used to try to develop that sound, but mine is not natural. They pull it up from the back of the throat. Singers that have that sound can sell records."

Hank says that when the Dixie Hummingbirds came to town, "it was like the Rolling Stones. They come out strutting and dancing, trucking, screaming, hollering. The women was crazy about 'em. I was hooked on

The Dixie Hummingbirds headlining at the Apollo, 1970s. Photo by Smooth Gary. Courtesy of Howard Carroll.

the Hummingbirds. I would use their melodies. I wasn't trying to steal or anything. I was just so crazy about 'em. I would call and tell 'em I just changed the lyrics. Now, if you ever get a copy of 'Work with Me Annie,' on the reverse side is a song called 'Until I Die.' Now, that's a Dixie Hummingbirds melody. I would take their songs and re-lyric it. Instead of saying 'God,' I said 'baby.'"[4]

By the middle 1960s, doo-wop and the early rock 'n' rollers were supplanted by new styles. While many white artists including Bob Dylan and the Beatles were changing rock music, the African American community brought gospel-inflected Motown and southern soul to the airwaves. The Impressions, Stevie Wonder, Marvin Gaye, the Supremes, the Miracles, James Brown, Wilson Pickett, and the Reverend C. L.'s daughter Aretha Franklin were among the genre's pioneers. This generation of performers would also carry on the influence of the Dixie Hummingbirds.

The 1960s "soul" pioneer Solomon Burke, Rock Hall of Fame inductee and native Philadelphian, credits the Dixie Hummingbirds with jump starting his career. Burke was fifteen years old in 1956 and already singing in his own gospel group, the Royal Cavaliers. After an impressive performance by the Cavaliers at the Liberty Baptist Church, Viola Williams, wife of Philadelphia's leading black disk jockey, Kae Williams, approached the group and, in Burke's words she said, "'Oh, you must come back when they're going to have the big program! They're going to have the Dixie Hummingbirds here and a big record contest. And you have to come back!' And I said, 'Oh, well I'd love to . . . ,' and we left it at that."

On performance night, the Cavaliers, tired of playing for little pay and getting nowhere, stayed home. Burke never forgot it. "The group refused to go with me to the gig!"

Burke recalls, "I borrowed a jacket from my uncle, shoes from my father, and pants from my other uncle. Then I remembered, oh, my God, my guitar is back at the bass player's house! But I had no time, so when I got to the church, I had no guitar." But, as promised, the Dixie Hummingbirds were present. "They were the big stars who brought everybody into Liberty Baptist Church." And Howard Carroll offered to lend the young Solomon Burke his guitar. "They were so kind to me! And I was so out of order compared to the gospel groups and the choirs that were there with their robes on."

> And one of the choir directors—Ruth Irving—was shouting out, "Oh, there's my little boy, Solomon Burke. Oh, I love him! That's the little singing, preaching boy. O-o-oh, just do it honey!" And I thought this is going to be great!
>
> So, Mr. Carroll handed me the guitar. And now I'm embarrassed because I have to tune the guitar to a special tuning because that was the only way I knew how to play. And I'm looking back and saying, "Don't be mad at me Mr. Guitar Man." My voice breaking up, but I have to tune these strings. And while I'm tuning, I'm preaching a little bit, getting the audience's attention. "Now, bear with me children. Oh, the Lord is going to *do* it! Sometime the Lord need to work with me and I need you all to work with me this *evening*!"
>
> And I'm doing my thing, singing while I'm tuning the strings. Doo doo doo doo. And I sing, "I was lost in sin and sorrow." Doo doo doo doo. I'm tuning. "On an isle of life's dark secrets." Doo doo doo doo. I got it now. "Oh, then when I saw." Do-o-o-o-o. That's my first guitar chord. "That old ship." I had it then! "I saw the captain beckon." It was all over! "My child I come to save you, step on board and follow me."

And I just kept on singing as I walked the floor. And I had to be careful because the suit pants were too big and the shoes a little long. 'C'mon church!' And everybody—including the Dixie Humming-birds—started singing. And this beautiful and fine-dressed white lady ran up with furs all around her neck, and they were flying and she had these diamonds all around her fingers. And she yelled out, "He's mine! He's mine! Oh, he's mine!"

The lady was Bess Berman from Apollo Records in New York City, and she said, "You are going to be on my label!" And another man walked up to me and said, "I'm Jimmy Bracken with Vee Jay Records and I want you for my label." And Don Robey from Peacock Records in Texas came over. "Boy, lookey here! My name is Don Robey!"

Well, I was just a kid, and Mrs. Williams came and rescued me. And I walked over and gave the guitar back to the Dixie Humming-birds. I can see it as if it was right now. I can feel it as if it was right this minute. God changed my life in the twinkling of an eye. And the Dixie Hummingbirds were right in the core. And two days later, I was on the front page of the *Philadelphia Tribune*. "Solomon Burke wins Apollo recording contract at Liberty Baptist Church."

To me, that memory says the Dixie Hummingbirds was the greatest group in the world. They could have been selfish like other groups and said, "We can't lend you our gee-tar, man. We can't do it." But the Dixie Hummingbirds handed me that guitar. They were stars![5]

Otis Williams—real name Otis Miles—was also brought up on the Hummingbirds in Texas and Detroit. "I was raised up going to church every Sunday and listening to the earlier groups back then, the Dixie Hummingbirds, the Nightingales, the Silvertones, the Harmonizing Four, the Alabama and Mississippi Blind Boys. It's been a big impact on my life."

In Detroit, Williams formed the Temptations, and by the early 1960s they had landed a contract with Berry Gordy's Motown Records. "Berry loved the Temps because he said our harmonies reminded him of the great gospel groups, because Melvin Franklin was singing down low, Eddie Kendricks was soaring up high, and we had that rich harmony in the middle."

As Williams recalls, in 1962, the Temps' love for gospel cost them a hit song. "Berry Gordy had originally written the Contours' 'Do You Love Me' for the Temptations."

But he couldn't find us because we were at King Solomon's Baptist Church, which was up on 14th. The Dixie Hummingbirds were head-lining. And each group came out and did their bit, and as the Hummingbirds came up to do theirs, the bass singer, Bobo, said, "Now, watch what *we* gonna do." And they got up there and turned the place out! And we just sat there saying, "Man, the Dixie Hummingbirds look something else." Next day, we went up to Motown and were telling them about the Hummingbirds at King Solomon's. And they said, "Well, Mr. Gordy was looking for you guys. He had "Do You Love Me" written for you and he couldn't find you all, so he gave it to the Contours."

That incident cemented a lasting bond between the Temptations and the Birds. "They were just electrifying. Like the gospel Temptations to me. Tucker would grab that ear and he'd start squalling, and we identi-fied with them. Their harmonies were impeccable and tight." Melvin Franklin and William Bobo were especially close. "Melvin loved the Hummingbirds," says Williams. "Him and Bobo used to sit and go over parts together. With Bobo being a natural bass and Melvin also, they would sit and exchange ideas and Melvin would listen at Bobo endlessly. We'd be in the dressing room singing their songs and that would be what we would harmonize on just to get into the flow of singing."[6]

In addition to influencing popular genres, black gospel itself was also transforming in the 1960s. New stylists—soloists and choirs—were emerging, and ultimately, piano and every conceivable type of instru-mental accompaniment from organ to electric guitar to the latest in synthesizers and full orchestrations became common. Gospel quartets remained popular but were moving toward "respected veteran" status, their viability as entertainers boosted by the expanding audience for the music outside the black community.

Impacted by the cataclysmic flashpoint events of the civil rights era, the Dixie Hummingbirds fulfilled their role as traditional spiritual enter-tainers, responding in song to the needs of the community. If they had recorded nothing else, their place in both gospel and American cultural history would have been assured. But as the 1970s unfolded, the Birds modernized their sound, teaming with some of pop's best-known stars to make a connection with younger audiences like few other groups of their generation. Weathering even the loss of one of their most beloved members, the Dixie Hummingbirds managed to press on, transcending both cultural and generational boundaries.

"One word can either break you or make you rich."

In the early 1960s, much of American pop music had reverted back to pre-rock 'n' roll blandness. *Billboard*'s rock 'n' roll charts included soporific singles like Percy Faith's "Theme from a Summer Place," the Highwaymen's "Michael Row the Boat Ashore," Connie Francis's "Everybody's Somebody's Fool," and Lawrence Welk's "Calcutta." The exciting material drew from R&B, including Sam Cooke's "Chain Gang," Ike and Tina Turner's "A Fool in Love" and "It's Gonna Work Out Fine," Bobby Bland's "Don't Cry No More" and "I Pity the Fool," and Hank Ballard's "Finger Poppin' Time."

Motown and soul were mere budding trends with Barrett Strong's "Money (That's What I Want)" and "Shop Around" by Smokey Robinson and the Miracles. On the soul front, James Brown hit with "Think," its funky rhythm a taste of things to come.

Peacock continued to release new gospel work, including sides by the Brooklyn All Stars, the 'Gales, Reverend Cleophus Robinson, and the Blind Boys. Label debuts included "Ain't Got Long Here" by Joe Ligon and the Mighty Clouds of Joy and "Stretch Out" by the Pilgrim Jubilees.

In the early 1960s, Peacock released a slew of entries by the Dixie Hummingbirds, now the label's most consistently best-selling gospel act. Over the years, Robey and Tucker, astute judges of material, had solidified an effective strategy. The Birds would go into the studio and record a half dozen tracks or more. Robey and Tucker would pick the strongest tracks and time-release them as singles spaced about four to six months apart. Typically, a Birds single would feature Tucker on one side and Walker on the other, or the two would share leads on both sides. Peacock followed this course throughout the decade.

Two Hummingbirds singles were released in 1960: Peacock 1808, Roxie Moore's "I Want to Feel the Holy Spirit" b/w "What a Friend," and Peacock 1817, "Leave Your Burdens There" b/w "Jesus Hold My Hand."

The Birds would have their next masterpiece in 1961. The first single of the year, Peacock 1831, paired Walker's "God's Goodness" with "He Cares for Me," a Tucker performance that evolved into a favorite over the years. Howard Carroll provided R&B-inflected guitar work as Tucker drew the lyric from a biblical tale. "I'm going to do like Simon Peter, when he was fishing out on the sea, I'm going to cast all my cares on Him, He cares for me." Their second release of the year proved to be the blockbuster: Peacock 1844, Walker's "Have a Little Talk with Jesus" was a first-rate soulful performance, but "In the Morning" was a supercharged tour de force, a high water mark in the Dixie Hummingbirds' recording career.

The song took off on a boogie-woogie guitar riff and the most prominent drum backbeat heard to date on a Birds track. A rocking piano and Bobo's pumping bass rounded out the ensemble. Tucker roared in like the west wind and maintained the velocity throughout. Occasionally, the studio engineer threw in a few strategic bursts of electronic echo. The searing energy of the performance made the song a standout.

> In the morning,
> In the morning,
> In the morn—morn—morn—morn,
> In the morning,
> I wanna be singing in the morning,
> When the dark clouds roll away.

R&B singer Jackie Wilson, once a member of the Dominoes but now out on his own, was especially taken with "In the Morning." Wilson would tell writer Arnold Shaw, "I liked the Dixie Hummingbirds and Ira Tucker, who could really scream." In 1962, Wilson took "In the Morning," rewrote it and recorded it himself as "I Just Can't Help It," freely acknowledging that he had taken the song from Ira Tucker.[7]

Tucker is pleased that Jackie Wilson loved his work enough to borrow but disappointed that he was not compensated. "Wilson cut my arrangement of 'In the Morning' to six bars," says Tucker. "When I called him, Jackie said to me, 'You right, you right, you right, baby—but count the bars!'" Wilson had changed it just enough to avoid copyright infringement and therefore legal liability. "And," adds Louise Tucker, "*they* made all the money!"

But Tucker sometimes "borrowed," too, as on Peacock 1861. Walker's track was a wailing rendition of his original, "Our Father's Children." The "hit" side, though, was "Bedside of a Neighbor," credited to Ira Tucker although he readily admits the song was not entirely his.

"Bedside," written in 1932 by Thomas Dorsey, was Dorsey's personal response to the untimely death of a close friend and neighbor. Titled "If You See My Savior," the song was recorded as "Bedside of a Neighbor" in the mid-1930s by at least three of Tucker's favorite groups: the Golden Gates, the Heavenly Gospel Singers, and the Norfolk Jubilees with

Norman "Crip" Harris. Tucker used Dorsey's melody and opening verses as a springboard to his own contemporary take on the song, a swinging romp tailored to Howard Carroll's guitar and the Hummingbirds' precision harmony skills.

> I was standing by the bedside of a neighbor,
> Who was just about to cross the swelling tide,
> And I asked him if he would do me a favor,
> Kindly take this message to the other side.

Tucker, of course, embellished the song from there, branding it with his own unique vocal gymnastics and additional lyrics.

> Well, you may chance to meet my mother or my father,
> Whoa, some friends whom I can't recall,
> You may chance to meet my brother or my father,
> But just try to see my savior first of all.

Howard Carroll contributed a hot guitar solo on the bridge, and when it was all done, "Bedside of a Neighbor" belonged to the Dixie Hummingbirds. Tucker never intended, though, to take credit for the song. At the time, Robey and company were handling the copyright arrangements from the Peacock offices. "It was a very big song," said Tucker, "but some really funny stuff happened."

> I got a statement saying "Ira Tucker—'Bedside of a Neighbor.'" I called and said, "Thomas Dorsey wrote that!" And the lady at Peacock said, "Oh, no he didn't. You wrote that." I said, "How you come to that?" She said, "Thomas Dorsey wrote 'If You See My Savior.'"
>
> I found out right then the technicalities of songwriting. One word can either break you or make you rich. Thomas Dorsey had his arrangement and I had mine.

"Bedside of a Neighbor" kept the Birds in the spotlight throughout 1962, and Peacock followed up with their second LP, *In The Morning*, featuring the Birds' three most recent "hits"—the title track plus "He Cares for Me" and "Bedside of a Neighbor." The remaining titles— composed by either Tucker, Walker, or Roxie Moore—were culled from previously recorded tracks that had been deemed not strong enough to stand on their own as singles. Both the Birds and the label benefited from the LP releases. The Hummingbirds had the prestige of their most recent work, including material that otherwise might not have been issued, collected in one attractive package, and sales of the LP generated income for Peacock's publishing arm, Lion Music, and additional royalties for the songwriters.

"When I did that verse, people was really going wild."

With all of its turmoil and violence, 1963 was a troubling year for the nation and for the Hummingbirds. In performances, they were expected to carry themselves with dignity, present themselves as worthy role models, and lift audiences above the difficult political and social challenges of that year. "The Bible says watch as well as pray," says Tucker, "and you've got to watch more than you pray."

"We were very much aware of what was happening at the time," says James Davis, "because we were out there and in it."

Davis describes how the group made light of the prejudices they encountered back then. "We used to joke with Beachey that he integrated our group because he was lighter than we were. I told him you act stuck up, . . . and Beachey, he just started talking trash. He had something funny to say about everything."

Apparently, even the more serious encounters. "We were in New Orleans," says Davis, "and Beachey, Bobo, and Howard had gone to town."

> They had walked almost back to where we were staying, but they got tired and Beachey, who was ahead of them, flagged down a cab. Beachey got in and told the driver to pick up Bobo and Howard. And the cab driver wanted to know what *was* Beachey. And Beachey said, "What do you mean, what am I?" And the cabbie said, "We can't ride Negro, so what are you?" Beachey got insulted and said, "I am a black man," and he got out of the car.
>
> He couldn't wait to tell Bobo and Howard what the cab driver had said. "We have to walk," he told them, "because of the way we look!" But he wasn't traumatized by any of that. None of us were. By then, we were used to it. Beachey and the guys didn't get angry. They just laughed it off.

Davis tells the story matter-of-factly, but then, as he ponders the memory, his dander comes through. "I'll tell you the truth," he says, "I have my theory about black and white."

I think that's the biggest hoax that's been played on the American people. Black and white. I've never seen anything in my life that's better because it had a different color. I thought about it a hundred times, and some of the worst people I've ever seen, some were as black as tar and some were as white as anything. So, there it is. Color doesn't make the person. Perception is what hurts people more than anything else.

And there's something else I get tired of listening to. The "Bible Belt!" That's what they call it. I'm so sick of that I don't know what in the world I'm going to do. Those "Bible Belt" people, they'll hang you before you can bat an eye.

Davis calls up the time they were traveling through the Carolinas in a couple of Cadillacs. "We were in Raleigh, on our way to a program."

Stopped at a corner and went into the grocery store to get something to munch on. And four women came walking up and they were talking loud. One of them said, "Better carry that white folk's car back home!" Then another woman comes up and says, "Hey! It's the Dixie Hummingbirds!" And you should have seen those others. They knew of us, but the one who thought we were chauffeurs in our boss's car, well, you could have bought her with a plug nickel!

Dignified behavior and appearance became more important than ever to the Hummingbirds as a sort of quiet resistance against prejudice. The Birds persevered, and, in 1963, Peacock 1889 was released. "Another Day" featured Tucker in a lilting hymn with guitar, drums, and church piano reminiscent of Sister Ernestine Washington. "If You Trust Him," a Walker composition, had the group singing half speed over a quick-time meter provided by stand-up bass, drums, and piano. These were solid journeymen tracks that kept the Birds active in the market that year.

Released in early 1964, Peacock 3012—the first for the Birds under a new numbering system—paired the old hymn favorite, "Come Ye Disconsolate," with what many regard as Walker's masterwork for the Birds, "Our Prayer for Peace." Audiences, shocked and dismayed by the assassination of President Kennedy, found solace in this track. The song also directly addressed the hatreds that were poisoning race relations in America, like Walker's 1953 "A Prayer for Tomorrow," the "message" song he had written for the Southern Sons. The Birds changed the feel and fitted it to their style.

Lyrically, "Our Prayer" remained essentially true to Walker's earlier version, but there were changes and, in added verses, a sharpening of the message.

> Let every man know, Father,
> Let them know that it is a sin,
> To hate his brother because,
> Of the color of his skin.

And an occasional line or two that anticipated themes that would surface seven years later in John Lennon's "Imagine."

> Oh, let me live in peace,
> Until that great day come,
> When everybody will be as one,
> When there will be no more,
> No more separating, Lord.

In the wake of the assassination, "Our Prayer for Peace" struck a note with the public. Walker, though, was so moved by the tragedy that he felt compelled to write a special verse. "President Kennedy was assassinated—I think it was on a Friday—and that Saturday I wrote a verse about the assassination. And we were in Jamaica, New York, and boy, when I did that verse, people was really going wild—because it had just happened."[8] The Birds would incorporate the new verse into their stage act and they performed it for a nationwide audience when they made their television debut on *TV Gospel Time* later that year.

The show, a syndicated program aimed at African American viewers, was attracting fans outside that demographic who appreciated the music more as folk tradition than religious expression. In a special gospel issue, *Billboard* reported that by the mid-1960s, *TV Gospel Time*, "seen in 50 markets across the country, . . . pointedly has no preacher nor does it display religious symbols" and is "viewed as entertainment in the most positive sense," demonstrating that "the broad mass of Americans, both Negro and white, can appreciate each other's cultural heritage and contributions."[9]

Each telecast of *TV Gospel Time* originated from a different city. The Dixie Hummingbirds traveled to Washington, D.C., for their appearance. Those who tuned in saw a gospel choir in shadow, hands upraised as they sang a rousing hymn; then, five silhouetted singers, *TV Gospel*

Time superimposed over their image. Then there was a cutaway to host, Frank Davis, who introduced the sponsors—this night, Sulfur-8, the medicated hair and scalp conditioner—and the evening's entertainment. "Yes, friends, today we have a wealth of talent for you. The Bibleway Joy Bell Singers! And from Chicago, the very talented Miss Myrtle Jackson! And to open our show, today we have one of the truly great names in gospel. Ladies and gentlemen, the ever-popular Dixie Hummingbirds!"

The Birds appeared in dark suits, subdued lighting, close formation, Ira Tucker out front, Davis and Bobo on either side, Thompson and Walker on risers above and behind, Howard Carroll in shadow off to the left. The group performed two numbers, "Bedside of a Neighbor" and "Maybe It's You" featuring Tucker.

They would come on again for the close, this time James Walker performing "Our Prayer for Peace" with his special verse about President Kennedy. Walker stood out front, Davis, Tucker, Thompson, and Bobo a level higher in a tight semicircle behind him, Howard Carroll behind and above them all. As Walker sang, he threw back his head, waved his arms, poured his heart into it as the Birds physically pulsed in and out behind him. Walker set up the Kennedy verse with a spoken aside. "There is one thing happened that really shook the nation. Listen!"

> In 1963, we all know it was on,
> The twenty-second of November,
> Tragedy! That happened,
> Way down in Dallas, Texas.
> Oh, hard to believe,
> The whole world will forever remember.
>
> Listen! President Kennedy, the one who fought so hard,
> For the human race,
> By the hands of a mad evil man,
> The day Kennedy was sleeping cold in his grave,
> He was only trying to tell the world—Listen!

At this, Walker broke into a wail and the Birds doubled the volume, stepping back abruptly and throwing their arms out wide, and then just as suddenly, pulling in close and dropping to hushed tones, Howard Carroll anchoring the transition with the perfect four-note guitar figure. The moment was poignant and riveting. Walker sang the final verse.

Together, together we will stand,
God said divided we'll fall,
Oh, Father, let all of this hatred cease,
Let us work and go to school together,
Let us all go in peace.

It was a brilliant performance, and, in its wake, the Birds were invited
to appear on *Jubilee Showcase*, a Chicago-based television program then
in its second year. The Birds worked the cameras like consummate
professionals. Unlike *TV Gospel Time*, the stage was well lit and the
Birds, with an elegant curtained backdrop behind them, played to a
small studio audience. The group was positioned to take advantage of
the camera angle—Tucker, Davis, Thompson, Walker, and Bobo facing
the viewers, Howard Carroll seated in the foreground, back to the
camera. The interplay between group members was beautifully
captured.

The audience broke into spontaneous applause when at the close of
"Let's Go Out to the Programs" Bobo descended one astonishingly low
note at a time on each syllable of "Let—My—Peo—ple—Go-o-o."

They also performed a bouncing version of "Didn't It Rain," Walker
on lead, the Birds flying behind with flashy sixth and ninth chord
harmonies and split-second call and response precision. Just like Café
Society, their performance was choreographed as they moved in perfect
coordination to the rhythm of the music. And like Café Society, television brought the Hummingbirds an impressive level of renown.

"I got so much to shout about!"

The appetite for gospel music remained healthy into the middle 1960s.
Don Robey had started the "Songbird" label, an adjunct to Peacock, and
to it signed the Sons of the Birds. James Williams of the Sons thought of
Songbird as a "second-string" or "farm club" label where up-and-comers
could record and be heard. In 1965, Robey told *Billboard* that "personal
appearance tours" were still the most important factor in driving gospel
record sales domestically, but that worldwide interest had boosted sales
in general. Robey named England, France, Germany, Sweden, Denmark,
and Japan as the best foreign markets for black gospel.

Although the basic outlet for the music was still "the circuit of
churches and halls which run through the Carolinas, Tennessee,
Georgia, Louisiana, Florida and reach up into Washington, New Jersey,

New York, and Chicago," lately black gospel was also routinely heard in "non-religious settings" like Disneyland and Las Vegas "where it is an accepted entertainment form."

Specialty Records producer and gospel promoter "Bumps" Blackwell made the observation that gospel had still not "crossed over the line," and that with the exception of Mahalia Jackson and Clara Ward, "the majority of hard-working gospel performers have not gained acceptance by white audiences." Long-established acts such as the "Original Alabama Blind Boys, Caravans, Mississippi Blind Boys, and the Harmonizing Four," he said, "are unknown outside the Negro circuit." Nonetheless, Blackwell saw potential in gospel's commercial crossover future. "The gospel market is still an untapped virgin area because there are many authentic acts unknown outside the circuit. Colleges and theaters could be lucrative areas if talent agencies would see the potential." He singled out a few groups that would do well, including the Harmonizing Four, the Swan Silvertones, the Alabama Blind Boys, and the Dixie Hummingbirds, noting that in recent years, the annual income of the Alabama Blind Boys before expenses was about $150,000.[10]

By 1965, the Dixie Hummingbirds, firmly established in the pure gospel market, had broadened their fan base through albums and TV appearances and the expanded interest in gospel. Although Robey had urged them for the past several years to take a shot at R&B, the Birds had always turned him down. Though they never considered the option seriously, in 1965 with Tucker and Carroll the "youngsters" of the group at forty years of age, they thought themselves too old to succeed in R&B. Moreover, the Birds, as always, remained committed to their intensely loyal fans and would not have been comfortable betraying their roots. If the Hummingbirds did not make concessions to pop music, however, pop grew closer to the Hummingbirds' tradition in the 1960s.

Rockers had taken an interest in "genuine" folk music and "message" songs in the wake of Bob Dylan's popularity and his influence on the Beatles to follow his lead. Songs with a social consciousness or rooted in cultural experience had currency with 1960s record buyers. Even in the world of R&B, message songs with the feel of soul gospel were beginning to chart. Performers like Curtis Mayfield and the Impressions led the way with hits like "Keep on Pushing" in 1964 and "People Get Ready" in 1965. By 1966, Motown's Stevie Wonder had hit with a cover of Bob Dylan's "Blowing in the Wind."

That same year, the Hummingbirds were invited to perform at the Newport Folk Festival. Prior to the festival, their recorded output was, as always, geared to a pure gospel fan base. A third Peacock album, PLP 115, released in late 1964 featured "Our Prayer for Peace," along with "Let's Go Out to the Programs," by then an "old" Birds favorite. Two singles were released in 1965, Peacock 3045 and 3073, the "hit" sides being Walker's waltz-time "Prayer for the Sick" and Tucker's soulful "You Don't Have Nothing." Those two tracks were quickly pressed into service as the centerpieces of PLP 127, the Birds' fourth LP, *Everyday and Every Hour*. The Birds' recent catalog, strong in entertaining and traditional material with a message that resonated with the sensibilities of the time, caught the attention of Newport Folk Festival organizers.

Festival planners that year were a "who's who" of the contemporary American folk music scene including Alan Lomax, Ralph Rinzler, Julius Lester, Jean Ritchie, Judy Collins, Theodore Bikel, Ronnie Gilbert and Pete Seeger of the Weavers, and Peter Yarrow of Peter, Paul, and Mary. George Wein, producer of the Newport Jazz Festival, also produced the Folk Festival. Assisting him was a team of budding young folk professionals that included scholar/writer Anthony Heilbut, five years away from publishing *The Gospel Sound*, his landmark book on the history of African American gospel music.

Both the Newport Jazz and Folk festivals had histories of presenting black gospel. Mahalia Jackson and Clara Ward had been the first with their appearances at the 1957 Jazz Festival. And prior to 1966, the Folk Festival had featured the Chambers Brothers (when they were strictly gospel), the Georgia Sea Island Singers, Alex Bradford, the Staple Singers, the Moving Star Hall Singers, the Wards, Reverend Gary Davis, and Reverend Robert Wilkins.

Certainly black gospel represented tradition, but an additional allure to the Festival board was the link between gospel and the "freedom songs" of the civil rights movement. Writing about the mid-1960s folk music scene, *New York Times* critic Robert Shelton quoted the Reverend Martin Luther King, Jr.: "The freedom songs are playing a vital role in our struggle," said King, and they "give the people new courage and a sense of unity . . . in our most trying hours." Shelton offered the example of a freedom song based on "Go Down, Moses," the new words improvised by "a young Negro, who talked of 'new-time religion.'"

> Go down, Kennedy,
> 'Way down in Georgia land,
> Tell old Pritchett,
> To let my people go.[11]

Straightforward spirituals like "We Shall Not Be Moved," "Over My Head," "We Shall Overcome," "Don't You Let Nobody Turn You 'Round," and "Ain't You Got a Right to the Tree of Life" had similar power. Traditional African American songs were now working to create a sense of harmony in a union of cultures dedicated to achieving social justice for all. The appearance of the Dixie Hummingbirds at the 1966 Newport Folk Festival represented all of these ideals. As Anthony Heilbut wrote in the 1966 Festival program notes, gospel singing is "one of the most exciting, profound, and imaginative forms of folk music in the country. It's about time the American public began supporting these great, much undervalued artists."[12] The Dixie Hummingbirds were receptive to that point of view and the notion that they could justifiably expand their domain as bona fide representatives of a proud tradition.

The Festival that year featured a breathtaking array of African American "folk" talent: the country blues of Son House, Bukka White, Skip James, and DeFord Bailey; the urban blues of Howlin' Wolf and Hubert Sumlin; the Caribbean ballads of Joseph Spence and Trinidad Tiger; the New Orleans jazz of the Preservation Hall Band; and the rocking blues of Chuck Berry. Representing the commercial gospel tradition along with the Dixie Hummingbirds were Claude Jeter and the Swan Silvertones,[13] and Dorothy Love Coates and the Gospel Harmonettes. The three veteran touring groups, featured together in a one-hour segment billed as a "Gospel Battle," performed on the main stage on Friday evening, the first day of the event.

As they might have at the Apollo, the groups were all seated on stage lending support as each performed in a circle of songs. The Gospel Harmonettes were dressed in flowing church robes, the Silvertones in shiny light-colored suits, the Birds in elegant dark suits. Host Willis James introduced the Birds and James Davis calmly greeted the crowd, giving no hint of the fire that was to come. "To the Master of Ceremonies and to all of these great artists, ladies and gentlemen, we are the Dixie Hummingbirds and very proud to be here. At this time, the Dixie Hummingbirds would like to take just a little ride in the Christian automobile." Howard Carroll played the opening chords on his road-worn Fender Stratocaster, and the Birds launched into the song.

The performance, as with all their live performances, was a departure from the recorded version. Tucker was at his guttural best, extending, improvising as Bobo pumped behind, the group in driving harmony. "Everybody. Every, every, every everybody's got a race to run ... Trust in Jesus, trust him in the morning, trust him in the evening, trust him in the mid, the mid, the mid, the mid, the midnight hour. . . . Prayer is your driver's license," and gradually slowing down for the close, "faith is your steering wheel," a flurry of chopped guitar chords and Tucker ended with a high falsetto flourish. The Birds retreated to their seats and the round robin turned to the Swan Silvertones. When the circle came around again to the Birds, they were reintroduced as "those very fine men of song from Philadelphia." They would stop the show with their performance of "The Reason I Shout" from their *Everyday and Every Hour* LP. Tucker cleared his throat and spoke to the crowd. "Are we having a good time?" They shouted back. "We want you to know you are free to clap your hands, pat your feet. And let's have a little church. Whatcha say?" They said, "Yeah." Tucker continued, "Whether you know it or not, it is a blessing to be here tonight. If you believe that, let me hear you say yeah!" They hollered back. "Do you feel all right, say yeah." Hollering louder this time. "If you feel"—Tucker screams it out—"*all right*, say *yeah*!" They do. "If you feel like clapping your hands, say yeah." Building. "If you feel like patting your feet, say yeah." Picking up speed. "If you've got anything to *shout* about, say yeah. . . . I like to tell you the reason I shout right here!" The guitar kicked in, the Birds double time handclapping as Tucker started singing.

"The Lord woke me up this morning." Group: "Right on time." Tucker: "When my eyes came open, I was in my right mind." Group: "In my right mind." Tucker: "I could move my limbs! And that's a mighty good reason to see me shout. I've got *so* much to shout about!" Tucker worked the audience, pointed to sections of the crowd and got them to clap along. Carroll and Bobo fell into a mesmerizing pattern as Tucker and Walker, hoarse from shouting, worked over the audience with their good old one-two gospel punch. Thompson and Davis chanted the mantra, "I got so much to shout about!" The performance lasted an incendiary eight and a half minutes, and when it was all over, the Birds had converted the crowd into the Newport Folk Festival Baptist Church.

There was an extended ovation with handclapping, whistling, and shouts for more. Davis stepped up to the mike breathlessly. "Thank you. Thank you. We highly appreciate the way you have received us." The crowd refused to let up. "Oh," says Davis, "we love you, too. We would love to do just a little more at this moment, I assure you, but it's time for us to go back to Birmingham." Introducing Dorothy Love Coates and the Gospel Harmonettes, the Harmonettes handled it with professional poise, thanking the Birds and moving into their next song. The 1966

Newport Folk Festival appearance was a glorious triumph for the Dixie Hummingbirds, and it would put them on the road to a wider popularity than they had ever before enjoyed.

"They have earned the title the 'Gentlemen of Song' throughout the world."

The appearance at the Newport Folk Festival provided impetus for the Birds to tour a wider circuit than ever before. Because they had not in any way compromised their material, the Birds were able to maintain their fan base at the same time they were playing nontraditional venues. The Birds toured their usual church circuit, the special programs and prestige events, the star-studded gospel extravaganzas, and now also the festivals and other secular venues like clubs and concert halls. Festival producer George Wein coordinated a number of similar events, and the Birds were regulars on his guest list. "This cat, George Wein," says Tucker, "he was the big man and we did a whole lot of things for him." In time, there would be traveling Newport events and the Birds would perform under that heading in New York, New Orleans, and Massachusetts' Tanglewood, among other places.

In the wake of their Festival appearance, Peacock released a "Best of" album, PLP 138, bringing together for the first time favorites like "Let's Go Out to the Programs," "In the Morning," "Bedside of a Neighbor," "Christian's Automobile," and "Our Prayer for Peace."

Two singles, Peacock 3084 and 3098, also debuted, with Tucker's "Confidential God" the strongest of the sides. Late in 1966, a sixth Dixie Hummingbirds album, PLP 144, *Your Good Deeds*, was released. The album's title track would be paired with James Walker's "What the Lord Is to Me" as a 1967 single, Peacock 3109. The amount of recorded product the Birds had on the market was a measure of their popularity during that period.

The Birds' progress was stalled by the assassination of the Reverend Martin Luther King, Jr., in 1968, an event with enormous repercussions that affected every aspect of the already strained relationship between the races. Popular music was not immune to the aftermath.

In the recording studios of Memphis and Muscle Shoals, Alabama, some of the hottest soul music in the land was being produced, brilliant collaborations between Anglo and African American musicians—Steve Cropper and Duck Dunn with Booker T, Otis Redding, and Sam & Dave at Stax; Chips Moman, Roger Hawkins, and Spooner Oldham with Wilson Pickett, Percy Sledge, and Aretha Franklin at Atlantic. The assassination of Dr. King changed everything. "It had a tremendous impact," said Jim Stewart, owner of Stax Records. "You knew things had changed and there's no way you could go back. Everybody started withdrawing, pulling back from that openness and close relationship that we felt we had.... Everybody went their separate ways. There wasn't that mixing and melting together like we had before."[14]

And indeed, the Dixie Hummingbirds would be derailed from the track they had been following, gently retreating from their pop inroads, moving closer to their traditional gospel constituency where they were not as vulnerable to the social forces that affected the commercial market. Yet during these transitional times, there continued to be cross-over in both directions as secular artists like Stevie Wonder and now Aretha Franklin made occasional forays into gospel while spiritual performers like the Staple Singers and Edwin Hawkins charted pop.

The Dixie Hummingbirds modernized their sound, embracing contemporary themes and instrumentation, drawing deeper on the very soul-feel they had helped inspire in the first place. They would release two singles in 1968: Peacock 3148, "The Inner Man" b/w "I'm Going On," and Peacock 3165, "Don't Let Me Fall," b/w "God Is Going to Get Tired." Of these, "The Inner Man" probably best exemplifies the updated Birds. Written by James Davis, the production is underpinned by prominent electric bass, drums, piano, and guitar. For the first time in a Birds recording, the instrumentals are on the same level in the mix as the vocals. The message "was in some sense," says James Davis, "a public relations thing for biased people. We were trying to show that we felt it wasn't what color a guy was, whether his eyes were slanted, whether he was nice looking, but that it was the inside of a man that counts." Davis's lyrics do indeed reflect the social currents of the day.

> It's the inner man,
> What's in a man,
> That counts.
> It's not his height,
> Not his size,
> Not the color of his eyes.
> It's the inner man,
> What's in a man,
> That counts.

"The Inner Man" combined the traditional gospel sound with contemporary sentiments. As Davis points out, "It doesn't say anything about Jesus or the Lord. The way things were with the black race of people and the white race of people, we wanted people to look at the thing from all angles."

The Birds' sound was also modernized by advances in recording technology. With multitrack stereo and a fuller frequency range, they now sounded state-of-the-art, their recorded performances on a par with the popular releases of the day.

With the 1968 release of their seventh album, PLP 153, *The Gentlemen of Song*, the Birds were inching closer to "elder statesmen" status. The Birds, of course, even early in their career had been called the "Gentlemen of Song," a reference to their elegant manner, appearance, and way with a tune. Wrote producer Richard Simpson in the liner notes, "Along with their character and living what they sing about, they have earned the title 'the Gentlemen of Song' throughout the world." There was no mention, however, that the album's release coincided with the Dixie Hummingbirds' fortieth anniversary in the business, the group not quite ready to play up their longevity.

The Gentlemen of Song was a fine showcase of spirited gospel with the Tucker/Walker vocal combo in fine mettle. Outstanding tracks included "I'm on the Battlefield," "I've Been Weighed," and "Prodigal Son," a tune that gave each of the Birds a moment in the vocal spotlight. *Gentlemen* sold well, and on its heels, Peacock released PLP-169, *Ye Shall Know the Truth*, another collection of standards and originals geared to traditional tastes. As the 1960s rolled over into the 1970s, it seemed that the Birds' primary recorded output had shifted from singles to long-playing albums, a reflection that their audience was growing older. By then, albums had become the favored music medium of the older, more settled generation.

The Birds would break back into the singles market again in 1970 with a novelty tune in the spirit of old-time sermonizers like Reverend J. M. Gates, who used to wrap serious content in entertaining packages with titles like "Clean the Corners of Your Mind" or "It's What You Think and Not What You Know." The Birds called theirs "Somebody Is Lying"; issued as Peacock 3191, it captured Tucker at his preaching best. It was the sort of tune the Birds loved to perform three quarters into the program, the reenergizer after the first plateau and just ahead of the way back up to the grand finale.

"Somebody Is Lying" was pure church-ifying, a slice-of-life rap with a modern day message. Howard Carroll opened with a wonderfully angular guitar figure that led into Tucker's spoken-word intro. "Friends, we are going to sing a song here that has to do with people. People in the hearing business. You know, people hear everything, including some of the things that they make up themselves. Ye-e-e-s, and sometimes it boils down to [pause] he said/she said. For the title of our song is— 'Somebody Is Lying.' Listen."

On this, Tucker and the group come in singing, their delivery sounding like rock 'n' roll's Coasters gone gospel. Do not, they warn, get involved in "He said–She said." "Look out!" cries Tucker. "Somebody is lying! Now that is the truth. Here is a conversation that could be going on w-a-a-a-ay across the nation or right across the street." He voiced all the parts, male and female.

> Well, did you see the pretty coat,
> That sister so-and-so wore to church?
> Yes, I saw it, but I heard that her husband,
> Wasn't making too much.
> Well, now, ah, I don't know but I was told,
> Somebody said that the coat was stole!
> Look Out! Somebody Is Lying!
>
> Well, did you hear about the Cadillac,
> So-and-so bought last week?
> You know what? You know, somebody said,
> That they had heard,
> That man couldn't hardly eat!
> Well, and then I heard he told his wife,
> Sunday morning in the church,
> You know what he told her?
> He said, "I got my Cadillac,
> Now honey, you got to go to work!"
>
> Please don't get involved in that "He said–She said."
> There's nothing but confusion all the time.
> If they say that you said,
> Somebody's going to say that they said,
> Look Out! Somebody Is Lying,
> And that is the truth!

The pure gospel preaching tradition reflected in "Somebody Is Lying" was indicative of the Birds' continuing commitment to their loyal fan base. Unfortunately, though, the market for singles by strictly gospel old-line quartets like the Birds had gone soft. Peacock would release no new Dixie Hummingbirds singles or LPs for the next two years, though an impressive back catalog would maintain the Birds' presence on records.

In 1971, the Birds accepted an offer to return to the recording studio, but not as the featured group and not on the Peacock label. Their old friend Marion Williams, who had quit the Ward Singers in 1958 to strike out on her own, had been exploring the boundaries of gospel in an Atlantic label series of albums that featured jazz sidemen. She was about to record a new album co-produced by Joel Dorn and Roberta Flack and backed by cutting-edge instrumentalists like Keith Jarrett, Ray Bryant, Hank Jones, and Joe Zawinul. The Dixie Hummingbirds signed on as back-up vocalists.

While the instrumental support may have seemed unconventional for gospel, the players laid down some very soulful tracks very much in keeping with the tradition. The material, however, stood well outside the standard gospel songbook. With the exception of the title track, Thomas Dorsey's "Standing Here Wondering Which Way to Go," the songs were culled from pop sources and, in the case of "Hare Krishna," from another faith altogether. Other cuts on the album included "Turn! Turn! Turn! (To Everything There Is a Season)," "He Ain't Heavy, He's My Brother," "Put Your Hand in the Hand," Percy Mayfield's "Danger Zone," Bob Dylan's "Wicked Messenger," and former Beatle George Harrison's "My Sweet Lord." Marion Williams performed masterfully in her trilling soprano and the Birds contributed "oohs" and "aahs" and occasional response to her call. Even though the Birds were not the record's central attraction, recording it put them back in the studio and in the public eye. More important, the song selections opened them to possibilities about to come their way. In fact, events in 1972 would waft the Birds to heights they could not have anticipated, even in their most ambitious dreams.

"I definitely wanted to do something with the Dixie Hummingbirds."

By the early 1970s, songs about faith or rooted in gospel returned to the *Billboard* pop charts. The number one hit for several weeks in early 1971 was the tune the Birds had just covered with Marion Williams, George Harrison's "My Sweet Lord." Later that year, Aretha Franklin peaked at number six with Simon and Garfunkel's "Bridge Over Troubled Water." The song had been inspired by Claude Jeter and the Swan

Silvertones. "Paul Simon and Art Garfunkel," explained Ira Tucker, "they used to go 'round to the gospel programs. So this night they were at a Swan Silvertones concert, and Jeter used to sing a song, 'Oh Mary Don't You Weep.' While Jeter was ad-libbing, he said, 'I can imagine Jesus said that Mary was like a bridge over troubled water,' and that's where Simon got his song."[15] Also in 1971, the Staple Singers were nominated for a Grammy as "Best R&B Group" for their gospel-styled "Respect Yourself." They had successfully made the transition from gospel to pop by retaining the spiritual integrity of their message. A year later, their label, Stax, ran a full-page ad in *Billboard* touting the Staples and the *Be Altitude/Respect Yourself* LP:

> The message that rock music is still looking for! You get it in the streets where people are looking for freedom. You hear it in tiny churches and one-room meeting halls where people are looking for truth. You find it at demonstrations where people are looking for peace and love through equality. . . . The new Staple Singers album. It picks up where the good book leaves off.[16]

Rather than urging gospel groups to record secular tunes, music promoters now highlighted a semblance to black gospel and biblical content as a selling point for rock 'n' roll/R&B. As the music world sought deeper meaning in their songs, the Dixie Hummingbirds began to get recognition for their place in the pantheon of American roots music. In 1972, the National Academy of Television and Recording Artists named the Dixie Hummingbirds the "Best Gospel Group of the Year." On the heels of that honor, Anthony Heilbut set up the Birds' appearance at the 1972 Newport Jazz Festival.

For the first time in its ten-year history, the Festival would not be taking place in Newport. Alluding to the "uncertainties and tumult of its place of origin," producer George Wein told a *New York Times* reporter, "The Newport Jazz Festival–New York City is now a permanent annual event." Festival concerts were spread over eight days—July 1–9, Sunday to Sunday—at scattered venues throughout the city with more than 600 artists performing at Carnegie and Philharmonic Hall, Yankee Stadium, Radio City Music Hall, Hudson River cruise boats, and on the streets of Harlem and Brooklyn. All in all, the best names in jazz and related music gathered to celebrate the tradition: Duke Ellington, Sarah Vaughan, Dizzy Gillespie, Thelonious Monk, Max Roach, Dave Brubeck, Stan Getz, Billy Eckstine, Cecil Taylor, Roland Kirk, Mary Lou Williams, Count Basie, Bill Evans, and on and on.[17]

The Dixie Hummingbirds would take part in one of the Festival's finale events, a July 9 Sunday morning two-hour Radio City Music Hall gospel extravaganza produced by Anthony Heilbut. More than 2,500 attended the event headlined by Marion Williams. "Her rich and powerful voice," wrote a *Times* reviewer, held "the audience rapt as it slid from deep, throaty whispers to sustained high notes.... Her encore of 'Amazing Grace' brought the audience to its feet." In fact, from his seat, one audience member broke into a spontaneous vocal solo. Ms. Williams, as it turned out, recognized him as Herbert Carson, who "used to drive and sing for Aretha Franklin and her father, Reverend Franklin." She passed him a mike so everyone could hear.

Willie Mae Ford Smith singing "from her 'sanctified soul,'" Jessy Dixon and his Dixon Singers demonstrating "a style that showed how closely gospel, jazz, and rhythm and blues are related in beats and rhythms," Dorothy Love Coates "talking and preaching," R. H. Harris "wailing in his falsetto, which brought ... memories of his late student, Sam Cooke," and the Consolers "singing what without the committed Christian message would have been the blues" were also on the program, along with the Dixie Hummingbirds, "first rate ... giving as good a display of great gospel choral singing as can be found in any black church."

The audience clapped along, stood in their seats, swayed to the rhythms, and shouted out encouragement. Anthony Heilbut was pleased with his choice of performers. "A terrific amount of soulful ad-libbing and note-bending combined with beautiful voices."[18] Paul Simon stood backstage with Anthony Heilbut checking out the Dixie Hummingbirds. He was looking to record with a gospel group on material he was developing for a solo album project. The Birds were a particular favorite.

Paul Simon had grown up in the city listening to R&B vocal harmony groups, but over the years he had developed a deep appreciation for the black gospel quartets that had spawned the doo-wop genre. "I listened to groups like the Moonglows," says Simon. "That was the first music that I heard." Doo-wop would be Simon's entrée into the world of gospel quartets. "I always liked that quartet singing. That quartet singing was the well from which doo-wop was drawn."[19] "Doo-wop," he would later tell writer Paul Zollo, "was the secular, urban, street-corner version of gospel. There was something very real and mysterious about the music because it was the first time that black culture entered the mainstream of American (white) culture."[20]

Paul Simon even took note of quartet singers early in his career, especially Sam Cooke of the Soul Stirrers, who would be a prime influence on Simon's singing style. "Sam Cooke's in a lot of my albums. Because my voice was never a hard and powerful voice, because it was a soft voice, . . . I was genuinely a Sam Cooke fan. . . . Because I had a similar voice, I learned Sam Cooke-isms."[21]

That morning at Radio City Music Hall, Simon was not immediately certain that the Dixie Hummingbirds were the right group for his project. He had also been thinking of the Swan Silvertones, the group that had inspired his earlier hit, "Bridge Over Troubled Water." The new song was "Loves Me Like a Rock," the seed idea coming from "My Rock," a track cut by the Silvertones for the Specialty label in 1952 and coincidentally one of Paul Owens's first with them after his unceremonious departure from the Hummingbirds. "Loves Me Like a Rock," explained Simon, was written "after 'Bridge Over Troubled Water' when I started to immerse myself in gospel. It came directly out of listening to gospel quartets. I definitely wanted to do something with the Dixie Hummingbirds, who were one of my favorite gospel groups. I also wanted to work very much with the Swan Silvertones, but the Swans had disbanded by then."[22] Anthony Heilbut nudged Simon in the direction of the Hummingbirds, and on the strength of their performance that morning the Birds got the call.

Louise Tucker remembers the night she first heard the song. "Ira came in, I guess 3 or 4 o'clock in the morning. He got me up and said he wanted me to listen to something, and I did. I said, 'Ummm hmmm . . . sounds good . . . Paul Simon . . . great.' Then I said, 'One thing, Ira, he didn't put in this song.' Ira said, 'What is it?' I said, 'the *soul*. The soul is left out. If you put the soul in it, you got a hit!' And there you go."

The Birds themselves were not immediately certain they ought to record the song. Recalls Louise Tucker. "There were guys in the group—I won't say who—would say, 'Oh, no! They'll kill us. We won't ever get nobody else to listen if we do this because this is blues or whatever you call it!'"

Don Robey and Evelyn Johnson at Peacock, however, had no second thoughts about it. "I got a call from Paul Simon," says Johnson. "I told him we would give it a thought. We had to sound important." Johnson recalled, "I did the same thing with Presley when they wanted to do 'Hound Dog.' Said, 'I'll get back to you in a couple of days.' And I said that on my knees! 'Please God, don't let 'em change their minds!'

[Johnson laughs] I had to make them feel they weren't doing us any favors."[23]

The Dixie Hummingbirds decided to go along for the ride. "Look at the words, what they say," James Davis later told a reporter. "'When I was a little boy and the devil would call my name, I'd say who do you think you're foolin'? I'm a consecrated boy, I sing on the choir.' To my mind, it fits in with us."[24] Says Simon, "I recorded it in New York City with me playing guitar and the Dixie Hummingbirds singing live." Howard Carroll remembers putting in several eight-hour daylong rehearsals with Simon and producer Phil Ramone in the studio. "Paul had a tape," says Carroll, "He'd play it and we just sat down and listened to it. A song like that, it didn't take no year to learn it." "And then," adds Simon, "the bass and drums were all overdubbed at Muscle Shoals, Alabama." In fact, "Loves Me Like a Rock" featured David Hood on bass and Roger Hawkins on drums, the same Muscle Shoals rhythm team that in the 1960s had helped shape the sound of soul greats like Aretha Franklin and Wilson Pickett.

The Birds also recorded some other songs at those sessions. Carroll recalls that some of them "leaned too much toward the secular" for the group to sing the actual words. "So, you might have heard us humming on a number of other things." One of those to make the album, the only other track featuring the Birds, was "Tenderness." Paul Simon had to convince them to record the tune,[25] and in the end, they thought it was a message they could support.

> What can I do,
> What can I do,
> Much of what you say is true,
> I know you see through me,
> But there's no tenderness,
> Beneath your honesty.

Sounding like a cross somewhere between Percy Mayfield and the Moonglows, the production was warm, gentle, and vulnerable. "I thought this was a nice idea," says Simon. "About people who are brutally honest, you know? And I thought the Dixie Hummingbirds were really great on it." New Orleans producer Allen Toussaint would do the horn arrangements for "Tenderness."[26]

Both tracks appeared on the album *There Goes Rhymin' Simon*, Columbia LP KC 32280, released in May 1973. "Kodachrome" would be the first to break, peaking at number two on the *Billboard* charts in July 1973. "Loves Me Like a Rock" followed with seven weeks in the top ten, leveling out at number two the week of October 6. The Dixie Humming-birds, name prominently emblazoned on the label just beneath Simon's, shared the top ten limelight those weeks with Marvin Gaye's "Let's Get It On," Al Green's "Here I Am (Come and Take Me)," Stevie Wonder's "Higher Ground," the Isley Brothers' "That Lady," and Gladys Knight's "Midnight Train to Georgia." After forty-five years, the Birds had a significant mainstream success.

Yet the Birds' "hit maker" status was a mixed blessing. Although they were able to command higher performance fees, the Birds continued to put fans first. James Davis remembers. "We lost money when Paul Simon decided out of the clear sky that he wanted to carry us around after we made 'Like a Rock.'" Not only money, but also a chance to perform internationally, because the Simon tour was worldwide.

> We were booked in five states and I guess he felt like he was big enough that if he wanted us, we should have dropped them, you know. Dropped all those people. But we thought about the fact that we been working with these people all those years and everything, and we were already booked. Naturally, we got in touch with them and asked what they thought. And everybody cried foul, you know. So we told Paul Simon as much as we'd like to go with him, we couldn't go.

Moreover, despite their chart success, the Birds had signed on to the project as studio musicians, paid a flat fee for their services with no further royalties.

Finally, "Loves Me Like a Rock" upset portions of the Birds' fan base. As Davis told a *Philadelphia Inquirer* reporter, initially putting a positive spin on it, "We didn't know that so many people cared about us. We got telephone calls and telegrams from all over. People said, 'Oh, no, the Dixie Hummingbirds, our favorites, are going rock!'" But the Birds did not regret their decision. "We were satisfied with the words to the song," says Davis, "so we did it."[27]

"That's the easiest Grammy that I've ever seen."

When "Loves Me Like a Rock" hit the charts in 1973, Peacock had not released a new single or LP by the Dixie Hummingbirds in more than two years. By then, the golden age of gospel had turned a tarnished bronze. But as Paul Simon and the Dixie Hummingbirds moved up the charts, esoteric regional and ethnic music became integrated into the musical establishment, and the major labels capitalized on the trends by absorbing the independents.

On May 23, 1973, Don Robey sold his Peacock/Duke labels complete with back catalog to ABC/Dunhill, one of the major players in the record industry. To Tucker's delight, Robey told the new owners that Tucker was one of his top producers. "He gave me a good name about it ... and ABC called me up ... and said, 'We need you as a producer.' Scared me to death, but I enjoyed that they asked Robey who was his producer, and he said 'Ira Tucker.'" Robey, too, would stay on, working as a consultant until his death in June 1975.

With the support of the new ABC/Peacock imprint, and in partnership with Don Robey, Tucker planned a new Hummingbirds album to both win back the traditional fan base and appeal to new listeners. The Birds brought together their usual traditional spirituals and gospel originals with contemporary material and contemporary performers, starting with "Loves Me Like a Rock."

Louise Tucker had always contended that the song needed a "soul" injection. Ira Tucker decided to re-record "Loves Me Like a Rock" in the Birds' own gospel style. He approached Paul Simon about it. "I asked Paul, 'Can I have a track on that?' And he said sure."[28] Tucker arranged to record in Philadelphia with hometown musicians and the help of Walt Kahn, a local R&B producer and owner of Queen Village Studios. The sessions took place immediately on the heels of the Birds' chart success with Paul Simon. The Birds' version of "Loves Me Like a Rock" came out with a real "swing down" feel. Tucker and Kahn produced it with a strong backbeat, tambourine, Carroll weaving a bluesy guitar figure throughout, and Thompson, Davis, Walker, and Bobo supplying full-stereo sharp vocal support. Tucker handled the lead vocals.

By 1973, meanwhile, the Tucker offspring—Linda, Sundray, and Ira, Jr.—were working in various capacities with Stevie Wonder who, as his music had matured, was reaching ever-higher plateaus of success. His groundbreaking album, *Talking Book*, had been released the year before and his follow-up, *Innervisions*, was receiving critical accolades as one of its tracks, "Higher Ground," was climbing the charts.

Linda Tucker had been the first to connect with Wonder. He had been impressed with her singing when he heard her in the late 1960s at a Detroit club called The Twenty Grand. Ira, Jr., fills in the story. "Wonder found out that she was my father's daughter. He knew about the Hummingbirds but had more of a feeling for my father than for the group. He admired my father's voice. And then he decided he was going to change the thing at Motown and do his *own* thing, so he hired Linda." She would sing background on Wonder's 1970 hit, "Signed, Sealed, Delivered, I'm Yours."

Meanwhile, Ira, Jr., was working as an educator in the Philadelphia schools. He had developed a system designed to "teach kids how to read through using contemporary music in the classroom. My concept was that if you could sing the lyrics, you could read them." One of the songs he used was "Do Yourself a Favor, Educate Your Mind," a popular track from Stevie Wonder's 1971 LP, *Where I'm Coming From.* Tucker extended an invitation through his sister for Wonder to visit the school. "Stevie was really important in me selling the program and 'Do Yourself a Favor' was a great song to kick off teaching them how to read. Stevie came to the school and stayed an entire day." The two of them hit it off and not long after, Tucker went to work for Wonder as his publicist. The job entailed duties ranging from the mundane to the handling of publicity, and in that context, Ira, Jr., thought about teaming up Stevie Wonder and the Dixie Hummingbirds.

The *Innervisions* album was released in 1973 and on it was a song, "Jesus Children of America," that Tucker thought would make the ideal connection. "I was trying to find a way to get them together, and I felt 'Jesus' would be a good song for the Hummingbirds to do. And then I thought that if I could get them to cover it, maybe I could get Stevie to perform with them on it. So, I talked to the Birds about the song. I let my father hear it, and he liked it." The song indeed was holy at its heart and had the kind of positive message that marked the best Birds material.

> Hello Jesus,
> Jesus children,
> Jesus loves you,
> Jesus children,
> Hello Children Jesus loves you of America.
>
> Are you hearing,
> What he's saying?
> Are you feeling,
> What you're praying?
> Are you hearing, praying, feeling,
> What you say inside.

In later verses, Wonder addressed courage ("Are you standing, like a soldier?"), integrity ("Are you standing for everything you talk about"), and the drug problem that had been plaguing the inner city ("Are you happy when you stick a needle in your arm?"). These were issues that resonated with the Birds, and so they decided to include their version of the song on their new album. "There were just some words my father wanted to change," says Tucker, Jr. "Wonder did 'Jesus Children of America,'" says Tucker, Sr., "and I did it 'Jesus, Children All Over the World.' And my son said, 'Stevie ain't going to like that.'" And Stevie called me and said, "I love it!"

"Jesus Children" would be the second track produced by Tucker and Kahn for the new Birds album. Howard Carroll recalls the session coming together in a whirlwind of activity. "Stevie came to Philadelphia one morning about 4:00 A.M. And he had Walt Kahn to call the union hall. And he called me and I got out of bed about 4:30 in the morning. And I went in and the studio was loaded with musicians. Stevie had every musician in town in the studio. [Howard lets out a laugh] I said, 'Stevie, we don't need all of this.' But Stevie was beautiful to work with and they all knew exactly what they were doing."

In the end, Wonder's participation in the session was limited to piano. "Stevie agreed to come in," says Tucker, Jr., "and the only thing was, Motown wouldn't let him sing, so he played the piano. He worked about five or six hours on the session and that was it. I remember he played a Fender Rhodes and it was a very warm sound and I remember him enjoying playing it. Stevie liked the arrangement the Hummingbirds had, so he really got into it with the piano, and it came out well." The Birds' take on "Jesus Children," while it retained the chord changes, melody, and most of the lyrics, was a radical departure from Wonder's original. The Birds infused it with gospel intensity, livened up the pace, and made it completely their own.

The album was filled out with a handful of originals produced by Tucker and Robey, including "Let It Alone," "In These Changing Times," "Hold On," "I've Been Born Again," and "God Is So Good." In 1973, ABC Records released the album, PLP 178, *The Dixie Hummingbirds/We Love You Like a Rock*, and two singles, Peacock 3198, "Loves Me Like a Rock," and 3203, "Jesus Children of America." The album liner notes were straightforward. "Paul Simon wrote it. The 'BIRDS' sang it. Then put the 'Rock' into the Simon Song. You may hear the author sing his song on his label, but you haven't heard anything till the 'BIRDS' have a go at it." And about "Jesus Children," "the rhythm gets to you, the chords move you in a modern 'new' Gospel way, how did this come about? Listen close, hear the electronic piano, that's the man, Stevie Wonder, he wrote it, he put it all together ..." *We Love You Like a Rock* was innovative Birds gospel. "So many 'new things' herein, a tuba, ... electro-comp synthesizer, ... the reggae beat.... The Dixie Hummingbirds, Don Robey, Ira Tucker and ... Walt Kahn had an idea. They put their idea into songs. All you have to do is love it like a rock." Even the cover photo signaled change. For the first time in their history, the Birds posed in everyday clothes around and on top of a rock in Philadelphia's Fairmont Park, James Davis in mauve pants and multicolored shoes self-consciously smiling out from the cover, his Hummingbirds posed dutifully beside and behind him.[29]

If there was any uncertainty on the part of the Birds, it dissipated with the acceptance of the album. Although the LP did not sell as well as the Birds had hoped, the single "Loves Me Like a Rock" entered the *Cash Box* top R&B 100 the week of September 15, 1973, and remained for eight weeks, peaking at the #34 spot. The Birds'—not Paul Simon's—recording of "Loves Me Like a Rock" won a Grammy that year in the category of "Best Soul Gospel Performance." "That song hit hard," says Ira Tucker. "That's the easiest Grammy that I've ever seen." And in fact, to date the only Grammy the Dixie Hummingbirds have won, although there would be nominations in the future. Winning in that category was particularly gratifying to the Birds, knowing that those who voted in that category tended to be gospel establishment insiders. For them, the award was a vote of confidence from their professional peers, and it also meant that young record buyers, black and white, were paying attention.

Years later, Paul Simon would tell filmmakers Ashley James and Ray Allen, "It was like recording with a national treasure; [it was] an honor to work with them. And the fact that *they* then recorded 'Loves Me Like a Rock' themselves and had a hit with it—and then won a Grammy with it—was even more pleasurable for me, even more pleasurable than if I had won a Grammy for myself—which I didn't."[30]

"They are afraid that we are going rock and roll."

The Birds became a hot commodity in the firestorm of publicity sparked by "Loves Me Like a Rock," in demand now at posh big city clubs and on their usual church circuit. Now two different Dixie Hummingbirds performed across the country: the conservative ones, singing good old-fashioned soul-stirring gospel for their own people, and the flashy ones, gospel entertainers working with the biggest names in R&B show business. As far as they were concerned, nothing had changed. They were drawing on their versatility to entertain the widest cross-section of people in the most wholesome way. Their intentions and message were the same, but the external packaging was subject to change pursuant to the venue. The Birds appear in one contemporary publicity shot in their nightclub wear: red suit jackets with wide lapels trimmed in white ribbing, red-checkered pants and vests, and red Cuban-heeled platform shoes adorned with silver lines and stars. The next day in church they dress conservatively in dark suits, ties, black shoes, and matching white handkerchiefs squared away in each lapel pocket. As James Davis would explain, "We recorded 'Jesus Children of America,' . . . but when we get serious, we don't sing that. People would not take us seriously if we sang rock." To that, James Walker added, "You can't get too far from gospel singing."[31]

The Birds talked to *Sepia* magazine in 1973 about what they perceived as the black community's failure to support their latest musical direction. *Sepia*, with an almost exclusively African American readership, offered the Birds a chance to communicate to their constituency. "The number we played with Paul Simon," said James Davis, "brought us a gold record each. The reason the number went so well is that it was played everywhere." Not, however, he points out, by black disk jockeys. "Some of them played it, but the number we did with Paul Simon was played by all of the white stations and that is the difference. If we could get that album of ours played by everyone, it would have been a big seller by now. But without the play, you are at a big disadvantage."

As to the all-important perception of their longtime fans, "We have already lost some of our audience," said Davis.

> The only thing in our favor is that we have gained more than we have lost. We have received letters. People write and tell us they hear this "Loves Me Like a Rock" everywhere and they want to know what it is. They say that we have been their number one favorite group for so many years. They are afraid that we are going rock and roll. . . .
>
> It would be a blessing if *Sepia* could help make it clear to our people that the Dixie Hummingbirds are religious men, living God-fearing lives who function as ambassadors for Jesus.[32]

With their forays into the pop world, the Birds also had to incorporate into their touring a support band—organist Tony Brockington, drummer Daryl Burgee, and bass guitarist Tony Beck, son of Philadelphia gospel trumpeter and sermonizer, Elder Charles Beck. Tony Beck would have a long association with the Hummingbirds, playing on their later recordings and working with Ira Tucker on producing records by local Philadelphia gospel performers.

In late November 1973, the Birds and band did a week with label mate Bobby Bland at the famed Whiskey Au Go Go in Los Angeles. Entertainment writer Bob Kirsch took in the show. "Opening nights in L.A. aren't generally the cause of any great excitement, but the combination of the blues of Bobby Bland and the gospel of the Dixie Hummingbirds was an exception. And for those who waited anxiously, the wait was justified." Kirsch praised Bland's "distinctive" voice, "letter perfect" phrasing, and "control," never mentioning, probably because he did not know, that Ira Tucker had been a prime influence on Bland in just those areas.

But Kirsch did have praise for the Birds, commenting on their "extremely smart move of mixing pure gospel with pop," and calling their harmonies "simply beautiful, the arrangements perfect and the overall effect on the audience . . . one of genuine appreciation."[33] Stevie Wonder dropped in one night and joined the Birds onstage for an exhilarating performance of "Jesus Children." Another night, a group of clergymen came by, Davis assumed to "check that the Hummingbirds hadn't gone to rock 'n' roll." To his relief and delight, they came backstage after the show and commended the Birds for "spreading the word of the Lord."[34] The Birds did well at the Whiskey. "We were turning people away," says Davis. "We stayed out there in California for a week and the man wanted to hold us over another week, but we wouldn't stay. One deal—an appearance in Charlotte—was holding us up, and we didn't call that deal off. That's how our group was made."

The following month, the Birds appeared as solo headliners at the trendy New York City club, Max's Kansas City. A reviewer for *Variety* magazine noted that the "almost-legendary . . . black gospel combo" is "finding a new lease on life via the rock cabaret scene," and that the sort of "rousing gospel" the Birds performed was new to most of the "wider ranging in age than usual" crowd who clapped along the whole time. "Some of them," said James Davis, "were trying to get on the stage with us, the music would all but invite them up there, you know."[35] Each of the Birds was singled out by name in the *Variety* review.

> Lead vocalist Ira Tucker, who goes from low to high, is an exciting
> performer, whose voice at *times* is almost operatic. Bass William Bobo

not only is a solid vocalist, but performs with facial contortions that are delightful. Strong support is supplied by Davis, the combo's leader, and tenor Beachey Thompson. James Walker is the happy expressive second lead vocalist, also far-ranging vocally, whose enthusiasm is catching. One number where Tucker and Walker divide leads in their response fashion is among the standouts. Guitarist Howard Carroll . . . joins vocally in the encore; impressions of other gospel acts, which is one of their many biggies.

Billy Altman, a writer for the rock 'n' roll magazine *Crawdaddy*, also witnessed the performance. Ira Tucker, "the man with a thousand voices," led the group through a "talking blues spiced song called 'Let It Alone,' which simply states that one should keep his nose out of other people's business." James Walker was the "loosest of the Birds, urging the audience to clap along, moving around on stage, and beaming" as he sang "Lord Take Care of Me." William Bobo "grabs the spotlight on the old hymn, 'Ezekiel Saw the Wheel,' his voice plummeting further and further down the scales as the audience gasps, then roars in approval." And James Davis "stands in the middle, proud and tall, happy to be approaching a new audience and obviously pleased by the enthusiastic response."[36] And, indeed, Davis would tell *Sepia*, "We feel in a nightclub something like we do in a church and we prove it to the people. When we were in New York, there is a number we did called 'Never Alone.' It got so that when we were introducing Walker . . . who does the lead on the song, people would rave. They ate us up as though we were in church. We never go over in church any better than we did there."[37]

That spring, the Birds opened for Stevie Wonder at Madison Square Garden, an all-important appearance that, unbeknownst to them, they almost lost to legendary blues singer Jimmy Reed. "Oh, man, I still feel the drama that surrounded that," says Ira Tucker, Jr., who was in on the planning. "Stevie asked me, 'Ira, do you think your father and the Birds would like to open up?' I said, 'Sure,' and I went to Mr. Davis and told him about it. Mr. Davis said okay, but he had to be sure it was real because he had some people who wanted that date. So I told him, 'Mr. Davis, that's for real. Stevie told me to come to you and tell you that.'" The Birds accepted.

Shortly thereafter, Ewart Abner, formerly of Vee Jay Records and then president of Motown Records, got involved in the concert plans. Abner was not a big gospel fan and suggested that instead of the Dixie Hummingbirds, they ought to consider "trying to do something for

Jimmy Reed. Stevie heard Reed was having problems and wanted to help. He asked me to call Jimmy and I do and find out that, yeah, Jimmy is broke and having a rough time." So Tucker was told to let the Birds know they were no longer on the show. "That's what it came down to. I was supposed to tell them that it wasn't happening—but I never did. I never told them because I was afraid of Mr. Davis."

Two weeks prior to the concert, however, Ewart Abner's plan to help Jimmy Reed backfired. Reed, it seemed, was adamant that Abner had ripped him off in the days when Reed recorded for Abner on the Vee Jay label. Reed refused to participate in the tribute, passing up not only a prestige gig but also what would have been a sizeable paycheck. As abruptly as the door had been closed on the Dixie Hummingbirds, it had now reopened.

Abner, unaware that the Birds never knew they had been dumped, asked Ira Tucker, Jr., if they were still available to perform. Tucker replied quite promptly and with a great deal of relief that they were. "The Hummingbirds," he says, "never knowing they'd been off the show, were the opening act. It was the first time they'd ever been in Madison Square Garden and the audience didn't know who they were. They came out in these checkered pants with the red jackets and the high heels. They cleaned the house! They got three encores—and they never even knew they were off the show!"

The Madison Square Garden concert was a sellout, with more than twenty thousand in attendance. *Billboard* hailed Wonder as "one of the leading forces in today's music market." As to the Birds, "they proved to be perfect for the occasion, blending a rich sound with strong stage presence."[38] Following the concert, there was a party at the Rainbow Room atop Rockefeller Center. Paul Simon as well as professional athletes, including basketball star Walt Frazier, attended.

In August, the Dixie Hummingbirds performed with Marion Williams at the prestigious Wolf Trap performing arts center just outside Washington, D.C. Following this string of concert events, Ira Tucker would team with Robey to produce more Birds projects and LPs by other gospel groups on the ABC/Peacock label—longtime colleagues like the Five Blind Boys and the Sensational Nightingales. He was also scouting Philadelphia for fresh talent and producing singles for local labels. The Birds' *Best of . . .* collection was followed by *Who Are We* in 1974, *Thanks to Thee* in 1975, and *Wonderful to Be Alive* in 1976.

The Birds continued to tour, but though they did quite a few club dates, they increasingly returned to their traditional venues. The once-

DIXIE HUMMINGBIRDS

The Dixie Hummingbirds in the mid-1970s. From left: Beachey
Thompson, Ira Tucker, Howard Carroll, James Davis, James Walker.

alienated audience unconditionally accepted them—the prodigal sons—back into the fold. The Birds still occasionally accepted outside projects such as doing backups on tracks for pop stars Melissa Manchester, Harry Chapin, and Leon Redbone.

On November 14, 1976, the Hummingbirds performed a live concert at one of their traditional stops, the Tabernacle Baptist Church, 239 George Street in New Brunswick, New Jersey. The program was the perfect blend of pop entries—"Loves Me" and "Jesus Children"; recent favorites—"Let It Alone" and "Hold On"; older favorites—"Prayer for Peace" and "Let's Go Out to the Programs"; and truly old-time classics—"Swing Low, Sweet Chariot" and "Two Little Fishes, Five Loaves of Bread." Few, if any, groups had this scope of a legacy to draw on, and the Birds took full advantage of it, showcasing almost a half-century of material. "Exactly what the jam-packed audience was waiting to hear," wrote Sundray Tucker in the notes to the album released on ABC/Peacock.

On April 28, 1976, in the wake of their two latest album releases, *Live* and *Wonderful to Be Alive*, William Bobo, bass singer with the Dixie Hummingbirds for more than thirty years, passed away. The story rocked Philadelphia's African American community and gospel fans and colleagues worldwide. "An original member of America's oldest gospel group died Wednesday night in a local hospital. William Bobo, 55, of the Dixie Hummingbirds, succumbed while a patient in West Park Hospital."[39]

Bobo had been ill and performing with the Birds only sporadically for almost three years. Even when he missed performances, Bobo was paid his share. "We took care of the guys," says James Davis. "He got his money the same way we got it."

The group had been scheduled to perform with Bobo on April 22 at the Main Point, a small folk club in Bryn Mawr, just outside Philadelphia, when Bobo suffered a stroke. The show was canceled and Bobo was hospitalized. The Birds, fully expecting him to recover, left town to honor previous commitments. His death twelve days later shocked them all. The Birds canceled appearances in Fort Wayne, Indiana, and Detroit, Michigan, to fly in for the funeral, a fitting tribute to a much beloved man who Tucker said was "born to sing bass."

"Nearly 2,000 Mourners Attend Final Rites for Dixie Hummingbirds' W. Bobo," read the *Philadelphia Tribune* headline. The main sanctuary of Enon Baptist Church at 19th and Green was jammed for the 8:00 P.M. two-and-a-half-hour "eulogistic" service laced through with "intermittent shouting and gaiety." The Brooklyn Skyways and the Sensational Nightingales sang in tribute. The Sons of the Birds were also to perform, but were "too overcome with emotion to sing." Roxie Moore read letters and telegrams from, among others, the Harmonizing Four, the Five Blind Boys, and Gertrude Ward, who had survived her daughter, the great Clara Ward, gone now almost three years. William Bobo was buried at Northwood Cemetery in Philadelphia, and the Birds were left to press on.[40]

Instead of immediately replacing William Bobo, Ira Tucker and James Walker took turns handling the bass parts. Tucker would later tell *Ebony* magazine, "When you work together for so long a time, you come to know each other's feelings and movements very well. . . . It's hard to get a guy today who can replace that kind of feeling and understanding. You might be able to find a guy who can sing better than the angels, but he may not be able to really capture the feeling of the group at all. So we put up a mike every night for Bobo, and we always say that if he was here he would really be working out on this number. And it seems as if that thought gives us a greater incentive to go forward, and it's almost as if our singing has gotten stronger since he died."[41]

James Davis worried about Tucker and Walker. "I told Tucker that I didn't think he and Walker could maintain their lead voices but so long the way they was singing bass. And they had gotten where they could really sing bass!" The Birds would invite bass singers to sit in with them, including a short stint in the 1980s with Jimmy Jones, Walker's old singing mate from both the Southern Sons and the Harmonizing Four. But Tucker and Walker continued to pick up bass parts. "I thought that an awful lot of bass for the lead singer was bad, but they were like children. They had a battle on, Walker trying to outdo Tucker and vice versa, singing against each other in some kind of way, being more versatile and showing it to the public." The Dixie Hummingbirds continued to tour internationally and release critically acclaimed albums, accruing honors and awards through the 1980s. After more than six decades together with no sign of stopping, they had earned the title, the "Iron Men of Gospel."

9
"Who Are We?"
(1977 AND BEYOND)

We've been singing for the master,
Ever since we were in our teens,
Riding down the highways,
And all of our pockets clean,

Who are we?
We're the Dixie Hummingbirds.

Well the road was rough, and the going was tough,
But we managed to sing every now and then,
Most of the time when we would render a program,
We'd always run in to Mister Slim,
You know Slim could be the difference,
In a meal or maybe none,
And Slim is when you look for three hundred people,
And you don't see but twenty-one.

Who are we?
We're the Dixie Hummingbirds,
And we love to sing . . .

—"Who Are We?"
The Dixie Hummingbirds

On a warm summer evening, June 28, 1998, the Birds celebrated their
70th anniversary with a grand dinner and roast coordinated by Ira
Tucker, Jr., at the African American Museum in Philadelphia on Arch

Street. More than 250 guests in gowns and tuxedos came out for the tribute. All the Philadelphia newspapers—white and black—covered the story. The room was set up with banquet tables and a long dais at the front for special guests. Each of the Birds—including eighty-two-year-old patriarch, Mr. James Davis—sat close at hand, family members at their sides, so that everyone there could enjoy their reactions as the evening unfolded. A mainstay of Philadelphia African American tradition, a gospel horn ensemble, the United House of Prayer for All People Brass Band, provided music with arrangements and chord changes rooted in the repertoire of the Dixie Hummingbirds.

The night began with the reading of a proclamation from Tom Ridge, at the time the governor of Pennsylvania. He wrote in part, "Over the last seventy years, you have entertained audiences with your strength and harmony. Throughout the Commonwealth and the world you have raised up your voices in glorious celebration. Through your music and its power you have educated and inspired countless citizens around the nation and the globe. Your influence has changed and shaped the foundation of gospel quartet singing.... As the Governor of the Commonwealth of Pennsylvania, I am pleased to take a moment to recognize the Dixie Hummingbirds for your commitment and dedication to the beauty of music. On behalf of all Pennsylvanians, I extend best wishes on your 70th anniversary. May you continue to enjoy many more years of service and success." Following the governor's salute, the mayor of Philadelphia, the Honorable Ed Rendell, awarded the Birds the "Liberty Bell," the city's highest civilian honor and, in the words of Tucker, Jr., "better than a key to the city."

Prominent Philadelphia businessman Lawrence Smallwood opened with a reminiscence of how his father had insisted that he and his brothers listen to Dixie Hummingbirds records before they went to church "because we weren't right for church until we listened to the Dixie Hummingbirds. I want you out there to understand," he said, "you are in the same space with living legends." At that, each invited luminary stood in turn and toasted the mighty Dixie Hummingbirds.

First to rise was Bobby Womack, coolly resplendent in black hat and sunglasses, one of the gospel Womack Brothers back in the 1950s, with the Valentinos on Sam Cooke's SAR label in the 1960s, and now an R&B survivor and star in his own right. "I'm up here on the pulpit with the big guys now," he said, and to the crowd, "Let's hear it for the Dixie Hummingbirds! 70 years more!"

Next to speak, Albertina Walker of the Chicago-based Caravans, a group that would spark out superstars Bessie Griffin, Inez Andrews, Cassietta George, Dorothy Norwood, and—still going strong—Shirley Caesar. "Somebody shout Hallelujah!" And then she recounted a conversation she once had with James Davis. "I was the manager of my group, and . . . Brother Davis was the manager of the Dixie Hummingbirds."

> The Birds . . . were such gentlemen. . . . "Brother Davis, how do you keep them in order?" He said, "We have rules and regulations . . ." And I said to him, "Brother manager, I have to be up at nighttime watching my girls, and I don't see your fellas out here, you know, socializing." And he said, "They're married, they got wives . . . They've sung and they go on to bed." . . . I watched the Dixie Hummingbirds, and this is the truth . . . Brother Davis . . . was on the case. . . . And I just want to commend the Dixie Hummingbirds . . . for standing up as men and being gentleman on the road and singing. Old Sam Cooke, if Sam were here today, he'd tell you that he got a lot of his learning from Ira Tucker. Amen. And I'm just glad to be here to say God bless you and I hope you can live to see another 70 years.

The baton passed to Willa Ward-Royster, sister of Clara Ward and original member of "those other Philadelphia gospel legends," the Ward Singers. "I'm so highly honored to be here. . . . I've known them for over 50 years—but I'm only 50 years old!" She remembered seeing the Birds for the first time. "My mother, Gertrude Ward, said, 'We're having this program and this fabulous group of men are coming here to sing.' Clara and I, we didn't particularly care about quartets. So, my mother said, 'You gonna like them.' . . . So, when we saw these handsome men come out there, and when they sang, we thought we had died and gone to heaven. They were so fabulous! The gospel community," she said, "was in for a fabulous surprise, when the Dixie Hummingbirds introduced their sound to Philadelphia."

> The "Birds," as they were . . . affectionately called, took us all to rare and glorious places, both musically and spiritually. From the beginning, they never looked back. . . . When I think of the seven species of hummingbirds, my mind's eye sees tiny little creatures whose songs I can't remember ever hearing. There's one species called the Dixie Hummingbirds, changed that image. Their presence is larger than life. . . . People, trust me, they can sing. Hallelujah! Congratulations on your anniversary!

Deniece Williams, former Stevie Wonder back-up singer, R&B soloist in her own right, and now back in the gospel fold, spoke next. "I'm telling you, my mother, my grandmother, ... wouldn't believe it to know that I was here with these guys tonight!" She told of the time her grandmother took her to see the Dixie Hummingbirds at one of the largest churches in town. "How fascinated I was, not only by their harmonies, but by their rhythm and how they carried themselves."

> And I've been working on the harmonies ever since. Kinda got a *little* of the rhythm. But I was so fascinated by their harmonies and their rhythms, and what they did with their voices, and I think I stole a little bit of that, surely a piece of that.... I know in my heart that that night, not a joint in town rocked as hard as we did than that church!
>
> We had a time that night. But it also conjures up in me some other memories, because at my church, ... on a good Sunday, they raised $40.00 in the offering. Now, that was a *good* Sunday.... And when I think about how [the Dixie Hummingbirds] would come to those churches and sing, ... knowing at the end *that* may be all they would have gotten.... Ask any gospel artist today to drive their car across the nation, to go and stay at the pastor's three-bedroom house, with him and his wife and twelve children. Eat Mother Evan's fried chicken, and you just ate sister so-and-so's chicken three, four churches ago, and to have someone hand you an offering like that, it speaks of the commitment ... they had to God....
>
> They broke ground for us.... It's a bit of a cost that ... the Dixie Hummingbirds have paid for us, so that we can go and do the things that we do in much more comfort. And it also causes me to think about the wives, and their love and their commitment.... And I tell you now, if there's anybody I feel that can write a book titled "Stand by Your Man," it's got to be these wives.
>
> Dixie Hummingbirds. You've given us a heritage, and you've given us an example. And we honor and we salute you tonight.

Next to stand was the Reverend Louise Williams, state legislator and host of a long-running gospel program on Philadelphia's WBAS. "Gospel," she said, "has come a long ways with the help of the Dixie Hummingbirds."

> They have made the pathway for where gospel is today.... The Dixie Hummingbirds have been green enough to grow.... They have been

broad enough to embrace whatever the trend was, as long as it was not a sacrilegious trend, and bring it into their style, and make it sound like the Dixie Hummingbirds. . . . And I say to all of us who sit here tonight, these are living legends. . . . So, hum on brothers, hum on!

The last to stand that night was Stevie Wonder, Motown recording artist, icon of twentieth century African American musical genius, steeped in gospel, and the most celebrated torchbearer of the Dixie Hummingbirds' legacy present that evening. "First question I want to know," said Wonder, playing on his sightlessness, "is, where *are* the Dixie Hummingbirds?"

He told a story from his days as a thirteen-year-old at the Michigan School for the Blind. Taught to get around campus by making sounds and listening for guiding responses from fellow students and teachers, Wonder liked to use Dixie Hummingbirds' songs as his personal radar.

Then, Wonder made an announcement that surprised everyone at the roast—including the Dixie Hummingbirds.

We are celebrating here in this, the African American Museum, a place that speaks of our culture, . . . our pain, . . . things we don't like to remember as African Americans, and that European Americans would like to forget, . . . a group of African American men [The Dixie Hummingbirds] who spanned 70 years.

Wonder talked about the beat-up van the Birds had been touring in for the past twenty years, rusting body, no air conditioning, uncomfortable seats, and a steel mesh cage welded in the rear to prevent the equipment from being stolen. Wonder declared that before he left Philadelphia, he wanted to drive that van. "And I am *very* particular about the things that I drive!" And then, his announcement. He would be presenting the Dixie Hummingbirds with a brand new van. "Hold on, hold on," he said, breaking into the applause. "There's one more thing. . . . Now, you will get the van, and that's all good, . . . but here's the twist. The only way you can get the van . . . is that *I* get the first chance to drive it! Ladies and Gentlemen, stand up for and let's give a hand to the Dixie Hummingbirds!"[1]

The tributes had been fitting and heartfelt. Throughout the 1980s and 1990s, the Birds had moved forward, weathering difficulties and disappointments, reaching further milestones, and finally pushing through to the twenty-first century when their continuity as a group would finally come into question.

"All things considered, this has been a great life."

The Hummingbirds—James Davis, Ira Tucker, James Walker, Beachey Thompson, and Howard Carroll—had adjusted to performing without William Bobo. Davis found the transition less rocky than anticipated. Bobo had missed quite a few dates during the period when he was ill, and the group had already learned to compensate. Walker and Tucker, judiciously alternating on bass under Davis's watchful eye, added an element of novelty and spectacle to the Birds' live show.

Although the Birds had always celebrated their anniversaries with a handful of select concerts, their fiftieth year together, 1978, was an especially meaningful and poignant milestone. The Birds entered the studio in 1977 and began working on an album to commemorate the occasion. The album, *Golden Flight*, was lovingly dedicated to their parents, with a special mention of James Davis's mother, Jannie. The liner notes, written by musicologist Birdis Coleman, Jr., provided substantive information about the Birds' history and accomplishments. Describing the Birds' "major influence on gospel music for fifty years," he spoke of their "melodic fluidity," "oratory," and "harmonic balance," qualities that, in his estimation, established the Birds as the "best quartet singers ever." William Bobo, wrote Coleman, "was one of the classic bass singers of all times. With incredible tonal depth, driving intensity and clarity, Bobo epitomized the 'pumping bass' of the quartet singer."[2]

With electric bass guitar, drums, and keyboards, *Golden Flight* presented the Birds at their contemporary best. For the first time, Howard Carroll added his voice to the recorded mix, taking on the role of second baritone. The album cover was eye-catching in design, adorned with a stained glass window in warm reds, yellows, and blues, a gold hummingbird in flight at the center—a fitting package for a fiftieth anniversary album.

Golden Flight was traditional in flavor. Ira Tucker produced and contributed originals, as did Walker, Roxie Moore, and James Davis. "Everybody gets to sing a lead on this album," Tucker told *Ebony*.[3] The record also reprised Birds' classics like Walker's "Only Jesus" and Tucker's "Somebody Is Lying" and "You Don't Have Nothing." The sound, clean and crisp, featured a southern soul groove and highly arranged interplay between voices and instruments. Released in 1978, *Golden Flight*, the Dixie Hummingbirds' twelfth LP, was a brisk seller.

Over the course of the year, the Birds garnered a generous amount of media exposure. They flew to California for a televised appearance on

The Dinah Shore Show, and then back to Philadelphia for *The Mike Douglas Show.* At the time, Douglas, who aired his unique mix of celebrity guests, chat, and musical performance out of Philadelphia, was revolutionizing daytime TV. His guest list ranged from high profile leaders like Martin Luther King, Jr., and Malcolm X to the best in African American musical entertainment ranging from Mahalia Jackson to Muddy Waters to Stevie Wonder. For the Dixie Hummingbirds, the appearance was a highlight in a year of highlights. They performed in elegant dark suits with vests, matching ties, flashy white shoes. Off to the side, a lone microphone stood in memory of William Bobo.

That year, the Birds were also featured in *Ebony* magazine. The top gospel group in the top African American magazine.

Within the frenetic show business world, any vocal group that can stay together for 10 or 15 years is exceptional, and any that can reach the lofty 25-year mark can rightly be considered a cultural institution. But this year, the Dixie Hummingbirds, ranked by many as the nation's number one gospel group, are celebrating their 50th anniversary. And amazingly, it appears that these well-matured gentlemen, who still perform like a bunch of spirited youngsters, are actually peaking in their later years.[4]

"I don't know what it is," said James Davis, then sixty-two years of age, "but everywhere we go, the people just don't want us to stop singing. . . . It's really hard for us to understand, but we love it." "Still traveling the gospel circuit," noted the magazine, the group "is now breaking its attendance records with every appearance, and young people are popping up at their concerts in ever greater numbers." A dividend, perhaps, from their collaborations with Paul Simon and Stevie Wonder.

Ebony also provided its readership a glimpse into the Hummingbirds' home lives. James Davis was pictured on his front porch stoop with Hortense, their sons, daughters, and grandchildren. Beachey Thompson sat in his favorite living room chair surrounded by twelve family members. Ira and Louise Tucker were shown smiling at each other while in an inset the Tucker offspring were pictured: Ira, Jr., with Stevie Wonder, Linda Tucker as one of the Supremes, and Sundray with Patti LaBelle's Bluebells and as one of the Three Degrees.

"When I first joined the fellows," said Beachey Thompson, "we were singing a lot of real sweet stuff. We don't get completely away from that now, but today we lean more or less toward numbers with an up-tempo that can get the people excited." James Davis was quick to add that a Hummingbird concert could be a "volatile experience." "When we appeared in Jacksonville, Florida, recently," he said, "they were taking people out on stretchers. And that was at a college performance."

Ebony noted that the Birds spent about eight months a year on the road at venues ranging from "mainstay southern country churches to major concert halls around the nation." *Ebony* also called the group a "major black institution," an indication that the Dixie Hummingbirds had transcended the ordinary and were now considered bona fide icons of African American musical tradition. Terms like "legendary" and "pioneering" would now be commonly affixed to their name. "All things considered," said James Davis, "this has been a great life."[5]

"Can't keep up with those younger men any longer."

The fiftieth anniversary had provided the Dixie Hummingbirds with yearlong activity, but as the decade wound down, the group came to the realization that they were increasingly dissatisfied with their recording label. Fruitfully associated with Peacock Records for more than twenty-five years, the Birds now found Peacock, in Don Robey's absence, corporate and impersonal. ABC/Peacock had flooded the market and had not effectively promoted the records.

In 1979, the Birds produced their own recording of a concert they performed at Lincoln Center. There they had been introduced by Dr. Wyatt Tee Walker, former chief of staff for the late Dr. Martin Luther King, Jr., a minister at the Canaan Baptist Church in Harlem, New York, and the author of a recently published book, *Somebody's Calling My Name: Black Sacred Music and Social Change*. Then the Birds took the stage and tore up the house with a play list of favorites that included "Loves Me Like a Rock," "Who Are We," "Our Prayer for Peace," "Nobody Knows the Trouble I've Seen," and "Help Me." It was the prototypical Birds rocket ride from easy start to catch-fire finale.

With the idea of taking more control of their career, and with Ira Tucker, Jr., now working closely with them, the Birds shopped the recording and struck a deal with Henry Stone, owner of TK records in Hialeah, Florida. Stone had broken through on the national pop scene in 1975 with two disco megahits by KC and the Sunshine Band: "Get Down Tonight" and "That's the Way (I Like It)." Stone, hoping to broaden his label's appeal, offered the Birds a $25,000 advance. In accepting Stone's offer, the Birds had made a pivotal business decision to exchange the security of a long-term label affiliation for the freedom to contract out an album at a time. In 1979, Stone's TK Productions released *The Dixie Hummingbirds Live in Concert* on the Gospel Roots label. From this point forward, the Birds would sink or swim on their own.

Stone was quick to release a follow-up LP, a Tucker-produced studio album, *Moving On*. The highlight was "The Dollar and the Devil," a Tucker performance that, with the charm of humor and clever lyrics, warned of what happens when greed takes over the home church. The idea for the song came from the title of a recitation Tucker's mother-in-law used to do as a little girl in church. "When the dollar rules the pulpit, the devil rules the pews." "I took the title," says Tucker, "and wrote new lyrics."[6] With a slow soul groove, Stevie Wonder-style keyboard, and minor key harmonies, Tucker and the group admonish, "But one thing please remember, just before you pay your dues, when the dollar rules the pulpit, then the devil rules the pews."

Even now, the Birds found primary sustenance on their traditional tour circuit. In 1981, a reporter for the *Philadelphia Inquirer* caught up with them at a Sunday afternoon concert at the Trinity Lutheran Church in Providence, Rhode Island.

> Every pew was jammed. There were old women in faded dresses, young women in flashy outfits, freshly scrubbed youngsters gazing in wonder at the ceiling, middle-aged couples in their prim and proper Sunday best, even a young man in a T-shirt who seemed to be stealing time for the Lord from his job.

The Birds wore "white three-piece suits, beige shirts and brown, dotted ties," and "spit-shined" shoes. They had just lifted the congregation to a "spine-tingling emotional high" with a performance of Tucker's "Moving On," the title track from their last LP, now almost two years old. "My body's getting weak," sang Tucker, "and I'm running out of time, but I've got my ticket, and I don't mind dyin'." Howard Carroll sat back in a folding chair accompanied by the simulated beat of an electronic drum machine. Davis, Tucker, Walker, and Thompson "stood with their hands folded in front of them, exuding . . . dignified calm. . . . Davis announced: 'We're thankful the Lord has spared us to sing one more time. We're gonna have a real good time!'" Clapping in rhythm, they launched into the next song.

Hand claps erupted from the audience as the voices of the five men blended into a rich, full harmony, enriched by Walker's silky falsetto. "It's the words and blessings of God that enable us to be heard today," shouted Walker.... "God has spared us! Thank you, Jesus!" ...

"Can I get a witness?" he sang over the background harmony as he began pacing back and forth, carrying the microphone stand. The congregation reacted with a sea of waving hands.

Davis mopped his brow and clenched his fist as he harmonized on the refrain, inclining his head as if pouring his soul into the mike. "I think that God is right here!" Walker sang, prompting several people to spring to their feet, clapping. Ira Tucker answered Walker's testimony with chilling high notes as he followed Walker down the aisle.

Suddenly, Walker sank to his knees, wailing "I'm down!" Tucker bent over him, singing exhortations and pulling him back up.

The two linked arms and, as they had done many times over the years, strutted up and down the aisle shouting, testifying, reaching out and shaking hands, the church responding in kind.

The Dixie Hummingbirds were clearly in fine form, although the slightest foreboding—the "running out of time," the "body getting weak," the "thanks for being spared"—had crept into their message. Beachey Thompson was battling diabetes. "This is my lifeline," said Thompson, referring to his medication. "Take this twice a day." They were beginning to look back, reminisce about the "old days," how they used to put their pants under a mattress "and sleep on them in order to press them"; how before gospel radio, they used to advertise "with megaphones running around the streets shouting 'Tonight! The Dixie Hummingbirds!'" How Davis forbade them to "hang around a pool hall" or play anything but "spiritual records" on a jukebox. Somebody brought up the irony that Davis—as subject to the rules as anybody—was the only one ever fined for the jukebox infraction. He had pressed the wrong button and instead of "Christian's Automobile," got Muddy Waters. Davis still paid the twenty-dollar fine.[7]

Beachey Thompson chided Davis for his iron hand. "If he says strawberries are ripe, even though snow's on the ground, I look for strawberries." But in the same breath, they praised him. "In my opinion," said James Walker, "Davis is one of the best managers in the business.... Whenever you're part of a group, anything can hurt the group." That he said was the reason for the rules and why the Birds to a man respected the authority of James Davis.[8]

James Davis had been the guiding force behind the Hummingbirds since before they were the Hummingbirds. He was tiring of the traveling life. "Can't keep up with those younger men any longer," he would say.[9] In 1983, he and the Birds appeared in a short educational film, *Eat Right*, sponsored by the American Heart Association. With actor Eddie Albert narrating, Davis and the Birds sang about proper diet and exercise. James Davis would also be called upon to do other public service films and announcements about the dangers of drug abuse. Clearly, he was viewed as a man who had credibility across the generations.

In 1983, the Birds released their latest album, *Mama*, on the Air label, a subsidiary of Atlanta International Records. Davis contributed "The Love of Joseph and Mary," his last recorded performance with the Birds. In 1984, at age sixty-eight and after fifty-six years at the helm, James Davis made the difficult decision to retire. Though he would not travel or perform with the group, the Birds still played by his rules, continued to pay him a share, and conferred with him in all matters of importance to the group. James Davis would remain an integral part of the Dixie Hummingbirds, if not in body, most definitely in spirit.

"Channels its subjects to inspirational heights."

"These Birds continue to soar" was typical of the story headlines that appeared in the wake of Davis's retirement. Ira Tucker took over as manager in place of James Davis, while the chore of booking would be passed to Beachey Thompson. The Reverend James Williams from the Sons of the Birds filled in the missing voice for the next two or so years, until William Bright, another of the Sons of the Birds, stepped in.

In 1986, the Hummingbirds—Tucker, Walker, Thompson, Carroll, and Bright—at last had the opportunity to tour Europe. Willie Leiser, a promoter based in Switzerland, contacted them. Leiser, booking gospel in Europe since the 1960s, also had an association with the famous Montreux Jazz Festival. "I first had the Hummingbirds over from April 25 to May 1," says Leiser. "We did four concerts in Switzerland and Germany. Basel. Bern. Meyrin on the outskirts of Geneva. Villingen, Germany. Not to mention a 30-minute affair in a concert hall for school children. And even without knowing much about this art, our people loved their concerts, clapped hands on the beat."[10] Over the years, Leiser would have the Hummingbirds back a number of times, often with drummer Kevin James filling in the rhythm tracks. In addition to

The Dixie Hummingbirds in Liège, Belgium, 1997. From left: Ira Tucker, Paul Owens, Robert Sacré (University of Liège professor and tour coordinator), Carl Davis, and Howard Carroll. Photo courtesy of Robert Sacré.

the concert halls, schools, and churches, the Birds would play the Montreux Jazz Festival in 1997.

The Birds returned from Europe feeling enriched and invigorated from the reception they had received. In spite of language and cultural differences, their performances had moved audiences. Back in the United States, they immersed themselves in touring and recording a series of LPs for Air Records, including the critically hailed *Smooth Sailing*, a concert album, *Live in Philadelphia*, and in 1988, *Our 60th*, a celebration of another important milestone.

The liner notes to *Our 60th* offered "special thanks," first to "God for life, health, and strength," and then to "Mr. James Davis, without whom the Birds would not have come together."[11] To celebrate their anniversary and the LP's release, the group traveled to Los Angeles for a special tribute. Among the stars who turned out to honor them were Bobby "Blue" Bland, Della Reese, Cab Calloway, and Kenny Gamble and Leon Huff, architects of the Philly soul sound.

That year would also mark the return of Paul Owens to the Dixie Hummingbirds after more than thirty years. Owens had been singing with Tommy Spann's Brooklyn All Stars when he learned that Tucker's brother had died. Owens came to the funeral and there was reunited with the Birds. "Howard Carroll said to me, 'Where you been?' I said, 'I've been right here in Philadelphia.'"[12] They had lost track of one another, and Tucker, who had been looking for him, immediately invited Owens back into the lineup.

Soon after Owens rejoined the group, the Philadelphia Music Foundation conferred an honor on the Dixie Hummingbirds—a place on the Philadelphia "Walk of Fame," a stretch of sidewalk in front of the Academy of Music on south Broad Street. The Birds—including James Davis in a rare public appearance—came out for the ceremony as a bronze plaque in their name was embedded in the pavement, joining fellow honorees maestro Eugene Ormandy, teen idol Frankie Avalon, folk musician Jim Croce, and light operatic duo, Jeannette McDonald and Nelson Eddy. Energized by the honor, and with Paul Owens back in the lineup, the Birds were in fine form, as strong a performing entity as they ever had been.[13]

In fact, with sparse new album releases and re-releases, the Hummingbirds still relied on personal appearances for income. In spite of their "legendary" status, they were working hard with a schedule as demanding as ever. However, in the early 1990s, with funding from the Pew Charitable Trust, the Ford Foundation, and the National Endowment for the Arts, filmmakers Ashley James and Ray Allen began shooting footage of the Birds for a documentary film. The filmmakers followed the group to performances, captured them in rehearsals, talked to them individually, and incorporated interviews with Melvin Franklin and Otis Williams of the Temptations, Bobby Womack, the Winans, Paul Simon, and Stevie Wonder. The camera would even accompany the Tucker family on a fishing outing.

Tragically, in the midst of filming, on October 30, 1992, James Walker passed away from the leukemia that had afflicted him for some time. He continued performing as long as possible as he carefully prepared a handpicked successor. "I know Walker as a good singer," reflected James Davis, "one who would give his all according to his condition each night. But we saw a different side of him that we didn't know when he got so sick. He knew he was going to die and he had found somebody who could sing a little like he did and tried to get him up." James Walker was sixty-six when he died. "He was one of the best to ever sing gospel music," Tucker would say. "He can never be replaced. It's like losing your brother."[14]

"He didn't want anybody to know he was that sick."

Walker had tried to anticipate the trauma of his own death by preparing a younger singer, Carl Davis, to take his place. Davis, born on June 27, 1934, in Richmond, Virginia, had grown up listening to the Harmonizing Four and the Dixie Hummingbirds. He began performing in the 1950s with Edna Gallmon Cooke's backing group, the Singing Sons. By the 1960s, Davis had formed his own group, the Miami-based Florida Robins. He left in 1965 to replace Claude Jeter in the Swan Silvertones, who at the time had decided to give up singing to go full time into the ministry. "I joined the Swans in Harrisburg, Pennsylvania," says Carl Davis. "Went on stage at 3:00 and sang in the background. At 8:00 that night, I was singing lead. Then we left straight out to Tampa and St. Pete."

Carl Davis had first met James Walker in Richmond during his tenure with the Harmonizing Four. "I got a chance to meet him. He was so down to earth and such a fine gentleman that he had time to talk to me, made me feel so good, and we hit it off right away." Over the years, when Carl Davis was himself singing professionally, Walker would come to hear him. Eventually, when Walker became ill, he talked to Davis about coming into the Birds, but not as a "replacement." "He never used that term," said Davis.

> He didn't want anybody to know he was *that* sick. And he always had a positive attitude about his sickness, that he was going to get well and be healed and continue to sing with the group. Once when he got sick and went into the hospital, Tucker and I went over to visit him and he said, "I'm doing fine. A few more days, I'm gonna be up and ready to go on tour." And he kept on saying he was fine, he was going to be all right, he was gonna have a good tour. But he got so weak that he couldn't get out of the bed. And then in October 1992, he passed away.[15]

James Walker would be laid to rest at the same Northwood Cemetery where William Bobo had been buried. Carl Davis would step into the lineup in 1992 and share screen time with the Birds as filmmakers Ashley James and Ray Allen continued filming their documentary. They chose not to let Walker's passing finish their story. "I didn't want to end on that note," Ashley James would say. "I changed the story around to reflect the Bird's continuum."[16]

When the film, *We Love You Like a Rock*, was released in 1994, it was heralded with excellent reviews and propelled the Birds as their new LP releases had done in the past. Unfortunately, though, amidst the high spirits surrounding the film's release, the Hummingbirds found themselves once again dealing with a loss.

Three years earlier, in January of 1991, Beachey Thompson had suffered a stroke and in 1992 was diagnosed with a heart condition. That year, he quit touring with the Birds, although he continued to handle the booking and would sing with them on special occasions. On June 28, 1994, Beachey Thompson passed away at the age of seventy-nine. He would be buried at Shelton Hills cemetery in Philadelphia. With sorrow in their hearts, the Dixie Hummingbirds pressed on with a heavy schedule of concerts and celebratory events prior to the release of the documentary.

In July of 1994, the Birds would play the Palladium on Sunset Boulevard in Hollywood, California, their old friend Bobby Womack officiating. A month later, they would be back on the East coast performing at the Philadelphia Folk Festival where they received a "thunderous ten-minute standing ovation." That Labor Day weekend, they were off to a three-day Smithsonian-sponsored festival in Johnstown, Pennsylvania, and a week after that in St. Louis highlighting a major blues festival. From there, it was a "mini tour of southern states before attending the scheduled October 1st New York Film Festival premiere" of the documentary.[17]

Following the premiere, the Birds—Ira Tucker, Paul Owens, Carl Davis, and Howard Carroll—traveled the country in concert with the film. They performed live at special screenings in festival and arts center settings in Philadelphia; San Francisco; Portland, Oregon; and at Washington, D.C.'s, Kennedy Center. In July 1995, Ira Tucker would travel to Newark, New Jersey, where the Newark Black Film Festival selected *We Love You Like a Rock* to receive the festival's Paul Robeson Award. Upon being introduced, Tucker "drew a fourteen-minute standing ovation." He thanked the filmmakers and then told the audience, "I'm here tonight because of . . . James B. Davis who founded the group in 1928 and started my professional career as a gospel singer, . . . and the main man, God, who made it all possible."[18]

In August 1995, they would return to Philadelphia to once again be honored by the city. At a concert hosted by the Newberry Singers at St. Paul's Evangelical Lutheran Church, Mayor Ed Rendell presented the Birds with an award designed especially for them. The trophy depicted each group member standing around a microphone and on the base was an inscription that cited the Birds as "a vital asset to the city."[19]

After four more years of touring and in preparation for their seventieth anniversary, a bevy of producers and musicians came together over a period of months in studios in Philadelphia, Detroit, Chicago, Hollywood, Nashville, and New York to create a tribute album. The Birds—Tucker, Owens, Carl Davis, Carroll, and now William Bright back in the fold—were joined on the tribute CD by a stellar cast of musical guests. Shirley Caesar, Isaac Hayes, Howard Hewitt, Wynona Judd, Mavis Staples, Deniece Williams, Vickie Winans, Bobby Womack, and, of course, Stevie Wonder and Paul Simon joined the Birds in a sampling of some of their finest material, including "How Great Thou Art," "Good Health," "Beaming from Heaven," "Come Ye Disconsolate," and other favorites. The highlight may have been "Loves Me Like a Rock," recreated in the studio by Paul Simon with the help of Stevie Wonder.

Paul Simon's arrival at Sigma Studios in Philadelphia in late September of 1998 made the front page of the *Philadelphia Inquirer*.[20] The studio was populated by young African American musicians looking more "hip-hop" than pop gospel. The Prayer for All People Brass Band was warming up. A young drummer and bass player were coordinating their parts. Session producer John Snyder was running around the control room, trying to get things in order for Paul Simon's pending entrance.

The door swung open and in breezed Simon. After a round of cursory greetings, Simon stepped into the main studio. Everybody was cranked up and playing and Simon gave it all a careful listen. He began taking control and the young instrumentalists immediately deferred to his authority. Simon sent the brass band packing. They did not fit his vision of this remake of "Loves Me Like a Rock." Simon pulled the drummer out of his isolation booth. He pulled a stool to the center of the studio and placed on it an empty plastic hard shell guitar case, saying that they could not record until they found a groove. Simon walked the drummer over to the guitar case, handed him some brushes, and got him tapping out a rhythm right on the case lid. Simon, meanwhile, picked up an Ovation guitar and began chording and singing "Loves Me Like a Rock." The drummer tapped along on the plastic guitar case. The Birds joined in singing. The performance was acoustic and spontaneous when Simon called out for the engineer to begin recording. Someone shouted something about "bleed-through," and Simon shouted back, "Bleed-through

Ira Tucker and Paul Simon at the Grammy MusiCares award ceremonies honoring Paul Simon (2001). Photo courtesy of Ira Tucker, Jr.

is all right!" and the tape machine began rolling. The performance took on its own character as all present realized this "Loves Me Like a Rock" would be nothing like the 1973 collaboration. A few weeks later, the master tapes would travel to New York City where Stevie Wonder would add his piano and voice to the mix.

The CD, *Music in the Air*, was subtitled an "All Star Tribute" to the Dixie Hummingbirds. Released on the House of Blues label, the album was a grand sendoff for the Birds' seventieth anniversary year, further highlighted by a July 1 appearance with Paul Simon and Stevie Wonder on the *Late Show with David Letterman*.

The Birds were in splendiferous dress with white tuxedos and tails. Paul Simon flanked them on the left, Stevie Wonder on the right. Simon launched into "Loves Me Like a Rock," and the sight was heartwarming to behold. Then, seventy-three-year-old Ira Tucker stepped up to the mike, taking the song to a place where only he could go. Paul Simon smiled humbly as he looked on, his words elevated by the power in Tucker's voice. Stevie Wonder took the next verse, drawing on every vocal nuance he had learned from Ira Tucker and other pioneers of gospel lead singing.

"To be or not to be? That is the question."

Past their anniversary year, the Hummingbirds were inducted into both the Gospel Music Hall of Fame and the Vocal Group Hall of Fame. In the fall of 2000 the National Endowment for the Arts declared the Birds "national treasures" and named them National Heritage Fellows. The honor came with a $10,000 gift, which the Birds used to support their continuous touring. "It's a great honor, it really is," Tucker would tell a reporter for the *Inquirer*. "What we try to do is get to the people who have been with us for years. We're not going to turn them down. Sometimes churches don't have the resources. We'll perform for 75, 100 people if that's what it takes."[21] The Birds would travel to Washington, D.C., where, along with other honorees, they were feted at special ceremonies and greeted by legislators and Endowment dignitaries.

Even approaching their seventy-fifth anniversary, an unprecedented milestone in gospel history, the Hummingbirds—Tucker, Owens, Carroll, Carl Davis, and Mr. James B. Davis—continued to live modestly, hustling to make ends meet when they should be resting on their laurels. Ira Tucker, Jr., vented his frustrations in a telling essay he wrote as much for himself as the public.

"To be or not to be? That is the question." These few words written by the immortal . . . Shakespeare centuries ago currently resound emphatically clear in the thoughts and hearts of the legendary gospel quartet, the Dixie Hummingbirds. After seventy-three years of being a viable, recognizable, iconic entity and influential force in Gospel music as well as Blues and R&B singing, the "Birds" . . . find themselves poised to answer Shakespeare's question . . . "To be or not to be?" . . . Have the "gentlemen of song," finally reached the end of the road? . . .

According to Ira Tucker, Sr., "we have truly experienced the slings and arrows, wounds and heartbreaks, suffered by all career entertainers surviving in such a competitive business. I would really like to see the group reach seventy-five. That would be an unparalleled achievement, something real special. However, our health is still the ultimate priority for any decision on retirement. Although I think the media and record companies have already written us off." Tucker's concerns could be valid since the sound of traditional gospel quartets seems to be rapidly disappearing from radio airwaves and concert tours across the country. Contemporary gospel music, choirs and R&B performers now attract the bulk of the media attention and radio airplay once garnered by traditional gospel artists. Tucker comments, "I don't know if there's a place for us today. I know the people still like us, but I just don't see any interest in quartet singing from the record companies or radio. I mean, sure, we're senior citizens, but baby, we can still cut it. We're still the Dixie Hummingbirds and those who've seen us or heard us know what that means."[22]

In the new millennium, the Dixie Hummingbirds may drive five grueling hours to be honored by the congregation of a small urban church. A group of local favorites open the program and, carried away, play long past their appointed time. The hour grows late, and by the time the Dixie Hummingbirds come on, a quarter of the audience has tired and gone home. The Birds, always professionals, put on a show as if the house was packed and the year was 1959. Afterward, the sanctuary now deserted, they tear down the equipment, load it in the van, and make the five-hour journey back home.

Two days later they may be in an airplane bound for Hollywood, where the National Academy of Recording Arts and Sciences (NARAS) has invited them to perform at the MusiCares' Person of the Year Tribute to Paul Simon. Michael Greene, president of NARAS, would write to them upon their return, "I don't believe there are words to describe the

The Hummingbirds in 2001. From left to right: William Bright,
Howard Carroll, Ira Tucker, Paul Owens, Carl Davis.

gratitude in my heart for the Dixie Hummingbirds' stunning performance. . . . You deserve another round of applause for your passion, for your humanity, as well as for music."

The Birds fully understand that their unpredictable lifestyle is the result of a choice they made decades ago when they elected to travel the gospel road. At the seventieth anniversary roast, James Davis credited "being able to do what you want for a living and make it" to "divine intervention" and the luck of meeting "the right ladies to stand behind and push us." Reflecting on the whole sweep of their career, says Davis, "when you look at it from all angles, may not look like we have got a whole lot to show, but we have got a whole lot out of life."

Ira Tucker, Sr., also has no regrets. At the anniversary roast, he said, "There have been a lot of people that have turned their backs on us. But you know what? The man upstairs sits high and looks low. That's who we have our faith and trust in, is God Almighty. I'd like to say this to you. It wasn't money that kept the Hummingbirds out here."

Although their compensation was never impressive, the Dixie Hummingbirds have clearly enjoyed the rewards of their long career. Spreading the good word. Joy in singing. Camaraderie on the road. The excitement of the show. Adulation. Grand moments of glory. And the simple knowledge that in the business of making people happy, they were a force for good in the world.

At the anniversary roast, Tucker left the podium saying: "I'm so happy to see all of you. God bless you and may heaven smile upon you. And just because this is our seventieth, don't think that we are finished. Don't think that we are finished." Would that they are not. Amen.

Notes

Chapter 1: "A Wheel in a Wheel, 'Way Up in the Middle of the Air"

1. Bernice Reagon, *We'll Understand It Better By and By* (Washington, DC: Smithsonian Institution Press, 1992), 18.

2. "Stephen Girard," *Encyclopedia Britannica* [Online] available: http://www.eb.com:180/bol/topic?eu=37634&SCTN=1.

3. *What Is It? in Greater Greenville*, Pamphlet published by Greenville Chamber of Commerce, approximate date, 1961.

4. Mamie Norris, telephone conversation with author, September 1996.

5. *Greenville News*, 3 January 1928.

6. Blanche McIver, telephone conversation with the author, September 1996.

7. Jim DuPlessis and Kathy Spencer, *Greenville News*, "The 100th Anniversary of Sterling High School," 13 July 1996.

Chapter 2: "I Just Got On My Travelin' Shoes"

1. Horace C. Boyer and Lloyd Yearwood, *How Sweet the Sound: The Golden Age of Gospel* (Washington, DC: Elliott & Clark, 1995), 61.

2. R. M. W. Dixon and J. Godrich, *Blues and Gospel Records 1902–1943* (Chigwell, Essex, England: Storyville Publications 1982).

3. *Detroit Plaindealer*, 17 January 1890, and the *Indianapolis Freeman*, 16 April 1890, in Doug Seroff, Ray Funk, and Lynn Abbott, "A Survey of Afro-American Music in 1890 as Recorded in the Black Community Press," *78 Quarterly* 1, no. 6 (1991): 51–63.

4. Doug Seroff and Lynn Abbott, "The Origins of Ragtime," *78 Quarterly* 1, no. 10 (1998): 130.

5. *The Indianapolis Freeman*, 24 March 1894, in Doug Seroff and Lynn Abbott, "The Origins of Ragtime," *78 Quarterly* 1, no. 10 (1998): 130.

6. Hans Nathan, *Dan Emmett and the Rise of Early Negro Minstrelsy* (Norman: University of Oklahoma Press, 1962), preface.

7. James Weldon Johnson, "The Origin of the Barbershop Chord," *The Mentor*, 29 February 1929, p. 53.

8. Ibid.

9. Paul Oliver, *The New Grove Gospel, Blues, and Jazz* (New York: W. W. Norton, 1986), 192.

10. Seroff and Abbott, "The Origins of Ragtime," 130.

11. Kip Lornell, *Happy in the Service of the Lord* (Urbana: University of Illinois Press, 1988), 12.

12. Ibid.

13. Keith Briggs, *Heavenly Gospel Singers, Volume One*, Document Records DOCD-5452, liner notes.

14. Anthony Heilbut, *The Gospel Sound: Good News and Bad Times* (New York: Limelight Editions, 1985), 354.

15. Ray Funk, *Carolina Gospel Quartets*, Document Records DOCD-5445, liner notes.

16. Oliver, *The New Grove Gospel*, 1–20.

17. Alan Young, *Woke Me Up This Morning* (Jackson: University Press of Mississippi, 1997), introduction.

18. Zora Neale Hurston, "The Sanctified Church," in *The Folklore Writings of Zola Neale Hurston* (Berkeley, CA: Turtle Island Foundation, 1981), 79–80.

19. For further discussion see William Barlow, "Cashing In: 1900–1939," in Jannette Dates and William Barlow, *Split Image: African Americans in the Mass Media* (Washington, DC: Howard University Press), 25–56.

20. Heilbut, *The Gospel Sound*, xxix.

21. Charles Reagan Wilson and William Ferris, eds., *Encyclopedia of Southern Culture* (Chapel Hill: University of North Carolina Press, 1989), 938.

22. Ray Barfield, *Listening to Radio, 1920–1950* (Westport, CT: Greenwood, 1996), 52.

23. Robert Hilliard and Michael C. Keith, *The Broadcast Century: A Biography of American Broadcasting*, 2d ed. (Boston: Focal Press, 1997), 65.

24. Wilson and Ferris, *Encyclopedia*, 938.

25. Barfield, *Listening to Radio*, 53.

26. Wilson and Ferris, *Encyclopedia*, 938.

27. Peter Grendysa, *The Golden Gate Quartet: Swing Down, Chariot*, Columbia Legacy CK47131, liner notes.

28. Thermon Ruth, conversation with the author, 16 March 1999.

29. Dixon and Godrich, *Blues and Gospel Records*.

Chapter 3: "Ain't Gonna Study War No More"

1. Anthony Heilbut, *The Gospel Sound: Good News and Bad Times* (New York: Limelight Editions, 1985), 37.

2. Curtis Rudolph, interview with the author, New Jersey, 11 August 1998.

3. R. M. Dixon and J. Godrich, *Blues and Gospel Records, 1902–1943* (Chigwell, Essex, England: Storyville Publications, 1982).

4. Robert Hardy, Interview with Doug Seroff and Ray Funk, Spartanburg, South Carolina, 12 may 1982. Jimmy Bryant would hook up with Robert Hardy and Blue Steel in 1939, seven months before he joined the Dixie Hummingbirds. He would convince Hardy to change the group's name to the Gospel Light Jubilee Singers, and under that rubric, record eight sides that would eventually be released on the Bluebird label. The sessions took place in Rock Hill, South Carolina. Coincidentally, Bryant's former group, the Heavenly Gospel Singers with William Bobo in the lineup were also cutting tracks for Bluebird at that same Rock Hill session.

5. The Evangelists would change their name to the Detroiters and in 1951 release a number of sides on the Los Angeles-based Specialty label. On those

sides, Jimmy Bryant is listed as a baritone, not a bass. By the middle 1950s, Bryant had dropped out of sight as a professional gospel singer.

6. Corroborated in an interview by Seamus McGarvey, *Blues & Rhythm, the Gospel Truth* (June 1986): 10–17.

7. Patria Ross, telephone conversation with the author, 26 February 2000. Holden Smith eventually left the Carolinas and resettled in Cincinnati, Ohio. There he founded the Jerriel Baptist Church Chorus and sang with them until his death in October 1990. His wife, Aurelia, and son, Kazava, have kept the Chorus going to this day.

8. *Sepia*, April 1974, pp. 60–64.

9. Richard Maltby, *Passing Parade* (New York: Oxford University Press, 1989).

10. Leonard Feather, *The New Edition of the Encyclopedia of Jazz* (New York: Horizon Press, 1960).

11. John Hammond, *From Spirituals to Swing*, Vanguard Recordings LP VRS-8523/4.

12. The American Recording Company, or ARC, was formed in 1932 as an amalgamation of record labels that came to include imprints like Romeo, Perfect, Conqueror, Banner, and Vocalion. Mitchell's Christian Singers—1st tenor William Brown, 2nd tenor Julius Daniels, baritone Louis Davis, and bass Sam Bryant—released sides on all these labels over the course of their recording career, 1934–1940. In addition to the live *From Spirituals to Swing* concert recording, their complete recorded works can be heard on Document Records DOCD-5493 and DOCD-5496.

13. Horace C. Boyer and Lloyd Yearwood, *How Sweet the Sound: The Golden Age of Gospel* (Washington, DC: Elliott & Clark Publishing, 1995), 53–159.

14. Minnie Lee Baker, telephone conversation with the author, 16 March 1999. Wilson Henry Baker was born in South Carolina on 28 September 1914.

15. In 1904, Mary McCleod Bethune founded the Daytona Normal and Industrial Institute for Negro Girls, known since 1929 as Bethune-Cookman College. She was the school's president until 1942. She was also an advisor to President Franklin Roosevelt.

16. Connie Karichoff, "Photographer William H. Jordan/A Portrait of Ansted's Black Community," *Goldenseal: West Virginia Traditional Life* (Winter 1998): 44–51.

17. Claude Jeter, telephone conversation with the author, 17 May 1999. Claude Jeter's West Virginia group, the Harmony Kings, should not be confused with the more famous Kings of Harmony of Alabama. Jeter's brief tenure with the Hummingbirds was as a temporary replacement for Jimmy Bryant.

Chapter 4: "Twelve Gates to the City"

1. Maya Angelou, telephone conversation with the author, 25 August 2000.

2. James Baldwin, *Go Tell It on the Mountain* (New York: Alfred A. Knopf, 1953).

3. Horace C. Boyer and Lloyd Yearwood, *How Sweet the Sound: The Golden Age of Gospel* (Washington, DC: Elliott & Clark Publishing, 1995), 57–64.

4. Robert Palmer, in *Rock & Roll: An Unruly History*, provides a nutshell overview of the Church of God in Christ: "The C.O.G.I.C., founded in Memphis in the mid-1890s, is a Pentecostal denomination whose members make direct contact with the Holy Spirit. Trance behavior—'getting happy'—

is widespread and encouraged, and no musical instrument is unworthy of singing God's praises."

In *How Sweet the Sound*, Horace Boyer provides more detail. He describes how, under the guidance of Charles Harrison Mason, the COGIC movement sought a "greater spiritual involvement" for its members. Mason was a preacher "who felt the need to stir his congregation with thematic songs at crucial moments in the service or sermon." He encouraged participation and performance from congregants. Members were expected to lead others in song. As Boyer describes it, "the responsibility of each member to lead songs resulted in the development of strong singers throughout the congregation. . . . While there was no overt competition among the singers, early on those singers who were able to ignite the congregation into a shout became congregational celebrities" (23–24). This dynamic, writes Boyer, first appeared in COGIC congregations in Los Angeles and spread south to cities like Memphis and eventually to the north. Sister Rosetta Tharpe, among other gospel luminaries, emerged from COGIC tradition.

5. Palmer, *Rock & Roll*, 47–49.

6. Maya Angelou, telephone conversation with the author, 25 August 2000.

7. *The Billboard Band Year Book*, "On the One-Nighter Trail," 26 September 1942.

8. The Angelic Gospel Singers were Margaret Allison, vocals and piano; Lucille Shird, Josephine McDowell, and Ella Mae Morris, vocals. Sisters Allison and McDowell started singing together in 1942 in a choir called the Spiritual Echoes. They began performing as the Angelics quartet in 1944. One of the members, Ella Mae Morris, was also a native of Greenville, South Carolina.

Clara Ward started performing in Philadelphia in 1935 as part of a family trio organized by her mother, Gertrude. In 1943, they launched themselves nationally via a performance at the National Baptist Convention, held that year in Philadelphia. Gertrude Ward was originally from Anderson, South Carolina.

The Sensational Nightingales formed originally in Philadelphia in 1942 with Howard Carroll, Paul Owens, William Henry, and Ben Joiner. Henry, of course, had earlier ties with the Dixie Hummingbirds. Carroll and Owens would be linked to the Birds in the future. By 1946, the Nightingales, through the efforts of Barney Parks, now no longer with the Dixie Hummingbirds, featured the "hard" gospel leads of the legendary Julius "June" Cheeks. Cheeks grew up in Spartanburg, South Carolina, and had been drawn to gospel by the Dixie Hummingbirds (Boyer and Yearwood, *How Sweet the Sound*).

9. Ashley James and Ray Allen, *We Love You Like a Rock*, Searchlight Films, 1994.

10. *The Philadelphia Inquirer* 25 July 1942, p. 5. A story in the paper reported "Thomas Maddox," an African American teenager, "had fled to Philadelphia from Elberton, Georgia, where he was wanted by authorities for "slashing a white motorist with a penknife during a quarrel on a Georgia road." Maddox's lawyer explained to Philadelphia Judge Clare Fenerty that the motorist had forced the Maddox car to a stop and then "demanded to know why a Negro had the temerity to pass a white man's car, and struck him with a jack handle." He also explained to the judge, "back in Elberton . . . authorities are holding Maddox's mother, two sisters, a brother and two brothers-in-law as hostages for his return." Maddox himself added that "he fears lynching if he is returned to Georgia." Judge Fenerty "assured the trembling youth that he

would not let him be 'subjected to mob violence.'" Said Fenerty, "As judge of this court it is my duty to see that no harm befalls this boy. . . . He belongs to one of our nation's minorities. But it makes no difference whether he is white or colored." Fenerty concluded by making reference to the war in Europe. "We all are fighting for democracy, and the black man, too, is risking his life to see that democracy stays alive on earth." With that, Fenerty ruled against extraditing Maddox back to Georgia.

11. Julius Caleb Ginyard was born in St. Mathews, South Carolina. He formed the Royal Harmony Singers in 1936 and recorded with them for Decca in 1941. The label sub-billed them as "The Florida Boys." The group evolved into the Jubalaires, recording for Decca in 1944 and King in 1947. Ginyard joined the Dixieaires in 1947. In 1952, he formed the Du Droppers, R&B pioneers with releases on RCA, Red Robin, and Groove. In 1955, Ginyard returned to gospel as a member of the Golden Gate Quartet. He recorded with them in Paris for Columbia records. In 1971, Ginyard moved to Switzerland and remained there as a solo performer until his death in 1978. Source: Vocal Group Harmony Web Site.

12. Seamus McGarvey, *Blues & Rhythm: The Gospel Truth* (June 1986).

13. Caleb Ginyard, III, *My Name Is Caleb N. Ginyard* (Hanover, PA: Akashic Books, 2002), 85.

14. Boyer and Yearwood, *How Sweet the Sound*, 45.

15. Ibid., 82.

16. *Billboard*, 27 February 1943, p. 6.

17. *New York Amsterdam News*, "Southernaires Got Started Eleven Years Ago in Church," 25 January 1941, p. 21.

18. *The Philadelphia Afro-American*, 20 March 1943, p. 8.

19. *The Philadelphia Inquirer*, 26 July 1942, p. 16.

20. *The Philadelphia Afro-American*, 14, 21 November 1942.

21. James and Allen, *We Love You Like a Rock*. 1994.

22. McGarvey, *Blues & Rhythm*, 11.

23. Bon Bon was George Tunnell, an African American vocalist who fronted the Jean Savitt big band in the late 1930s. Newspaper ads in the early 1940s billed Tunnell at Philadelphia clubs as "Bon Bon and His Buddies."

24. John Hammond with Irving Townsend, *John Hammond on Record: An Autobiography* (New York: Ridge Press/Summit Books, 1977), 10.

25. Ibid., 30.

26. John Koenig, "John Hammond/An American Original," *Goldmine* (7 September 1990): 11–14.

27. Hammond, *John Hammond*, 64.

28. Ibid., 67–68.

29. Koenig, "John Hammond," 12.

30. Hammond, *John Hammond*, 200.

31. Ibid., 206.

32. Billie Holiday with William Dufty, *Lady Sings the Blues* (New York: Lancer Books, 1965), 42.

33. Jim Haskins, *The Cotton Club* (New York: Random House, 1977), 36–37.

34. Lewis Erenberg, *Swingin' the Dream* (Chicago: University of Chicago Press, 1998), 145–46.

35. Whitney Balliett, "Profiles," *The New Yorker*, 9 October 1971, pp. 50–92.

36. Michael Denning, *The Cultural Front: The Laboring of American Culture in the Twentieth Century* (London: Verso, 1996), 325.

37. Erenberg, *Swingin' the Dream*, 145–46.

38. Balliett, "Profiles," 50–92.

39. Hammond, 207–10.

40. Balliett, "Profiles," 54.

41. Dan Morgenstern, *Café Society*, Onyx Records #210, liner notes.

42. Erenberg, *Swingin' the Dream*, 145–46.

43. *The Jazz Record*, 15 June 1943, p. 4.

44. Holiday, *Lady Sings the Blues*, 79.

45. Ibid., 83.

46. Erenberg, *Swingin' the Dream*, 327.

47. Balliett, "Profiles," 54.

48. Ibid., 55.

49. *Philadelphia Afro-American*, 10 October 1942, p. 5.

50. Truly a family group, brothers Russell, 1st tenor; Lander, 2nd tenor; Wallace, baritone; Melvin, bass; and Everette, guitar; along with Danny Owens, tenor, first recorded for the Newark-based Manor label in 1943. They used the profits from records and radio appearances to establish the Coleman Hotel in Newark, catering to an African American clientele. They also went on to appear post-1943 at Café Society. Their early sides are collected on Document CD 5551, *Early Black Vocal Groups, Volume 3*.

51. Some assumed White had been the Hummingbirds' original connection to Café Society, since Davis and White had grown up together in Greenville. The truth was that White had no involvement. If anything, there may have been residual tension between the two. Davis had at one time been engaged to marry Josh White's sister, Deborah. "She and I went to the same church," says Davis. The relationship, however, fell apart. "I was in love with her before I married my wife. "

Over the years, Josh White was in a position to help the Birds, both as a popular attraction at Café Society, and with Decca records, for whom he recorded. But he never did. "Josh was a little controversial," says Tucker. "He was a pretty good thinking guy, but he never had anything to do with the Hummingbirds making records or playing at Café Society. Josh was kind of funny. Like, some guys if they're bigger than you, they let you know. He was like that. He didn't bother with us too much. I put it because maybe Davis didn't marry his sister. There might have been some tension there."

Davis, on the other hand, has good feelings about his encounters with Josh White during the Café Society days. "The only time we saw Josh White was when he came down to the club," says Davis. "And he was tellin' me that he sure was happy that I had sense enough to not get hooked up in that fast life like he did."

52. This Lester Young sextet was never recorded, but Rudi Blesh in *Combo, U.S.A.* writes that they did work Café Society in 1942 (p. 100). That same year, Norman Granz brought Young and Red Callendar together with Nat Cole on piano to record for the California-based label Philo, later renamed Aladdin.

53. Davis and Tucker, interview with the author, 1998.

54. *Billboard*, 12 September 1942.

55. *Variety*, 11 November 1942, p. 44.

56. Balliett, "Profiles," 55.

57. Denning, *The Cultural Front*, 324–33.

58. Ibid., 324–33

59. Paul Robeson, *Songs of Free Men*, Columbia Records M-534. Circa 1940s.

60. Josh White, *Ballads and Blues*, Decca Records, 1947.

61. Denning, *The Cultural Front*, 352.

62. Barry Olivier, *Sonny Terry & Brownie McGhee: Back to New Orleans*, Fantasy Records 24708, liner notes

63. Denning, *The Cultural Front*, 338.

64. *New York Times*, 14 March 1943, Section II, p. 7.

65. *Philadelphia Afro-American*, 12 December 1942, p. 9.

66. *Variety*, 20 January 1943.

Chapter 5: "Move On Up a Little Higher"

1. Jannette Dates and William Barlow, *Split Image: African Americans in the Mass Media* (Washington, DC: Howard University Press, 1990), 209–19.

2. William Barlow, *Voice Over: The Making of Black Radio* (Philadelphia: Temple University Press, 1999), 143.

3. Gilbert Williams, *Legendary Pioneers of Black Radio* (Westport, CT: Praeger, 1998), 10.

4. Darryl Williams, telephone conversation with the author, 28 September 2001.

5. Steven Kinzer, "The Man Who Made Jazz Hot," *New York Times*, 28 November 2000, Section B, p. 1.

6. Ray Charles and David Ritz, *Brother Ray* (New York: Dial Press, 1978), 120–121.

7. Paul Denis, "The Negro Makes Advances," *Billboard*, 2 January 1943, p. 38.

8. *The Philadelphia Inquirer*, 1 April 1943, p. 13.

9. *The Philadelphia Afro-American*, 29 May 1943, p. 10.

10. *The Philadelphia Afro-American*, 20 November 1943, p. 8.

11. The ban on shellac was actually derived from a ban on the recording of new music imposed in 1942 by James Petrillo, then president of the American Federation of Musicians. On the surface, the purpose of the Petrillo ban was to conserve shellac as a prime ingredient in the manufacture of explosive weapons. In truth, Petrillo's primary motive was to use the shellac issue as leverage in a dispute with the major labels—Victor, Columbia, Decca—over the displacement of live performance in public venues by jukebox recordings. Petrillo's actual motive was the economic well-being of his constituents, professional musicians. More on the ban can be read in Scott Deveaux, "Bebop and the Recording Industry: The 1942 AFM Recording Ban Reconsidered," *Journal of the American Musicological Society* (1988): 126–65.

12. *The Philadelphia Afro-American*, 7 August 1943, p. 8.

13. *The Philadelphia Afro-American*, 27 November 1943, p. 10.

14. Randall Grass, "Making a Joyful Noise," *The Philadelphia Inquirer*, 19 April 1981, p. 15.

15. Beachey Thompson, telephone conversation with Ray Funk, 13 June 1982.

16. Ibid.

17. After Thompson left, the Willing Four evolved into the Trumpeteers, then later, incorporating their radio network affiliation, the C.B.S. Trumpeteers. Another of the important groups of gospel's golden age, the Trumpeteers released numerous recordings on labels such as Score, King, Okeh, and Nashboro. Their best-known side was "Milky White Way." The

driving force behind the Willing Four/Trumpeteers was baritone Joe Johnson. He was "a go-getter," says Beachey Thompson. "He was some kind of salesman. He didn't have a voice but he would make you forget his sound and look at him. He would do it all. Joe Johnson was a sales person!"

18. Beachey Thompson, telephone conversation with Ray Funk, 12 June 1982.

19. Ibid.

20. Rick Kennedy and Randy McNutt, *Little Labels—Big Sound* (Bloomington: Indiana University Press, 1999), introduction.

21. Arnold Shaw, *Honkers and Shouters: The Golden Years of Rhythm & Blues* (New York: Collier Books, 1978), 132.

22. *Billboard*, 20 February 1943, p. 21.

23. *Billboard*, 9 December 1944, p. 16.

24. *The Philadelphia Tribune*, 1 September 1945, p. 9.

25. *The Philadelphia Tribune*, 10 November 1945, p. 15.

26. Interviews with the author, Senior Wheels East, Philadelphia, 18 July 2000.

27. *The Philadelphia Tribune*, 10 November 1945, p. 15.

28. *The Philadelphia Tribune*, 19 January 1946, p. 12.

29. *The Philadelphia Tribune*, 11 May 1946, p. 13.

30. *The Philadelphia Afro-American*, 11 May 1946, p. 8.

31. *The Philadelphia Tribune*, 19 January 1946, p. 12.

32. *The Cleveland Call and Post*, 19 September 1942, p. 15. The Live Wires were a venerable Cleveland-based group that, though they had never recorded, had a history going back to 1929. Frank Vaughn was a founding member and leader of the Wires at that time; the group also included the Huff brothers—Curtis, James, and Ralph—along with LeRoy Gaines, the Reverend Paul Spivey, and Robert Ross.

33. Galen Gart, *The American Record Label Directory and Dating Guide, 1940–1959* (Milford, NH: Big Nickel Publications, 1994).

34. *Billboard*, 3 August 1946, p. 22.

35. *New York Amsterdam News*, 28 December 1942, p. 2.

36. Phillip Groia, *They All Sang on the Corner* (West Hempstead, NY: Phillie Dee Enterprises, 1983), 29.

37. Curtis Rudolph, interview with the author, New Jersey, 11 August 1998.

38. Shaw, *Honkers and Shouters*, 138.

39. Andy Razaf, *Philadelphia Tribune*, 16 September 1950, p. 12.

40. *The New York Amsterdam News*, 15 February 1947, p. 23.

41. In 1957, with personnel changes and a new label, the Five Royales would write and record "Dedicated to the One I Love," an R&B hit for them and in 1959, an early rock 'n' roll million-seller for teen doo-wop girl group the Shirelles.

42. Linda Saylor-Marchant, *From the Church to the Apollo Theater—Life Story of Thermon T. Ruth* (privately published, no date).

43. Tommy Hunt, telephone conversation with the author, 6 April 2001.

44. *The Philadelphia Tribune*, 3 December 1949, p. 12.

Chapter 6: "My Record Will Be There"

1. Leonard Feather, *The New Edition of the Encyclopedia of Jazz* (New York: Horizon Press, 1960).

2. Steve Rowland and Larry Abrams, producers, *Tell Me How Long Trane's Been Gone*, CultureWorks Ltd., 2001.

3. Prentiss Barnes, telephone conversation with the author, 13 December 2000.

4. Horace C. Boyer and Lloyd Yearwood, *How Sweet the Sound: The Golden Age of Gospel* (Washington, DC: Elliott & Clark Publishing, 1995), 197.

5. Bobby Womack, *Say It Loud!* VH1 Network Web site, 8 October 2001.

6. The Bay States—Willie Comborne, Robert Furrell, William Wright, and Owens's brothers-in-law, Frank, Charles, and Billy Mickens—were one of the more popular quartets around Philadelphia and had their own local radio show. As for Paul Owens, he would jump from group to group over the years, one time or another joining the Swan Silvertones, the Brooklyn All Stars, and the Dixie Hummingbirds—twice.

7. Cheeks had recorded for Decca in 1949 with his group, the Singing Sons. A year later, the Sons released a second record on the Freedom label. Cheeks joined the Nightingales in 1951 as their lead singer, and soon after, their star began to rise. He had a full-toned, cutting voice that he could break up into gravel, driving the audience into a frenzy.

8. Boyer and Yearwood, *How Sweet the Sound*, 236–37. Barney Parks would finish out his career as a promoter, eventually marrying and managing the career of Edna Gallmon Cooke, former schoolteacher turned gospel diva. Cooke studied music at Temple University and began performing profession- ally in Washington, D.C. Between 1949 and 1966, she recorded a string of sermons in song, mostly on the Nashville-based Nashboro label, and often with male quartet accompaniment, including the Radio Four and June Cheek's former group, the Singing Sons. Parks and Cooke worked together in partner- ship over the course of her illustrious career until her death in 1967.

9. Willa Ward-Royster, telephone conversation with the author, 6 November 2000.

10. Willa Ward-Royster and Toni Rose, *How I Got Over: Clara Ward and the World-Famous Ward Singers* (Philadelphia: Temple University Press, 1997), 98.

11. Boyer and Yearwood, *How Sweet the Sound*, 114–15.

12. Ibid., 112.

13. Bernice Johnson Reagon, ed., *We'll Understand It Better By and By* (Wash- ington: Smithsonian Institution Press, 1992), 12.

14. Boyer and Yearwood, *How Sweet the Sound*, 42.

15. Mark Lisheron, "Rhythm-and-Jews: The Story of the Blacks and Jews Who Worked Together to Create the Magic of R & B," *CommonQuest* (Summer 1997): 23.

16. Jeffrey Melnick, *A Right to Sing the Blues: African Americans, Jews, and American Popular Song* (Cambridge, MA: Harvard University Press, 1999).

17. Lisheron, "Rhythm-and-Jews," 25.

18. Ibid., 23.

19. Ibid.

20. Tony Collins, *Rock Mr. Blues: The Life and Music of Wynonie Harris* (Milford, NH: Big Nickel Publications, 1995), 74.

21. Steven Tracy, *Going to Cincinnati: A History of the Blues in the Queen City* (Urbana: University of Illinois Press, 1993), 120–121.

22. Ira Tucker, Jr., telephone conversation with the author, 10 September 2001.

23. *Billboard*, 3 August 1946, p. 32.

24. *Billboard*, 20 July 1946, p. 36.

25. Paul Fine, telephone conversation with the author, 27 June 2000.

26. Pleasant Joseph and Harriet Ottenheimer, *Cousin Joe: Blues from New Orleans* (Chicago: University of Chicago Press, 1987), 117.

27. Morris Ballen, telephone conversation with the author, 19 June 2000.

28. A similar title, "Why I Like Roosevelt, Parts 1 & 2," was released a year later in 1947 as Aladdin #2018 by R. H. Harris and the Soul Stirrers with Willie Eason on lead.

29. Ed Sprouse, telephone conversation with the author, 8 September 2001.

30. Morris Ballen, telephone conversation with the author, 19 June 2000.

31. Margaret Allison, telephone conversation with the author, 29 March 2001.

32. Contract between Ivin Ballen and the Royal Harmony Singers, July 2, 1949. Courtesy of Bruce Bastin, Interstate Music, Ltd., East Sussex, U.K.

33. Margaret Allison, telephone conversation with the author, 29 March 2001.

34. Ibid.

35. Session logs indicate that by 1952, Ernest James was recording with the Nightingales. He would remain with the 'Gales for at least the next three years.

36. Anthony Heilbut, *The Gospel Sound: Good News and Bad Times* (New York: Limelight Editions, 1985), 192.

37. The 45-rpm serial numbers are not shown in discographies, but they are listed in undated catalogs issued by Gotham in the early 1950s.

38. *The Philadelphia Tribune*, 9 December 1950, p. 12.

39. Horace Clarence Boyer, telephone conversation with the author, 28 June 2001.

40. Margaret Allison, telephone conversation with the author, 29 March 2001.

41. Ibid.

42. Boyer, 28 June 2001.

43. *The Philadelphia Tribune*, 30 December 1950, p. 6.

44. *The Philadelphia Tribune*, 11 August 1951, p. 9.

45. The Griffith Park event in Washington, D.C., occurred on Sunday evening, July 2, 1950, and was a special Fourth of July concert with fireworks. The program was billed as the "First Annual Spiritual Pilgrimage and Fireworks Display." Headliners were Sister Rosetta Tharpe and Madame Marie Knight, Sister Rosetta's mother, Katie Belle Nubin, with special guests, the Golden Gate Quartet, Elder Smallwood E. Williams, the Sunset Harmonizers, and, of course, the Harmonizing Four. M.C.s were Miss Francis White of WOOK radio and Jon Massey of WWDC radio.

46. *The Philadelphia Tribune*, 25 August 1951, p. 12.

47. *Wedding Ceremony of Sister Rosetta Tharpe*, Decca DL 5382, liner notes.

48. *The Philadelphia Tribune*, 31 July 1951, p. 12.

49. Galen Gart, *First Pressings: The History of Rhythm & Blues, Volume 1: 1951*, (Milford, NH: Big Nickel Publications, 1991), 5, 12, 17.

50. Brian Rust, *The American Record Label Book: From the 19th Century Through 1942* (New Rochelle, NY: Arlington House Publishers, 1978), 212–17.

51. Gart, *First Pressings: Volume 1*, 41.

52. Arnold Shaw, *Honkers and Shouters: The Golden Years of Rhythm & Blues* (New York: Collier Books, 1978), 445–50.

53. Galen Gart, *First Pressings: The History of Rhythm & Blues, Volume 2: 1952* (Milford, NH: Big Nickel Publications, 1992), 16.

54. Cedric Hayes and Robert Laughton, *Gospel Records, 1943–1969: A Black Music Discography* (London: Record Information Services, 1992).

55. Marie Knight, telephone conversation with the author, 26 October 2001.

56. The Evangelist Singers would change their name to the Detroiters and have some success on Art Rupe's Specialty label in the 1950s. At one time, former Dixie Hummingbird Otis Jackson recorded with the Evangelists, as did Jimmy Bryant.

57. Heilbut, *The Gospel Sound*, 48.

Chapter 7: "Let's Go Out to the Programs"

1. *The Philadelphia Tribune*, 21 November 1953, p. 2.

2. Jerry Butler, telephone conversation with the author, 8 August 2001.

3. *The Chicago Defender*, 10 September 1955, p. 1.

4. *The Philadelphia Tribune*, 23 August 1955, p. 3.

5. Big Bill Broonzy, "Black, Brown, and White Blues." Vogue Records 134.

6. *Rock and Roll: The Early Days*. An Archive Film Production (TFBI Associates, 1984).

7. *Time*, 23 April 1956, p. 31.

8. Dr. Gadson Graham, interview with the author, Paterson, New Jersey, 7 April 2001.

9. Bernice Johnson Reagon, ed. *We'll Understand It Better By and By* (Washington: Smithsonian Institution Press, 1992), 201.

10. *The Pittsburgh Courier*, 8 August 1953, p. 19.

11. *The Pittsburgh Courier*, 27 March 1953, p. 18.

12. *The Pittsburgh Courier*, 13 June 1953, p. 18.

13. *The Pittsburgh Courier*, 24 April 1953, p. 20.

14. Willa Ward-Royster, telephone conversation with the author, 6 November 2000.

15. Gertrude Ward, letter to James S. Hill, 16 November 1954.

16. *The Pittsburgh Courier*, 19 April 1955, p. 15.

17. *Newsweek*, 2 September 1957, p. 86.

18. *The Chicago Defender*, 24 January 1953, p. 7. An article on 1952 as an entertainment year was headlined, " 'Packages' Among the Things Fans Liked the Best." The piece went on to describe a number of secular package shows that did well that past year.

19. Program Booklet, "The Gospel Train," 1952.

20. *New York Amsterdam News*, 16 February 1952, p. 13.

21. Galen Gart, *First Pressings: The History of Rhythm & Blues, Volume 2: 1952* (Milford, NH: Big Nickel Publications, 1992), 50.

22. *The Philadelphia Tribune*, 12 September 1952, p. 12.

23. Gart, *First Pressings, Volume 2*, 33.

24. Horace C. Boyer and Lloyd Yearwood, *How Sweet the Sound: The Golden Age of Gospel* (Washington, DC: Elliott & Clark Publishing, 1995), 174. In the late 1950s, Lou Rawls would join the lineup of the Pilgrim Travelers, eventually moving on and dueting with Sam Cooke on the R&B standard, "Bring It On Home to Me."

25. From the funeral program of Archie Brownlee, 12 February 1960. Brownlee was born in Turil, Arkansas, in 1925. He lost his sight in infancy and entered the Piney Woods School at age six in 1931. He began singing professionally in 1943, organizing a group called the Jackson Harmoneers, later known as the Original Five Blind Boys of Jackson, Mississippi. After Brownlee

died, Woodard, Abrams, and Clinkscales maintained the group as singers like Roscoe Robinson and Willie "Little Ax" Broadnax passed through. The Blind Boys also recorded over the years with some of the finest backing musicians in the business, including organist Maceo Woods and guitarists Wayne Bennett, Lefty Bates, and Arthur Crume.

26. Gart, *First Pressings, Volume 2*, 14, 50.

27. Boyer and Yearwood, *How Sweet the Sound*, 179.

28. Ibid., 117.

29. Russ Cowans, "Robey Rolls to Top in Hard-to-Crack Recording Business," *The Chicago Defender*, 28 February 1953, 18–19.

30. Information here was culled from these sources: Galen Gart and Roy C. Ames, *Duke/Peacock Records: An Illustrated History with Discography* (Milford, NH: Big Nickel Publications, 1990); Rick Kennedy and Randy McNutt, *Little Labels—Big Sound* (Bloomington: Indiana University Press, 1999), 73–88.

31. Evelyn Johnson, telephone conversation with the author, 6 December 2000. In 1947, with Robey acting as his manager, Gatemouth cut four sides for Leo and Ed Mesner's Los Angeles Aladdin label, but the poorly promoted records went nowhere. Robey was enthusiastic enough about Brown's talent that he decided to bank on it. He launched a management company, the Buffalo Booking Agency, and a record label, Peacock, both on the chance that the singer/guitarist would break through in a big way.

32. Galen Gart, *First Pressings, The History of Rhythm & Blues, Volume 1: 1951* (Milford, NH: Big Nickel Publications, 1991), 56.

33. Gart, *First Pressings, Volume 2*, 36.

34. *Philadelphia Tribune*, 19 April 1952, p. 12.

35. Evelyn Johnson, telephone conversation with the author, 6 December 2000.

36. Gart, *First Pressings, Volume 2*, 4, 75.

37. Cowans, "Robey Rolls to Top," 18–19.

38. Charles White, *The Life and Times of Little Richard* (New York: Harmony Books, 1984), 37–38.

39. Alan Young, *The Pilgrim Jubilees* (Jackson: University Press of Mississippi, 2001), 113–14.

40. Alan Govenar, *The Early Years of Rhythm & Blues: Focus on Houston* (Houston, TX: Rice University Press, 1990), 8–10.

41. Evelyn Johnson, telephone conversation with the author, 6 December 2000.

42. Joe Ligon, telephone conversation with the author, 4 January 2001.

43. Govenar, *The Early Years*, 8–10.

44. Seamus McGarvey, "An Interview with Ira Tucker of the Dixie Hummingbirds," *Blues & Rhythm: The Gospel Truth* (June 1986): 10–17.

45. Young, *The Pilgrim Jubilees*, 64.

46. LeRoy Crume, telephone conversation with the author, 27 November 2000.

47. Howard Carroll, unpublished interview with Per Notini and Jonas Bernholm, Sweden, 18 May 1999.

48. Arthur Crume, telephone conversation with the author, 27 November 2000.

49. McGarvey, "An Interview with Ira Tucker," 10–17. The actual sequence of Tucker's remarks has been altered with his approval for the sake of "readability."

50. Willie Dixon and Don Snowden, *I Am the Blues: The Willie Dixon Story* (New York: Da Capo, 1989), 159–160.

51. Anthony Heilbut, *The Gospel Sound: Good News and Bad Times* (New York: Limelight Editions, 1985), 50.

52. Roger Wood, "Behind the Scenes: Evelyn Johnson and the Crucial Link Between Houston and Memphis in the Evolution of R&B," unpublished manuscript, 2001.

53. Evelyn Johnson, telephone conversation with the author, 6 December 2000.

54. James M. Salem, *The Late Great Johnny Ace and the Transition from R&B to Rock 'n' Roll* (Urbana: University of Illinois Press, 1999), 70.

55. Lula Mae Watts, telephone conversation with the author, 9 July 2001.

56. Galen Gart, *First Pressings: The History of Rhythm & Blues, Volume 3: 1953* (Milford, NH: Big Nickel Publications, 1997), 79.

57. The program booklet for the event offered the following about the Harmonizing Four: "It was 25 years ago . . . that four boys in the Dunbar Elementary School Glee Club in South Richmond decided to see what they could do with some close four part harmony. The director of the glee club encouraged their first efforts and pretty soon the Harmonizing Four developed to the point that they were invited to sing for civic meetings, clubs, schools, and churches all over the city."

58. Roxie Moore, telephone conversation with the author, 3 November 2001.

59. Ira Tucker, from the transcript of an interview by David April broadcast live on his program "The Gospel Train," Delaware Valley public radio station WRDV, 6 June 1994.

60. Gart, *First Pressings, Volume 3*, 100

61. Jerry Butler, telephone conversation with the author, 8 August 2001.

62. *Chicago Defender*, 16 January 1954, p. 7.

63. Galen Gart, *First Pressings, The History of Rhythm & Blues, Volume 4: 1954* (Milford, NH: Big Nickel Publications, 1990), 13–14.

64. Gart, *First Pressings, Volume 4*, 3.

65. Joe Williams, interview by David April, public radio station WRDV, 6 June 1994.

66. McGarvey, "An Interview with Ira Tucker," 10–17.

67. Ashley James and Ray Allen, *We Love You Like a Rock*, Searchlight Films, 1994.

68. Givens started his singing career in Newark, New Jersey, and by 1941 was recording with the Southern Sons on RCA and its subsidiary, Bluebird. When the draft decimated the Sons' lineup, Givens pressed on, first with the original Ink Spots and later with the Golden Gate Quartet. By 1954, Givens had crossed over from gospel to R&B, joining the Dominoes with Jackie Wilson in place of Clyde McPhatter as the group's lead singer.

69. Marc Ryan, *Trumpet Records: An Illustrated History with Discography* (Milford, NH: Big Nickel Publications, 1992), 7–9.

70. James and Allen, *We Love You Like a Rock*.

71. Steve Schickel, "Controversy Nips Spirituals' Power," *Billboard*, 29 January 1955, pp. 57–68.

72. *Chicago Defender*, 17 September 1955, p. 7.

73. *Chicago Defender*, 26 November 1955, p. 7.

74. *Philadelphia Tribune*, 29 December 1955, p. 5.

75. Galen Gart, *First Pressings: The History of Rhythm & Blues, Volume 5: 1955* (Milford, NH: Big Nickel Publications, 1990), 81.

76. Schickel, "Controversy Nips Spirituals' Power," 57–68.

77. *Philadelphia Tribune*, 24 September 1955, p. 11.

78. *Philadelphia Tribune*, 7 and 14 January 1956.

79. Ted Fox, *Showtime at the Apollo* (New York: Holt, Rinehart and Winston, 1983), 225–27.

80. Jack Schiffman, *Uptown: The Story of Harlem's Apollo Theater* (New York: Cowles, 1971), 91.

81. Thermon Ruth with Linda Saylor-Marchant, *Gospel: From the Church to the Apollo Theater* (Brooklyn, NY: T. Ruth Publications, no date, no page numbers).

82. Boyer and Yearwood, *How Sweet the Sound*, 91.

83. Fox, *Showtime*, 228.

84. *Chicago Defender*, 10 December 1955, p. 6.

85. Fox, *Showtime*, 232.

86. Galen Gart, *First Pressings: The History of Rhythm & Blues: Volume 6, 1956* (Milford, NH: Big Nickel Publications, 1991), 9.

87. *Chicago Defender*, 3 March 1956, p. 15.

88. *New York Amsterdam News*, 1 September 1956, p. 28.

89. Ruth, *Gospel* (no page numbers).

90. Ibid., 229.

91. Fox, *Showtime*, 231.

92. Willa Ward-Royster with Toni Rose, *How I Got Over: Clara Ward and the World-Famous Ward Singers* (Philadelphia: Temple University Press, 1997), 106.

93. Crume, telephone conversation with the author, 27 November 2000.

94. Ruth, *Gospel* (no page numbers).

95. Crume, telephone conversation with the author, 27 November 2000.

96. Boyer and Yearwood, *How Sweet the Sound*, 121.

97. Joe Williams, interview by David April, 6 June 1994.

98. Carrie Thompson, telephone conversation with the author, 28 September 2001.

99. Mabel Carroll, telephone conversation with the author, 23 December 2001.

100. *The Philadelphia Tribune*, 27 September 1956, p. 1.

101. *The New York Amsterdam News*, 1 June 1957, p. 15.

102. Galen Gart, *First Pressings: The History of Rhythm & Blues, Volume 7: 1957* (Milford, NH: Big Nickel Publications, 1993), 93.

103. *The Philadelphia Tribune*, 28 December 1957, p. 15.

104. Jim Dawson, *The Twist: The Story of the Song and Dance That Changed the World* (Boston: Faber & Faber, 1995), 9–11.

105. *The Philadelphia Tribune*, 19 October 1957, p. 15.

106. Morgan Babb, telephone conversation with the author, 18 August 2001. Also, *The Nashville Commentator*, 14 July 1956, p. 3.

107. Ligon, 4 January 2001.

108. Fox, *Showtime*, 232–33.

109. *New York Amsterdam News*, 22 February 1958, p. 14.

110. *New York Amsterdam News*, 7 June 1958, p. 13.

111. The label had issued jazz LPs by Betty Carter and Sonny Criss in 1958.

112. Gart, *First Pressings, Volume 7*, 5–19.

113. *New York Amsterdam News*, 23 May 1959, p. 13.

114. Dr. Gadson Graham, interview with the author, 7 April 2001.

Chapter 8: "Loves Me Like a Rock"

1. Charles Sawyer, *The Arrival of B. B. King* (Garden City, NY: Doubleday, 1980), 52.

2. Ted Fox, *Showtime at the Apollo* (New York: Holt, Rinehart and Winston, 1983), 237.

3. James Hudson, telephone conversation with the author, 12 July 2000.

4. Hank Ballard, telephone conversation with the author, 6 November 2000.

5. Solomon Burke, telephone conversation with the author, 31 May 2001.

6. Otis Williams, interview with the author, State College, Pennsylvania, 5 May 2001.

7. Arnold Shaw, *Honkers and Shouters: The Golden Years of Rhythm & Blues* (New York: Collier Books, 1978), 442–443.

8. Ashley James and Ray Allen, *We Love You Like a Rock*, Searchlight Films, 1994.

9. *Billboard*, 23 October 1965, p. 36.

10. Eliot Tiegel, "From Prayer House to Plush Nightclub: Gospel Music Spreads the Word," *Billboard*, 23 October 1965, pp. 81–94.

11. Robert Shelton, *The Face of Folk Music* (New York: Citadel Press, 1968), 169–199.

12. Anthony Heilbut, *Newport Folk Festival Program* (July 1966).

13. By 1966, former Hummingbird Paul Owens had departed the Silvertones and was now singing with the Brooklyn All-Stars.

14. Rob Bowman, *Soulsville, U.S.A.: The Story of Stax Records* (New York: Schirmer Books, 1997), 146.

15. Seamus McGarvey, "An Interview with Ira Tucker of the Dixie Hummingbirds," *Blues & Rhythm: The Gospel Truth* (June 1986): 10–17.

16. *Billboard*, 26 February 1972, p. 59.

17. McClandish Phillips, "Newport Festival Is Here to Stay, Wein Says," *New York Times*, 9 July 1972, p. 46.

18. Les Ledbetter, "Gospel Concert Is Short but Oh! So Sweet," *New York Times*, 10 July 1972, p. 38.

19. Paul Simon, interview with the author, Philadelphia, 24 September 1998.

20. Paul Zollo, *Paul Simon 1964–1993*, WEA/Warner Brothers, 28 September 1993.

21. Daniel Levitin, "Paul Simon: The Grammy Interview," *Grammy Magazine*, September 2001, p. 44.

22. Zollo, *Paul Simon*.

23. Evelyn Johnson, telephone conversation with the author, 6 December 2000.

24. Billy Altman, "The Dixie Hummingbirds: After 45 Years, a Pop Success," *Crawdaddy*, March 1974, p. 32.

25. Ibid.

26. Zollo, *Paul Simon*.

27. Randall Grass, "Making a Joyful Noise," *The Philadelphia Inquirer*, 19 April 1981, p. 12.

28. McGarvey, "An Interview with Ira Tucker," 14.

29. *The Dixie Hummingbirds: We Love You Like a Rock*, Peacock PLP 178.

30. Ashley James and Ray Allen, *We Love You Like a Rock*, Searchlight Films, 1994.

31. Grass, "Joyful Noise," 15.

32. Patrick and Barbara Salvo, "45 Years of Gospel Music," *Sepia*, April 1974, p. 60.

33. *Billboard*, 24 November 1973, pp. 26–27.

34. Salvo, 60.

35. Ibid., 62.

36. Altman, "The Dixie Hummingbirds," 32.

37. Salvo, 62.

38. *Billboard*, 13 April 1974, p. 20.

39. *The Philadelphia Tribune*, 1 May 1976, p. 1.

40. Culled from reports that appeared in the *Philadelphia Tribune*, May 1, 4, 8, 1976.

41. *Ebony*, October 1978, p. 60.

Chapter 9: "Who Are We?"

1. All the quotes from a transcript of the Hummingbirds roast, Philadelphia, 28 June 1998.

2. Birdis Coleman, Jr., *Golden Flight*, Peacock Records PY-59237.

3. *Ebony*, October 1978, pp. 56–60.

4. Ibid.

5. Ibid.

6. Randall Grass, *Philadelphia Inquirer*, 19 April 1981. Clipping from a Dixie Hummingbirds press kit.

7. Daniel Rubin, *Philadelphia Inquirer*, 21 June 1998.

8. Grass, 1981.

9. Rubin, 1988.

10. Willie Leiser, correspondence by e-mail, 5 February 2002.

11. *Our 60th*, Air 10141.

12. Paul Owens, interview with the author, Annapolis, Maryland, 12 December 1999.

13. *Philadelphia Tribune*, 5 April 1988, p. 1.

14. *Philadelphia Inquirer*, Obituaries, 6 November 1992.

15. Carl Davis, interview with the author, Paterson, New Jersey, 7 April 2001.

16. Lee Hildebrand, *Billboard*, 11 November 1994. Clipping from a Dixie Hummingbirds press kit.

17. From an undated Dixie Hummingbirds press release.

18. Ibid.

19. Ibid.

20. *Philadelphia Inquirer*, 1 October 1998, p. 1.

21. Ibid.

22. Ira Tucker, Jr., from an unpublished private correspondence, 13 September 2001.

Bibliography

Books

Adell, Sandra. *Dictionary of Twentieth Century Culture: African American Culture.* Detroit: Gale, 1996.

Albert, George, and Frank Hoffman. *The Cashbox Black Contemporary Singles Charts, 1960–1984.* Metuchen, NJ: Scarecrow Press, Inc., 1986.

Allen, Ray. *Singing in the Spirit.* Philadelphia: University of Pennsylvania Press, 1991.

Anderson, Jervis. *This Was Harlem 1900–1950.* New York: Farrar, Straus, & Giroux, 1982.

Baldwin, James. *Go Tell It on the Mountain.* New York: Alfred A. Knopf, 1953.

Barfield, Ray. *Listening to Radio, 1920–1950.* Westport, CT: Greenwood, 1996.

Barlow, William. *Looking Up at Down: The Emergence of Blues Culture.* Philadelphia: Temple University Press, 1989.

———. *Voice Over: The Making of Black Radio.* Philadelphia: Temple University Press, 1999.

Bastin, Bruce. *Red River Blues: The Blues Tradition in the Southeast.* Chicago: University of Illinois Press, 1995.

Blesh, Rudy. *Combo: U.S.A.* Philadelphia: Chilton, 1971.

Blockson, Charles L. *Black America Series: Philadelphia 1639–2000.* Charleston, SC: Arcadia Publishing, 2000.

Bowman, Rob. *Soulsville U.S.A.: The Story of Stax Records.* New York: Schirmer Books, 1997.

Boyer, Horace C., and Lloyd Yearwood. *How Sweet the Sound: The Golden Age of Gospel.* Washington, DC: Elliott & Clark Publishing, 1995.

Butler, Jerry, with Earl Smith. *Only the Strong Survive.* Bloomington: Indiana University Press, 2000.

Cantor, Louis. *Wheelin' on Beale.* New York: Pharos Books, 1992.

Charles, Ray, and David Ritz. *Brother Ray.* New York: The Dial Press, 1978.

Cohadas, Nadine. *Spinning Blues into Gold.* New York: St. Martin's Press, 2000.

Collins, Tony. *Rock Mr. Blues: The Life and Music of Wynonie Harris.* Milford, NH: Big Nickel Publications, 1995.

Cooper, Ralph, with Steve Dougherty. *Amateur Night at the Apollo.* New York: HarperCollins, 1990.

Courlander, Harold. *Negro Folk Music, U.S.A.* New York: Columbia University Press, 1963.

Dates, Jannette, and William Barlow. *Split Image: African Americans in the Mass Media*. Washington, DC: Howard University Press, 1990.

Davis, Gerald. *I Got the Word in Me and I Can Sing It, You Know: A Study of the Performed African American Sermon*. Philadelphia: University of Pennsylvania Press, 1985.

Dawson, Jim. *The Twist: The Story of the Song and Dance That Changed the World*. London: Faber & Faber, 1995.

Denning, Michael. *The Cultural Front: The Laboring of American Culture in the Twentieth Century*. London: Verso, 1996.

Dixon, R. M. W., and J. Godrich. *Blues and Gospel Records 1902–1943*. Chigwell, Essex, England: Storyville Publications, 1982.

Dixon, Willie, and Don Snowden. *I Am the Blues: The Willie Dixon Story*. New York: Da Capo, 1989.

Edwards, Joe. *Top 10s & Trivia of Rock & Roll and Rhythm & Blues, 1950–1973*. St. Louis, MO: Blueberry Hill, 1974.

Epstein, Dena, J. *Sinful Tunes and Spirituals: Black Folk Music to the Civil War*. Urbana: University of Illinois Press, 1977.

Erenberg, Lewis. *Swingin' the Dream*. Chicago: University of Chicago Press,1998.

Evans, David. *Big Road Blues*. Berkeley: University of California Press, 1982.

Feather, Leonard. *The New Edition of the Encyclopedia of Jazz*. New York City: Horizon Press, 1960.

Fox, Ted. *Showtime at the Apollo*. New York: Holt, Rinehart and Winston, 1983.

Gart, Galen, ed. *First Pressings: The History of Rhythm & Blues. Volume 3, 1953*. Milford, NH: Big Nickel Publications, 1989.

———. *First Pressings: The History of Rhythm & Blues. Volume 5, 1955*. Milford, NH: Big Nickel Publications, 1989.

———. *First Pressings: The History of Rhythm & Blues. Volume 4, 1954*. Milford, NH: Big Nickel Publications, 1990.

———. *First Pressings: The History of Rhythm & Blues. Volume 1, 1951*. Milford, NH: Big Nickel Publications, 1991.

———. *First Pressings: The History of Rhythm & Blues. Volume 6, 1956*. Milford, NH: Big Nickel Publications, 1991.

———. *First Pressings: The History of Rhythm & Blues. Volume 2, 1952*. Milford, NH: Big Nickel Publications, 1992.

———. *First Pressings: The History of Rhythm & Blues. Volume 7, 1957*. Milford, NH: Big Nickel Publications, 1993.

———.*The American Record Label Directory and Dating Guide, 1940–1959*. Milford, NH: Big Nickel Publications, 1994.

Gart, Galen, and Roy C. Ames. *Duke/Peacock Records: An Illustrated History with Discography*. Milford, NH: Big Nickel Publications, 1990.

Ginyard, III, Caleb. *My Name Is Caleb. N. Ginyard: A Father and Son Autobiography of a Spiritual Music Genius*. Hanover Township, PA: Akashic Press, 2002.

Goreau, Laurraine. *Just Mahalia, Baby*. Waco, TX: Word Books, 1975.

Govenar, Alan. *The Early Years of Rhythm & Blues: Focus on Houston*. Houston, TX: Rice University Press, 1990.

Groia, Phillip. *They All Sang on the Street Corner*. West Hempstead, NY: Phillie Dee Enterprises, 1983.

Hammond, John, with Irving Townsend. *John Hammond on Record: An Autobi-ography*. New York: Ridge Press/Summit Books, 1977.

Harris, Michael. *The Rise of Gospel Blues*. New York: Oxford University Press, 1992.

Haskins, Jim. *The Cotton Club*. New York: Random House, 1977.

Hayes, Cedric, and Robert Laughton. *Gospel Records, 1943–1969: A Black Music Discography*. London: Record Information Services, 1992.

Heilbut, Anthony. *The Gospel Sound*. New York: Limelight Editions, 1985.

Hilliard, Robert, and Michael C. Keith, *The Broadcast Century: A Biography of American Broadcasting*. 2d ed. Boston: Focal Press, 1997.

Hinson, Glenn. *Fire in My Bones: Transcendence and the Holy Spirit in African American Gospel*. Philadelphia: University of Pennsylvania Press, 2000.

Hirshey, Gerri. *Nowhere to Run: The Story of Soul Music*. New York: Penguin Books, 1984.

Holiday, Billie, with William Dufty. *Lady Sings the Blues*. New York: Lancer Books, 1965.

Hurston, Zora Neale. *The Folklore Writings of Zora Neale Hurston*. Berkeley, CA: Turtle Island Foundation, 1981.

Jackson, John. *American Bandstand: Dick Clark and the Making of a Rock 'n' Roll Empire*. New York: Oxford University Press, 1997.

———. *Big Beat Heat: Alan Freed and the Early Years of Rock & Roll*. New York: Macmillan, 1991.

Jackson, Mahalia, with Evan McLeod Wylie. *Movin' On Up*. New York: Hawthorn Books, 1966.

Johnson, James Weldon. *The Book of American Negro Spirituals*. New York: Viking Press. 1925.

Jones, Arthur. *Wade in the Water: The Wisdom of the Spirituals*. Maryknoll, NY: Orbis Books, 1993.

Joseph, Pleasant, and Harriet Ottenheimer. *Cousin Joe: Blues from New Orleans*. Chicago: University of Chicago Press, 1987.

Kennedy, Rick, and Randy McNutt. *Little Labels—Big Sound*. Bloomington: Indiana University Press, 1999.

Kukla, Barbara J. *Swing City: Newark Nightlife, 1925–50*. Philadelphia: Temple University Press, 1991.

Lornell, Kip. *Happy in the Service of the Lord*. Urbana: University of Illinois Press, 1988.

Lowe, Allen. *American Pop from Minstrel to Mojo on Record 1893–1956*. Redwood, NY: Cadence Jazz Books, 1997.

MacDonald, J. Fred. *Don't Touch that Dial! Radio Programming in American Life from 1920 to 1960*. Chicago: Nelson Hall, 1979.

Maltby, Richard. *Passing Parade*. New York: Oxford University Press, 1989.

Margolick, David. *Strange Fruit: Billie Holiday, Café Society, and an Early Cry for Civil Rights*. Philadelphia: Running Press, 2000.

Marsh, J.B.T. *The Story of the Jubilee Singers with Their Songs*. New York: Negro Universities Press, 1969.

Melnick, Jeffrey. *A Right to Sing the Blues: African Americans, Jews, and American Popular Song*. Cambridge, MA: Harvard University Press, 1999.

Nathan, Hans. *Dan Emmett and the Rise of Early Negro Minstrelsy*. Norman: University of Oklahoma Press, 1962.

Odum, Howard, and Guy Johnson. *The Negro and His Songs: A Study of Typical Negro Songs in the South*. Chapel Hill: University of North Carolina Press, 1925.

Oliver, Paul. *Songsters and Saints: Vocal Traditions on Race Records*. Cambridge: Cambridge University Press, 1984.

———. *The New Grove Gospel, Blues, and Jazz*. New York: W.W. Norton, 1986.

Otis, Johnny. *Upside Your Head! Rhythm and Blues on Central Avenue*. Hanover, NH: Wesleyan University Press/University Press of New England, 1993.

Palmer, Robert. *Rock & Roll: An Unruly History*. New York: Harmony Books, 1995.

Reagon, Bernice, ed. *We'll Understand It Better By and By*. Washington, DC: Smithsonian Institution Press, 1992.

Rust, Brian. *The American Record Label Book: From the 19th Century through 1942*. New Rochelle, NY: Arlington House Publishers, 1978.

Ruth, Thermon, and Linda Saylor-Marchant. *Gospel: From the Church to the Apollo Theater*. Brooklyn, NY: T. Ruth Publications (no date).

Ryan, Marc. *Trumpet Records: An Illustrated History with Discography*. Milford, NH: Big Nickel Publications, 1992.

Sacré, Robert, ed. *Saints and Sinners: Religion, Blues, and (D)evil in African-American Music and Literature*. Liège, Belgium: Societé Liégeoise de Musicologie, 1996.

Salem, James M. *The Late Great Johnny Ace and the Transition from R&B to Rock 'n' Roll*. Urbana: University of Illinois Press, 1999.

Sawyer, Charles. *The Arrival of B. B. King*. Garden City, NY: Doubleday, 1980.

Schiffman, Jack. *Uptown: The Story of Harlem's Apollo Theater*. New York: Cowles, 1971.

Seroff, Doug. *Birmingham Quartet Scrapbook*. Smithsonian Program Booklet, 1980.

———. *Gospel Arts Day/Nashville*. Smithsonian Program Booklet, 1988.

———. *Home of the Heroes*. Smithsonian Program Booklet, 1990.

Shaw, Arnold. *Honkers and Shouters: The Golden Years of Rhythm & Blues*. New York: Collier Books, 1978.

Shelton, Robert. *The Face of Folk Music*. New York: Citadel Press, 1968.

Tracy, Steven. *Going to Cincinnati: A History of the Blues in the Queen City*. Urbana: University of Illinois Press, 1993.

Tyson, Timothy B. *Radio Free Dixie*. Chapel Hill: University of North Carolina Press, 1999.

Wald, Elijah. *Josh White: Society Blues*. Amherst: University of Massachusetts Press, 2000.

Walker, Wyatt Tee. *"Somebody's Calling My Name": Black Sacred Music and Social Change*. Valley Forge, PA: Judson Press, 1979.

Ward, Andrew. *Dark Midnight When I Rise: The Story of the Jubilee Singers Who Introduced the World to the Music of Black America*. New York: Farrar, Straus, & Giroux, 2002.

Ward, Geoffrey C., and Ken Burns. *Jazz: A History of America's Music*. New York: Knopf, 2000.

Ward-Royster, Willa, and Toni Rose. *How I Got Over: Clara Ward and the World-Famous Ward Singers*. Philadelphia: Temple University Press, 1997.

Warner, Jay. *American Singing Groups*. New York: Da Capo Press, 2000.

Whitburn, Joel. *Billboard's Top 10 Charts, 1958–1988*. Menomonee Falls, WI: Record Research, 1988.

White, Charles. *The Life and Times of Little Richard: The Quasar of Rock*. New York: Harmony Books, 1984.

Williams, Gilbert A. *Legendary Pioneers of Black Radio*. Westport, CT: Praeger, 1998.

Williams, Martin. *The Jazz Tradition*. New York: Oxford University Press, 1970.

Wilson, Charles, and William Ferris, eds. *Encyclopedia of Southern Culture*. Chapel Hill: University of North Carolina Press, 1989.

Wolff, Daniel. *The Life and Times of Sam Cooke*. New York: William Morrow, 1995.

Young, Alan. *Woke Me Up This Morning*. Jackson: University Press of Mississippi, 1997.

———. *The Pilgrim Jubilees*. Jackson: University Press of Mississippi, 2001.

Articles

Alland, Alexander, Jr. "'Possession' in a Revivalistic Negro Church." *Journal for the Scientific Study of Religion* 1 (1962): 204–13.

Altman, Billy. "The Dixie Hummingbirds: After 45 Years, a Pop Success." *Crawdaddy*, March 1974, pp. 32–33.

Balliett, Whitney. "Profiles." *The New Yorker*, 9 October 1971, pp. 50–92.

Burnim, Mellonee V. "Functional Dimensions of Gospel Music Performance." *Western Journal of Black Studies* 12, no. 2 (1988): 112–21.

Boggs, Beverly. "Some Aspects of Worship in a Holiness Church." *New York Folklore* 3 (1977): 39–44.

Boyer, Horace. "Contemporary Gospel Music." *The Black Perspective in Music* 7 (1979): 5–58.

Cowans, Russ. "Robey Rolls to Top in Hard-to-Crack Recording Business." *The Chicago Defender*, 28 February 1953, pp. 18–19.

Danchin, Sebastian. "Spiritual and Gospel Music and the Rise of an Afro-American Identity in U.S. Radio," in *Saints and Sinners*, edited by Robert Sacré. Liège, Belgium: Societé Liégeoise de Musicologie, Etudes & Editions 5, 1996.

Denis, Paul. "The Negro Makes Advances." *Billboard*, 2 January 1943, p. 38.

Deveaux, Scott. "Bebop and the Recording Industry: The 1942 AFM Recording Ban Reconsidered." *Journal of the American Musicological Society* (1988): 126–65.

Dorsey, Thomas. "Gospel Music." In *Reflections on Afro-American Music*, edited by D. de Lerma. Kent, OH: Kent State University Press, 1973.

Feintuch, Burt. "A Noncommercial Gospel Group in Context: We Live the Life We Sing About." *Black Music Research Journal* 1 (1980): 37–50.

Grass, Randall. "Making a Joyful Noise." *The Philadelphia Inquirer*, 19 April 1981, 15.

Hurston, Zora Neale. "Spirituals and Neo-Spirituals." In *The Sanctified Church*. Berkeley, CA: Turtle Island [1934], 1983.

Johnson, James Weldon. "The Origin of the Barbershop Chord." *The Mentor*, 29 February 1929.

Jules-Rosette, Bennetta. "Song and Spirit: The Use of Songs in the Management of Ritual Contexts." *Africa* 45 (1975): 150–66.

Karichoff, Connie, "Photographer William H. Jordan/A Portrait of Ansted's Black Community." *Goldenseal: West Virginia Traditional Life* (Winter 1998): 44–51.

Kinzer, Steven. "The Man Who Made Jazz Hot." *New York Times*, 28 November 2000, Section B, p. 1.

Koenig, John. "John Hammond/An American Original." *Goldmine*, September 7, 1990, pp. 11–14.

Kroll-Smith, J. Stephen. "The Testimony of Performance: The Relationship of an Expressive Event to the Belief System of a Holiness Sect." *Journal for the Scientific Study of Religion* 19 (1980): 16–25.

Ledbetter, Les. "Gospel Concert Is Short but Oh! So Sweet." *New York Times*, 10 July 1972, p. 30.

Levitin, Daniel. "Paul Simon: The Grammy Interview." *Grammy Magazine*, September 2001, p. 44.

Lisheron, Mark. "Rhythm-and-Jews: The Story of the Blacks and Jews Who Worked Together to Create the Magic of R & B." *Common Quest* (Summer 1997): 23.

McGarvey, Seamus. "An Interview with Ira Tucker of the Dixie Hummingbirds." *Blues & Rhythm, the Gospel Truth* (June 1986): 10–17.

Newman, Kathy. "The Forgotten Fifteen Million: Black Radio, the 'Negro Market,' and Consumer Activism." Unpublished paper, 1998.

Phillips, McClandish. "Newport Festival Is Here to Stay, Wein Says." *New York Times*, 9 July 1972, p. 46.

"On the One-Nighter Trail." *The Billboard Band Year Book* (26 September 1942).

Rein, Richard. "After 50 Years, the Dixie Hummingbirds Are Still Music's Sweet Bird of Youth." *People*, 26 March 1979, pp. 109–12.

Salvo, Patrick, and Barbara Salvo. "45 Years of Gospel Music." *Sepia*, April 1974, pp. 60–64.

Seroff, Doug, and Abbott, Lynn. "Polk Miller and the Old South Quartette," *78 Quarterly* 1, no. 6 (1991).

———. "The Origins of Ragtime." *78 Quarterly* 1, no. 10 (1998).

Schickel, Steve. "Controversy Nips Spirituals' Power," *Billboard*, 29 January 1955, pp. 57–68.

Tiegel, Eliot. "From Prayer House to Plush Nightclub: Gospel Music Spreads the Word." *Billboard*, 23 October 1965, pp. 81–94.

Wood, Roger. "Behind the Scenes: Evelyn Johnson and the Crucial Link between Houston and Memphis in the Evolution of R&B." Prepublication manuscript, 2001.

Zolten, Jerry. "Don't You Let Nobody Turn You 'Round." *Rejoice* 3, no. 6, (1991/1992).

Periodicals

Billboard, 1942–1994.

The Chicago Defender, 1954–1956.

The Cleveland Call and Post.

Ebony, 1978.

The Nashville Commentator, 1956.
The New York Amsterdam News, 1941–1959.
Newsweek, 1957.
The Philadelphia Afro-American, 1942–1946.
The Philadelphia Inquirer, 1942–1998.
The Philadelphia Tribune, 1945–1976.
The Pittsburgh Courier, 1953–1955.
Soul, 1974.
Time, 1956.
Variety, 1942.

Interviews

Interviews are by author unless otherwise indicated.

Allison, Margaret (The Angelic Gospel Singers). 29 March 2001.

Angelou, Maya. 8 September 2000.

Babb, Morgan (The Radio Four). 18 August 2001.

Baker, Minnie Lee. 16 March 1999.

Ballard, Hank (The Midnighters). 6 November 2000.

Ballen, Morris (Gotham Records). 19 June 2000.

Barnes, Prentiss (The Moonglows). 13 December 2000.

Boyer, Horace Clarence (The Boyer Brothers). 28 June 2001.

Bradley, Carey (The Kings of Harmony). 9 July 2001.

Bright, William (Sons of the Birds). 12 June 1999.

Burke, Solomon. 31 May 2001.

Butler, Jerry (The Impressions). 8 August 2001.

Carroll, Howard. 7 May 1999.

———. Interviewed by Per Notini and Jonas Bernholm, 18 May 1999.

———. 27 April 2001.

———. 23 December 2001.

Carroll, Mabel. 23 December 2001.

Crume, Arthur (The 5 Blind Boys of Mississippi, the Highway QCs, The Sensational Nightingales, The Soul Stirrers). 27 November 2000.

Crume, LeRoy (The Soul Stirrers). 27 November 2000.

Davis, Carl. 7 April 2001.

Davis, James. 7 February 1995.

———. 16 April 2000.

———. 30 March 2001.

———. 8 June 2001.

Davis, James, and Ira Tucker, 12 June 1998.

Fine, Paul (Gotham Records). 27 June 2000.

Freeman, Isaac (The Fairfield Four). 25 May 2000.

Graham, Dr. Gadson. 7 April 2001.

Hardy, Robert (Hardy Blue Steel). Interviewed by Doug Seroff and Ray Funk, 12 May 1982.

Hudson, James "Pookie" (The Spaniels). 12 July 2000.

Hunt, Tommy. (The Flamingos). 6 April 2001.

Jeter, Claude (The Swan Silvertones). 17 May 1999.

Johnson, Evelyn (Peacock Records). 6 December 2000.

Knight, Marie. 26 October 2001.

Lawrence, Linda Tucker (The Supremes). 8 October 2001

Leiser, Willie, correspondence by e-mail. 5 February 2002.

Ligon, Joe (The Mighty Clouds of Joy). 4 January 2001.

McIver, Blanche. 10 August 1996.

Merchant, Jimmy (Frankie Lymon and the Teenagers). 23 April 2001.

Moore, Roxie. 3 November 2001.

Norris, Mamie. 10 August 1996.

Owens, Paul. 12 December 1999.

Parks, Barney. 8 August 1996.

———. 9 March 2000.

Rudolph, Curtis. 11 August 1998.

Ruth, Thermon (Selah Jubilee Singers, the Larks). March 16, 1999.

Senior Wheels East Community Center. 18 July 2000.

Simon, Paul. 24 September 1998.

Smith, Aurelia. 26 February 2000.

Sprouse, Ed (The Blue Ridge Quartet). 8 September 2001.

Thompson, Beachey. Interviewed by Ray Funk, 13 June 1982.

Thompson, Carrie. 28 September 2001.

Tucker, Ira. 13 November 1996.

———. 10 May 1998.

———. 6 June 1998.

———. 12 June 1998.

———. 5 December 1998.

———. 17 February 2000.

———. 3 August 2000.

———. 21 April 2001.

———. 21 September 2001.

———. 24 October 2001

Tucker, Jr., Ira. 7 September 1995.

———. 10 September 2001

———. 13 December 2001.

———. 27 December 2001.

Tucker, Louise and Ira. 21 September 2001.

Tucker, Sundray (The Three Degrees). 6 June 2001.

Ward-Royster, Willa (The Famous Ward Singers). 6 November 2000.

Watts, Lula Mae. 9 July 2001.

Williams, Darryl. 28 September 2001.

Williams, James (Sons of the Birds). Interviewed by David April, 6 June 1994.

———. 29 December 2001.

Williams, Otis (The Temptations). 5 May 2001.

Recordings

Broonzy, Big Bill. "Black, Brown, and White Blues." Vogue Records 134.

Café Society. Onyx Records #210.

Carolina Gospel Quartets. Document Records, DOCD-5445.

Early Black Vocal Groups, Volume 3. Document DOCD-5551.

From Spirituals to Swing. Vanguard Recordings. LP VRS-8523/4.

The Golden Gate Quartet. *Swing Down, Chariot*. Columbia Legacy CK47131.

The Heavenly Gospel Singers. *Complete Recorded Works in Chronological Order, Volume One*. Document Records, DOCD-5452.

Mitchell's Christian Singers. *Complete Recorded Works in Chronological Order*. Document Records DOCD-5493 and DOCD-5496.

Robeson, Paul. *Songs of Free Men*. Columbia Records M-534.

Simon, Paul. *Paul Simon 1964–1993*. WEA/Warner Brothers.

Terry, Sonny, and McGhee, Brownie. *Back to New Orleans*. Fantasy Records 24708.

Testify! The Gospel Box. Rhino Entertainment.

Tharpe, Sister Rosetta. *The Wedding Ceremony of Sister Rosetta Tharpe*. Decca DL 5382.

White, Josh. *Ballads and Blues*. Decca Records.

Films and Radio Documentaries

April, David. "The Gospel Train." Delaware Valley Public Radio WRDV, 6 June 1994.

James, Ashley, and Ray Allen. *We Love You Like a Rock*. Searchlight Films, 1994.

Rock and Roll: The Early Days. An Archive Film Production. TFBI Associates. 1984.

The Dixie Hummingbirds on Record

Singles

Decca

James Davis (T), Wilson Baker (T), Barney Parks (Bar), Jimmy Bryant (Bass)   1939

7645	When the Gates Swing Open Joshua Journeyed to Jericho
7656	Motherless Children Has a Hard Time The Stone That Was Hewed Out of the Mountain
7667	Wouldn't Mind Dying Little Wooden Church
7677	I'm Leaning on the Lord Moving Up the Shining Way
7688	I Looked Down the Line What a Time
7715	Sleep On, Mother Walking on the Water
7746	God's Got Your Number Lord If I Go

Regis-Manor-Kay Ron

James Davis (T), Beachey Thompson (T), Ira Tucker (Bar), William Bobo (Bass)   1944

1008–1074–1004	Book of the Seven Seals [IT] I Just Couldn't Keep It to Myself [JD]

Regis-Manor-Arco

With Sister Ernestine Washington   1944

1007–104–1244	If I Could Just Make It In Savior Don't Pass Me By

Apollo

James Davis (T), Beachey Thompson (T), Ira Tucker (Bar), William Bobo (Bass)   1946

104	In the Storm Too Long [IT] Every Knee Surely Must Bow [IT]
108	My Record Will Be There [IT] Amazing Grace [IT]

132	One Day [JD, IT] Don't You Want to Join That Number [IT]	1947
155	Just a Closer Walk with Thee [JD, WB] Ezekiel Saw the Wheel [IT, WB]	
183	Wrestlin' Jacob [IT] Nobody Knows the Trouble I've Seen [IT]	
191	If We Ever Needed the Lord Before [IT] Journey to the Sky [JD, IT]	
196	Guide My Mind [IT] God Is Now Speaking [IT]	1948
201	Jesus I Love You [IT, JD] I'll Forever Stand [IT, WB]	
220	Jesus Has Traveled This Road Before [IT] The Holy Baby [WB]	

Gotham

James Davis (T), Beachey Thompson (T), Ira Tucker (Bar), William Bobo (Bass)   1949

G614	Lord Come See About Me [IT,WB] I'll Be Satisfied [IT]
G628	Move On Up a Little Higher [IT] We Shall Walk Through the Valley [IT]
G632	Search Me Lord [IT] Two Little Fishes and Five Loaves of Bread [IT, BT]
G641	I Must Have Jesus [IT] Is There Anyone in Heaven That You Know [WB, BT]

Ernest James (T), Beachey Thompson (T), James Davis (Bar), Ira Tucker (Bar),   1950
William Bobo (Bass)

| G686 | Beaming from Heaven [IT]
You've Got to Live So God Can Use You [IT] |
| G697 | What Then [IT, EJ]
Down on Me [JD] |

With the Angelic Gospel Singers
Margaret Allison, Lucille Shird, Josephine McDowell, Ella Mae Norris, Doc Bagby (Organ)

G663	Jesus Will Answer Prayer [MA, EMN, IT] In the Morning [MA, EMN, IT, JD, BT, EJ]
G683	Dear Lord, Look Down upon Me [MA, IT] Standing Out on the Highway [MA, EMN, IT]
G694	Glory, Glory, Hallelujah [MA, EMN, IT, JD, BT, EJ] I'm on My Way to Heaven Anyhow [IT]

Okeh-Columbia

Paul Owens (T), Beachey Thompson (T), James Davis (Bar), Ira Tucker (Bar),   1951
William Bobo (Bass)

| 6864-G31086 | I'll Never Forget [IT, PO]
I'll Live Again [IT, PO] |

With the Angelic Gospel Singers (add Bernice Cole and, in place of Ernest James, Paul Owens)

6858-G31086*   Today (Evening Song) [BC, PO, IT]
                         One Day [BC, PO, IT]
       *Released March 1952

Peacock

Paul Owens (T), Beachey Thompson (T), James Davis (Bar), Ira Tucker (Bar),   1952
William Bobo (Bass)

1594*   What Are They Doing in Heaven Today [PO]
                         Wading Through Blood and Water [IT]

       *Released April 1952

1705   I Know I've Been Changed
                         Trouble in My Way*

       *Earlier take recorded with Paul Owens unreleased. This take with Howard Carroll in place of Owens

Beachey Thompson (T), James Davis (Bar), Ira Tucker (Bar), William Bobo (Bass), Howard Carroll (G)

1713   Lord If I Go [IT, JD]
                         Eternal Life [IT]

1722*   Let's Go Out to the Programs [IT]   1953
                         I'll Keep on Living After I Die [IT]

       *Released November 1953

1727   Live Right, Die Right [IT, BT]   1954
                         (Original Title: "Crossed Jordan in a Calm Time")
                         Prayer Wheel [IT]

Beachey Thompson (T), James Davis (T), Ira Tucker (Bar), James Walker (Bar), William Bobo (Bass), Howard Carroll (G)

1736*   Christian Testimonial [IT]
                         Will the Lord Be with Me [IT, JW]

       *Released October 1954

1740   I'm Not Uneasy [IT]
                         Sinner, Sin No More [IT, JW]

1742   It Must Have Been the Lord (That Touched Me) [IT]   1955
                         Take Care of Me [JW]

With Otis Jackson

1753*   The Life Story of Madame Bethune, Parts 1 & 2

       *Released September 1955

1757   Poor Pilgrim of Sorrow [IT]   1956
                         Devil Can't Harm a Praying Man [IT]

1763   Troubles Will Be Over [IT, JW]
                         Way Up on High [JW]

1764   Thank You Lord for One More Day [IT]
                         Get Right Church [IT]

1770	Loving Hand [JW]	1957
	Cool Down Yonder [IT]	
1773	Live On Forever [IT, JW]	
	Just Trusting [IT]	
1780*	Christian's Automobile [IT]	
	Stop by Here [JW]	

*Released November 1957

1783	Walls of Zion [IT]	1958
	Just a Little While [JW, IT]	
1788	I Don't Know Why (I Have to Cry Sometime) [WB]	
	Let's Go Out to the Program No. 2	
1791	Make One Step [IT]	
	Come On and See About Me [[IT]	
1803	Nobody Knows the Trouble I See [IT]	1959
	The Final Edition [IT]	
1808	I Want to Feel the Holy Spirit [IT]	1960
	What a Friend [JW]	
1817	Jesus Hold My Hand [IT, JW]	
	Leave Your Burdens There [IT, JW]	
1831	He Cares for Me [IT]	1961
	God's Goodness [JW]	
1844	Have a Little Talk with Jesus [JW]	
	In the Morning [IT]	
1861	Our Father's Children [JW]	1962
	Bedside of a Neighbor [IT]	
1889	Another Day [IT]	1963
	If You Trust Him [JW]	
3012	Our Prayer for Peace [JW]	1964
	Come Ye Disconsolate [IT]	
3045	Lord, I Come to Thee [JW]	1965
	If Anybody Asks You [IT, JW]	
	(Original Title: "Anybody You Ask")	
3073	Prayer for the Sick [JW]	
	You Don't Have Nothing [IT]	
3084	The Old Time Way [JW]	1966
	Gabriel [IT]	
3098	Only Jesus [JW]	
	Confidential God [IT]	
3109	Your Good Deeds [IT]	1967
	What the Lord Is to Me [JW]	
3148	The Inner Man	1968
	I'm Going On [IT]	
3165	Don't Let Me Fall [IT, JW]	
	God Is Going to Get Tired [JW]	
3179	Payday	1969
	Somebody [IT]	
3191	Somebody Is Lying [IT]	1970
	Lord, If You Don't Help Us [JW]	

| 3198 | Loves Me Like a Rock [IT]
 I've Been Born Again [IT] | 1973 |
| 3203 | Jesus Children of America [IT]
 Hold On [IT] | |

Albums

Peacock-ABC-MCA-Song Bird

Beachey Thompson (T), James Davis (T), Ira Tucker (Bar), James Walker (Bar), William Bobo (Bass), Howard Carroll (G)

PLP-100	*The Dixie Hummingbirds and a Christian Testimonial*	1959
PLP-108	*In the Morning*	1962
PLP-115	*Our Prayer for Peace*	1964
PLP-127	*Every Day and Every Hour* (Produced in Chicago by Lafayette Leake)	1965
PLP-138	*The Best of the Dixie Hummingbirds*	circa 1966
PLP-140	*Golden Gems of Gospel* (Compilation includes "Bedside of a Neighbor")	circa 1966
PLP-144	*Your Good Deeds*	circa 1967
PLP-153	*The Gentlemen of Song* (Produced by Richard Simpson)	1967
PLP-166	*The World's Greatest Spiritual and Gospel Artists* (Compilation includes "I'm Going On," "I've Been Weighed")	1969
PLP-169	*Ye Shall Know the Truth* (Recorded at Sam Phillips Studio, Memphis, TN)	1969
PLP-178 (ABC)	*We Love You Like a Rock*	1973
GLS-1974	*The World's Greatest Gospel Artists Sing the Favorite Gospel Music of Our Time* (One Track: "This Evening")	
Song Bird-235	*A Holiday Gift Just For You* (One Track: "Christian's Automobile")	
Song Bird-240	*Mother's Favorite Songs* (One Track: "Come Ye Disconsolate")	1974
PLP-59205	*Who Are We*	1974
ABCD-4013	*Sixteen Great Performances*	1975
PLP-59217	*Thanks to Thee*	1975
PLP-59226	*Wonderful to Be Alive*	1976
PLP-59231	*The Dixie Hummingbirds Live*	1977
PLP-59237	*Golden Flight*	1978
ABC PY-59235	*Perpetual Moments* (One Track: "Loves Me Like a Rock")	
MCA-28119	*In These Changing Times* (A repackaging that combines Side A of PLP-178, "We Love You Like a Rock," with Side B of PLP-59226, "Wonderful to Be Alive")	1983

MCA-L33–1101   *Gospel's Golden Greats*
               (One Track: "Loves Me Like a Rock")

MCA-22017   *More Gospel Sound*   1990
               (One Track: "Loves Me Like a Rock")

Atlanta International Records (Gospel AIR)

AIR 10061   *Mama*   1983

AIR 10078   *Smooth Sailing*   1984

AIR 10121   *Live in Philadelphia*   1987

AIR 10141   *Our 60th*   1989

AIR 10181   *In Good Health*   1993

Anthologies and Collections

Apollo

481   *Spiritual Moods*   1959
               (Three Tracks: "Don't You Want to Join That Number,"
               "Just a Closer Walk with Thee," "Ezekiel Saw the Wheel")

18 Top Hits

BR-40   *Bonus Selection*   Circa early 1960s
               (Four Tracks from Apollo Sessions: "If We Ever
               Needed the Lord Before," "Nobody Knows the
               Trouble I See," "Journey to the Sky," "Jesus Has
               Traveled This Road Before")

Constellation

LP-100   *Scripture in Song*   1964

               (Tracks culled from Gotham Sessions: "Lord Come See
               About Me," "I'll Be Satisfied," "Move On Up a Little
               Higher," "We Shall Walk Through the Valley," "Search Me
               Lord," "Two Little Fishes and Five Loaves of Bread,"
               "Beaming from Heaven," "You've Got to Live So God Can
               Use You," "What Then," "Down on Me")

Arctic

LP-1002   Concert Performance at the Hotel Philadelphia   1966
               (Two Tracks: "I Know I've Been Changed" and
               "The Little Wooden Church")

HOB

LP-296   *The Dixie Hummingbirds and the Angelic Gospel Singers/*   1966
               Move On Up a Little Higher
               (Unreleased or Alternate Tracks from Gotham Sessions:
               "Cool Down Yonder," "Young Man," "Get Away Jordan,"
               "I'll Be Satisfied," "Move On Up a Little Higher")

Gospel Roots

5041	*The Dixie Hummingbirds Live in Concert*	1979
5050	*Moving On*	

51 West 1979

QR-16058	*Pray On* (One Track: "I'll Live Again")
QR-16059	*Wake Up in Glory* (One Track with the Angelic Gospel Singers: "One Day")

Folk Lyric 1986

FL-9045	*A Cappella Gospel Singing* (One track: "I Looked Down the Line")
FL-9046	*The Golden Age of Gospel Singing* (One Track with the Angelic Gospel Singers: "Dear Lord, Look Down upon Me")

Gospel Heritage 1988

HT 318	*Dixie Hummingbirds* (Gotham Sides alone and with the Angelic Gospel Singers)

Krazy Kat

KK-836	*Amazing Grace* (Two Unreleased Takes from Gotham Sessions: "Born to Die," "Dear Lord Look Down Upon Me")	1989

Gospel Jubilee

RF-1405	*In the Storm Too Long* (Anthology of Decca, Regis, and Apollo sides)	1991

Spirit Feel 1991

SF 1012	The Gospel Sound of Spirit Feel (Two Tracks: "Prayer Wheel," "Maybe It's You")

Columbia/Legacy-CSP

CG 31086	*The Gospel Sound* (Four Tracks from the Okeh Sessions: ""One Day" and "Today" with the Angelic Gospel Singers; "I'll Never Forget," and "I'll Live Again" on their own)	1971
BS 16924	*His Shining Light* (One Track with Thomas Dorsey: "I'm Waiting for Jesus")	1983
CK 57163	*The Essential GospelSampler* (Two Tracks: "When the Gates Swing Open," "Hide Me in Thy Bosom")	1994
CK 67007	*They Sing Praises* (One Track with the Angelic Gospel Singers: "One Day")	1995

CDs and Videos

Mobile Fidelity

MFCD 751   *We Love You Like a Rock/Every Day and Every Hour*   1976
                     (Remastered Repackaging of Two Previous Peacock LPs)

MFCD 771   *Dixie Hummingbirds Live*   1977
                     (Remastered Repackaging of Peacock LP)

MCA

MCAD-22043   *The Best of the Dixie Hummingbirds*   1991

MCAD-11882   *The Dixie Hummingbirds: Thank You for One More Day*   1998
                     (70th Anniversary Retrospective)

MCAD-11896   *Great Gospel Groups*   1998
                     (One Track: "Christian's Automobile")

MCAD-088112–864–2   *20th Century Masters/ The Millennium Collection,*   2002
                     The Best of the Dixie Hummingbirds

Rhino

R2 70288   *Jubilation! Great Gospel Performances*   1992
                     (One Track: "Christian's Automobile")

Air

10184 (Video)   *Live in Atlanta*   1993
                     (Complete Concert Performance)

AC 7005 (Video)   *Air Gospel Presents the Video Collection*   1997
                     (Performance of "Christian's Automobile")

AIR 10229   *Quartet Legends*   1997
                     (Two Tracks from *Our 60th:* "Satan Is Mad at Me,"
                     "You Ought to Change")

Sony/Columbia Legacy

CK 57160   *The Gospel Sound, Volumes 1 & 2*   1994
                     (Reissue of earlier LP Collection)

CK 57163   *The Essential Gospel Sampler*   1994

CK 57164   *Precious Lord: Recordings of the Great Gospel Songs of*   1994
                     Thomas A. Dorsey
                     (Three Tracks with Thomas Dorsey: "Hide Me in Thy Bosom,"
                     "I'm Waiting for Jesus," "When the Gates Swing Open")

CK 67007   *They Sing Praises*

J2K 65804   *Sony Music 100 Years/ Soundtrack for a Century/ Folk,*
                     Gospel, Blues: Will the Circle Be Unbroken
                     (One Track: "I'll Never Forget")

Vanguard

77014–2   *Gospel at Newport*   1995
                     (Two Tracks from the 1966 Newport Folk Festival:
                     "Christian's Automobile," "I've Got So Much to Shout About")

Document

DOCD-5462	*Sister Ernestine Washington/Complete Recorded* *Works in Chronological Order (1943–1948)*	1996
	(Two Tracks: "If I Could Just Make It In," "Savior Don't Pass Me By")	
DOCD-5491	*The Dixie Hummingbirds/Complete Recorded* *Works in Chronological Order (1939–1947)*	1996
DOCD-5585	*Gospel Singers and Preachers* (One Track: "Jesus I Love You")	1997

Collectibles

COL 6103	*The Very Best of the Dixie Hummingbirds and the Angelics:* *Up in Heaven*	1998
COL 6000	*Good Lord I've Been Saved: The Best of Old School Gospel.* (Two Tracks: "I Cannot Tell a Lie," Marching On In")	no date

House of Blues

5141614612	*Music in the Air: The Dixie Hummingbirds 70th Anniversary* *Celebration and All Star Tribute* (Newly recorded tracks with Paul Simon, Stevie Wonder, Patty LaBelle, Wynona Judd, Shirley Caesar, Vickie Winans, and others. Birds Personnel: Ira Tucker, Howard Carroll, Paul Owens, Carl Davis, William Bright)	1998

DCC/3X Platinum

TXP-1001	*The Dixie Hummingbirds: Looking Back—A Retrospective*	1998

Frank Music

FM5531	*The Dixie Hummingbirds: Move On Up a Little Higher*	2000

P-Vine

PCD-5818	*The Dixie Hummingbirds: Journey to the Sky* *The Legendary Recordings 1946–1950*	2001

Properbox

Properbox 42	Good News, 100 Gospel Greats (Six Tracks: "The Book of the Seven Seas," "Every Knee Surely Must Bow," "Amazing Grace," " Don't You Want to Join That Number," Just a Closer Walk with Thee," "Ezekiel Saw the Wheel")

Collaborations

Atlantic

SD-8289	Marion Williams *Standing Here Wondering Which Way to Go* (Backing Vocals)	1971

Bell

| Bell-130 | Melissa Manchester *Bright Eyes* (Backing Vocals) | 1974 |

Warner Brothers

| BS 2971 | Leon Redbone *DoubleTime* (Backing Vocals on One Track: "If We Ever Meet Again This Side of Heaven") | 1977 |

Elektra/Asylum

| 6E-142 | Harry Chapin *Living Room Suite* (Backing Vocals) | 1978 |

Green Linnet

| GLCD 2123 | The Kennedys *Life Is Large* (Backing Vocals) | 1996 |

Sources

Apollo Records Catalogue

Billboard Magazine

Gotham Records Catalogue (Courtesy of Bruce Bastin)

"The Dixie Hummingbirds Discography 1939–1959." *Blues & Rhythm and the Gospel Truth* (June 1986).

Dixon, R.M.W., and J. Godrich. *Blues & Gospel Records* 1902–1943. Chigwell, Essex, England: Storyville Publications, 1982.

Gart, Galen, and Roy C. Ames. *Duke/Peacock Records: An Illustrated History with Discography*. Milford, NH: Big Nickel Publications, 1989.

Hayes, Cedric, and Robert Laughton. *Gospel Records* 1943–1969: *A Black Music Discography*. London: Record Information Services, 1992.

Credits

General Index

Index of Groups

Gospel Song Titles